The
TEXAS HILL COUNTRY
Book
A Complete Guide

One of the many water-level gauges along Hill Country roads, which are prone to flooding.

THE
TEXAS HILL COUNTRY
BOOK
A Complete Guide
INCLUDING AUSTIN AND SAN ANTONIO

THIRD EDITION

ELEANOR S. MORRIS

Berkshire House Publishers
Lee, Massachusetts

On the Cover and Frontispiece
Front cover: *Gillespie County wildflowers: bluebonnets and white prickly poppies.* Photo © Laurence Parent.
Frontispiece: *One of the many flood gauges along Hill Country roads, which are prone to flooding.* Photo © Eleanor S. Morris.
Back cover: Author's photo by Herman Morris.

THE TEXAS HILL COUNTRY BOOK: A COMPLETE GUIDE
THIRD EDITION — 2003

ISBN: 1-58157-066-X
ISSN: 1056-7968 (series)

Editor: Elizabeth Tinsley. Managing Editor: Philip Rich. Design and composition: Dianne Pinkowitz. Cover design and composition: Jane McWhorter. Maps: Ron Toelke Associates. Index: Diane Brenner.

Berkshire House books are available at substantial discounts for bulk purchases by corporations and other organizations for promotions and premiums. Special personalized editions can also be produced in large quantities. For more information, contact:

Berkshire House Publishers
480 Pleasant St., Suite 5; Lee, Massachusetts 01238
800-321-8526

Manufactured in the United States of America

10 9 8 7 6 5 4 3 2 1

No complimentary meals or lodgings were accepted by the author or reviewers in gathering information for this work.

Berkshire House Publishers'
Great Destinations™ travel guidebook series

Recommended by NATIONAL GEOGRAPHIC TRAVELER and TRAVEL & LEISURE magazines.

. . . a crisp and critical approach, for travelers who want to live like locals.
USA TODAY

Great Destinations™ guidebooks are known for their comprehensive, critical coverage of regions of extraordinary cultural interest and natural beauty. The authors in this series are professional travel writers who have lived for many years in the regions they describe. Each title in this series is continuously updated with each printing, in order to insure accurate and timely information. All of the books contain over 100 photographs and maps.

Neither the publisher, the authors, the reviewers, nor other contributors accept complimentary lodgings, meals, or any other consideration (such as advertising) while gathering information for any book in this series.

Current titles available:
The Adirondack Book
The Berkshire Book
The Charleston, Savannah, & Coastal Islands Book
The Chesapeake Bay Book
The Coast of Maine Book
The Finger Lakes Book
The Hamptons Book
The Hudson Valley Book
The Monterey Bay Big Sur & Gold Coast Wine Country Book
The Nantucket Book
The Napa & Sonoma Book
The Santa Fe & Taos Book
The Sarasota, Sanibel Island, & Naples Book
The Shenandoah Valley Book
The Texas Hill Country Book
Touring East Coast Wine Country

If you are traveling to, moving to, residing in, or just interested in any (or all!) of these enchanting regions, a **Great Destinations™** guidebook is a superior companion. Honest and painstakingly critical, full of information only a local can provide, **Great Destinations™** guidebooks provide you with all the practical knowledge you need to enjoy the best of each region. Why not own them all?

Acknowledgments

A bit of the magic of the Texas Hill Country is found in the attitude of the friendly, open folks who inhabit the region. There are too many to name them all here, but I'd like to thank everyone I spoke with along the many miles I covered while writing the guide, as well as those at the local Convention and Visitors Bureaus and Chambers of Commerce who were so helpful in providing information on their counties and towns. Special thanks to Cynthia Maddox, director of the Austin Visitors Bureau; Ernest J. Loeffler, Jr., and his helpful staff at the Fredericksburg Convention and Visitors Bureau; and Patricia Moore of the Bandera County Convention & Visitors Bureau. These people were very busy but always ready to help.

Thanks, too, to the folks at Berkshire House — Elizabeth Tinsley, editor; Jean Rousseau, publisher; Carol Bosco Baumann, marketing and sales director; Leslie Ceanga, office manager; and Philip Rich, managing editor. They helped me put everything together.

Contents

CHAPTER ONE
A Land Worth Fighting for
HISTORY
1

CHAPTER TWO
On the Trail
TRANSPORTATION
11

CHAPTER THREE
The Violet Crown
AUSTIN AND TRAVIS COUNTY
20

CHAPTER FOUR
Out in the Territory
HILL COUNTRY WEST AND SOUTH OF AUSTIN
BLANCO, BURNET, GILLESPIE, HAYS, KIMBLE, LLANO, & MASON COUNTIES
78

CHAPTER FIVE
Along the River
SAN ANTONIO AND BEXAR COUNTY
166

CHAPTER SIX
Old West and Old Country
**THE HILL COUNTRY WEST AND
NORTH OF SAN ANTONIO**
BANDERA, COMAL, KENDALL, KERR, MEDINA, REAL, & UVALDE COUNTIES
201

CHAPTER SEVEN
Hill Country Help
INFORMATION
281

Introduction

Welcome to the third edition of this guide to the Texas Hill Country.

Since the last edition, Austin and San Antonio have continued to grow at a fast pace, nevertheless retaining their charm. These two vibrant metroplexes offer an astounding array of places to see and things to do, mixing and merging the traditional and the contemporary and a variety of cultural influences. The two cities also serve as gateways to a lesser-known but deeply treasured gift of nature and history: the Texas Hill Country.

The Hill Country has been slower to change — a good thing. To many, the Hill Country is a magical place. Part of the charm is the Old Country *Gemütlichkeit* of towns like Fredericksburg and Boerne. Then there's the authentic cowboy ambiance of Bandera, the serenity of Utopia, and the beauty of the Lost Maples at Leakey. And best of all, it's true; it's not the imagination of a bewitched few. In the Hill Country the horizon is farther, the views greater, the air clearer, the rivers and streams cleaner, the people friendlier — and the road is all yours.

You'll find neither traffic nor crime; what you will find is that Nature has smiled on the Hill Country with rivers, lakes, deep caverns, and, of course, the hills. Hills high and low, hills undulating and steep, hills and valleys with panoramic views as far as the eye can see (and in Texas that can be pretty far). Small valleys contain scattered farms and ranches where fat cattle or sheep graze among the rocks and cedar. Many farmhouses and other buildings are built of the limestone, rocks pried from the soil and blocks quarried from the hills. Oak and mesquite line the roads, and every once in a while cactus, either yucca or prickly pear, appears in the underbrush amid the rocks.

Drive for miles and miles, and you won't see a billboard or sign of any kind. In fact, if you ignore the telephone and power lines along the way there'd be nothing except the wooded hills, broad ranchlands, and wide vistas. Good rural roads take you winding through the hills and valleys, down to low-water crossings (read the gauges; flash floods can occur), over wild roller-coaster roads, and up and away to the highest, most picturesque spots. In between, small towns welcome you with their history, art, regional foods, crafts, and festivals. Some towns have several motels and inns, others may have only one, but Texas Hill Country hospitality is everywhere.

When the Texas Department of Commerce queries out-of-state visitors on what impresses them most about Texas, the number-one answer is "the friendliness of the people."

Where is the Hill Country? The geographical boundaries of the Hill Country are rather hard to describe, but loosely the region encompasses the area of spring-fed streams and hills along the southern edge of the Balcones Escarpment south of the Edwards Plateau and east to the boundaries of Travis and Bexar Counties along Interstate 35.

The Balcones Escarpment is a lower extension of the Great Plains stretching from the High Plains of northwest Texas at the foot of the Rocky Mountains southward to the Rio Grande. The escarpment, which angles across the state from south to north, causes heavy warm air from the Gulf of Mexico to release most of its moisture on the lower eastern portion of the state, saving the Hill Country from the arid climate of the western part.

The Burnet-Llano Basin lies at the junction of the Colorado and Llano Rivers in Burnet and Llano Counties on the northern reaches of the Hill Country. Minerals were found in abundance here; the town of Llano was once known as the Pittsburgh of the South.

The Highland Lakes north from Austin to Burnet and Llano Counties offer some of the finest fishing in the entire state. They were formed by a series of dams impounded along the Colorado River, beginning with Lake Buchanan to the north. This large reservoir, and the one to the south, Lake Travis in the western part of Travis County, form the boundaries of the Highland Lakes. In between, from north to south, there are three small reservoirs: Inks Lake, Lake LBJ (originally called Granite Shoals), and Lake Marble Falls. Lake Austin is just north of the city of Austin, and Town Lake flows through the city, making possible the pleasant outdoor activities that add so much to the Austin experience.

So you might say that the Hill Country is mound after mound of undulating hills all the way to the Edwards Plateau south of Staked Plains — the Llano Estacado. The farther west you go, the higher the hills become, until they almost seem like small mountains, before they drop down to the Badlands, the desert where outlaws like John King Fisher lurked in the old days.

Amid the rocky soil and undulating hills there is water, water, everywhere. Ten rivers (counting Onion Creek) flow through the Hill Country, providing fishing, swimming, rafting, and canoeing much of the year: the Colorado, Frio, Guadalupe, Llano, Medina, Nueces, Pedernales, Sabinal, San Antonio, and San Marcos, to take them alphabetically. Cool, even cold, and especially popular in the hot Texas summer, are the springs along the eastern rim of the Hill Country: Barton Springs at Austin, San Marcos Springs at San Marcos, Comal Springs in New Braunfels, and several in San Antonio.

Eleanor S. Morris
Austin, Texas

THE WAY THIS BOOK WORKS

The Hill Country of Texas covers a large area in the center of the state and is composed of an assortment of counties and towns, each of them prizing their separate identities as well as being part of a whole entity, also prized: the "Hill Country." The sixteen counties covered by this book have been divided into four main regions:

The gateways to the Hill County:
Austin and Travis County
San Antonio and Bexar County

The remaining counties of the Hill Country:

The seven Hill Country counties west and south of Austin:
Blanco, Burnet, Gillespie, Hays, Kimble, Llano, and Mason.

The seven Hill Country counties west and north of San Antonio:
Bandera, Comal, Kendall, Kerr, Medina, Real, and Uvalde

While we have divided the Hill Country in this way to make such a large area manageable, we also want to make clear that the Hill Country is one homogeneous area, both geographically and culturally — although, of course, each county treasures its particular history and the unique features of its landscape. However, except for a small sign by the side of the road naming which county you are entering, you'll generally find that it is indistinguishable from the one you are leaving as you cross the county line.

Within these geographical groupings, listings are arranged alphabetically — first by town or topic, and then by establishment names. Some entries, such as those in the "Shopping" sections, are usually arranged by category; hence, all the craft shops appear together.

Factual information was researched at the latest possible time before publication, but be advised that many of these "facts" are subject to change. Chefs and innkeepers come and go, hours change, shops appear and disappear. When in doubt, phone ahead.

Specific information (such as addresses and location, telephone numbers, hours of business, and a summary of special features or restrictions) is presented in the left-hand column or at the beginning of a listing.

Because actual prices for lodgings and restaurants are constantly changing, we have noted price ranges instead, explained below:

Lodging prices are given for a per-room rate, double occupancy. It's a good idea to phone ahead for any price changes or other information and for reservations:

Lodging Rates:

Inexpensive	Up to $65
Moderate	$65 to $100
Expensive	$100 to $175
Very Expensive:	Over $175

These rates do not include room taxes or service charges.

Restaurant prices indicate the cost of an individual's meal, which includes appetizer, entrée, and dessert, but does not include cocktails, wine, tax, or tip. Restaurants with a prix-fixe menu are noted accordingly.

Dining Rates:

In Austin and San Antonio:

Inexpensive	Up to $20
Moderate	$20 to $30
Expensive	$30 to $50
Very Expensive	Over $50

Out in the counties:

Inexpensive	Up to $10
Moderate	$10 to $20
Expensive	$20 to $35
Very Expensive	Over $35

Meals are abbreviated as follows:
B: Breakfast
L: Lunch
D: Dinner
SB: Sunday Brunch

Credit cards are abbreviated as follows:
AE: American Express
CB: Carte Blanche
D: Discover
DC: Diner's Club
MC: MasterCard
V: Visa

The
TEXAS HILL COUNTRY
Book
A Complete Guide

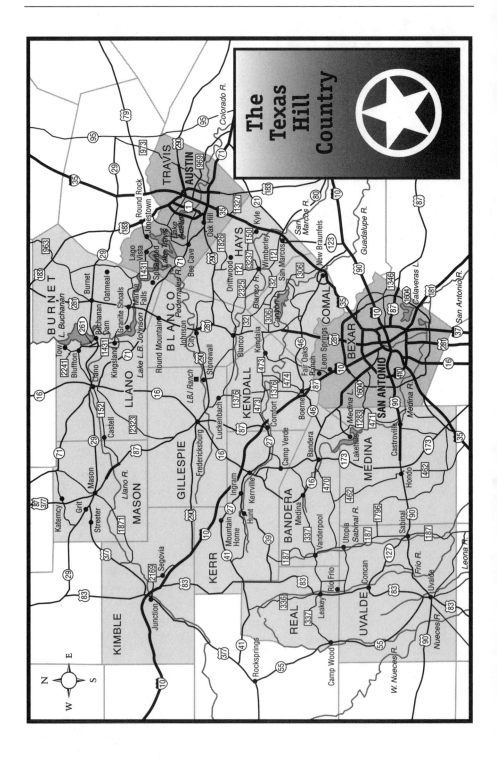

CHAPTER ONE
A Land Worth Fighting Over
HISTORY

Eleanor S. Morris

The massive dome of Precambrian pink granite for which Enchanted Rock State Natural Area in Gillespie County is named.

From the beginning, Texas has been a place coveted by all who passed this way, and the Hill Country fought over practically to the present day. First came the Paleo-Americans, then the fierce Plains Indians. Then the French came, seeking land for France; and then the Spanish, seeking gold, silver, and souls for Spain. Their colonists — Mexican-Indians, and the Anglos enticed there with promises of land — also strove to claim the territory as their own.

Why did they want this land, this hilly, rocky, thin-soiled ground covered with cacti and mesquite, unsuitable for farming? The Anglo settlers who finally tamed the Hill Country with their settlements became ranchers, raising herds of cattle, sheep, and goats. Here they could take advantage of the Hill Country's clear and plentiful spring water, magnificent rivers, and invigorating air and enjoy the beauty of the open space.

These days, of course, it's friendliness, not fighting, that is found throughout the Hill Country, from the sophisticated mix of cultures and creativity of Austin and San Antonio to the down-home informality out in the surrounding counties.

NATURAL HISTORY

HILL COUNTRY GEOGRAPHY

To begin to understand the Hill Country geologically, it helps to divide the region into three areas. The larger area to the north of the Hill Country is the Llano Estacado (Staked Plains), itself divided into the North and South Plains. The Edwards Plateau, forming more than half of the lower regions of the Llano Estacado, extends eastward toward the Balcones Escarpment or fault, a rugged, flat limestone table that stretches from the Rio Grande at Del Rio eastward to San Antonio and north to Austin on the Colorado River. The Balcones Escarpment, rising to heights of 300 to 1,000 feet, provides a clear break between the High Plains/Edwards Plateau and the coastal plains.

The area of the Edwards Plateau that lies on the edge of the Balcones fault is divided into two sections: the Hill Country, the popular name for this land of hills and spring-fed streams, and the Burnet-Llano Basin, lying at the junction of the Colorado and Llano Rivers in Burnet and Llano Counties. For our purposes the latter is also included in the Hill Country.

Geologically, the hilly central Texas basin is in an intermediate stage of erosion between the youth of the Edwards Plateau and the old age of the central lowlands. Separated from the coastal plains by the fault zone, the Hill Country rises with low, wooded areas along the uplifted side of the limestone fracture.

ROCKS AND WATER EVERYWHERE

A shallow sea covered much of Texas during the Cretaceous Period, about 100 million years ago. The land was part of a reef system inhabited by shelled sea creatures. As these creatures died and their shells decomposed over the millennia, thick beds of limestone were formed that make up the Edwards Plateau.

For millions of years, layer after layer built up over the Edwards until powerful earthquakes uplifted the land, forming hills and shearing the rock, exposing sections of the limestone formations. Water filtered through the cracks, dissolving millions of holes in the porous limestone, forming both large caves and tiny honeycomblike holes in the rock.

If you peeled away the tops of many of the hills of the Hill Country, you'd find lots of these holes, carved over the millions of years by underground rivers and streams. Many are still filled with water today; others, relatively dry, form networks of caves that have become tourist attractions. Others are home to creatures that have adapted to life in the underground. Scientists have discovered dozens of rare species, such as a blind cave millipede and a harvestman (a relative of the spider), which have evolved over hundreds of thousands or millions of years, totally isolated underground.

With only a thin layer of topsoil barely covering the limestone bedrock, the Hill Country is not conducive to agriculture, even with its wealth of water. Barton Creek, for instance, rises from limestone strata in the Balcones Fault formed millions of years ago when the area west of Austin uplifted to create the Edwards Plateau. The thin limestone-based soil does support cedar, mesquite, post oak, and live oak in abundance, along with laurel, sumac, prickly pear cactus, and range grass. And parts of the Hill Country, those near reliable water sources, are famous for their peaches: Stonewall and Fredericksburg, in particular, lay claim to exceptionally tasty fruit.

GOATS, SHEEP, CATTLE — AND ARMADILLOS

The land of the Hill Country is more suited for the grazing of cattle, sheep, and goats, and rural residents are usually ranchers rather than farmers. There is grass for the cattle, weeds for sheep, and tree foliage for goats — the region is the nation's leading producer of angora and mohair as well as one of the country's leading sheep and wool areas. Angora goats from Turkey were introduced to the Hill Country in 1849. Just about all the angora goats in the United States live on ranches between Uvalde in the Hill Country and San Angelo to the west; Texas produces 97 percent of all U.S. mohair.

White-tailed deer, jackrabbits, possums, raccoons, and wild turkeys all inhabit the brush, and the roads are strewn with the bodies of one of nature's most interesting animals, the armadillo — so many that the nine-banded armadillo (*Dasypus novemcinctus*) is a Texas joke as well as a Texas symbol.

In 1981 a resolution that the armadillo be officially declared the "state mammal" — joining the bluebonnet, the mockingbird, the longhorn, the pecan tree, and chili as a state symbol — was presented to the legislature. The House of Representatives OK'd it, but the Senate balked when adversaries offered the opossum, buffalo, and even the unicorn in opposition. So that was the end of the "official" armadillo.

SOCIAL HISTORY

THE FIRST TEXANS

Historians believe that tens of thousands of years before recorded history, the first humans to take possession of Texas soil were people who crossed the narrow land bridge that rose after the Ice Age to connect Asia with Alaska.

Archaeologists named these original Texans Paleo-Americans. Hunters and scavengers, they roamed across the High Plains, leaving behind nothing more than traces of their tools and bones from Clovis, New Mexico, through Abilene, Texas. Walking from cactus to mesquite in search of food, these early Texans evidently had learned to make fire, perhaps to protect themselves with basic cloth-ing, and to make simple tools of bone and stone. Moving eastward, they came to the Llano Estacado, hunting the mastodon and the massive forerunner of today's buffalo, until they came to the banks of the Hill Country's Pedernales River, just above the Balcones Escarpment.

Then they disappeared, to be replaced by newer arrivals across the land bridge. Europeans later gave these newcomers the name of Indian. While many of them went south into Mexico and Central and South America, others scat-tered across the High Plains of Texas into the central plateaus, chasing the bison across the arid land. These groups of "Llano Man," as anthropologists named them, are identified by their hunting tool, a primitive flint spear called the Clo-vis fluted point.

Those who penetrated farther into the Hill Country, to the spectacular scenery formed by ancient limestone above the Balcones Escarpment, discov-ered they could live on deer and smaller game, until they, too, vanished, leaving evidence of some form of ritual cannibalism from the Archaic Age.

NATIVE AMERICANS

Next, a succession of Indian peoples appeared in various areas of Texas: the Karankawas in the coastal bend; the Caddos in the piney woods of East Texas; the Coahuiltecans, who came the closest to the Hill Country; and the Tonkawas, who roamed over the Balcones Escarpment, ranging from the Ed-wards Plateau east to the Brazos Valley.

A far fiercer tribe held sway over the richest hunting grounds of the Pleis-tocene Age, the High Plains above the central Texas plateau with its millions of bison, antelope, deer, and elk: the Apache. Distinct from the Western Apache (the Navaho, San Carlos, Chiricahua, and Mescalero, who settled in Arizona and New Mexico), these Eastern Apache (Lipan, Palomas, Carlanas, and Jicaril-los) made themselves masters of the High Plains, learning to live off buffalo and warring with the Tonkawas.

THE SPANISH IN TEXAS

In 1540 Texas was invaded from the south by a new contender. Alvar Nuñez Cabeza de Vaca, from Spain, had already made landfall, shipwrecked on the Gulf Coast in 1528; his records were the first written mention of the land. Along came Francisco Vásquez de Coronado, annoyed but undaunted by his failure to find the famed cities of gold in Arizona or New Mexico. (What he expected to be the fabled city of Cibola turned out to be a dusty Zuni pueblo.) With his retinue of 300 Spaniards, Mexican Indians, and priests determined to convert the na-tives to Christianity, Coronado pursued his dream of fabulous New Spain gold and silver into what was to become Texas. Refusing to return to Spain as a fail-ure, he and his horde sowed the seeds of their own destruction.

For the Spanish brought horses, animals unknown in the Southwest at the time. Freely helping themselves to the animals, the Apaches successfully harried and discouraged the Spanish for the next 200 years. Swooping down from the plains on horseback, they burned the missions and presidios (forts) in San Antonio and elsewhere that the Spanish were desperately trying to establish.

Meanwhile, the horse had filtered northward, and by the early 1700s a group of fierce Plains Indians called Comanche by the Spanish also found a natural affinity for horseback hunting and warfare. Mounted, they believed themselves invincible. Historians have compared them to the mounted hordes of Genghis Khan as they came thundering south to the Llano Estacado and the Balcones Escarpment to plunder a far richer concentration of bison than anything seen on their barren plains.

They learned to ride for thousands of miles, to strike and turn back, and they attacked the Lipan Apache, driving them south. One hundred fifty years before the white settlers of Texas learned to dread the "Comanche Moon," the Apache first and then the Spanish knew that on nights when the moon was bright enough to see by and the grass tall and fresh to feed their horses, the Comanches were sure to strike.

THE FRENCH THREAT

Eleanor S. Morris

Now a museum, the French Legation was built in 1841 by Alphonse Dubois de Saligny, French chargé d'affaires in the Republic of Texas

A t the same time as the Spanish were establishing their missions, the French, spilling over from Louisiana, were attempting to establish a foothold in this part of the New World. Robert Cavelier de La Salle (who came to a bad end in East Texas at the hands of either Karankawas or his own men; nobody knows for sure) and others of his ilk are important to the Texas story mainly because they were perceived as a threat by the Spanish.

Failing to settle colonists north of the Rio Grande through the missions, even as the French were spreading into Texas from the east, the Spanish attempted at least to establish the "rancheros" that were successful in New Spain (northern Mexico), ranches that gave rise to the vaquero (cowboy) and other icons of today's Western culture. But the Indian peril never stopped: Apaches still struck from the west, and from the north Comanches never ceased their moonlight raids in spring and fall.

The combination of hostile Indians, the failure of widespread conversion of the less warlike Indians to Christianity, and the decline of Spanish colonies above the Rio Grande contributed to the end of the Spanish attempt to gain dominion over Texas at this time. By the beginning of the 18th century, all was abandoned as they finally retreated south, leaving behind them only the ruins of one or two missions and lean and longhorn cattle.

For the three centuries following Cabeza de Vaca and Coronado, the missions, and the encounters with the French, Texas remained virtually unoccupied by Europeans — except for three small settlements that the Spanish, in response to the French threat, had established by 1800: San Antonio on the southern edge of the Hill Country, Goliad south toward the border, and Nacogdoches in East Texas. (It would not be until the 20th century that Hispanic influence of any weight would be felt in Texas as a whole; in the Hill Country this would be mainly in San Antonio.) Attempting to ensure their continued presence in this part of Texas, the Spanish devised a novel plan to populate the area — although it was one that proved to be their undoing. This was the "empresario system," whereby they offered huge grants of land to those who would undertake to bring in large groups of settlers.

EARLY ANGLO SETTLERS

A round the time of the American Revolution, hardy Anglo frontiersmen had pushed their way from the Atlantic seaboard to the banks of the Mississippi. Several thousand new American citizens emigrated west to Missouri and Upper Louisiana, and they prospered. Why not invite these hardened pioneers to settle Texas? the Spanish reasoned. But the land still belonged to Spain; to alleviate the danger of an Anglo takeover, two conditions were imposed: The settlers had to swear allegiance to the king of Spain and embrace Catholicism.

Having little or no connection with the revolution that had raged behind their backs as they forged westward, frontiersmen such as Daniel Boone, William Morgan, and their fellows had no qualms about complying with the first condition; as for the second, so long as they agreed to convert to Catholicism, they were assured officially that their religious practices would not be scrutinized. Under these circumstances, how could they refuse the title of *empresario*, which came with enormous acreages of free land?

But while the Spanish sought to attract these Anglos to Texas and ensure their loyalty to Spain, they overlooked those few Mexicans who had earlier taken advantage of the empresario system. The Mexican-born Spanish colonists and Mexican-Indian mestizos became impatient with Spanish rule. Their rebellion in 1810 led to the Mexican War of Independence, and Mexico became a sovereign nation.

One American who had taken advantage of the Spanish land offer, swearing allegiance to Spain, was Moses Austin; in 1821 he was granted permission to settle 300 colonists on his land. But he died six months later, leaving it to his son, Stephen Fuller Austin, who formed the first Anglo colony in Texas.

Every Texas schoolchild knows the story of Stephen F. Austin's "First Colony" of 300: After the elder Austin's death, Mexico at first refused to honor the land grant. A year's worth of protest by Stephen Austin finally convinced the Mexican government to recognize the claim, but it was only on the condition that Mexican law prevail among the settlers.

Soon other Anglo colonists followed. By the mid-1830s around 30,000 were living in Texas, outnumbering the Mexicans by about four to one and rejecting the Spanish language and Spanish-Mexican culture in favor of their own. The Mexican government viewed their growing numbers with alarm, but attempts to discipline and disarm them failed.

THE TEXAS WAR OF INDEPENDENCE

Fighting erupted at the Anglo settlement of Gonzales on October 2, 1835, when the Mexicans demanded the town's cannon from the colonists. Told to "Come and get it!" the Mexicans lost the first battle of the Texas Revolution, and the taunt has served as the Gonzales motto ever since.

In December colonists captured San Antonio, held by Mexicans, who then agreed to withdraw to Mexico. But on March 2, when Texans were meeting at Washington-on-the-Brazos to declare their independence by establishing the Republic of Texas, General Antonio López de Santa Anna arrived to recapture San Antonio.

There followed the famous Battle of the Alamo. The Mexicans began a siege of the presidio on February 24. The fort was defended by 155 men, including Davy Crockett, James Bowie, and Colonel William Travis. "We consider death preferable to disgrace. . . . For God's sake and the sake of the country, send us reinforcements," Travis wrote, threatened by more than 5,000 Mexicans. Refusing to surrender to Santa Anna, all the Texans perished in hand-to-hand fighting.

After the Alamo fell, Colonel James Fannin, commanding 100 men at Goliad, was ordered to retreat; but before he could do so, he was overtaken by the Mexicans. Again greatly outnumbered, he surrendered after a hopeless battle. Imprisoned in Goliad, the entire force was slaughtered in cold blood by order of Santa Anna.

This outrage gave the Texans a double battle cry: "Remember the Alamo! Remember Goliad!" The two forces met for the last time at San Jacinto near today's city of Houston. In a surprise attack during the Mexicans' siesta, General Sam Houston prevailed over the larger force, and Santa Anna, caught unawares, was captured. (He was later freed.)

THE REPUBLIC OF TEXAS

The republic endured for ten years; Sam Houston was elected president on July 23, 1836. However, it was a straggling frontier community with barely more than 40,000 people, and recognition, if not annexation, by the United States was an attractive solution to the problems of a republic with no economy and no money, no banks, no improved roads, no schools, and, worse, with a territory still occupied by hostile Indians, especially in the Hill Country, the High Plains, and the Panhandle.

A resolution for statehood fared badly in both the Senate and the House. Northerners, ignorant of Texas geography, were afraid that adding Texas to the United States would expand slavery throughout the Southwest (even though slavery had come as far as it could go — the narrow belt of cotton plantations along the Brazos).

The Texas solution to this impasse was to pretend indifference to whether or not it became part of the Union. Stephen Austin leaked the information that if the United States was not prepared to extend aid and recognition, Texas might have to look elsewhere — England, for example. Neither Austin nor Houston seriously considered becoming involved with Great Britain, but the idea of a new British colony in the middle of America finally made an impression on the

This display in the Sophienberg Museum in New Braunfels honors the organization formed in the 19th century to encourage German settlement.

Eleanor S. Morris

antiexpansionists of the Northeast. Andrew Jackson capped his career as president by recognizing Texas. And in 1845, still fearing Britain's motives, the United States Congress narrowly approved the annexation of Texas.

Houston was elected to the Senate soon after and spent nearly fourteen years in office, until 1859. He was then elected governor of Texas but was deposed when his pleas for national unity were rejected by the people of Texas, who voted to secede from the Union during the Civil War.

Although Texan participation in the War Between the States was limited to supplying men, material, and services, it cost her dearly. Ninth state in the union in terms of wealth per capita in 1860, Texas was 36th when Reconstruction ended in 1880. Texas also was one of the last Confederate states to be readmitted to the Union — not until 1870.

SETTLING THE HILL COUNTRY

B ack in the days of the republic, Texas was still working on the problem of underpopulation. Just as the Spanish and Mexicans had before, the new government employed the empresario system to populate the empty frontier. German-born Henry Fisher had acquired a huge land grant north and west of Austin, in country still held by the Comanche. He was commissioned by Sam Houston to represent the republic to the German states of the Rhine to attract colonists to the Hill Country. The timing was perfect: Life was hard in the Rhineland in the 1840s, with crop failure and economic depression. Twenty-five altruistic noblemen had formed an organization to support emigration and to encourage the Germans, once in Texas, to stay together. This was the *Adelsverein*, a Society for the Protection of German Immigrants to Texas.

Under the leadership of Prince Carl of Solms-Braunfels, the Adelsverein raised $80,000 to purchase land and settle German pioneers. Enter Fisher, who in June of 1844 convinced the gullible Prince Carl to spend $9,000 on the purchase of 4,000,000 of his own acres. Misrepresenting the land, he claimed that it was accessible, fertile, and perfectly suited for coastal commerce; never mind that it was Comanche territory. The first contingent of immigrants was to arrive in December, and Prince Carl sailed to the new land to prepare for their arrival.

Once there, he saw how he had been taken. There was nothing to be done but to make other arrangements, and he looked for a second site where his people could settle and organize their resources before expanding into Indian country. He found 9,000 acres on the Guadalupe River 30 miles northeast of San Antonio, and there at the foot of the Balcones Escarpment he laid out a town that he called — what else? — New Braunfels.

This done, he sailed for home to retrieve his bride, Princess Sophie. But the princess balked at the idea of adventure in a raw, uncivilized new land, and Prince Carl never returned to Texas. When in Galveston to board the ship home, however, he had met the man who replaced him. This was another nobleman but, unlike the prince, one who renounced his title. Baron von Meuesbach became plain John O. Meuesbach, citizen of Texas, fated to become the salvation of the town of Fredericksburg.

The history of the German settlers in the Hill Country is told in greater detail in the stories of their counties later on in this guide. Suffice it to say that many of the customs, crafts, and traditions of the "old country" have been carefully preserved by the descendants of these hardy pioneers.

But the story of Hill Country settlement is not exclusively about German immigrants, although they have contributed much to the culture of the area, outranking Mexicans as the second most numerous ethnic group in Texas. Other Hill Country settlers came from the east and southeast United States and from other places in Europe — Danes, Dutch, Belgians, French, Norwegians, Slavs, and Swedes purchased land from the holders of Spanish or Mexican land grants. Like the Germans, they began communities that have retained their distinctive ethnic qualities.

Henri Castro, the Texas consul general in Paris from 1839 to 1842, was also a successful colonizer, bringing several hundred Alsatians to the Medina River south of San Antonio in the early 1840s. There they began a thriving community that retained the Alsace-Lorraine ethnic culture and cuisine that are an important part of the Hill Country to this day.

Sturdy houses of hand-quarried limestone bear witness to the determination of the settlers to endure with some comfort Hill Country weather, with extremes from 100-degree summer temperatures to below-20 degrees of a winter "blue norther" blowing down from the far northern reaches of Canada. The new residents of the Hill Country held the land dearly, building by hand miles of stone fences outlining fields and pastures.

THE HILL COUNTRY TODAY

Hill Country people strongly identify with their cultural heritage and are eager to share these many and diverse blessings with all comers. The land once fought over is today a land of friendly hospitality, delighting visitors with the rich variety of Hill Country traditions and attractions, new and old.

CHAPTER TWO
On the Trail
TRANSPORTATION

Eleanor S. Morris

The River Walk in San Antonio is a favorite spot for visitors to enjoy the sunshine, see the sights, and perhaps stop in a nearby cafe.

Folks came here first on horseback and in covered wagons; the first supplies for building Austin came by mule train. The San Antonio story offers a little more glamour: Here was the beginning of the Chisholm Trail, route of the cattlemen driving their herds north to the stockyards of Kansas City. The Old Spanish Trail from Laredo cut across the southeast corner of the territory that would become the city; the stagecoach route to El Paso passed straight through San Antonio from east to west — a century or two of steady traffic that shows no sign of letting up.

Today U.S. Highway 90 follows the same east-west trail through San Antonio that the stagecoach once plied — but it's a safe bet those passengers wouldn't recognize the route now. Both Austin and San Antonio are centers of growth and therefore traffic, with congestion possible throughout the day and into the

TEXAS HILL COUNTRY ACCESS

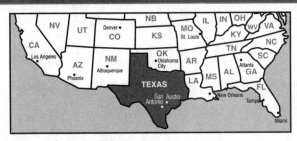

Approximate distances from outside Texas

From	To Austin	To San Antonio
Albuquerque	890 miles	818
Atlanta	917	993
Chicago	1245	1320
Denver	1067	945
Los Angeles	1428	1356
New Orleans	527	560
New York	1762	1838
Oklahoma City	390	466
Phoenix	1059	990
Washington, DC	1525	1600

Approximate distances within Texas

From	To Austin	To San Antonio
Austin	—	78
Brownsville	329	283
Dallas	201	279
El Paso	590	582
Houston	163	201
San Antonio	78	—
Texarkana	352	430

early evening. Drivers here are urged to be "Texas friendly" in all their comings and goings. (Construction is underway on a new state highway to run parallel to and east of I-35 between Austin and San Antonio.)

However, on the way out to the Hill Country, you'll find quieter, slower, and wonderfully scenic routes — the farm to market road and the ranch road. Leaving Austin and San Antonio behind via these smaller and less traveled roads, you'll feel as though the clock has been turned back and that you're seeing the same inspiring views that lured the Spanish, the cowboys, and the pioneers to these parts in the first place.

This chapter lists the many ways — plane, car, train, and bus — that you can arrive at the Hill Country's two gateway cities, Austin and San Antonio. It also details the modes of transportation available to you within these two cities: airport transit, taxi, limousine, local bus, rental car (and your own car). When you are ready to sally forth into the hills, you'll see several ways to get to and around the Hill Country — by bus or by car (your own or a rental).

GETTING TO THE HILL COUNTRY GATEWAY CITIES

Austin

GETTING TO AUSTIN BY AIR

Since Austin is both the capital of the state of Texas and the site of the main campus of the University of Texas (with a student enrollment that swells the population of the city by some 50,000 every year), most major airlines have frequent flights to the city from anywhere in the U.S.

Austin-Bergstrom International Airport (512-530-ABIA; www.ci.austin.tx .us./newairport; 3600 Presidential Blvd., Austin, TX 78719) is Austin's new airport (replacing Robert Mueller Municipal Airport), located at the site of the former Bergstrom Air Force Base. It is planned to meet Austin's air traffic needs far into the 21st century. The airport opened in the spring of 1999 with the potential for international passenger service, which Mueller Airport did not have. The 45,000-square-foot terminal building is the result of years of work by airport planners to meet the growing demand for expanded airport facilities. For reservations and information on flights, call:

America West	800-235-9292
American	800-433-7300
Continental	800-525-0280
Delta	800-221-1212
Northwest	800-225-2525

Southwest	800-435-9792
United	800-241-6522
USAir	800-428-4322

Airport Transit Service

| Super Shuttle | 512-258-3826 |

Taxicab Service

Metered service, set by city ordinance, is based on $1.75 for pickup and $1.75 per mile. Average fare from the airport to downtown is about $30.

American Yellow Checker Cab Company	512-452-9999
Austin Cab Company	512-478-2222
Roy's Taxis	512-482-0000

The Hill Country covers a lot of territory and is best experienced by car. However, if you're with a group — or want to pamper yourself — more than a dozen companies offer limousines, sedans, vans, "whatever is needed." Here are several:

Limousine Service

Austin Area Limousines	800-767-4090	512-386-8600
Lone Star Limousines	512-990-8482	
Roy's Limousines	512-293-1494	

GETTING TO AUSTIN BY BUS

| Greyhound Bus Lines | 800-231-2222 | 512-458-3823 |
| Kerrville Bus Company | 800-335-3722 | 512-389-0319 |

GETTING TO AUSTIN BY TRAIN

Amtrak Station (800-872-7245; www.amtrak.com; 250 N. Lamar Blvd. and W. Cesar Chavez St.) The Amtrak Eagle, a two-level passenger train, provides daily direct service to major U.S. hubs. Consult the Web site for information and fares. Reservations are required.

GETTING TO AUSTIN BY CAR

Austin has one major interstate freeway leading into the city from north and south — **Interstate 35,** which begins in Laredo and goes through San Antonio and Austin up to Duluth, MN. As in any other large city, it's a good idea to avoid the 7 to 9am and 5 to 7pm rush hour traffic if possible.

San Antonio

GETTING TO SAN ANTONIO BY AIR

San Antonio International Airport (210-207-3450; www.ci.sat.tx.us/aviation; 9800 Airport Blvd., San Antonio, TX 78216) is 13 miles from the Downtown River Walk and is directly linked via the McAllister Freeway (U.S. 281) to Broadway, which will take you straight to the Alamo in the heart of downtown San Antonio.

Terminal One:

Aerolitoral	800-237-6639
Delta	800-221-1212
Mexicana	800-531-7921
Northwest	800-225-2525
Southwest	800-435-9792

Terminal Two:

Aeromexico	800-237-6639
America West	800-292-2274
American	800-433-7300
Continental	800-525-0280

Airport Transit Service
SATRANS: For reservations and fares, call 210-281-9900.

Taxicab Service
Metered service based on $1.50 per mile from 5am to 9pm. Additional fare other times. Time to central business district is approximately 15 minutes, with the average fare being $15 plus tip, regardless of number of persons. Fare is subject to change.

San Antonio Taxis	210-444-2222
Yellow Checker Cab	210-222-2222

GETTING TO SAN ANTONIO BY BUS

Greyhound Bus Lines/Trailways	800-231-2222
Kerrville Bus Company	210-227-5669

GETTING TO SAN ANTONIO BY TRAIN

Amtrak has service to San Antonio via Austin, Ft. Worth, Dallas, Little Rock, St. Louis, Springfield, and Chicago. Call 210-223-3226; toll-free reservations: 800-872-7245.

GETTING TO SAN ANTONIO BY CAR

San Antonio has four major interstate freeways (Interstates 10, 35, and 37 and Interstate 410, a loop around the city) and four U.S. highways (U.S. 90, 181, 87, 281) leading into it from every direction. All highways lead into the central business district (or to connections to this district), which is linked directly to the airport by the McAllister Freeway (U.S. 281). As in Austin, the morning and afternoon rush hour traffic is best avoided.

Interstate Highways
I-35: Laredo, TX-San Antonio-Duluth, MN
I-10: Jacksonville, FL-San Antonio-Los Angeles, CA
I-37: Corpus Christi, TX-San Antonio
I-410: Circumferential Loop around San Antonio

GETTING AROUND AUSTIN AND SAN ANTONIO

S treet parking in bustling Austin and San Antonio is both limited and metered; the meters offer various time options and are regularly checked.

Austin's Capitol and trolley.

Eleanor S. Morris

However, both cities have open parking lots and covered parking garages (for a fee). Visitors to both cities can walk comfortably and safely around the downtown areas and can use public and tourist transportation (described below), some of it for free.

Austin

Public transportation within and around the city of Austin offers visitors and residents some convenient choices:

In the capitol area, Capital Metro Dillo, consisting of the Red Dillo, Blue Dillo, Gold and Silver Dillos, is "free for the taking" (512-474-1200). You can park free at two Park & Ride lots, one at Toomey Road (south of Town Lake off South Lamar) and the other at Austin High School (MoPac Expressway and West 1st St.), and the Dillo will take you to downtown, the UT campus, the state office complex, and restaurants and clubs along 6th Street. In the rest of town, **Capital Metro** offers forty-eight routes downtown and around town; fare 50¢ (512-474-1200, 800-474-1201).

Renting a Car in the Hill Country

Even with the abundance of car rental agencies in Austin and San Antonio (and at the two airports), it's a good idea to reserve ahead.

Austin

Advantage	800-777-5500	512-388-3377
Alamo	800-327-9633	
Avis	800-831-2847	512-476-6137
Budget	800-527-0700	512-478-6438
Dollar		512-530-7368
Enterprise	800-325-8007	
Hertz	800-654-3131	
National	800-227-7368	
Payless	800-729-5377	
Thrifty	800-847-4389	

San Antonio

A&P Recreational Vehicles Rentals	210-667-1838	
Advantage	800-777-5500	210-341-8211
Alamo	800-327-9633	210-828-7967
Avis	800-831-2847	210-826-6332
Budget	800-527-0700	210-828-8888
Enterprise	800-325-8007	210-224-6363
Hertz	800-654-3131	210-225-3676
National Car Rental	800-227-7368	210-824-7544
Thrifty	800-367-2277	210-341-4677

The Austin Downtown Rangers are also at your service, on the alert for lost or displaced tourists. It's easy to spot their distinctive uniforms: a white polo shirt and bike helmet with a red star, plus black cycling shorts with a red stripe. Armed with maps of the city and two-way communication equipment, they provide assistance to visitors, answering questions and reporting problems to city agencies.

San Antonio

Public transportation in San Antonio also offers choices:
VA Metropolitan Transit Service (210-362-2020) is the city bus company.
Via Transit (210-362-5050) for the disabled.
Via Information (210-362-2020).

San Antonio streetcars run on five downtown routes, taking you to the Alamo, Spanish Governor's Palace, La Villita, Institute of Texan Cultures, and the King William Historic District. Fare: varies locally; local 75¢, express $1.60; seniors and children 5–11, local 35¢, express 75¢, transfers 15¢.

GETTING TO AND AROUND THE HILL COUNTRY

A car (your own or a rental) is your best bet for traveling through the Hill Country beyond the major cities. First of all you'll want a map. To get a free travel guide and map by mail, write to the Texas Department of Transportation, Travel Center, 112 East 11th St., Austin TX 78701, or call 800-452-9292. Or you can buy a road map at any gas station in the state.

From Austin

Depending upon your destination, you have a choice of four major highways out of Austin: **U.S. Hwy. 183** goes northwest through Travis County to Burnet County; **State Hwy. 71** goes northwest through Travis County to Llano County; **U.S. Hwy. 290** goes west through Travis County to Hays, Blanco, Gillespie, and Kimble Counties; and **I-35** South skirts the eastern boundaries of Travis, Hays, and Comal Counties. Once you've headed west, U.S. Hwy. 83, stretching north and south between I-10 and U.S. Hwy. 90, goes through Kimble, Kerr, Real, and Uvalde Counties.

From San Antonio

Depending on your destination in the Hill Country, you have a choice of five major highways out of San Antonio: **U.S. Hwy. 90** goes west to Medina and

Uvalde Counties; **State Hwy. 16** goes northwest through Bexar County to Bandera, Kerr, Gillespie, and Llano Counties; **I-10** goes northwest through Bexar County to Kendall, Kerr, and Kimble Counties; **U.S. Hwy. 281** goes north through Bexar Country to Comal, Kendall, Blanco, and Burnet Counties; **U.S. Hwy. 87** goes northwest through Bexar County to Kendall, Kerr, Gillespie, and Mason Counties. **I-35** skirts the eastern boundaries of Comal, Hays, and Travis Counties. Once you've headed west, **U.S. Hwy. 83**, stretching north and south between I-10 and U.S. Hwy. 90, goes through Kimble, Kerr, Real, and Uvalde Counties.

Farm to market roads and ranch roads: To get away from it all, once outside of Austin or San Antonio, take the numerous good but small roads between the larger highways to experience even more of the Hill Country (identified as FM and RR on your Texas highway map). Instead of traffic, you'll see scenic hills, the foliage of oak, mesquite, and cactus, and maybe a deer or armadillo sharing your road.

CHAPTER THREE
The Violet Crown
AUSTIN AND TRAVIS COUNTY

Eleanor S. Morris

The Governor's Mansion on Colorado Street, diagonally across from the Capitol.

For all its rapid growth, Austin, the capital of Texas, remains a city that is very much a part of the landscape. Even in its most bustling commercial areas, you never feel cut off from the natural beauty of the Texas Hill Country. The surrounding county, Travis, is the gateway west to the Hill Country.

To make it easy to navigate both city and county, this chapter explores Austin first: the city's history; its lodgings, restaurants, and food purveyors; its culture, recreational opportunities, and places to shop. Then Travis County's offerings are described.

AUSTIN HISTORY

The imagination of even the romantic will not be disappointed on viewing the Valley of the Colorado, and the fertile and gracefully undulating woodlands and luxuriant prairies at a distance from it.
— Mirabeau B. Lamar, vice president of the Republic of Texas, 1838

Austin was named for Texas hero Stephen F. Austin, but it wasn't easy. In 1835 the trader Joseph Harrell established a small settlement along the mouths of three streams — Waller, Shoal, and Barton Creeks, all draining into the Colorado River — and he called it Waterloo. In 1838 his friend Mirabeau B. Lamar, vice president of the Texas Republic, came visiting to hunt buffalo. Camping on the banks of the Colorado, Lamar was greatly impressed with the beauty of the area. In the following years he battled with Sam Houston — elected president of the republic in 1836 — not only for political power but also over the choice of a new site for the state capital, then Washington-on-the-Brazos, where Texas had originally declared its independence.

When Lamar succeeded Sam Houston as president in 1838, he quickly sent his agent to Waterloo to build a new capital city for the republic. It was to be named for Stephen F. Austin, father of Texas. That spring 200 workmen arrived in ox-carts. Lots were sold at auction (for about $120) and grand 120-foot-wide Congress Avenue became lined with not-so-very-grand log cabins and plank houses.

But then Houston was reelected president in 1842. The first thing he did was to move the capital seat to Houston, and then he moved it back to Washington-on-the-Brazos. All, that is, but the General Land Office, the repository of the republic's archives. In this he was thwarted by the heroic efforts of one Angelina Eberly, doyenne of a nearby boardinghouse.

Fervently believing that the archives belonged in Austin, Eberly set off the cannon usually employed to warn of Indian raids. The people came to the rescue, routing Houston's men who had come to take away the archives and sending them back empty-handed. The archives remained safely stashed away in the Eberly boardinghouse, and this little contretemps has gone down in local history as the "Archives War."

In 1844 new president Anson Jones moved the capital back to join the archives in Austin. When Texas joined the United States in 1845, Austin remained as the capital, albeit shakily; the issue wasn't settled until it passed two statewide voter referendums, one in 1850 and another in 1852.

The city flourished, growing from 856 people in 1840 to 3,494 in 1860. A limestone capitol was built in 1853, but it was gutted by fire. The new building, of fossilized red granite from Hill Country quarries, was built in 1888. This engendered a Texas boast: the dome is 14 feet higher than that of the U.S. Capitol in Washington, D.C. The Governor's Mansion was built in 1856, and the oldest surviving office building in Texas, the General Land Office, was built around

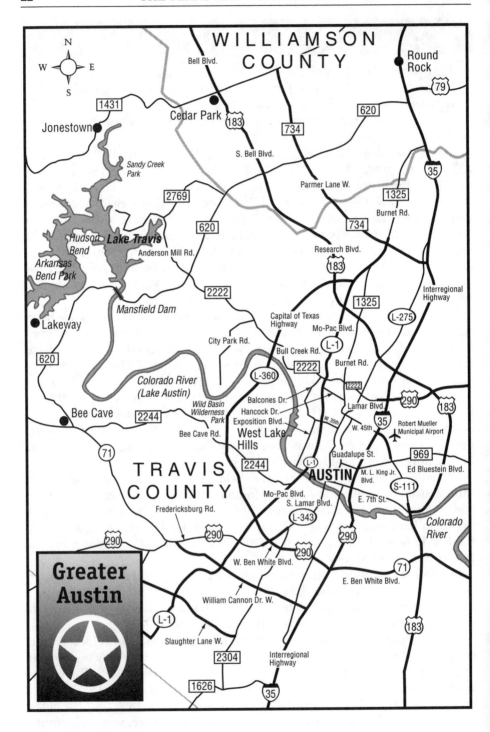

Downtown
Austin

L-1

W. 34th St.
W. 31st St.
Guadalupe St.
W. 29th St.
E. 30th St.
W. 281/2 St.
Adams Park
Shoal Creek
Greenbelt
W. 28th St.
W. 27th St.
Lamar Blvd
L.B.J.
Library and
Museum
W. 26th St.
University
of Texas
Texas
Memorial
Museum
W. 24th St.
W. 24th St.
Neill-
Cochran
Museum
Pease Rd.
Rio Grande.
Fine Arts
Complex
W. 23rd St.
Guadalupe St.
W. Lynn St.
Pease
Park
Harry
Ransom
Center
Speedway
Memorial
Stadium
Enfield Rd.
W. 21st St.
Martin Luther King Jr. Blvd.
W. Lynn St.
West Austin Park
Maroon
Stadium
W. 15th St.
West Ave.
Rio Grande.
E. 15th St.
Congress Ave.
Red River St.
Erwin
Special
Events
Center
1
W. 12th St.
Baylor St.
Lamar Blvd.
Duncan
Park
W. 11th St.
2
State
Capitol
W. 6th St.
W. 5th St.
W. 8th St.
3
E. 10th St.
E. 12th St.
E. 11th St.
E. 9th St.
Red River St.
W 1st St.
(Cesar Chavez St.)
Shoal Creek
Greenbelt
L-343
Guadalupe St.
Lavaca St.
E. 7th St.
E. 6th St.
E. 5th St.
San Jacinto St.
Neches St.
35
W. 4th St.
W. 3rd St.
Colorado St.
Congress Ave.
Brazos St.
Trinity St.
Red River St.
4
E. 7th St.
Colorado River
Lamar Blvd.
Dawson Rd.
W. Riverside Drive
Butler
Civic Center
Coliseum
5
E. 1st St.
Congress Ave.
Barton Springs Rd.
Dougherty
Cultural Arts
Center
Palmer Auditorium
and Convention Center
L-343
290

N
W   E
S

1. Recreation Center
2. Travis Co. Court House
3. Post Office
4. O. Henry Home and Museum
5. Austin Convention Center

1857. In the 1890s short-story writer William Sydney Porter (known by his pseudonym, O. Henry), who lived for a while in Austin, was so taken with the surrounding hills that he described the city as set in the hills like a "Violet Crown."

In 1938 the Lower Colorado River Authority began building the series of dams that gave the Austin area and the Hill Country the Highland Lakes. It has been said that the lower lakes — Lake Austin and Lake Travis — added still more jewels to Austin's "Violet Crown," a crown now set over the heads of more than half a million inhabitants and still growing.

It's the mix of country, hills, and clear-water lakes with an educated, philosophical population comfortable with different cultures and ethnicities that makes Austin the community everyone loves to love. You're apt to see a fellow in a Gucci suit sporting a ponytail as well as ponytailed workers doing street repairs. And drive 10 or 15 minutes in any direction and you're out under the stars in quiet, calm, unspoiled country of hills and wide horizons.

In spite of its constant growth, Austin has remained as laid back as it ever was, an open-minded, down-home kind of place that, in spite of its growth from a low-tech sleepy town to a high-tech bustling city, not only tolerates but also likes and respects people who are different. During a recent high-tension football game here between the Fighting Irish of Notre Dame and the valiant Longhorns of the University of Texas, the local paper printed this advice: "In Rome do as the Romans do; in South Bend do as the Irish do; in Austin do whatever the heck you wanna do!" The latest thing seen around town is a proliferation of "Keep Austin Weird" bumper stickers. Check it all out at www.keepaustinweird.com.

While 6th Street has long been a popular restaurant, club, and shopping venue, Austin's diverse community lately has come to recognize South Congress Avenue, just south of the Congress Avenue Bridge over Town Lake, as a cultural and retail hub for the city. The stores, restaurants, bars, and other businesses that now line the avenue give the area its appealing personality, making it a vital link beween between South Austin and the downtown area.

AUSTIN LODGING

As the seat of state government and a major university town, Austin has an abundance of places to stay. Visitors should note that the highest demands for lodging tend to occur in March, for major basketball games and other popular events, and in May, when the University of Texas and other colleges around town hold commencement exercises. For comprehensive listings of places to stay, visit the Web site: austin.citysearch.com.

HOTELS

Like any large city, Austin has its share of large national-chain hotels, such as Doubletree (800-222-8733), **Embassy Suites** (800-362-2779), **Hilton** (800-445-

8667), **Hyatt** (800-233-1234), **Radisson** (800-333-3333), **Renaissance** (800-468-3571), **Marriott** (512-478-1111), and **Westin** (800-228-3000). Uniquely Austin, however, are **The Driskill,** for its history and architecture, and the **Four Seasons,** for its location on Austin's glory, Town Lake.

THE DRISKILL
Manager: Jeffrey Trigger.
512-474-5911, 800-252-9367.
www.driskillhotel.com.
604 Brazos St., Austin, TX 78701.
Price: Expensive.
Credit Cards: AE, CB, D, DC, MC, V.
Handicap Access: Yes.
Special Features: Walking tours of the historic property by appointment.

The Driskill is an Austin treasure, opened in 1886 with a grandeur that was a rarity on the Texas frontier. Having recently undergone yet another of its many transformations, the emphasis has been not on renovation but on restoration, on returning the hotel to its original turn-of-the-century Victoriana.

The four-story L-shaped building has three grand entrances, arched windows, balconies, columns, corbels, gargoyles, and more. The hotel welcomes dignitaries, heads of state, legislators, and lobbyists. It has 177 luxuriously appointed rooms and 12 suites, a full-service restaurant, the Driskill Grill for dinner, and the 1886 Cafe and Bakery, open for breakfast, lunch, and dinner, as well as a coffee bar, 24-hour room service, gift shop, concierge desk, valet parking — and it's right on the corner of Brazos and 6th St., Austin's famed entertainment district. (Rooms on the east side have an entertaining view right down 6th St.) Additional work has taken the hotel to even greater heights with a rooftop swimming pool and a health club.

FOUR SEASONS HOTEL
Manager: Tom Segesta.
512-478-4500, 800-332-3442.
austin.citysearch.com,
search: Four Seasons Hotel.
98 San Jacinto Blvd., Austin, TX 78701.
Price: Very Expensive.
Credit Cards: AE, MC, V.
Handicap Access: Yes.

The hotel prides itself on pampering guests in the manner of fine European hotels, amidst a Southwest decor that somehow manages to be elegant even though a rugged crystal and iron chandelier hangs over the lobby. There are sofas upholstered in brown-and-white steerhide, tables of genuine mission doors with ox-yoke legs, and an elk head mounted over the fireplace. Half of the 292 guest rooms have a view over Town Lake, and there's an outdoor pool on the lake, too. (Nobody swims in the lake.) Special are the Sunday brunch and dinners in the hotel restaurant, the Cafe at Four Seasons.

BED & BREAKFASTS

For those who want a more intimate, less anonymous place to spend the night, the good news is that the bed & breakfast idea has caught on in the Southwest. Listed here is a selection of romantic, historic, convenient, and sociable inns that will pamper you and help you find your way around town and out of it.

CARRINGTON'S BLUFF BED AND BREAKFAST
Innkeeper: Phoebe Williams.
512-479-0638, 888-290-6090.
www.carringtonsbluff.com.
1900 David St., Austin, TX 78705.
Price: Moderate to Expensive.
Credit Cards: AE, D, MC, V.
Handicap Access: No.

This inn, just minutes from downtown, is set on a tree-covered bluff overlooking Pease Park. Built in 1877, one of the first homesteads in Austin, it seems like a quiet country cottage, and that's the feeling the innkeepers have nurtured. The five rooms in the main house are named for Carrington family members. The Writer's Cottage across the street got its name from three writers whose names grace the rooms; the carriage house has two guest rooms and its own private porch.

GOVERNOR'S INN
Innkeeper: Lisa Wiedemann.
512-477-0711.
www.austinbedand breakfast.com.
611 W. 22nd St., Austin, TX 78705.
Price: Expensive.
Credit Cards: AE, D, MC, V.
Handicap Access: Yes.

This award-winning inn is in a quiet neighborhood just a few blocks from the University of Texas and the Texas State Capitol. The mansion was built in 1897 and for years was known as the Kenny-Lomax House before it began a new life as a fraternity house. Inspired by the Governor's Mansion nearby, all the 10 rooms are named for Texas governors, beginning with the first one, Sam Houston, and not forgetting colorful Ma and Pa Ferguson. High-ceilinged rooms have four-poster beds, baths have claw-foot tubs, and rockers and swings offer relaxation on the wraparound porch. Breakfasts are ample, with the likes of sausage-and-chili quiche or Eggs Governor with strawberry cream-cheese bread; you may want to ask for a recipe!

THE MILLER-CROCKETT HOUSE
Innkeeper: Kathleen Mooney.
512-441-1600, 888-441-1641.
www.millercrockett.city search.com
112 Academy Dr., Austin, TX 78704.
Price: Moderate to Expensive.
Credit Cards: AE, MC, V.
Handicap Access: Yes, in the cottages.

Just two blocks from downtown, with a spectacular view of Austin's skyline, this bed & breakfast has three guest rooms, each with bath and balcony, and two private cottages. The 1888 building "has a historical marker," Kathleen Mooney says happily.

For breakfast you might be fed delicious eggs Benedict, a French toast soufflé, or huevos rancheros along with sausage or bacon and Texas Ruby Red grapefruit with strawberries, kiwi, and crystallized ginger — very tasty. You can then work it off on one of the inn's 12 mountain bikes along nearby Town Lake's Hike and Bike Trail.

Eleanor S. Morris

Named for the daughter of a Texas provisional governor, Woodburn House is now a bed & breakfast inn.

WOODBURN HOUSE
Innkeepers: Sandra and Herb Dickson.
512-458-4335.
austin.citysearch.com, search: Woodburn House.
4401 Avenue D, Austin, TX 78751.
In historic Hyde Park just north of downtown.
Price: Moderate to Expensive.
Credit Cards: AE, MC, V.
Handicap Access: No.

Here's a chance to stay in Austin's Hyde Park neighborhood, one of the areas the Austin Visitor Center suggests for touring for its lovely old homes. This bed & breakfast, an Austin landmark, is named for a former occupant, Bessie Hamilton Woodburn, the daughter of a Texas provisional governor after the Civil War. The spacious mansion has porches both upstairs and down and five guest rooms, all with private bath and lace curtains at the long windows.

Breakfast is often Mexican — "real Mexican, not Tex-Mex," says Sandra, whose family hails from Guadalajara. She grows her own Mexican spices and makes her own salsa. But not to be scorned are the Belgian waffles, French toast, and quiches that Herb serves.

Nearby is a very informal all-American eatery, the Hyde Park Grill — another plus.

AUSTIN RESTAURANTS AND FOOD PURVEYORS

According to those who know such things, Austinites eat out more than the denizens of any other city in Texas. Perhaps part of the attraction for dining out is explained by yet another fact from the same sources: Austin also has more restaurants per capita than any other American city. Which leads to a vast number of cuisine choices, from chicken-fried steak and cream gravy to grilled tenderloin of ostrich with sauce porcini; from pit-cooked brisket barbecue to curried lamb with basmati rice; from enchiladas in salsa verde to chipotle shrimp over mushroom and rice pilaf.

To open a restaurant anywhere is cited as a tricky business venture at best. Faced with such an array of competitive establishments, Austin restaurants tend to come and go. One advantage of this form of natural selection is that there is absolutely no room for bad restaurants; they just don't make it. So in almost any eating emporium in Austin you're pretty sure to be served excellent cuisine in any category: American, Western, Southwestern, Mexican, French, Italian, Spanish, Chinese, Japanese, Taiwanese, Korean, Indian, Greek, Indonesian, Indian, Middle Eastern. . . .

As for decor, this, too, goes from one extreme to another, from barbecue-stand informality to French cafe coziness, from limestone walls to romantic candlelight, from Mexican cliché to Victorian gentility.

What to wear? Austin is informal; many restaurants subscribe to the City Grill's definition and dress code: "Classy and refined, yet casual enough to wear your jeans." Just don't get so laid back that you flout the health code: shirt and shoes worn at all times.

All of Austin's restaurants are nonsmoking. This caused quite a flap when it was instituted, but things have settled down considerably, and folks seem to eat out as often as before. Following is the result of a considered selection from all the many good restaurants in Austin, along with some food purveyors, specialty shops reflecting the area's German and Spanish traditions, and the eclectic interests of an increasingly sophisticated clientele. Check the restaurant's Web page for more information, or visit the Austin Web site: www.austin.city search.com.

CHEZ NOUS
512-473-2413.
www.cheznous.citysearch
.com
510 Neches St., Austin, TX 78701.
Price: Moderate to Expensive.
Cuisine: French.
Serving L, D.
Credit Cards: AE, DC, MC, V.
Reservations: No.
Handicap Access: Yes.

This personable and friendly small French bistro just around the corner from 6th St. serves delicious, authentic French cuisine. The simple decor is enlivened by French posters on the walls, lace curtains on the windows, flowers in aperitif bottles and candles on the tables. Service is friendly and attentive. The prix fixe menu du jour includes a choice of soup, appetizer or salad, one of three daily specials, and dessert, all delicious.

CHUY'S
512-474-4452.
austin.citysearch.com,
search: Chuy's.
1728 Barton Springs Rd.,
Austin, TX 78704.

Funky Chuy's is Austin at its most whimsical. A thousand wooden fish dangle from the ceiling of the bar, and hubcaps cover the ceiling of the dining room. The result is hilarious. Walls are Mexican pink and green; piñatas dangle invitingly, asking to be smacked (but they never are — too messy); and

Just south of downtown.
Price: Inexpensive.
Cuisine: Tex-Mex.
Serving: L, D.
Credit Cards: AE, D, MC, V.
Reservations: No.
Handicap Access: Yes.

there's a memorial altar to Elvis by the front door. The crowd most nights testifies to the great taste of the Tex-Mex fare. The menu may be limited, but regulars favor the taco salad, the blue corn tortillas, the barbecued chicken tacos, and the chips and salsa.

CITY GRILL
512-479-0817.
austin.citysearch.com,
 search: City Grill.
401 Sabine St., Austin, TX
 78701.
One block west of I-35
 between 4th and 5th Sts.
Price: Moderate.
Cuisine: Mesquite Grill.
Serving: D.
Credit Cards: AE, CB, D,
 DC, MC, V.
Handicap Access: Yes.

The City Grill, specializing in mesquite-grilled steaks and seafood, is in a refurbished 1890s warehouse. The old wood floors and beamed ceilings contrast with the elegance of the candles and the linen tablecloths, all of which live up to the restaurant motto: "classy and refined, yet casual enough to wear your jeans." You'll find the beef tender and the grilled fish moist and tasty, all in line with the popular restaurant's reputation.

County Line on the Lake, great barbecue in Austin.

Eleanor S. Morris

COUNTY LINE ON THE LAKE
512-346-3664.
austin.citysearch.com,
 search: County Line on
 the Lake.
5204 FM 2222, Austin, TX
 78731.
0.25 mile east of Loop 360.

Always popular, so you may have to wait, but the beautiful Hill Country view makes that easy. Continue to enjoy it by eating outdoors if the weather is nice (which is most of the time in the Hill Country!), and enjoy the view from the hill while digging into the big meaty ribs, lean brisket, and special sausage the County Line is famous for throughout the Southwest. The atmosphere here is

Price: Moderate.
Cuisine: Barbecue.
Serving: L, D.
Credit Cards: AE, CB, D,
DC, MC, V.
Reservations: Only for 10
or more.
Handicap Access: Yes.

upscale roadhouse. From the Longneck Bar we downed ice-cold beer and frozen margaritas as we watched the view of Bull Creek as it runs into Lake Austin. For dessert, the Kahlúa pecan brownie is a must.

EL SOL Y LA LUNA
512-444-7770.
www.elsolylaluna.city
search.com.
1224 S. Congress, Austin,
TX 78701.
Price: Inexpensive.
Cuisine: Mexican.
Serving: B, L, D.
Credit Cards: AE, D, MC, V.
Handicap Access: No.

Named one of the best Hispanic restaurants in the country, the decor here features El Sol (the sun) and La Luna (the moon). Try the enchiladas zacatecanas, creamy with avocado sauce. Or the four-cheese gorditos, a Tuesday specialty snatched up in a hurry. And not only great food — on Weds., Thurs., Fri., and Sat. evenings there's lively, live Latin American music.

GREEN MESQUITE BBQ & MORE
512-479-0485.
austin.citysearch.com,
search: Green Mesquite.
1400 Barton Springs Rd.,
Austin, TX 78704.
Corner of South Lamar.
Price: Inexpensive.
Cuisine: Barbecue, Tex-Mex,
Cajun.
Serving: L, D.
Credit Cards: AE, D, DC,
MC, V.
Reservations: No.
Handicap Access: Yes.
Special Features: Bluegrass,
blues, and country-
western music live on Fri.,
Sat., and Sun. nights.

This rustic and homey Austin tradition serves up music from local bands on weekends, along with the food: chicken-fried steak, catfish, jambalaya, and "bubba tacos" — soft flour tortillas stuffed with your choice of barbecued beef, turkey, or chicken and topped to the gills with lettuce, tomato, and shredded cheddar cheese, served with a homemade salsa and a choice of two sides. The beans were a little too sweet and the Cajun rice a little oily, but the big chunky coleslaw was seasoned just right, and the potato salad was mellow. The po' boy sandwiches are as authentic as any you'll get in New Orleans, and of course all the pies are homemade. Present owners Tom and Liz Davis are carrying on the welcoming tradition of this little old shack on an important corner (right on South Lamar) begun before Harry Truman was president.

GREEN PASTURES
512-444-4747.
austin.citysearch.com,
search: Green Pastures.
811 W. Live Oak, Austin,
TX 78704.

Shades of the Old South! This white mansion, surrounded by manicured grounds and strutting peacocks, is instant Scarlett O'Hara-Rhett Butler ambiance. Retro Southern gentility and the best Sunday brunch in Texas make this an Austin classic. Everybody likes not only the good taste of the food

Live Oak is about 1.5 miles south of downtown; turn right off Congress for 9 blocks.
Price: Expensive.
Cuisine: Southern, Continental.
Serving: L, D, SB.
Credit Cards: AE, D, MC, V.
Reservations: Yes.
Handicap Access: Yes.

HULA HUT
512-476-4852.
austin.citysearch.com, search: Hula Hut.
3826 Lake Austin Blvd., Austin, TX 78703.
On Lake Austin.
Price: Moderate.
Cuisine: Polynesian Mexican.
Serving: L, D.
Credit Cards: D, DC, MC, V.
Reservations: No.
Handicap Access: Yes.

but also the sheer abundance of the spread — a large assortment of cheeses and fruits, shrimp, salads, maybe a choice between prime rib and grilled blue marlin tampico (tomato, green pepper, onion sauce), three or four vegetables, and at least four desserts. The peach and plum strudel and the Green Pastures bread pudding are recommended.

The mix may sound weird, but once you try it, you're hooked. You can dine inside or out over the lake, where boaters tie their craft up by the giant fish guarding the pier bar. We began with the Huli Huli Luau Platter of BBQ ribs and chicken tacos, grilled chicken nachos, chicken flautas, little garlic-roasted potatoes, and chili con queso. Then we went on to Hawaiian grilled chicken: a grilled breast topped with fresh poblano chilies, grilled pineapple slices, jack cheese, and crispy smoked bacon.

The tacos and enchiladas have to be the largest ever seen; the taco stuffed with char-grilled mahi mahi, red cabbage, cilantro, and jalapeño lime sauce was pretty peppy.

The popular Hyde Park Bar & Grill in Austin.

Eleanor S. Morris

HYDE PARK BAR & GRILL
512-458-3168.

Hyde Park Bar & Grill's super lentil soup is on the menu daily, and there's also a soup of the day if you want a change. We like their stir-fry and

austin.citysearch.com,
search: Hyde Park Bar &
Grill.
4206 Duval St., Austin, TX
78751.
Historic Hyde Park
neighborhood north of
downtown.
Price: Inexpensive.
Cuisine: American.
Serving: L, D, Sat. & Sun.
Brunch.
Credit Cards: AE, D, DC,
MC, V.
Reservations: No.
Handicap Access: Yes.

the spicy chicken salad, but the spinach salad is delicious, too, in this very informal all-American eatery.

IRON WORKS BARBECUE
512-478-4855.
www.ironworksbbq.com.
100 Red River, Austin, TX
78701.
East edge of downtown.
Price: Moderate.
Cuisine: Barbecue.
Serving: L, D.
Credit Cards: AE, MC, V.
Reservations: No.
Handicap Access: Yes.

Delicious brisket, chicken, sausage, and ribs are to be had in this rustic tin shed, for years the home of Weigl Iron Works, near the Convention Center. The classic barbecue plate comes with a choice of two out of three side dishes: beans, salad, or coleslaw. Top this off with a slice of pecan, apple, or cherry pie or peach cobbler while you enjoy deciphering the dozens of brands burned into the wooden walls.

JEFFREY'S
512-477-5584.
www.jeffreysofaustin.com.
1204 West Lynn, Austin, TX
78703.
Bet. 6th St. and Enfield Rd.
just west of downtown.
Price: Very Expensive.
Cuisine: New Texan,
Continental.
Serving: D daily.
Credit Cards: AE, D, DC,
MC, V.
Reservations:
Recommended.
Handicap Access: Yes.

Talk about adventurous cuisine — this fine dining establishment in the historic Clarksville neighborhood takes high honors indeed. Chef David Garrido, acclaimed by the James Beard Foundation, makes magic with an amazing array of flavors. For starters, how about shredded goose on a small blue corn taco sauced with fresh mango puree? Or crispy oysters on root chips (sea sprouts) with habañero honey aïoli? Or skookum oysters with caviar and chervil lemon mignonette? "I've tried leaving oysters off the menu," Chef David says, "but our patrons raised the roof." He has published a cookbook, *Nuevo Tex-Mex*, with recipes using all the flavors that he says "make a good marriage."

The portabella mushroom with Brie on pureed maple sweet potato garnished with baby bok choy was yet another delicious starter. Sturgeon, pecan-wood smoked for sweetness and served in an orange champagne sauce, was accompanied by a black Oregon truffle in a wine-butter-shallot sauce; elk was served with hazelnut wild rice and huckleberry thyme sauce; lamb was flavored with roasted shallot custard, ginger, honey, and saffron.

Orange saffron crème brûlée, hazelnut mascarpone cheesecake with plum compote, and apple spice cake with macadamia and rum raisin sauce raised dessert to the heights. The menu varies, but a must, like the oysters, is chocolate intemperance, a dense, bittersweet chocolate mousse with a brownie crust covered with melted chocolate.

KATZ'S DELI & BAR
512-476-3354.
www.katzneverkloses.com.
618 W. 6th St., Austin, TX
  78701.
Downtown, west of
  Congress Ave.
Price: Inexpensive to
  Moderate.
Cuisine: New York Deli.
Serving: B, L, D.
Credit Cards: AE, D, DC,
  MC, V (no checks).
Reservations: No.
Handicap Access: Yes.
Special Features: Open 24
  hours a day.

"We Never Klose" is the boast of this establishment, which has been providing Austinites with their kosher-style deli fix since 1979, introducing "bagel" and "deli" into the Texas vocabulary. Bagels abound, of course, from the basic $1.95 toasted with butter to the legendary $8.95 cream-cheese-slathered roll thick with lox and lettuce, tomato, and purple onion. The chicken-in-a-pot contains award-winning consommé, both noodles and matzo balls, vegetables, and a whole quarter chicken; the homemade cheese blintzes come with a choice of apple, blueberry, or hot fudge topping.

KERBEY LANE CAFE
512-445-4451.
austin.citysearch.com,
  search: Kerbey Lane Cafe.
2700 S. Lamar Blvd., Austin,
  TX 78704.
South of downtown.
Price: Inexpensive.
Cuisine: American Diner,
  Tex-Mex.
Serving: B, L, D.
Credit Cards: AE, D, DC,
  MC, V.
Reservations: No.
Handicap Access: Yes.
Special Features: Open 24
  hours a day.

It's true what they say: Austin couldn't get along without its supply of wholesome food available any hour of the day or night, and this homegrown restaurant is the place for it. Breakfast, lunch, and dinner all feature fresh, locally grown produce and are served round the clock every day in this and three other locations: 2606 Guadalupe (512-477-5717; University area), 3704 Kerbey Ln. (midtown), and 12602 Research Blvd. (512-258-7757; North). Lots of green vinyl and light wood and a bucolic mural of hills and fields set the tone; the waitstaff wear whatever they're comfortably casual in, and the service is friendly and snappy. Legendary among the healthy and wholesome offerings are Kerbey Lane's pancakes, sandwiches, crisp salads, and all sorts of imaginative specials. The migas (eggs scrambled with crispy tortilla bits) with spicy red sauce are recommended.

OLD PECAN STREET CAFE

512-478-2491.
austin.citysearch.com,
search: Old Pecan Street Cafe.
310 E. 6th St., Austin, TX 78701.
At Trinity and San Jacinto.
Price: Inexpensive.
Cuisine: Texas-Style American.
Serving: L, D, Sat. & SB.
Credit Cards: AE, D, MC, V.
Reservations: No.
Handicap Access: Partial.

The menu here doesn't change from week to week, so when you find something you really like, you can count on its being there (although there are certain favorites for each night, too) — like the Old Pecan Street chicken, a chicken breast flattened, spread with pesto, rolled up, and simmered in brandy. That the pecan pie is a perennial favorite goes without saying. The building is the historic Platt-Simpson, in 1871 part of a livery stable, in 1901 a hardware store. Inside are stone walls and wooden floors; outside you'll find a historic plaque on the red brick, and bright blue awnings shade the restaurant windows.

SHADY GROVE

512-474-9991.
www.theshadygrove.com.
1624 Barton Springs Rd., Austin, TX 78704.
Price: Inexpensive.
Cuisine: American.
Serving: L, D.
Credit Cards: AE, DC, D, MC, V.
Handicap Access: Yes.

Here's another laid-back Austin eatery, where you can dine indoors or out under the pecan trees in a real grove that once was a trailer park. It's the place for either "burgers and beer" or the special Hippie Sandwich of grilled zucchini, eggplant, mushrooms, roasted bell peppers, tomato, and arugula on a seven-grain bun. Indoors there's a full bar, rock walls, stone pillars, and a cozy fireplace. On Thursday nights in the summer, there's live music under the pecan trees.

SHORELINE BAR & GRILL

512-477-3300.
www.shorelinegrill.com.
98 San Jacinto Blvd., Austin, TX 78701.
On Town Lake at 1st St.
Price: Moderate.
Cuisine: Seafood.
Serving: L, D.
Credit Cards: AE, D, MC, V.
Reservations: Recommended.
Handicap Access: Yes.

This is the place for watching the Austin bats at sunset (see the "Nature" section in this chapter) while looking out over Town Lake and enjoying a memorable seafood or prime rib meal. We had the grilled prime rib and the grilled shrimp and crab cake entrée, both served with a fresh vegetable medley of green and wax beans, squash, and bell peppers. We topped it off with the Shoreline special of crème brûlée and chocolate "intensive," a triple chocolate confection that becomes more decadent with each bite.

THREADGILL'S

512-472-9304.
www.threadgills.com.
310 Riverside Dr., Austin, TX 78704.

Here's the same good old Threadgill's, now opened just south of downtown — called their "world headquarters" — so there's no need to go to the original one up at 6416 North Lamar. You'll have

South of Town Lake at
  Barton Springs Rd.
Price: Moderate.
Cuisine: American food,
  Southern style.
Serving: L, D.
Credit Cards: D, MC, V.
Reservations: No.
Handicap Access: Yes.

to do without the musical memories of the original Threadgill's, where Janis Joplin used to sing, but there's often live music here on Thursday evening. The new Threadgill's is next door to the late Armadillo World Headquarters and contains a large collection of memorabilia from the musical heyday of Austin, in the 1970s. And this is still the place for tried-and-true chicken-fried steak and cream gravy on homemade biscuits. There are plenty of neon signs and old beer clocks on the walls to transport you back in time as you chow down on pork roast and liver and chicken and dumplings with black-eyed peas and okra. He-man portions, great vegetables, and fresh home cooking make this Austin landmark a winner. As for that chicken-fried steak, lots of our friends say it's the best in town.

WEST LYNN CAFE
512-482-0950.
www.westlynn.citysearch
  .com.
1110 West Lynn, Austin, TX
  78703.
Bet. 6th St. and Enfield Rd.
  just west of downtown.
Price: Inexpensive.
Cuisine: Vegetarian.
Serving: L, D, Sat. & SB.
Credit Cards: AE, D, DC,
  MC, V.
Reservations: No.
Handicap Access: Yes.

The scent of food is so delicious as you enter the cafe, it makes you want to become a vegetarian if you aren't one already. The zucchini poblano — a casserole of fresh zucchini, corn, and poblano peppers — is baked in a fresh tomato sauce with New Mexico spices and a hint of fresh cilantro, topped with melted jack cheese.

The innovative menu includes such dishes as spanakopita, a classic Greek dish of flaky filo dough layered with spinach, eggs, sliced almonds, fresh dill, oregano, and ricotta and feta cheeses. A Caribbean stir-fry is a mélange of fresh vegetables and tofu with cashews and tropical fruit in a ginger sauce, served with black beans. Dishes on the menu that are starred can be prepared zero cholesterol/nondairy if you wish.

Sandwiches, salads, smoothies, fresh juices, and natural sodas are on the menu in this attractive cafe, where you can eat outdoors under an arbor or indoors under a slanted ceiling decorated with stars and squares. A changing art show is mounted on the walls.

Z TEJAS GRILL
512-478-5355.
austincitysearch.com, search
  Z Tejas Grill.
1110 W. 6th St., Austin, TX
  78703.
West edge of downtown.
Price: Inexpensive.

There's a climb here, up the front steps to the restaurant's outdoor and indoor dining, but the exertion is worth it. The crunchy catfish beignets served with jalapeño tartar sauce and the chicken and sausage gumbo ya-ya got us off to a great start. Voodoo tuna was served with black peppercorn vinaigrette and soy mustard sauce, and the Z'green

Cuisine: Southwestern.
Serving: B, L, D, Sat. & SB.
Credit Cards: AE, D, DC, MC, V.
Reservations: No.
Handicap Access: No.
Special Features:
  Complimentary valet
  parking in evening.

salad was mixed greens with roma tomatoes and colored peppers with a sun-dried tomato-basil dressing. Another specialty is the pork tenderloin, stuffed with chorizo, jack cheese, grilled onions, and poblano peppers in a roasted garlic cream sauce.

AUSTIN FOOD PURVEYORS

BAKERIES

Old Bakery and Emporium (512-477-5961; www.austin360.com, search: Old Bakery and Emporium; 1006 Congress Ave., Austin, TX 78701; year-round Mon.–Fri. 9am–4pm, Dec., prior to Christmas, Sat. 10am–2 pm) Dating from 1876 and built by Swedish immigrant Charles Lundberg, the bakery sells baked goods as well as handicrafts made by Austin senior citizens.

Sweetish Hill Bakery (512-472-1347; austin.citysearch.com, search: Sweetish Hill Bakery; 1120 W. 6th St., Austin, TX 78703; Mon.–Sat. 6:30am–7pm, Sun. 6:30am–5pm) There's luncheon-only service at Portabla (4818 6th St.) but here's where all the baking is done and where the main action is, especially on a Saturday morning. The bakery celebrated its 28th anniversary in 2003 and boasts of being Austin's first "from-scratch" bakery, using real butter and fresh eggs for such goodies as sticky buns and Cyprus horns, a delicious cinnamon and almond croissant. It offers gourmet lunches, such as ham and Brie on a baguette, plus other sandwiches and hot dishes. The coffee is Anderson's, a fresh-roasted blend made especially for Sweetish Hill. "We use only local stuff," is a bakery byword.

Texas French Bread (512-499-0035; austin.citysearch.com, search: Texas French Bread; 2900 Rio Grande, Austin, TX 78705; Mon.–Fri. 7am–7pm, Sat. 7am–6pm, Sun. 7am–5pm) Here's a true Texas success story: Early in the 1980s Judy Willcott began baking out of her house for friends and a few restaurants. Today there are Texas French Bread establishments all over Austin — but the one on Rio Grande is where most of the culinary work is done. It's also where you can enjoy outdoor Austin: There are cafe tables in front and picnic tables under the big tree alongside the garden that grows all the herbs used in the bakery.

There's hardly a party in Austin where the food doesn't include a Texas French Bread French bread. But also popular are the sourdough bread, the baguettes, and the bollos (crusty rolls). The Hyde Park chocolate cake is a marvel, but so are all the other cakes in the display case, plus scones, croissants, muffins, and Texas-shaped cookies in butter, ginger, and chocolate. You can get coffee, tea, and lunch here as well — one of the popular specials is the TFP, a vegetarian salad bursting at the seams.

COFFEE SHOPS

Joe's Bakery and Coffee Shop (512-472-0017; austin.citysearch.com, search: Joe's Bakery; 2305 E. 7th St., Austin, TX 78702; daily 7am–3pm) Joe says he's now more of a restaurant than a coffee shop. "That's what I named it when I opened," he says. But you can still get great coffee, along with fresh, made-on-the-premises Mexican pastries like empanadas and pan dulce, "from my own recipes," Joe promises.

Jo's (512-444-3800; 1300 S. Congress, Austin, TX 78704; Sun.–Mon. 7am–6pm, Tues.–Fri. 7am–9pm, Sat. 7am–10pm) Part traditional Texas icehouse, part gourmet coffee shop, Jo's serves up delicious drinks and fresh sandwiches daily.

Quack's 43rd Street Bakery (512-453-3399; 411 E. 43rd St., Austin, TX 78751; Mon.–Fri. 6:30am–11pm, Sat. & Sun. 8am–11pm) You can get your coffee fix here just about any time of the day or night. Quack's is a bakery and a coffee shop, "half and half," so you can be sure of delicious pastries to go along with your coffee.

FARM, ORCHARD, AND PRODUCE MARKETS

Central Market (512-206-1000, 800-360-2552; austin.citysearch.com, search: Central Market; 4001 N. Lamar Blvd., Austin, TX 78756; daily 9am–9pm) The sheer magnitude of this indoor market has made it a tourist attraction, one of the first things locals love to show off to visitors. "Have you seen Central Market yet?" is the cry, and it's off to what must be one of the largest selections of comestibles most anywhere. How about 7 kinds of bananas, 10 varieties of potatoes and 11 of mushrooms, 18 to 40 kinds of apples, 19 styles of olives, 20 choices of sushi, 25 kinds of salad greens, 37 varieties of coffee beans, 2,500 different wines — you get the idea.

And you can get your fill of samples as you wander thorough all 68,000 square feet of food. Sample a tasty sharp cheese in the cheese department, bite-size bits of amandine tart in the bakery, Mom's spaghetti sauce on a bit of pasta, Mamo's garlic sauce for chicken and fish in the sauce department, Oka's dressing for salad and dip on both a tortilla chip and in a tiny cupful of lettuce, or albino salmon hot in coconut sauce in the fish department. There's almost no need to adjourn to the Central Market Cafe, although the food there, indoors or out on the covered patio (with fans for cooling), is an adventure as well, especially the Texas-size breakfast tortilla served daily until 11am.

Specializing in high-quality food free from chemicals, the market offers more than 500 organic products throughout the store, including produce, olive oil, wine, and dairy products. Regularly scheduled cooking courses are also offered, such as the fancy hors d'oeuvre class taught by the chef of a local catering service.

And now you can duplicate the same experience on the south side of town at Central Market Westgate, 4477 S. Lamar Blvd. (512-899-4300), with the same fresh produce, exotic specialties, cafe, and tempting samples as the original.

South Austin Farmers' Market (2910 S. Congress, Austin, TX 78704, in El Gallo parking lot; Sat. 9am–1pm year round) Rain or shine, hot or cold, this long-time weekly market sells seasonal fresh vegetables, fruits and flowers, and occasional products such as jams and jellies.

There's barbecuing right on the pavement at the Travis County Farmers' Market.

Eleanor S. Morris

Travis County Farmers' Market (512-454-1002; austin.citysearch.com, search: Travis County Farmers' Market; 6701 Burnet Rd., Austin, TX 78757; daily 8am–6pm) There's not as much going on under the roofs of this open-air market as there used to be, but still to be had among the produce are such Texas specialties as the 1015 onion (which wins over even the Vidalia in sweetness and size), vine-grown tomatoes, watermelons and fabulous Hill Country peaches. BBQ World Headquarters (www.bbqworldheadquarters.com) at the market serves special certified Angus beef — the brisket melts in your mouth — and 100 percent pure pork sausage "made especially for us," says owner Kathy Bischoff. Texas Primitive Furniture is big on Texas primitive armoires and cabinets. The cabinets are stocked with local products made by farmers, such as salsa, chilies, and spices.

HEALTH AND NATURAL FOODS

Sun Harvest Farms (512-444-3079; austin.citysearch.com, search: Sun Harvest Farms; 4006 S. Lamar Blvd., Austin, TX 78703; daily 8am–10pm) This specialist in all-natural foods offers a farmers' market of organic produce, meats untreated with antibiotics, vegan (no animal products) baked goods, gourmet organic cheeses, homeopathic vitamins, herbs, and remedies, and a cafe and juice bar, here and at their north location, 2917 W. Anderson Ln., Austin, TX 78757.

Whole Foods Market (512-476-1206; austin.citysearch.com, search: Whole Foods Market; 601 N. Lamar Blvd., Austin, TX 78703; daily 8am–10pm) Whole Foods considers itself alone in the entire nation for a quality standard prohibiting artificial color, flavors, additives, preservatives, chemicals, and growth hormones in any Whole Foods products. Food that has been irradiated and grains and grain products that have been bleached or bromated are not sold here.

AUSTIN CULTURE

A ustin natives and visitors alike enjoy the rich bounty of cultural opportunities here that reflect not only the area's history and traditions but also the latest trends in the arts and entertainment.

ARCHITECTURE

Eleanor S. Morris

The LBJ Library is one of Austin's most striking architectural landmarks.

A ustin has some wonderful old buildings to view on foot or by car. First and foremost, the red granite **Texas State Capitol**, downtown at 11th and Congress Ave., has always been deep in the heart of Texas. Built in 1888, it was declared a National Historic Landmark in 1986 and was recently renovated. It's constructed of native granite eons old — if you get up close you can see fossils imbedded in the stone. The dome, crowned by a statue of woman holding aloft a star, is 14 feet higher than the Capitol dome in Washington, D.C.

The dome is special for more than its height. Travelers to Paris, Florence, and Rome marvel at three of the four examples in all the world of a "floating dome," while the fourth is right here in Austin. (A floating dome is an inner dome constructed within an outer one.) The Texas floating dome can be viewed from the fourth balcony display area, where you can look down from a dizzying height to the beautiful mosaic floor of the rotunda below, or up to the bronze star and the letters T-E-X-A-S on the ceiling.

Tours start every 15 minutes Mon.–Fri. 8:30am–4:30pm, and every half hour Sat. and Sun. 9:30am–4:30pm, beginning next to the Information Desk left of the front entrance on the first floor. Parking is free at Capitol Visitor Parking Garage east of the Capitol between 12th and 13th Sts.

Also in Austin's **downtown area** are elegant business houses, dating from 1850 to 1940, along Congress Avenue and 6th Street. In the Bremond Block, view fashionable Victorian-era residences. **Hyde Park**, just north of downtown, is a still-viable neighborhood of Victorian and Craftsman homes. The **Texas State Cemetery** is the final resting place of many Texas patriots, including Stephen F. Austin.

Detailed brochures with maps are available at the **Austin Convention and Visitors Bureau, Visitor Information Center** (512-478-0098, 800-926-2282; www.austintexas.org; 201 E. 2nd St., Austin, TX 78701; Mon.–Fri. 8:30am–5pm, Sat. 9am–5pm, Sun. noon–5pm).

Three free **guided walking tours** depart from the south entrance of the State Capitol (weather permitting). The 60-minute Capitol grounds tour leaves at 2pm on Sat., 9am on Sun. The 90-minute Bremond Block tour leaves at 11am on Sat. and Sun. The Congress Avenue and E. 6th Street tour, also 90 minutes, departs at 9am on Thurs., Fri., and Sat. and at 2pm on Sun.

Free visitors' parking lots are at 15th and Congress, and 12th and San Jacinto. For information, call 512-454-1545 during the day or 800-926-2282, ext. 7226, to leave a message at any time.

DANCE

Ballet Austin (512-476-2163; www.balletaustin.org; 300 Guadalupe St., Austin, TX 78705) Austin's first professional ballet company is known for both classical and contemporary works presented during the fall-to-spring season. An annual offering is *The Nutcracker* every December.

Tapestry Dance Company (512-474-9846; www.tapestry.org; TDC Studios, 507-B Pressler, Austin, TX 78703) A professional multiform dance organization, Tapestry performs often at Austin's Paramount Theater. It also holds classes in the Tapestry Dance Academy, located on Pressler near 5th St.

University of Texas (512-471-1444, 800-687-6010; www.utexas.edu/cofa/theatre; Dept. of Theatre and Dance, University of Texas at Austin, Austin, TX 78712; box office: Bass Concert Hall, 23rd St. and E. Campus Dr.) The Department of Theatre and Dance offers performances regularly.

GALLERIES

Take a walk along 6th Street — and South Congress — for some interesting galleries.

Art on 5th Fine Art Gallery (512-481-1111; 1501 W. 5th St., Austin, TX 78703; Mon.–Sat. 10am–6pm) More than 100 artists are represented in this eclectic gallery. Miró, Picasso, and Chagall share space with emerging local artists.

f8 Fine Art Gallery (512-480-0242; www.f8fineart.com; 1137 W. 6th St., Austin, TX 78703; Tues.–Sat. 10am–6pm, Sun. 1pm–5pm) Photography and painting by regional and international artists are shown here.

Fire Island Hot Glass Studio (512-389-1100; austin.citysearch.com, search: Fire Island Hot Glass; 3401 E. 4th St., Austin, TX 78202; Tues.–Sat. 9am–4pm) All sorts of handblown glass is for sale here: paperweights, vases, perfume bottles, oil lamps, drinking glasses, Christmas ornaments, glass bead jewelry, fish, even refrigerator magnets. You can watch it being blown, too. Demos take place Sat. 9am–noon.

Gallery Soco (512-442-5144; 1714-A S. Congress, Austin, TX 78704; Tues.–Sat. 11am–6pm, Sun. 1pm–5pm) Fine art, with more than 300 artists represented.

Gallery 1313 (512-441-6500; 1313 S. Congress, Austin, TX 78704; Mon.–Fri. 10am–7pm, Sat. 10am–7pm, Sun. noon–5pm) Contemporary fine art gallery.

Guadalupe Arts Center (512-473-3775; 1705 Guadalupe St., Austin, TX 78701; Tues.–Sat. 10am–6pm) This gallery offers 1,800 square feet of diverse works by resident and local artists.

Stephen Clark Gallery (512-477-0828; 1101 W. 6th St., Austin, TX 78703; Tues.–Sat. 10am–4pm) This gallery presents fine art photographs with an emphasis on Mexico and the American Southwest.

Texas Folklife Resources (512-441-9255; 1317 S. Congress, Austin, TX 78704; Tues.–Thurs. 1pm–6pm, Sat. 1pm–5pm) This gallery showcases Texas folk art.

Wally Workman Gallery (512-472-7428; www.wallyworkmangallery.com; 1202 W. 6th St., Austin, TX 78703; Tues.–Fri. 10am–5pm) Specializing in excellent fine art, the gallery features original works by many Austin artists.

Women and Their Work (512-477-1064; 1710 Lavaca St., Austin, TX 78701; Mon.–Fri. 9am–5pm, Sat. noon–4pm) This statewide nonprofit contemporary art gallery and gift shop has featured Texas women artists for more than 50 years.

HISTORIC HOMES

In addition to the historic homes you can see in Austin's Bremond Block and Hyde Park neighborhood (see "Architecture") are these mansions open to the public.

GOVERNOR'S MANSION OF TEXAS
512-463-5516.
www.governor.state.tx.us/mansion.
1010 Colorado St., Austin, TX 78701.
Open: Tours every 20 minutes Mon.–Thurs. 10am–noon.
Admission: Free.

Master builder Abner Cook built this Greek Revival mansion in 1856, and every Texas governor since then has called it home. Outside, the two-story fluted columns were built of Bastrop pine, and inside its brick walls were plastered by an African-American slave. Governor Elisha Pease was the first occupant, and he was pleased to be able to view the Fourth of July fireworks from the balcony.

THE NEILL-COCHRAN MUSEUM HOUSE
512-478-2335.
2310 San Gabriel St., Austin, TX 78705.
Open: Weds.–Sun. 2pm–5pm.
Admission: $2.

A blend of Greek Revival architecture and native Texas materials makes this mansion a unique Austin landmark. Abner Cook, the master builder who also built the Governor's Mansion, used native limestone and pine from Bastrop to construct this home in 1855 for Washington L. Hill. It was home to a succession of owners (during the Civil War, Federal soldiers were hospitalized here, and some are buried near the house) until it was purchased in 1958 by the Colonial Dames of America.

LIBRARIES

AUSTIN HISTORY CENTER
512-974-7480.
www.ci.austin.tx.us/library/lbahc.htm.
810 Guadalupe St., PO Box 2287, Austin, TX 78768.
Open: Mon.–Thurs. 10am–9pm, Fri. & Sat. 10am–6pm, Sun. noon–6pm.
Admission: Free.

The history center is housed in another of Austin's historic buildings, this one an Art Deco interpretation of Renaissance Revival style. It was built in 1933 as the Austin Public Library and is still fondly referred to as "Old Main." (The new building, ultramodern glass and cement, is right next door.) Everything ever printed or recorded about Austin and Travis County is zealously collected and protected within its walls, and the library is run by a very helpful and friendly staff.

CENTER FOR AMERICAN HISTORY AT THE UNIVERSITY OF TEXAS AT AUSTIN

If you're looking for Texas history, you'll find it here in 120,000 volumes of Texana. Stephen F. Austin's papers and those of his father, Moses

The University of Texas displays the Santa Rita No. 1 oil rig. The gusher from this well was the first to provide revenues for the university.

Eleanor S. Morris

512-495-4515.
www.cah.utexas.edu.
2.101 Sid Richardson Hall,
Austin, TX 78712.
University of Texas campus
on Red River next to the
LBJ Library.
Open: Mon.–Sat. 9am–5pm.
Admission: Free.

Austin, are here, as are the Bexar Archives, the Barker Texas History Collections, and other important historical materials dealing with the settling of the state. A closed-stack library, it's open for research to anyone abiding by the rules.

**JOHN HENRY FAULK
CENTRAL LIBRARY**
512-499-7599.
austin.citysearch.com,
search: John Henry Faulk
Central Library.
800 Guadalupe St., Austin,
TX 78701.
Open: Mon.–Thurs.
9am–9pm, Fri.–Sat.
9am–6pm, Sun.
noon–6pm.
Admission: Free.

This four-story main branch of the Austin library system offers business information, books, children's programs, consumer services, and periodicals dating back to the 1800s. Out in front is one of the city's Art in Public Places, *Eagle II* by David L. Deming, made of Cor-Ten steel.

**LYNDON BAINES
JOHNSON LIBRARY
AND MUSEUM**
512-721-0200.
www.lbjlib.utexas.edu.
2313 Red River St., Austin,
TX 78705.

The presidential library houses 40 million pages covering the entire public career of Lyndon Baines Johnson as well as those of close associates (used primarily by scholars). Year-round exhibits from the permanent historical and cultural collections include gifts from foreign heads of state, a moon rock, and a replica of the Oval Office. Visitors'

Open: Daily except
  Christmas 9am–5pm.
Admission: Free.

remarks suggest the library's scope and impact: "I don't know when I've seen a place so educational, so beautiful, or emotional in my life" and "This is what a presidential library should be like."

Don't miss the First Lady's Room, a comprehensive exhibit of Lady Bird Johnson's life and times.

TEXAS STATE LIBRARY AND ARCHIVES COMMISSION
512-936-INFO (-4636).
www.tsl.state.tx.us.
1201 Brazos St., PO Box 12927, Austin, TX 78711.
Open: Mon.–Fri. 8am–5pm;
  Genealogy Dept.
  Tues.–Sat. 8am–5pm.
Admission: Free.

Some of Texas's most important historical documents and collections are housed in the Texas State Library, including genealogy records. In the lobby of the building — named for an elected interim vice-president of the Texas republic — a 13-foot by 45.5-foot mural, painted by Peter Rogers in collaboration with Peter Hurd, depicts events and personages of the republic. Also in the lobby are exhibits displaying artifacts of the Texas republic, and on the second floor is a colorful display of every flag that played a part in Texas history. A large statue of Sam Houston stands at the entrance to the building.

MUSEUMS

Austin museums reflect the history of both the city and the state, as well as the sometimes esoteric interests of its residents.

THE AUSTIN MUSEUM OF ART DOWNTOWN
512-922-4246.
www.amoa.org.
823 Congress Ave., Austin, TX 78701.
Open: Tues.–Sat.
  10am–6pm, Thurs. to 8pm, Sun. noon–5pm.

The goal of this newer branch of the art museum, housed in what was once the First City Bank but is now the 823 Congress Building, is to make exhibitions accessible and exciting for the widest audience possible, through the exhibits themselves, tours, and special programs.

THE AUSTIN MUSEUM OF ART AT LAGUNA GLORIA
512-458-8191.
www.amoa.org.
3809 W. 35th St., Austin, TX 78703.
Open: Tues.–Sat. 10am–5pm, Thurs. 10am–8pm, Sun. noon–5pm.

Set on 12 green acres of lovely grounds once owned by Stephen F. Austin, who purchased the land in 1832 but died before he could build on it, the museum is nationally known for its art exhibits, sculpture gardens, and educational programs. The museum building was once the home of Clara Driskill Servier, considered a heroine for her work in preserving the Alamo for posterity, and was deeded to the Texas Fine Arts Commission in 1943. The grounds, in the middle of the city, are secluded, shady, and spacious, with meandering walks,

Admission: Adults $2, students $1, children 12 and under free.

sunken sculpture gardens, and rock terraces down to the shores of Lake Austin. (The museum has been under extensive renovation, and hours and admission may change.)

Eleanor S. Morris

The new Texas-size Bob Bullock Museum.

THE BOB BULLOCK TEXAS STATE HISTORY MUSEUM
512-936-TSHM (-8746).
www.TheStoryofTexas.com.
1800 N. Congress. Ave.,
Austin, TX 78712.
Open: Mon.–Sat. 9am–6pm,
Sun. noon–6pm.
Admission: Adults $5,
seniors $4.25, under 18 free.
IMAX Theater: Adults $6.50,
seniors $5.50, under 18 $4.50.

Not surprisingly, this is a Texas-size museum. The expansive lobby features a four-story rotunda rising over a 40-foot terrazzo design incorporating themes from Texas's past. Passing through the rotunda, visitors enter the Grand Lobby to stand on a 50-foot granite map of the state. There are three floors of state-of-the-art exhibits and 17 different media and interactive experiences tracing Texas history. The museum boasts Austin's only IMAX Theater with 2-D and 3-D capabilities, as well as the special effects Texas Spirit Theater. Other facilities include a 200-seat indoor/outdoor cafe, a store with a Texas Fair theme, classrooms, and an underground parking garage. There's also a free oudoor parking lot across the street from the museum.

ELISABET NEY MUSEUM
512-458-2255.
www.ci.austin.tx.us/
elisabetney.
304 E. 44th St., Austin, TX
78751.
Open: Weds.–Sat.
10am–5pm, Sun.
noon–5pm, closed Mon. &
Tues.
Admission: Free.

Elisabet Ney was Texas's first sculptor, and she was famous well before she settled in Austin in 1892. Born in Münster, Germany, in 1833, she was the first woman to be accepted into the Munich Art Academy. She sculpted such notables as Bismarck, Garibaldi, and Ludwig II of Bavaria, whose life-size likenesses may be seen in the restored former home and studio today. She and her Scottish husband, Dr. Edmund Montgomery, moved to the United States to escape the Franco-Prussian War. After a 20-year hiatus, she resumed her career in 1892 when she received commissions to model Sam Houston and Stephen F. Austin for the Columbian Exposition in Chicago.

Today these marbles are in the Texas State Capitol, but the plaster models are in the museum. A plaster model of Lady Macbeth, which Ney considered her masterpiece, stands in the full light of the large studio window. Sculpted between 1902 and 1905, the marble statue has been in the collection of the Smithsonian in Washington, D.C., since 1916.

THE FRENCH LEGATION MUSEUM
512-472-8180.
www.frenchlegation
museum.org.
802 San Marcos St., Austin,
TX 78702.
Open: Tours Tues.–Sun.
1–4:30pm.
Admission: adults $4,
seniors $3, students and
teachers $2, under 5 free.

This Greek Revival bayou-style mansion, built in 1841, is Austin's oldest standing building. Preserved by the Daughters of the Republic of Texas, it was built by Alphonse Dubois de Saligny, named chargé d'affaires to the Republic of Texas when King Louis Philippe of France recognized the republic in 1839. But the French nobleman never occupied the legation; he left in a huff because of the "Pig War." The pigs on a neighboring site ate Saligny's corn and, perhaps worse, chewed on some table linens he had purchased in New Orleans on his way to this outpost of civilization. His servant shot the pigs, the animals' owner beat the servant, and the "war" was on.

The legation's kitchen is the only authentic reproduction of an early Creole kitchen in the United States. There's a bang-up Bastille Day celebration every July 14th.

JACK S. BLANTON MUSEUM OF ART
512-471-7324.
www.blantonmuseum.org.
University of Texas Art
Building at 23rd & San
Jacinto Sts.

These galleries are home to 20th-century art from both North and Latin America as well as the Michener Collection, deeded to the university by novelist James A. Michener and his wife. You can also see a Gutenburg Bible printed in 1455, plus exhibits of photography and the theater arts. The mu-

Mail: Blanton Museum of Art, 23rd & San Jacinto Sts., Austin, TX 78712. Open: Mon.–Fri. 9am–5pm, Thurs. to 9pm, Sat. & Sun. 1pm–5pm. Admission: Free.

seum has acquired the Suida-Manning Collection, one of the most important collections of Old Masters in private hands.

O. HENRY MUSEUM
512-472-1903.
www.ohenryfriends.com.
409 E. 5th St., Austin, TX 78701.
Open: Weds.–Sun. noon–5pm.
Admission: Free.

Austin is proud to boast that William Sidney Porter, otherwise known as short story master O. Henry, once lived in Austin, from 1893 to 1895. His 1886 Queen Anne-style cottage contains his desk, writing materials, and other period furnishings. The first weekend in May the museum sponsors the O. Henry Pun Off competition. Open to the public, it's held in the backyard, where both a book fair and a country-western concert are going on at the same time. All three trophies — first, second, and third — are of "the rear end of a horse."

TEXAS MEMORIAL MUSEUM
512-471-1604.
www.tmm.utexas.edu.
2400 Trinity St., Austin, TX 78705.
Open: Mon.–Fri. 9am–5pm, Sat. 10am–5pm, Sun. 1–5pm.
Admission: Free.

An eclectic mix of Texas's cultural and natural history and science, with dinosaur fossils, antique firearms, wildlife dioramas, native American artifacts, rare gems and minerals, and the original Goddess of Liberty statue removed from the Capitol dome during a recent restoration. Gift shop.

UMLAUF SCULPTURE GARDEN & MUSEUM
512-445-5582.
www.umlaufsculpture.org.
605 Robert E. Lee Rd., Austin, TX 78704.
Open: Weds.–Fri. 10am–4:30pm, Sat. & Sun. 1–4:30pm.
Admission: Adults $3.50, seniors $2.50, students $1, children 6 and under free.

In 1985 Charles and Angeline Umlauf gave their home, studio, and work to the city of Austin. The museum was built with private funds and contains more than 200 sculptures by Charles Umlauf, an internationally known sculptor. The works are displayed by rotation in 6 acres of gardens. The setting is lovely, with a waterfall, streams, and ponds under tall cedars and oaks. The works are executed in diverse materials, from exotic woods to terra-cotta, bronze to alabaster, and range from detailed realism to lyrical abstraction. A 10-minute video shows the late artist talking about his work and philosophy.

MUSIC AND NIGHTLIFE

Austin celebrates music all year long, indoors and out. Here music and nightlife are synonymous: Austin lays claim to the title "Live Music Capital of the World," and there's certainly enough going on all over town — all the time — to merit the title. Through the years Austin has been a magnet for creative souls, giving rise to the live-music culture in which many popular rock 'n' roll, blues, jazz, and country-western singers like Willie Nelson got their start. The legacy of Stevie Ray Vaughan, Janis Joplin, Jerry Jeff Walker, the Fabulous Thunderbirds, and others has made Austin a music mecca. Famous for its clubs, Austin's line both sides of East 6th St. (once Old Pecan Street) and spill out over to 5th, to South Congress, all over downtown. The SXSW Festival (South by Southwest; www.sxsw.com), held in March, brings thousands of musicians and listeners from all over the world, as far away as Australia. The Austin City Limits Music Festival (www.aclfestival.com) was held in Zilker Park in September 2002; coordinators hope to make it an annual event. Free outdoor concerts are held regularly ar Auditorium Shores and Waterloo Park.

There is even music at Austin's Bergstrom Airport, two live music stages for your entertainment while you wait for your flight to depart (www.ci.austin .tx.us/austinairport/musicartstours.htm).

You can find information on clubs, restaurants, and shops at the **Austin Convention and Visitors Bureau, Visitor Information Center** (512-474-5171, 800-926-2282; www.austin360.com/acvb; 201 E. 2nd St., Austin, TX 78701). Austin nightspots pack in patrons with high-energy levels for music live and lively, other entertainment, and food. Look for well-known music venues like the Continental Club (www.continentalclub.com), Saxon Pub (www.thesaxonpub.com), and Stubb's (www.stubbsaustin.com). Especially famous is **Antones** for the blues; at the **Elephant Room** there's great jazz. For country-western music and dancing, the **Broken Spoke** on S. Congress is a classic Texas dance hall; Willie Nelson got his start here.

What makes Texas music so varied, so rich? Those in the know credit the intermingling of so many cultures — Hispanic and Spanish, German, Black, Czech, and Anglo — all celebrated in the "Live Music Capital of the World."

And it's not only blues, jazz, rock 'n' roll, and country that move musical Austin; Austinites have a vibrant interest in classical music as well. The Austin Symphony Orchestra, for instance, has a dedicated following; more than 200,000 people attend the orchestra's performances each year.

Austin Symphony (512-476-6064; www.austinsymphony.org; 1101 Red River St., Austin, TX 78701) The oldest symphony orchestra in Texas is under the leadership of Maestro Peter Bay. With its high level of musicianship, the orchestra delights Austin music lovers. Performances are at Bass Hall at the University of Texas, at Palmer Auditorium, Riverside Dr. and S. 1st St., and other venues around town.

University of Texas Performing Arts Center (512-471-1444, 800-687-6010; www.ut pac.org; PO Box 7818, Austin, TX 78713) The center includes Bass Concert Hall, Bates Recital Hall, McCullough Theater, and B. Iden Payne Theater, and hosts music, dance, Broadway, and comedy performances regularly, with major stars, great diversity, artistic integrity, and just plain fun. The center is a flagship institution in the state of Texas; when the English National Opera's production of Prokofiev's *War and Peace* came to the United States, it played in only two venues — the Metropolitan Opera and UT's Bass Concert Hall, where the facilities, amenities, and audiences are first class. Call for more information.

THEATER

The theater arts are thriving in Austin, with a host of offerings noted for both creativity and professionalism. Ticket services include **Austix** (512-454-8497), which gives information on half-price "day of performance" tickets and full-service theater tickets.

Esther's Follies (512-320-0553; www.esthersfollies.com; 525 E. 6th St., Austin, TX 78701; Thurs. 8pm, Fri. & Sat. 8pm and 10pm) One of Texas's premier musical and comedy troupes performs hilarious original satire and musical parody. Both revered and feared for its biting wit, the Follies is a centerpiece of the 6th St. entertainment strip. The large store window on the street behind the stage reveals passersby who stop in wonder at what's going on inside, which adds to the fun.

Hyde Park Theatre (512-452-6688; austin.citysearch.com, search: Hyde Park Theatre; 511 W. 43rd St., Austin, TX 78751) Productions range from comedy to tragedy and everything in between, performed by a variety of groups in this theater on the northern edge of the city's Hyde Park Historical District.

Paramount Theatre (512-472-5470; www.theparamount.org; 713 Congress Ave., Austin, TX 78701) Classic movies on a big screen and local and national touring artists are on the bill in this movie palace. Built in 1915, one of those opulent beauties that drew crowds in vaudeville and early movie days, the Paramount has been beautifully restored and is considered one of the country's most richly detailed historic theaters.

State Theater Company (512-472-5143; www.theaustintheatrealliance.org; 719 Congress Ave., Austin, TX 78701) The theater performs new, innovative productions as well as traditional theater pieces. Performances are usually year-round, from October to September.

Zachary Scott Theatre Center (512-476-0541; www.zachscott.com; 1510 Toomey Rd., Austin, TX 78704) Named for the Austin native turned movie star, this organization is actually two theaters in one: the main stage in the larger building and the Arena Stage around the corner, a theater-in-the round. The long season runs virtually year-round, so interested visitors ought to be able to catch something. Productions in this regional theater, which uses both local and national talent, include musicals, contemporary comedy, and drama.

SEASONAL EVENTS

There's something — often more than one something — happening every month of the year in Austin. The **Austin Convention and Visitors Bureau, Visitor Information Center** (512-474-0098, 800-926-2282; www.austin360.com /acvb; 201 E. 2nd St., Austin, TX 78701) has a complete list.

In JANUARY, the Austin Yacht Club welcomes the New Year with **sailboat races** on Lake Travis (512-266-1336; www.austinyachtclub.org).

FEBRUARY celebrates **Black History Month** as well as **Mardi Gras** — feasting, partying, and parading on 6th St. before Lent (512-499-0980; www.mardi grasaustin.com) — and bawdy, Rio-style **Carnaval Brasileiro** at City Coliseum (512-452-6832; www.sambaparty.com).

MARCH is the time for the **Zilker Park Kite Festival,** one of the oldest in the nation, drawing thousands of professional and amateur kite-flyers (512-453-7174; www.zilkerkitefestival.com). There is also Austin's famous music celebration, **South by Southwest (SXSW),** a massive gathering each year of local and national critics who come to judge musicians from all over the world hoping to make their mark. Austin isn't called the Music Capital of the World for nothing. Workshops, panel discussions, and hundreds of concerts performed at more than 25 city venues bring 15,000 music aficionados to the streets and clubs of Austin (512-467-7979; www.SXSW.com). (See "Music and Nightlife" above for more information.)

For the athletes among us there's the renowned **Capitol 10,000** (512-472-3254; www.runtex.com), an event that puts thousands of runners on the downtown streets. Part of the show: the unique costumes that appear among the racers.

Later in the month and into April, Austin goes cowboy for the **Star of Texas Fair & Rodeo**. PCRA competitors hit the arena, and area students exhibit prize livestock. There's headline entertainment, too, at the Texas Exposition Center (512-919-3000; www.staroftexas.org).

As for APRIL, for the more sophisticated crowd, the annual **Texas Hill Country Wine & Food Festival** gathers together the state's chefs, food consultants, food writers, and gourmets. A highlight is the Hill Country wine auction (512-329-0770; www.texaswineandfood.org). The **Austin Fine Arts Festival,** formerly known as the Fiesta at Laguna Gloria, features 200 nationally juried artists, local musicians, and hands-on art activities for children at Republic Square, 5th and Guadalupe (512-458-6073; www.austinfinearts festival org).

Music this month can be found at the **Bob Marley Festival,** which pays tribute to the king of reggae with music, arts and crafts, and Jamaican food at Auditorium Shores (512-773-5177; www.austinmarleyfest.com/AustinMarley.html). And a new event, designed to preserve Austin's parks as the best of the best, is the **Austin ParksFest,** featuring a concert, a barbecue cook-off, the Capital of Texas Triathlon, and a fun run (512-477-1566; www.austinparksfest.org).

MAY brings the **Old Pecan Street Spring Arts and Crafts Festival,** turning East 6th St. (known in the mid-1880s as Pecan Street) into a lively street fair with more than 400 art, crafts, and food booths, and live music (512-441-9015; www.roadstarproductions.com). **Cinco de Mayo** celebrates Mexico's 1862 battle for independence from France in a lovely fiesta with mariachi music and Tex-Mex food at Fiesta Gardens and other locations (512-499-6700; www.austin-cincodemayo.com).

JUNE brings **Juneteenth,** when African-Americans commemorate their heritage with music, food, and stirring speeches at Waterloo Park (512-928-1989).

JULY is ushered in with one of Austin's most popular traditions. 50,000 Austinites gather at Zilker Park for the **Fourth of July Fireworks & Symphony.** The Austin Symphony hosts this annual concert of patriotic music that ends with the *1812 Overture* on the Auditorium Shores outdoor stage as a fantastic fireworks show explodes over Town Lake.

Bastille Day at the French Legation celebrates the French Independence Day on July 14th. Once the headquarters of the French chargé d'affaires to the Republic of Texas (see "Museums"), the legation is the site of festivities with gourmet wines and pastries, French fashions, French singers, and even fencing duels (512-472-8180).

AUGUST brings the **Austin Chronicle Hot Sauce Festival.** Join amateurs and pros alike as they compete with their hottest sauces in a taste-off at Waterloo Park (512-454-5766; www.austinchronicle.com).

In SEPTEMBER, Austin celebrates **Diez y Seis** on the 16th with music, food, and other fun festivites to celebrate Mexico's independence from Spain, at Plaza Saltillo and various other sites (512-472-0516). The **Austin City Limits Music Festival** brings the magic of the famed public TV series *Austin CIty Limits* outside the studio and into Austin's beloved park, Zilker. The **Old Pecan Street Fall Festival** turns 6th St. into a lively street fair with musicians, food vendors, artists, and craftspeople (512-441-9015; www.roadstarproductions.com).

OCTOBER brings the **Texas Wildlife Expo** to the Texas Parks and Wildlife Headquarters (512-389-2901; www.tpwd.state.tx.us/expo; 4200 Smith School Rd., Austin, TX 78744), with hands-on activities and educational, fun lessons about wildlife management, conservation, hunting, fishing and camping. The **Austin Film Festival,** recognized as one of the top film festivals in the country, shines the spotlight on top-billed films and indies alike at the Paramount Theatre and various other locations (512-472-2901; www.the paramount.org). For the athletes, Austin's own three-time Tour de France champion Lance Armstrong leads the pack during **Ride for the Roses Weekend,** a program of bike events and galas that raises money for cancer research (512-236-8820; www.laf.org).

Be forewarned that **Halloween on 6th Street** brings some 60,000 costumed revelers to fill the barricaded seven blocks of Austin's best-known entertainment area, 6th St.

NOVEMBER heralds the Texas Book Festival, with readings and signings by popular authors as well as live music and poetry readings at the Texas State Capitol (512-477-4055; www.texasbookfestival.org). **Chuy's Christmas Parade** ushers in the season of giving with a procession of giant balloons, marching bands,vintage cars, floats, and celebrities along Congress Ave. (888-439-2489; www.chuysparade.com).

Victorian Christmas on 6th St. transforms Austin's entertainment district into 19th-century London so that Thanksgiving weekend shoppers can get a head start on their Christmas shopping. Booths are filled with holiday craft and gift items (512-441-9015; www.roadstarprodutions.com).

DECEMBER is ushered in with one of Austin's best-loved holiday traditions. Every year **Trail of Lights and Zilker Christmas Tree** begins with the lighting of the 165-foot tree, seen from miles away. Surrounding the tree is a mile-long trail of lights, an extensive and impressive display of holiday figures and winter scenes (512-499-6700).

The **Armadillo Christmas Bazaar** is a unique Austin holiday market, with renowned Southwest artists selling their handiwork. In keeping with the Southwestern theme, you can nibble on tasty Tex-Mex food and move to ubiquitous live Austin music while you shop (512-447-1605; www.armadillobazaar.com).

AUSTIN RECREATION

A ustin prides itself on being in tune with nature. The city lives and breathes within a beautiful natural environment, embracing a total of 191 parks, and is a leading innovator in environmental issues in the nation.

BOATING AND WATER SPORTS

Emma Long Metropolitan Park (512-346-1831; austin.citysearch.com, search: Emma Long Metropolitan Park; 1600 City Park Rd., FM 2222 west of Loop 360) With boat ramps and camping facilities in Austin's largest park, the public can launch boats on Lake Austin all year long.

Town Lake, the section of the Colorado River that bisects Austin, is a year-round training spot for many U.S. collegiate rowing teams, clubs, and amateurs just out to enjoy the water, the weather, and the scenery. **Austin Canoe and Kayak** (512-719-4386; austin.citysearch.com, search: Austin Canoe and Kayak) and **Zilker Park Canoe Rental** (512-478-3852) are handy if you haven't brought your own canoe.

CAMPING

G iven Austin's usually mild weather, the camping season is year-round. August to October is the most popular time at both public parks and private

RV parks, as well as March, an event-filled month. Reservations for these times at least one month in advance are recommended.

Austin Lone Star RV Resort (512-444-6322, 800-284-0206; www.gocamping america.com/lonestar; 7009 S. IH-35, Austin, TX 78744) This national-award-winning park has log cabins, full hookups for RVs, tent camping areas, a pool, and the Hitchin' Post shop offering gifts with a Texas flair. On IH-35 barely 5 miles southeast of the State Capitol.

Crestview RV Park (512-295-2308; S. IH-35, exit 200 south; PO Box 1028, Buda, TX 78610) 80 sites with full hookup, 100 sites total.

Emma Long Metropolitan Park (512-346-1831; 1600 City Park Rd., FM 2222 west of Loop 360) Austin's largest park, with two boat ramps, fishing, water-skiing, and swimming. 20 utility campsites with electricity, 50 tent sites. Entry fee $5 per car, $6 per night.

Pecan Grove RV Park (512-472-1067; 1518 Barton Springs Rd., Austin, TX 78704) 13 three-way hookups, self-contained RVs only.

Royal Palms RV Park (512-385-2211; www.gocampingamerica.com/royal-palms; 7901 E. Ben White Blvd., Austin, TX 78741) 64 sites with full hookups, group facilities, no tents.

FAMILY FUN

Families with children will find plenty of activities in the Austin area. The free brochure *101 Things for Kids to Do in Austin* is available at the **Austin Convention and Visitors Bureau, Visitor Information Center** (512-474-5171, 800-926-2282; www.austin360.com/acvb or www.austintexas.org; 201 E. 2nd St., Austin, TX 78701).

AUSTIN CHILDREN'S MUSEUM
512-472-2499.
www.austinkids.org.
201 Colorado St., Austin, TX 78701.
Open: Tues.–Sat. 10am–5pm, Weds. to 8pm, Sun. noon–5pm.
Admission: $4.50, children under 2 free; free admission Weds. 5pm–8pm and Sun. 4pm–5pm.

This museum's philosophy is that learning is fun. Exhibits and programs are designed to appeal to children's interest in science and technology, how people live, and creative expression. Popular permanent exhibits are the Whole Foods Market, where children learn about nutrition while "playing store"; the Music Room, where they can play simple instruments and dance; and the Sound Track Studio, equipped with keyboard and microphone.

AUSTIN NATURE AND SCIENCE CENTER
512-327-8180.

The center offers hands-on education programs about ecology and exhibits about science, natural history, and botany. The Nature Center is on 80

www.ci.austin.tx.us/nature-
science.
301 Nature Center Dr.,
Austin, TX 78746.
Located in Zilker Park off
Stratford Dr.
Open: Mon.–Sat. 9am–5pm,
Sun. noon–5pm.
Admission: Free.

acres of canyons, meadows, and trails just west of Zilker Park.

**JOURDAN-BACHMAN
PIONEER FARM**
512-837-1215.
www.pioneerfarm.org.
11418 Sprinkle Cut-Off Rd.,
Austin, TX 78754.
Open: Year-round, Sun.
1pm–5pm; June–Aug.,
Mon.–Thurs.
9:30am–1pm; Sept.–May,
Mon.–Weds. 9:30am–1pm.
Admission: Adults $4,
children 3–12 $3, under 3
free.

This living-history museum tells the story of life as it was lived in the 1850s on a 2,000-acre cotton farm. Docents in costume demonstrate the work of those days. Depending on the day and time of year, youngsters can watch cows being milked, horses being shod by a blacksmith, or food cooking on an old wood-burning stove. Children can also help plant or pick cotton and watch it being spun into yarn, and they can plan on scrubbing clothes on a washboard anytime.

STEAM TRAINS

Austin Steam Train Association (512-477-8468; www.austinsteamtrain.org) operates three separate excursions on the 143-ton Southern Pacific Locomotive 786, built in 1916: Hill Country Flyer, River City Flyer, and Twilight Flyer. The locomotive pulls 1920s Pennsylvania day coaches and post-World War II streamlined lounge and parlor-sleeper cars.

Hill Country Flyer: Runs year-round from Cedar Park to Burnet and back again, 68 scenic miles each way. The five-hour excursion starts at the station behind Cedar Park City Hall (north of Austin on U.S. 183 near RR 1431), and there's a short layover in small-town Burnet for some entertainment (an enactment of a Wild West shoot-out). Check their Web site (www.austinsteam train.org) for the current schedule.

River City Flyer: Runs June through November, with 90-minute round-trips every Saturday and Sunday from Cedar Park to Austin, with a 2.5 hour layover downtown for shopping and dining. Check their Web site (www.main. org/flyer) for the current schedule.

Twilight Flyer: Seasonal celebrations or theme entertainment on selected Saturday and holiday evenings, round-trip from Cedar Park. Check their Web site (www.main.org/flyer) for the current schedule.

WATER EXCURSIONS

Austin Duck Adventure (512-477-5274; www.austinducks.com; 1605 W. 5th St., Austin, TX 78703) Tour Austin's historic and scenic streets, then splash into Lake Austin for a spin in a unique amphibious vehicle.

Capital Cruises (512-480-9264; www.capitalcruises.com; Hyatt-Regency Boat Dock, Town Lake) Bat-watching excursions; nightly one-hour cruise departing 30 minutes before sunset. Also public sightseeing cruises Sat. & Sun. 1pm, as well as hourly rentals of canoes, pedal boats, kayaks, and electric boats.

Lone Star Riverboat (512-327-1388; austin.citysearch.com, search: Lone Star Riverboat; south shore of Town Lake between the Congress and First St. Bridges) A real old-fashioned paddle wheeler, the *Lone Star* takes sailors for a 90-minute scenic cruise on Town Lake. Mar.–Oct., Sat.–Sun. 3pm. Also additional bat-watching sunset tours Apr.–Oct.

GOLF

Eleanor S. Morris

Golfers ponder their strategy at the Lions' course.

A ustin lays claim to one of the country's premier golf locations. Proof is in the huge number of courses: 20 public ones and 18 large country clubs in the area. Listed below are half a dozen. For more information, contact the **Austin Convention and Visitors Bureau, Visitor Information Center** (512-474-0098, 800-926-2282; www.austin360.com/acvb; 201 E. 2nd St., Austin, TX 78701) or check out www.mygolf.com/golf/courses/TX/Austin for a comprehensive review of public golf in and around Austin.

Bluebonnet Hill Golf Course (512-272-4228; austin.citysearch.com, search: Bluebonnet Hill; 9100 Decker Ln., Austin, TX 78724) Greens fees: weekdays $16 to walk, $26 to ride; weekends $27 to walk, $36 to ride.

Butler Park Pitch & Putt (512-477-4430; austin.citysearch.com, search: Butler Park; 201 Lee Barton Dr., Austin, TX 78704) $6 for 9 holes.

Circle C Golf Club (512-288-4297; austin.citysearch.com, search: Circle C; 7401 Hwy. 45, Austin, TX 78739) Greens fees (includes cart): Mon.–Fri. $39, Sat.–Sun. $49.

Hancock Public Golf Course (512-453-0276; austin.citysearch.com, search: Hancock Public Golf; 811 E. 41st St., Austin, TX 78751) Established in 1899, this is the oldest golf course in Texas. It's for walkers. Greens fees: $7.50 for 9 holes on weekdays, $8.50 weekends; $14 for 18 holes on weekdays, $15.50 weekends; seniors $7.50 for 9 or 18 holes weekdays or weekends; juniors (under 18) $6.50 for 9 or 18 holes weekdays or weekends.

Lago Vista Golf Club (512-267-1170; austin.citysearch.com, search: Lago Vista; 4616 Rimrock Dr., Lago Vista, TX 78645) Greens fees: $35 weekdays, $40 weekends.

Lions Municipal Public Golf Course (512-477-6963; austin.citysearch.com, search: Lions Municipal Golf; 2901 Enfield Rd., Austin, TX 78703) Greens fees: $14.50 weekdays, $16 weekends and holidays.

Morris Williams Public Golf Course (512-926-1298; austin.citysearch.com, search: Morris Williams Golf; 4300 Manor Rd., Austin, TX 78723) Greens fees: $13.50 weekdays, $15 weekends.

HIKING, BIKING, AND RUNNING

Austin offers an excellent 30-mile network of trails, 18 of them on well-surfaced scenic paths following natural greenbelts into all areas of the city. An additional 14 miles of trails are natural surface. No motor vehicles are allowed at any time, and all trails have a 10pm–5am curfew. Dogs must be controlled; Austin has a leash law enforced by the Austin Park Police (Rangers). For maps of the seven Hike and Bike Trails of Austin, contact the **Austin Parks and Recreation Department** (512-499-6700; Mon.–Fri. 8am–5pm; www.ci.austin.tx.us/parks).

Barton Creek Greenbelt: Some runners and bikers prefer paths that follow picturesque creeks. Here you'll find 7.5 miles of natural surface both east and west of MoPac Expressway (Loop 1).

Town Lake Greenbelt: A host of joggers and bikers enjoy Town Lake Trail because of the visual beauty of its 10-plus miles of granite gravel and concrete. Loop A, from MoPac Bridge to Lamar Boulevard, is 2.9 miles; Loop B, Mo-Pac Bridge to South 1st Street, is 4.1 miles.

The Veloway: This 3.1-mile paved asphalt loop wanders through creeks and meadows on more than 100 acres of parkway. Catch it on south Loop 1 or from Bowie High School (512-414-5247; 4103 Slaughter Ln.). Open from dawn to dusk.

Cyclists on the 10-mile Hike and Bike Trail around Town Lake.

Eleanor S. Morris

Waller Creek Walkway: Just east of the main downtown area, Waller Creek Walkway follows the creek from 15th St. down where it flows into Town Lake, 0.75 mile of granite gravel, concrete, and brick surface. The Waterloo Park area, 15th St. south to 10th St., is 0.25 mile. Lower Waller Creek Development, 10th St. south to Town Lake, is 0.5 mile.

Bike rentals are available at **University Cyclery** (512-474-6696; www.ucycle austin.com; 2901 N. Lamar Blvd., Austin, TX 78705) and **Bicycle Sport Shop** (512-477-3472; www.bicyclesportshop.com; 1426 Toomey Rd., Austin, TX ; or 512-345-7460; 10947 Research Blvd., Austin, TX 78759).

NATURE AND NATURE PRESERVES

Austin's greenbelts are parks that follow rivers, creeks, and scenic ravines. These areas of scenic beauty are designed to accommodate walking, hiking, jogging, running, bicycling, and even rock climbing in some places. Another special feature of Austin's many natural attractions is its bat colony.

AUSTIN'S BATS
Bat Conservation International (512-327-9721; www .batcon.org) or *Austin American Statesman* (512-416-5700, ext. 3636). Congress Avenue Bridge.

A natural phenomenon unique to Austin is, of all things, its bat colony. Just after sunset between March and November the largest urban colony of Mexican freetail bats in North America (about 1.5 million at last count) flies out from under Town Lake's Congress Avenue Bridge. Clouds of them blot out the sky as they zoom out on their nightly

Open: Daily at sunset
	Mar.–Nov.
Admission: Free.

quest for dinner fare — insects, about 10,000 to 30,000 pounds a night, for which Austin is mighty grateful.

**BRIGHT LEAF STATE
	NATURAL AREA**
512-459-7269.
Dry Creek south of RR 2222
and Mesa.

These 216 acres of pristine Hill Country, an oasis of peace and beauty in the midst of Austin, are home to abundant wildlife, including gray foxes and migratory songbirds.

**KARST NATURE
	PRESERVE**
512-327-8181.
austin.citysearch.com,
search: Karst Nature
Preserve.
3900 Deer Ln., Austin, TX
	78749.
Open: Dawn to dusk.

Karst originally referred to a limestone plateau in Germany, but the word now means any area with limestone rocks, deep fractures, and caves that feed rainwater directly into underground lakes and streams. This 10-acre preserve over the Edwards Aquifer Recharge Zone features caves, sinkholes, and honeycomb outcroppings along the ⅛-mile trail, a pleasant winding walk of about 20 minutes (including stops for bird watching and inspecting the caves and sinkholes). However, don't explore the caves on your own. Wildlife has the run of most of the caves, and others are too risky to head down alone. Call the Austin Nature Center, 327-8181, to arrange for access.

**LADY BIRD JOHNSON
	WILDFLOWER CENTER**
512-292-4100.
www.wildflower.org.
4801 La Cross Ave., Austin,
	TX 78739.
Open: Grounds Tues.–Sun.
	9am–5:30pm.; visitors
	gallery Tues.–Sat.
	9am–4pm, Sun. 1pm–4pm.
Admission: Adults $4,
	students and seniors
	$2.50, children 4 years
	and under free.

Formerly the National Wildflower Research Center, this nonprofit educational organization is unique in its focus on native plants, resource conservation, and ecologically sensitive design. Created by Lady Bird Johnson in 1982 as part of a national beautification project, the center will give you an eyeful of natural beauty — this is the only institution in the nation dedicated exclusively to conserving and promoting the use of plants native to North America, including 75 species of wildflowers. The 42-acre site includes numerous research display gardens, landscaped areas, theme gardens, preserved woodlands, and natural grassland. The gift shop is open Tues.–Sat. 9am–5:30pm, Sun. 1pm–4pm; the Wildflower Cafe is open Tues.–Sat. 9am–4pm, Sun. 11am–4pm.

**WILD BASIN
	WILDERNESS
	PRESERVE**
512-327-7622.
www.wildbasin.org.

These 227 acres of beautiful Hill Country were set aside in the mid-1970s to preserve the land through active management, nature education, and research. Operated with the help of trained volun-

805 N. Capital of Texas Hwy., Austin, TX 78746. Open: Daily, sunrise to sunset. Admission: Voluntary $2 adults, $1 students and children, $6 maximum per family.

teers, about 2.5 miles of trails pass through woodland, grassland, and streamside habitats. (Part of a pedestrian-only trail is wheelchair accessible.) Wild Basin is home to some threatened and endangered species of plants, animals, and birds, such as the golden-cheeked warbler and the black-capped vireo, as well as hundreds of both common and unique species. The office and gift shop are open Mon.–Fri. 9am–4:30pm, Sat. & Sun. 9am–4pm.

ZILKER NATURE PRESERVE 512-480-3060. www.ci.austin.tx.us/ cepreserves/zilker. 302 Nature Center Dr., west of Loop 1 (MoPac); park on Barton Springs Rd. Mail: Austin Parks & Recreation Dept., 200 S. Lamar Blvd., Austin, TX 78704. Open: Dawn to dusk.

On the west end of Zilker Park, this 60-acre preserve with 2 miles of trails features a creek bed (sometimes there's water there, sometimes not) edged with meadows and high cliffs with shallow caves. Foot trails begin under the Loop 1 (MoPac) Bridge and lead up to the dry areas that are endemic to the Edwards Plateau, abundant with mountain laurel, myrtle croton, and croton bush. A rock-walled ramada (an open, covered shelter) overlooks both the preserve and the Austin skyline.

PARKS

Austin enjoys 320 beautiful days a year, so when visitors want to be outdoors, they can be sure to find Austinites already there, taking advantage of the city's 191 parks. Austinites are outdoor people. No matter how large the city is getting, there are parks aplenty for fun, fitness, and relaxation for everyone. It's a rare neighborhood that doesn't have its own park — and rarer still to see one empty. Austin has the distinction of being cited as one of the four best cities in the nation for parks.

Emma Long Metropolitan Park (512-346-1831; austin.citysearch.com, search: Emma Long Metropolitan Park; 1600 City Park Road, off FM 2222 west of Loop 360) is Austin's largest park, with 1,147 acres. The public can launch boats on Lake Austin year-round as well as camp, fish, water ski, and barbecue.

Mayfield Park and Preserve (512-474-9692; www.ci.austin.tx.us/cepreserves .mayfield; 3808 W. 35th St.) is also a preserve; its 22 acres are on Barrow Brook Cove at Lake Austin. On the grounds are lily ponds, peacocks and hens, and trails meandering through woods and over creek bridges and foot stones. On display is a home typical of suburban lake cottage retreats of the late 1800s. Open daily 8am–5pm.

McKinney Falls State Park (512-243-1643, 800-792-1112; www.tpwd.state.tx.us/

park/mckinney; 5808 McKinney Falls Pkwy.) is a 744-acre state park just 13 miles southeast of the State Capitol. The park offers 3.5 miles of hiking and biking trails as well as fishing, picnicking, camping, and viewing such wildlife as birds, white-tailed deer, raccoons, squirrels, and armadillos. Open year-round. Entrance fee $1 per person 13 and over.

Mount Bonnell Park (512-974-6700; austin.citysearch.com, search: Mount Bonnell; 3800 Mt. Bonnell Dr.) is Austin's most romantic park, established in the 1850s and famed for trysts at sunrise and sunset. It's the highest scenic spot (you'll climb 99 steps) for viewing Austin and the surrounding Hill Country. The mountaintop park is 775 feet above sea level, and there's a shade structure and picnic tables on the bluff overlooking Lake Austin. The park is open 5am–10pm.

Pease District Park (512-974-6700; austin.citysearch.com, search: Pease Park; 1100 Kingsbury St., on Shoal Creek along Lamar Blvd.) was the first city park, dedicated in 1876 by Governor Pease himself. One of the city parks with a picnic area for large groups, it also has a wading pool and children's playground, and it's popular for informal volleyball and softball games.

Symphony Square (also downtown, at Red River and 11th Sts.) was given to the city by the state in 1982. Waller Creek runs underneath the street, separating the theater and four restored 100-year-old buildings open for touring. The Jeremiah Hamilton home is the only original one — the other three were moved here from other locations. Jeremiah Hamilton had been the slave of A. J. Hamilton, a governor during Reconstruction. He was a carpenter, and he built this two-story limestone house, making it triangular in order to wedge it into the lot bordered by Waller Creek, Red River, and 11th Street. The Austin Symphony Society saved it from destruction, and it serves as a refreshment venue when the symphony performs outdoor musical events here. The other three houses date from 1870 (old Wilson Mercantile), 1880 (Doyle House), and 1887 (Hardeman House).

Woolrich Park, a bright green square with a charming white gazebo, is set in the middle of downtown on Guadalupe between 9th and 10th Sts. One of four parks deeded in the original city plan when Edwin Waller came to survey the city, it has been the scene of countless weddings, political rallies, and the occasional city council swearing-in.

Zilker Park (512-472-4914; austin.citysearch.com, search: Zilker Park; 2100 Barton Springs Rd. on Town Lake) is one of Austin's most popular parks. Originally the site of temporary Franciscan missions in 1730, the 400-acre downtown park along the shores of the lake counts Barton Springs Pool among its attractions. Zilker Gardens in the park includes an Oriental garden, a meditation trail, a famous rose garden, a Swedish log cabin from the 1840s, and a fine garden center as well as the Austin Nature and Science Center (www.ci.austin.tx.us/nature-science). Open daily 5am–10pm.

SKATING

Chaparral Ice Center at Northcross Mall (512-451-5102; www.austin360.com, search: Chaparral Ice Center; 2525 W. Anderson Ln., Austin, TX 78757) . You can catch a taste of real winter every day in this ice-skating rink located inside a shopping mall. Open Mon., Weds. 10am–11:15am, adults only; noon–5pm; 7pm–9pm; Tues. 10am–1pm; Fri. 10am–5pm; Sat. 12:30pm–9pm; Sun. noon–6pm (subject to change). For a truly professional ice-skating facility, check out Chaparral Ice's new 40,000-square-foot rink in North Austin (512-252-8500; 142000 IH-35 N. at Wells Branch Pkwy.).

SWIMMING

Austin's soaring summer temperatures and Austinites' love of outdoor sports make swimming a popular pastime here.

Barton Springs Pool is open year-round.

Eleanor S. Morris

BARTON SPRINGS POOL
512-867-3080.
austin.citysearch.com, search: Barton Springs Pool.
2100 Barton Springs Rd., Austin, TX 78746.
Located in Zilker Park.
Open: 5am–10pm daily, except Thurs., when it closes at 7pm for maintenance.
Admission: Adults $2.50 weekdays, $2.75 weekends; children 12–17 75¢, children 11 and under 50¢.

Barton Springs Pool is a local institution, regardless of the chilliness of the water. The spring-fed water that gushes up from the Edwards Aquifer to fill Austin's favorite swimming pool is said to remain a constant 68 degrees. Although to many it may feel absolutely arctic, water enthusiasts swim all year long in the 944-foot chlorine-free pool. Lifeguards are on duty 9am–8pm.

McKINNEY FALLS STATE PARK
512-389-8900, 800-792-1112. www.tpwd.state.tx.us/park /mckinney.
5808 McKinney Falls Pkwy., Austin, TX 78744.
Open: Daily year-round.
Admission: $2 per person 13 and over.

Two creeks, Onion and Williamson, form quiet pools and waterfalls at the park. There's an excellent visitor center, hiking and interpretive trails, campsites, a playground, and fishing as well as swimming. Historically interesting are the preserved circa 1850 ruins of the homestead of one of Stephen F. Austin's original 300 colonists, Thomas F. McKinney, for whom the park is named. For modern fun, check out the Texas State Park Store.

STACY PARK & WADING POOL
512-476-4521.
700 E. Live Oak, Austin, TX 78704.
Open: Year-round, Mon.–Fri. 6am–8pm, Sat. & Sun. noon–7pm (subject to change).
Admission: Free.

This is another of the Hill Country's spring-fed swimming holes. Warm, steamy water is the attraction to this outdoor pool during cooler months.

TENNIS

Austin offers more than fifteen tennis facilities totaling 200 courts. For information on public courts all over the city, call the **Austin Parks & Recreation Dept.** at 512-480-3020.

AUSTIN SHOPPING

Austin can boast of a remarkably eclectic shopping scene — you can easily shop till you drop, from the sidewalk arts and crafts market on "the Drag" (Guadalupe Street alongside the University) and South Congress Avenue to malls like Barton Creek, with its panoramic views of both the Austin skyline and the outlying hills.

ANTIQUES

You can pick up a guide, map included, of 21 Austin-area antique shops at the **Austin Convention and Visitors Bureau, Visitor Information Center** (512-478-0098, 800-926-2282; www.austin360.com/acvb; 201 E. 2nd St.; Mon.–Fri. 8:30am–5pm, Sat. 9am–5pm, and Sun. noon– 5pm).

BOOKS

A ustin's bookstore sales are the highest per capita of the fifty largest cities in the U.S. Here are several venues for this highly regarded pastime.

Barnes & Noble (512-418-8985; austin.citysearch.com, search: Barnes & Noble; 10000 Research Blvd., Austin, TX 78759; daily 9am–11pm) This giant bookstore in the Arboretum also has a cafe (serving Starbucks coffee) and a music department. Check out the Web site for Barnes & Noble's four other locations.

Book People (512-472-5050, 800-853-9757; www.bookpeople.com; 603 N. Lamar, Austin, TX 78703; daily 9am–11pm) One of America's largest bookstores is the boast here, with four floors containing more than 300,000 titles, a 2,000-title newsstand, cards and stationery, comfortable chairs and couches, an espresso bar, and even jewelry and arts and crafts from around the world.

Half Price Books (512-454-3664; austin.citysearch.com, search: Half Price Books; 8868 Research Blvd., Austin, TX 78758; Mon.–Sat. 10am–10pm, Sun. noon–9pm) This Texas institution has three locations stocked with new, used, academic, and out-of-print titles, CDs, cassettes, LPs, and videos; most merchandise is half the publisher's price — or less.

TravelFest (512-469-7906; 1214 W. 6th St., Austin, TX 78703; and 512-418-1515; Gateway Center, 9503 Research Blvd., Austin, TX 78758; both stores open daily 9am–9pm) Largest collection of travel books in Texas, plus a wide assortment of travel gear, travel agents, and other services.

University Co-op Bookstore (512-476-7211; www.coop-bookstore.com; 2224 Guadalupe St., Austin, TX 78705; Mon.–Fri. 8:30am–7:30pm, Sat. 9:30am–6pm, Sun. 11am–5pm) Across from UT on the Drag, the Co-op has been an Austin landmark for more than 90 years. With a Barnes & Noble bookstore taking up space next door, the Co-op now mainly stocks textbooks, UT clothing and souvenirs, and art supplies, but they have an extensive search service from their Web site and offer discounts on over 500,000 trade books.

CLOTHING AND ACCESSORIES

V isitors looking for authentic western attire will find the real thing at the following shops, generally open daily:

Allen's Boots (512-447-1413; 1522 S. Congress, Austin, TX 78704) "We know Western wear" is the motto here, with just about every brand of boot made as well as hats, shirts, jeans, and accessories.

Callahan's General Store (512-385-3452; www.callahansgeneral-store.com; 501 Bastrop Hwy., Austin, TX 78741) A little bit east of town out on the Bastrop Highway (Hwy. 183) is this picturesque farm and ranch store, with seed, garden tools, and baby chicks and ducks amidst the boots and saddles.

Cavender's Boot City (512-892-4747; www.cavenders-boots-city.com/scape;

4435 S. Lamar Blvd., Austin, TX 78741) Another big western mart, this one claiming to be the "World's #1 Boot Dealer."

Rewards (512-502-9799, 800-292-0195; austin.citysearch.com, search: Rewards; 9722 Great Hills Trail, Austin, TX 78759) Handwork and jewelry of contemporary artists of the Southwest, such as Hopi jewelry and handcrafted belts and buckles.

CRAFTS

Antigua (512-912-1475; 1508 S. Congress, Austin, TX 78701; 10am 'til whenever) A delightful shop filled with crafts from around the world.

Clarksville Pottery & Galleries (512-454-9079; clarksvillepotterycentral.citysearch.com; 4001 N. Lamar, # 200, Austin, TX 78756; Mon.–Sat. 10am–6:30pm, Thurs. until 8pm, Sun. 11am–5pm) A fine crafts gallery representing 300 artists, about a third of them Texans, the rest out of state. "All-American" creations are featured, including pottery, blown glass, gold and silver jewelry, and wooden ware such as boxes and clocks.

Craftown Gallery (512-331-4252; 13945 N. Hwy. 183, at Hwy. 620, Austin, TX 78717; Mon.–Sat. 10am–6pm, Sun. noon–5pm) An interesting collection of booths offering homier arts and crafts for the home, such as hand-painted wall hangings, floral arrangements, country dolls, candles, and ceramics.

Eclectic Ethnographic Art Gallery (512-477-1816; eclectic.citysearch.com; 700 N. Lamar Blvd., Austin, TX 78703 Mon.–Sat. 10am–6pm, Sun. noon–6pm) Primitive and ancient arts, distinctive furnishings, rugs, belts, jewelry, and adornments.

James Avery Craftsman, Inc. (512-327-6342; www.jamesavery.com; 2901 S. Capital of Texas Hwy., Austin, TX 78746; Mon.–Sat. 10am–9pm, Sun. noon–6pm) Avery handcrafts his work at his studio in the Hill Country in Kerrville, but it's for sale here in Austin at the Barton Creek Square Mall. You'll find unique sterling and 14K gold jewelry, bronze paperweights, and other fine pieces made with the lost wax method and hand finished.

Renaissance Market (512-397-1468; austin.citysearch.com, search: Renaissance Market; on the Drag at 23rd and Guadalupe Sts., Austin, TX 78705; Mon.–Sun. 10am–sunset) An outdoor market of sidewalk artisans across from the university.

Tesoros Trading Company (512-479-8377; www.tesoros.com; 209 Congress Ave., Austin, TX 78701; daily 10am–6pm) Folk art and other treasures (*tesoro* is Spanish for treasure) from around the world, with an emphasis on preserving the crafts of Latin America.

GIFTS

Austin Museum of Art Shop (512-477-0766; www.amoa.org; 823 Congress Ave., Austin, TX 78701; Mon.–Sat. 10am–6pm, Thurs. 10am–8pm, Sun. noon–

5pm) You'll find art gifts, jewelry, decorative accessories, books, T-shirts, gift wrap, and cards plus terrific things for children.

El Interior (512-474-8680; austin.citysearch.com, search: El Interior; 1009 West Lynn St., Austin, TX 78703; Mon.–Sat. 10am–6pm, Sun. noon–5pm) Colorful Mexican folk art: hand-painted wooden animals, pottery and rugs from Oaxaca, terra-cotta pieces from Puebla and Jalisco, lacquer work from Guerrero, and traditional Mexican clothing.

Necessities and Temptations (512-473-8334; austin.citysearch.com, search: Necessities and Temptations; 1202 W. 6th St., Austin, TX 78703; Mon.–Sat. 10am–6pm, Sun. 11am–3pm) Austin and Texas souvenirs, T-shirts, bolo ties, postcards, and such, all handily downtown just west of Congress Avenue.

Pecan Square Emporium (512-477-4900; austin.citysearch.com, search: Pecan Square Emporium; 1122 W. 6th St., Austin, TX 78703; Mon.–Sat. 10am–6pm, Sun. 11am–4pm) A European-style gift shop with Swiss music boxes and German nutcrackers as well as other gifts and jewelry.

Wild About Music (512-708-1700; www.wildaboutmusic.com; 721 N. Congress Ave., Austin, TX 78701; Mon.–Sat. 11am–7pm, Sun. noon–6pm) Everything with a musical motif: apparel, T-shirts, caps and accessories, stationery, collectibles, even art. Also specializing in items related to the Austin/Texas music scene and contemporary jazz.

SHOPPING MALLS

A ustin's shopping malls are generally open daily (although not every shop opens on Sunday).

The Arboretum (512-338-4437; www.austin360.com, search: Arboretum; 10000 Research Blvd., Austin, TX 78759) An outdoor mall with an upscale collection of specialty shops.

Barton Creek Square Mall is one of the city's largest shopping malls.

Eleanor S. Morris

Barton Creek Square Mall (512-327-7040; 2901 S. Capital of Texas Hwy., Austin, TX 78746) Four miles from the center of town, this indoor mall offers a fantastic view of Austin's skyline in addition to Dillard's, Foley's, JC Penney, Montgomery Ward, and Sears, and 180 other fine shops.

Highland Mall (512-454-9656; austin.citysearch.com, search: Highland Mall; 6001 Airport Blvd., Austin, TX 78752) More than 180 specialty shops plus a food court, cart marketplace, and Foley's, Dillard's, and JC Penney at this indoor mall.

Northcross Mall (512-451-7466; austin.citysearch.com, search: Northcross Mall; 2525 W. Anderson Ln., Austin, TX 78757) Located at Burnet Rd., this indoor mall has 60 specialty shops as well as larger stores like Beall's and Oshman Sporting Goods and the only mall ice-skating rink around, Chaparral Ice.

TRAVIS COUNTY

In 1840, when Austin became the Texas capital, Travis County was created from a portion of Bastrop County, the county to the east. But it wasn't fully organized until 1843, when it was named for Alamo commander and hero Colonel William B. Travis. The main business of the county is government, education, and recreation, along with a little farming and ranching. The rolling hills of Travis County, on the edge of the Hill Country, are the setting for Austin, the Colorado River, and Lake Travis. The city of Austin, its suburbs, and its lake — Lake Austin — take up most of the county. The county's other main attraction is Lake Travis, which offers swimming, boating, camping, picnicking, and otherwise enjoying the sunshine and fresh air. Cedar, oak, live oak, pin oak, and pecan trees abound; flowering trees, such as redbud and crape myrtle, also flourish both in the countryside and in the city.

TRAVIS COUNTY LODGING

Once you leave Austin, most accommodations are on Lake Travis, either resorts or bed & breakfast inns, all of them generally open year-round.

RESORTS

BARTON CREEK RESORT & SPA
Manager: James Walsh.
512-329-4000, 800-336-6158.
www.bartoncreek.com.
8212 Barton Club Dr.,
Austin, TX 78735.

Barton Creek calls itself the "Golf Capital of Texas," and with reason: four championship golf courses, including the No. 1 and No. 2 Fazio Canyons and Fazio Foothills. Located in the Texas Hill country just 15 minutes west of downtown Austin, the four-star resort features 300 rooms, 16

Price: Expensive to Very Expensive.
Credit Cards: AE, D, DC, MC, V.

spacious suites, a fitness center and spa, a tennis center, and two restaurants offering casual and gourmet fare as well as Tex-Mex, of course. Room rates at this spread-out resort include doorman fees, luggage handling, golf-ball handling, transportation within the resort, complimentary lobby coffee, a daily newspaper, and use of the fitness center, pools, and nature trails. But the many special packages include, variously, daily breakfast, a round of golf or a sleeve of golf balls, a spa treatment, and other amenities, and all sorts of spa and golf options can be added to any booking. The resort's Golf Advantage School offers a simple approach: "Good fundamentals combined with good mechanics leads to effective results."

LAKEWAY INN
Manager: David McGregor.
512-261-6600, 800-LAKEWAY.
www.lakewayinn.com.
101 Lakeway Dr., Austin, TX 78734.
Price: Expensive to Very Expensive.
Credit Cards: AE, D, DC, MC, V.
Handicap Access: Yes.
Special Features: "A concierge who knows everything."

The inn's 239 guest rooms and suites — 16 with fireplaces — all have views of Lake Travis or the marina, so there's water everywhere. The decor is southwestern and the scenery Hill Country. The resort offers the Travis Room Restaurant for dining and a pub for more casual fare, as well as two swimming pools, two 18-hole golf courses, tennis, boat rentals, a fitness center and spa, nearby horseback riding, and hiking, biking, and jogging trails.

RESORT RANCH OF LAKE TRAVIS
Manager: Gary Baker.
512-264-2533, 800-888-5253.
www.resortranch.com.
Rte. 1, Box 27H, Spicewood, TX 78669.
Price: Inexpensive (tent sites, RV sites, screened cabins) to Expensive (cottages).
Credit Cards: AE, D, MC, V.
Handicap Access: Yes.

The substantial-looking cottages are built of native Texas stone and can sleep six. Spacious living-dining areas have wood-burning fireplaces and large windows overlooking covered decks and views of the Hill Country. Rustic screened cabins, built of wood, are under the trees, with picnic tables and grills right outside. Swimming is either in the large tree-and-deck-surrounded pool or in the lake. Wildflowers in the spring and deer all year long make this a pleasant country resort that also offers tennis, BBQ and picnic areas, a children's playground, horseback riding, a cafe, a country store, lake cruises, waterfront facilities, softball, horseshoe and washer pits, and basketball, volleyball, and tetherball courts.

BED & BREAKFASTS

**ROBIN'S NEST BED &
BREAKFAST ON LAKE
TRAVIS**
Innkeepers: Robin Maisel
and Shelly Carls.
512-266-3413.
www.robinsnestlaketravis
.com.
1007 Stewart Cove, Austin,
TX 78734.
Off RR 620 on Lake Travis.
Price: Moderate to Very
Expensive.
Credit Cards: AE, D, MC, V.
Handicap Access: No.

This cozy getaway has ten rooms in three rustic buildings, many with Jacuzzis and decks overlooking the lake. The inn boasts 100 feet of waterfront, so there's plenty of opportunity for all sorts of water sports. Take breakfast in the kitchen (and read the paper as you would at home) or have it served on the front porch or upper deck. You might be treated to shrimp migas (scrambled eggs, corn tortillas, cheese, tomatillos, and peppers with the shrimp) along with pinto beans and a pistachio fruit salad.

**TRAIL'S END BED &
BREAKFAST**
Innkeepers/Managers:
JoAnn and Tom Patty.
512-267-2901, 800-850-2901.
austin.citysearch.com,
search: Trail's End.
16708 Trail's End Cove,
Leander, TX 78641.
Off Hwy. 183 in Cedar Park.
Price: Moderate to
Expensive.
Credit Cards: AE, D, MC, V.
Handicap Access: No.

The Pattys built their dream house way out in the country, so it's aptly named. The large two-story house has two guest rooms with private baths, plus there's a small cottage equipped with full kitchen and all the amenities. Bird-watching, hiking, a gazebo, and a swimming pool in the woods, with a view out over the hills, make this a most attractive hideaway. Yet you're not too far from the shops and restaurants of nearby Cedar Park or from the Hill Country Flyer, a renovated steam train that takes to the hills every weekend (see "Family Fun").

TRAVIS COUNTY RESTAURANTS, NIGHTLIFE, AND CULTURE

Just in case Austin doesn't have enough restaurants, here are several recommendations outside the city limits.

**THE BELGIAN
RESTAURANT**
512-328-0580.
austin.citysearch.com,
search: Belgian Restaurant.

This elegant restaurant brings to the Texas Hill Country fine meats and seafood graced with continental sauces. "Even Belgians eat steaks," says owner Felix Florez, as he describes one of the restau-

3520 Bee Caves Rd., Austin, TX 78746.
In the western suburb of West Lake Hills.
Price: Expensive.
Cuisine: Continental.
Serving: L, D.
Credit Cards: AE, D, DC, MC, V.
Reservations: Recommended.
Handicap Access: Yes.

rant's specialties, Belgian-style Surf and Turf. A 7-ounce tenderloin is topped with a veal sauce brandy demi-glace, accompanied by sautéed Maine lobster in a white wine seafood crème sauce. Another specialty, Dover sole cardinale, presents the whole fish poached in champagne, stuffed with sautéed spinach, and smothered in a lobster/ Swiss cheese sauce. The venison au poivre is venison tenderloin flambéed in cognac and topped with a green peppercorn crème sauce.

The menu is topped off with rich desserts such as the Belgian sundae, a concoction of vanilla bean ice cream in an almond tuille. The sauce is a ganache of dark Belgian chocolate, and the whole is covered with whipped cream.

CANYONSIDE CAFE AND GRILLE

512-263-4205.
3595 RR 620 S., Austin, TX 78738.
Price: Moderate.
Cuisine: American traditional.
Serving: L, D, SB. Closed Mon.
Credit Cards: AE, DC, D, MC, V.
Handicapped Access: Yes.

The CanyonSide, up a flight of stairs (there's an elevator), overlooks the 30,000-acre Balcones Nature Preserve. Dine inside or outside on the covered deck with its magnificent Hill Country view. Popular at lunch are the hot buffet and salad bar, each with a choice of three entrées, as well as items on the menu, such as the Asian Chicken Salad, the Greek Salad, and sandwiches and burger, too. For dinner, specials are the grilled salmon with lemon-dill butter, and the marinated pork tenderloin in honey-ginger sauce. All the breads, muffins, cornbread, and rolls, are made in-house. As for desserts, "All our desserts are special," says restaurateur Bill Tulloch of Chef Sherry Crickmer's creations.

CIOLA'S ITALIAN-AMERICAN RESTAURANT

512-263-9936.
www.ciolas.com.
1310 Hwy 620 South, suite C-1, Austin, TX 78734.
In the town of Lakeway, in a shopping center.
Price: Moderate to Expensive.
Cuisine: Italian.

Dan Ciola takes pride in both the family motto, "Remember, it's the sauce that counts!" and in the fact that his Uncle Dominick, in his 80s, is still supervising the kitchen in the family's original restaurant in Virginia. That one was established in 1949; the Texas restaurant was opened in 2002, and it's going strong. Happy groups gather around red and white checkered tablecloths digging into pasta, seafood, and steak along with fine wines from a comprehensive wine list. As for delectable food — linguini and clams, fettuccini Alfredo, saltimbocca, veal or chicken marsala, piccata, or parmigiana —

Serving: L, D Mon.–Fri.; D
Sat.– Sun.
Credit Cards: AE, D, MC, V.
Reservations: Yes.
Handicap Access: Yes.

**THE EMERALD
RESTAURANT**
512-263-2147.
www.virtual-restaurants
.com/Emerald.
13614 Hwy. 71 W., Austin,
TX 78733.
Price: Very Expensive.
Cuisine: Irish and
Continental.
Serving: D.
Credit cards: AE, DC, D,
MC, V.
Handicap Access: Yes.

the extensive menu leaves out nothing of renowned
Italian cuisine. Mangia, mangia, mangia!

The Kinsella family, Marge and Paul, with
daughters and sons, have transferred their nostalgia for County Mayo in Ireland to a 1927 limestone and wood cottage here in the Hill Country, but
with a twist. Not only do they serve up Irish dishes
in a most sophisticated manner, but many things on
the menu are very gourmet continental. The soda
bread is served with tasty butters; the "Leprechaun
Irish Stew" has a drop of Creazure flavoring it. Specialties include monkfish seasoned with Irish mustard from Galway Bay, and quail served with
old-fashioned Irish dressing and sauce made with
Irish Mist and herbs. Portions, surrounded by fresh
vegetables, are very generous. The restaurant has a
full bar.

**HUDSON'S ON THE
BEND**
512-266-1369.
www.austin360.com, search:
Hudson's on the Bend.
3509 RR 620, Austin, TX
78734.
Located 1.5 miles west of
Mansfield Dam.
Price: Expensive to Very
Expensive.
Cuisine: Game,
Contemporary.
Serving: D.
Credit Cards: AE, DC, MC,
V.
Reservations: Yes.
Handicap Access: No.

Chefs Jeff Blank and Becky Barsch Fisher didn't
plan to specialize in exotic game, but when they
featured dishes such as grilled ostrich tenderloin
with a porcini mushroom sauce, medallions of kangaroo with fresh kiwi, and even armadillo and rattlesnake, the restaurant got written up in magazines
and newspapers. Thus Hudson's acquired a reputation for wild game. But other dishes are delicious,
too, such as the pork tenderloin stuffed with homemade chorizo (sausage) and served with a mango-
jalapeño sauce. (The restaurant specializes in such
sauces, all of which you can find bottled for sale at
Austin's Central Market.) But no matter what you
order, save room for the corn pudding.

THE OASIS
512-266-2442.
austin.citysearch.com,
search: Oasis.
6550 Comanche Trail,
Austin, TX 78732.

You can't say you've been to Austin if you
haven't gone out to the Oasis. It began in 1982
with five outdoor decks over Lake Travis with seating for 300. It's grown to 28 decks and several indoor dining rooms, with seating for 1,500. "Great

On Lake Travis.
Price: Moderate.
Cuisine: Tex-Mex.
Serving: L, D Mon.–Sat., SB.
Credit Cards: D, DC, V.
Reservations: No.
Handicap Access: Yes.

food, great times — and a terrific view" are what bring the crowds out.

Always a top area attraction because of the view over the lake, especially at sunset, the Oasis is even better these days because the food has greatly improved. We began with crab-stuffed mushrooms — succulent crabmeat topped with Monterey jack cheese in a buttery mushroom cap — then went on to the Oasis super combo of beef enchilada, chile relleno, and a soft chicken taco. Key lime pie and sopapillas (little Mexican puff pastries served with honey to pour inside) were a perfect finish.

And when the sun sets spectacularly over the lake, the music begins. Live entertainment might be anything: blues, jazz, a samba band, or maybe an oldies group. Call to find out who's playing on your night.

... SAM HILL?
   WATERFRONT GRILL
512-266-2811.
16405 Clara Van Trail,
   Austin, TX 78734.
Price: Moderate.
Cuisine: Tex-Mex, Korean,
   Steak, Seafood.
Serving: L, D daily.
Credit Cards: AE, D, MC, V.
Reservations: No.
Handicap Access: Usually
   (depends on level of lake).

You're sure to ask yourself, "What in Sam Hill?" when you see that there is absolutely nothing left off the menu at this waterfront grill, from oysters and fried green tomatoes to bee bim bop (a Korean dish) and eggs Benedict (for brunch). The certified 12-ounce Angus strip steak was served with roasted red potatoes; the lemon pepper tuna, seasoned with a lemon pepper rub, was char-grilled and served with fresh lemon and herbed wild rice. With our specialty drinks like prickly pear margarita and cowboy colada, we got to take home our ... Sam Hill? mugs as souvenirs.

Upstairs above the restaurant is a bar, poolroom, and a band, with eclectic music playing most nights.

NIGHTLIFE

THE BACKYARD
512-263-4146.
www.thebackyard.net.
13101 W. Hwy. 71 W.,
   Austin, TX 78768.
At Hwy. 620 in the town of
   Bee Cave.

The Backyard is a bar and outdoor amphitheater that's the scene of music for every taste ("except symphony"). So for country and country-western, blues and jazz, flamenco guitar, classic rock, and much more, this is the place to come and hear regional and national artists — among them Sheryl Crow, Lyle Lovett, the Neville Brothers — perform in the fresh air of Travis County. Tickets are available at Star Tickets (512-469-SHOW), Albertson's (a local grocery chain), and Waterloo Records.

Eleanor S. Morris

Willie Nelson is a frequent visitor — and performer — at Poodie's Hilltop Bar & Grill in Spicewood, Travis County.

POODIE'S HILLTOP BAR & GRILL
512-264-0318.
www.poodies.com.
22308 Hwy. 71 W.,
Spicewood, TX 78669.

Spicewood is a small community strung along several miles of Rte. 71, and the entertainment here is Poodie's, on the east side of the highway. "Poodie" is Poodie Locke, Willie Nelson's road manager (Willie lives in the neighborhood).

From 11am to 2am daily, the restaurant serves up hamburgers, chili, and chicken-fried steak. The entertainment usually runs from Tues. through Sat. The Troubadillos — the house band — play on Tues., Jimmy Lee Jones hosts open mike on Weds., and a roster of other guests are scheduled for Thurs. through Sat.

With Willie in the vicinity, big-name musicians often drop in — people like Merle Haggard, Toby Key, Pat Green, Cory Morrow, Pauline Reese, and Rusty Weir.

TRAVIS COUNTY FOOD PURVEYORS

Flip's Satellite Cafe (512-301-1883; 7101 W. Hwy. 71, Austin, TX 78735; Mon.–Thurs. 8am–9pm, Fri.–Sat. 7am–10pm; Sun. 8pm–10pm) Although Flip's is technically in the city, it's so close to the city limits at the "Y" at Oak Hill — the crossroads of Hwys. 71 and 290 west to the hills — that it's more in the country than the city. So on the way to Blanco and Gillespie Counties, stop here for breakfast or lunch or a snack. You'll find coffee in the form of cappuccino, latte, and breve, and homemade pastries. A deli-ful of eat-in or take-out sandwiches, chicken salad, and other foods will send you on your way.

Hill Country Cellars Winery (512-259-2000; 1700 N. Bell Blvd., Cedar Park, TX 78613; Fri.–Sun. noon–5pm). A 200-year-old native grapevine, threatened by destruction due to development, was saved in 1990 by the owners, who moved it to this location. A tasting room is located in a 50-year-old limestone ranch house, and a covered patio offers a great spot to enjoy both the wine and the view. The chardonnay is particularly recommended.

Slaughter Leftwich Winery (512-266-3331; 107 RR 620 South, Box 22 F, Austin, TX 79734; Sat.1pm–5pm, but can be irregular; you might want to call ahead) Not only are the chardonnay vineyards here the oldest in Texas, but the wine from these grapes wins the most awards in the state. The sauvignon blanc is pretty special, too. But judge for yourself at the wine tastings. The vineyards are about 3,000 feet above Lake Travis, which gives the grapes a lovely view.

SEASONAL EVENTS

Lago Vista

In APRIL the **Lago Vista Lions Club Chili Cookoff** includes — in addition to the daytime tastings of the entries of expert chili cooks — a beauty contest, arts and crafts for sale, and a Saturday night barbecue and dance.

MAY is the time for the **Turnback Regatta,** with yachts sailing from the Austin Yacht Club to Bar-K Point on Saturday, then back again on Sunday. Meanwhile, during the two-day event, the Lago Vista Volunteer Fire Department puts on a delicious, and partly fiery, barbecue.

Lakeway

In APRIL the **Bluebonnet Bash** celebrates spring with an art exhibit featuring the works of local artists. Visitors can tour both artists' studios and galleries at the Oasis Restaurant and the Slaughter Leftwich Winery.

JULY brings **Under a Texas Sky**, a Fourth of July weekend pops concert by the Austin Symphony Orchestra.

In DECEMBER there's more music, a **Carol Concert** at the Lakeway Inn, with songs by the New Texas Festival Singers.

TRAVIS COUNTY RECREATION

Travis County is one huge playground, centered around Lake Travis. During the long summer, Austinites beat the heat by taking to the water here. Weekends on the lake are a central Texas ritual for sailors, swimmers, water-skiers, scuba divers, fishermen (and women), and windsurfers. The latest rage here is the wakeboard, a combination of a surfboard and water ski.

BOATING AND WATER SPORTS

Dutchman's Landing Marina (512-267-4289; austin.citysearch.com, search: Dutchman's Landing; 17900 Easy St., Jonestown, TX 78645) On Lake Travis; has boat slips as well as boat rentals — including a party barge — and fishing.

Wet & Wild Watercraft Rentals can be found at two locations (360 Bridge on Lake Austin and Yacht Harbor Marina on Lake Travis; 512-266-3644). They pride themselves on having the latest equipment, pleasure boats, ski boats (drivers available), pontoon boats, personal watercraft such as Sea Doo, Tiger-shark, and Polaris, as well as kneeboards, waverunners, tubes, and wakeboards. Hourly and daily waterskiing is offered, and although their regular hours are 9am–8pm daily, "if somebody calls us and wants to go skiing at 7am when the water's really nice, we'll go. . . ."

CAMPING

Travis County has a number of campgrounds, set in a variety of scenery. Two of them don't require reservations — you can just drop in and pitch your tent.

Arkansas Bend Park (512-473-9437, 800-776-LCRA [Lower Colorado River Authority]; www.co.travis.tx.us/tnr/parks; on Lake Travis) Tent sites, boat ramp. $5 per vehicle day use, $10 camping per night.
Camper Resort on Lake Travis (512-266-1562; 17317 W. Beach Rd., Austin, TX 78732; 3 miles from FM 620 near Mansfield Dam on Lake Travis) Hookups, by reservation only.
Cypress Creek (512-473-4083, 800-776-LCRA; www.co.travis.tx.us/tnr/parks; Anderson Road at FM 2769 at Lake Travis) Tent sites, boat ramp. $5 per vehicle day use, $10 camping per night. No reservations.
Mansfield Dam Park (512-473-9437, 800-776-LCRA; www.co.travis.tx.us/tnr/parks; FM 620 at Mansfield Dam Rd.) Picnic areas, rest rooms, boat ramp, tent sites, swimming. $5 per vehicle day use, $10 camping per night.
Pace Bend Park (512-473-9437, 800-776-LCRA, 512-264-1482 for RV reservations; www.co.travis.tx.us/tnr/parks; FM 2322, 4.6 miles east of Hwy. 71) Twenty "improved" RV sites, over 200 tent sites, picnic areas, potable water, boat ramp. $5 per vehicle day use, $10 camping per night, $15 improved sites.
Resort Ranch of Lake Travis (512-264-2533; www.resortranch.com; 1300 N. Pace Bend Rd., Spicewood, TX 78669) Tent sites, RV sites, cabins.

FAMILY FUN

AUSTIN ZOO
512-288-1490, 800-291-1490.
www.austinzoo.com.
10807 Rawhide Trail,
Austin, TX 78736.
Open: Daily (except
Christmas) 10am–6pm.
Admission: Adults $6,
students $5, seniors and
children 2–12 $4, children
under 2 free.

West of Hwy. 71, 20 minutes from downtown Austin, this private zoo offers the whole family a hands-on experience with animals from around the world. The zoo's mission is to foster empathy, understanding, and conservation of nature. A bright red train takes kids for a ride around the zoo ($2).

FISHING

Mike Hastings of **Git Bit** is at your service as a fishing guide (512-280-2861), as is Allen Christianson (512-441-6682). Black and white and stripers (striped bass) and Guadalupe bass abound in Lake Travis. If you're thinking of fishing on your own, please note that access to bank fishing on Lake Travis is limited.

HORSEBACK RIDING

What would any part of Texas — even as urban an area as Austin and Travis County — be without horses and horseback riding? And not just Western cow ponies — you can go English saddle, dressage, hunting, jumping, or just mosey along a trail.

Golden Vista Equestrian (512-243-3500; www.goldenvistaequestriancenter.com; 9513 S. Hwy. 183, Austin, TX 78747) Trail rides (weekends only), over 50 acres in Travis County; indoor and outdoor arenas for lessons in Western, English, hunter-jumper, dressage, and cross-country.

Resort Ranch of Lake Travis (512-264-2533, 800-888-5253; www.resortranch.com; 1300 N. Pace Bend Rd., Spicewood, TX 78669) Horseback riding.

NATURE

Nature reigns in Travis County, thanks to the average 320 beautiful days you can count on each year. Austinites and visitors alike are drawn to Lake Travis and to the nature areas bordering the city.

WEST CAVE PRESERVE
830-825-3442.
www.westcave.org.
FM 3238, Round Mountain,
TX 78663.
Open: Guided tours only,
Sat. & Sun. 10am, noon,
2pm, 4pm, weather
permitting, year-round.
Admission: Donations
accepted.

Many rare and endangered plants are preserved in this 30-acre sanctuary for the golden-cheeked warbler and other rare birds. Stands of ash juniper and live oak are to be found here, as well as grassland savannas with wildflower meadows.

SWIMMING

Bob Wentz Park at Windy Point (512-854-9437; www.co.travis.tx.us/tnr/parks; Comanche Trail off Hwy. 620) This popular Lake Travis beach has a little bit of sand shoreline, which makes it good for windsurfing. There's also some jetskiing and scuba diving. Open: Sept. 10–Oct. 31, 9am–7:30pm; Nov. 1–Feb. 28, 9am–6pm; Mar. 1–Apr. 30, 9am–7:30pm; May 1–Sept. 9, 8am–9pm. Admission: $5 per vehicle.

Hamilton Pool Preserve (512-264-2740; www.co.travis.tx.us/tnr/parks; FM 3238, Hamilton Pool Rd., 30 miles from Austin off Hwy. 71) Hamilton Pool is a unique natural area formed thousands of years ago when the dome of an underground river collapsed. This created a pool and a grotto that attracted the area's first inhabitants, who left artifacts there 8,000 years ago. The grotto and the downstream area support lush and diverse flora and a variety of wildlife. Open: 9am–6pm daily, weather permitting (call for daily updates); no entry after 5:30pm. Admission: $5 per vehicle.

Hippie Hollow Park (512-473-9437; www.co.travis.tx.us/tnr/parks; Comanche Trail off Hwy. 620) Pick your way carefully down the rocks to reach the water at this Lake Travis beach, the only clothing-optional beach (you must be 18 or over to enter). No lifeguards on duty here. Open: Sept. 10–Oct. 31, 9am–7:30pm; Nov. 1–Feb. 28, 9am–6pm; Mar. 1–Apr. 30, 9am–7:30pm; May 1–Sept. 9, 8am–9pm. Admission: $5 per vehicle.

Mansfield Dam (512-473-9437; www.co.travis.tx.us/tnr/parks; Mansfield Dam Rd., 5 miles south of Hwy. 620 and FM 2222) Sixty-five acres with picnic tables and barbecue grills, a boat launch, and a great little cove for swimmers that's especially favored by scuba divers. Sailboats like it, too. (Cars used to be able to drive over the dam, but no more — now the road is open to walkers only.) Open: Year-round sunrise to 9pm. Admission: $5 per vehicle.

TRAVIS COUNTY SHOPPING

In Bee Cave in the mid-1840s, there was a general store, a cotton gin, and a cigar factory by the side of the road. Now there's a small shopping area along the west side of Hwy. 71, next to Wilson's Furniture Store and Tea Room.

House of Harriette & John (512-263-5103; 12719 W. Hwy. 71, Austin, TX 78736; open 10:30am–5:30pm daily except Mon.) These two small white-trimmed brown cottages are surrounded by greenery with a little patio separating them. John, son of Harriette, is a gemologist, and his shop is a treasure trove of minerals and gems. But be prepared — he'll show you a lovely hunk of blue stone and challenge you to identify it. Here's a clue: it's the Texas state gem. John's specialty in gemstones is the Lone Star Cut, the star of Texas faceted in a gem. The shop holds a fascinating array of gems, mineral specimens, and fossils as well as curios created from natural stones.

Harriette's house across the way is packed with antiques, handmade apparel, crafts, toys, and "all sorts of oddities." The work of nationally known artists, many signed and dated, are shown here, such as Carolyn Pfleferer's angels, Karen Germany's black dolls, and Linda MacDonald's Nativity pieces. "When you shop with us, your friends will remember their gifts," Harriette promises.

Living Desert Cactus Nursery (512-263-2428; 12719 W. Hwy. 71, Austin, TX 78736; daily 10am–5:30pm) This shop is covered inside and out with cacti, succulents, and all sorts of related specialty items — mobiles, gourds, pottery vessels. Cacti are propagated from cuttings or grown from seeds: "We don't go around digging up the Hill Country," says Yvonna Dunten, owner. In addition to indigenous cacti, there are fascinating ones from faraway places like Africa and Brazil. "We're only limited by our imagination," says Darrell Dunten of the wild assortment of things in the nursery.

Serendipity Gifts (512-263-7100; 12705 W. Hwy. 71, Austin, TX 78736; Mon.–Sat. "10-ish to 6-ish") This delicious-smelling little shop is full of a medley of things: antiques, jewelry, fine wedding, birthday, and thank-you gifts, original art, fun gifts like puzzles and games, and even edible gifts such as mouthwatering jellies, candies, and condiments, and gift baskets full of the same.

CHAPTER FOUR
Out in the Territory
HILL COUNTRY WEST AND
SOUTH OF AUSTIN
Blanco, Burnet, Gillespie, Hays, Kimble,
Llano, & Mason Counties

Eleanor S. Morris

The Blanco County Chamber of Commerce in Johnson City.

To make such a large territory as the Hill Country manageable, we've divided the 14 counties around Austin and San Antonio (in every direction except east) into two chapters. This chapter covers the seven counties closest to Austin: Blanco, Burnet, Gillespie, Hays, Kimble, Llano, and Mason (in alphabetical order). Chapter Six describes the seven counties around San Antonio.

In all the counties, you'll find a friendly interest in strangers, pride in that specific corner of the land (wild and hostile territory not so long ago), and much the same cuisine, which features Mexican and Tex-Mex dishes, barbecue, and that all-Texan favorite, chicken-fried steak. (However, there's a new note lately, as many eateries offer more "gourmet" dishes on their menus along with old-time favorites.) The cedar and pine of the Hill Country landscape, as well as the

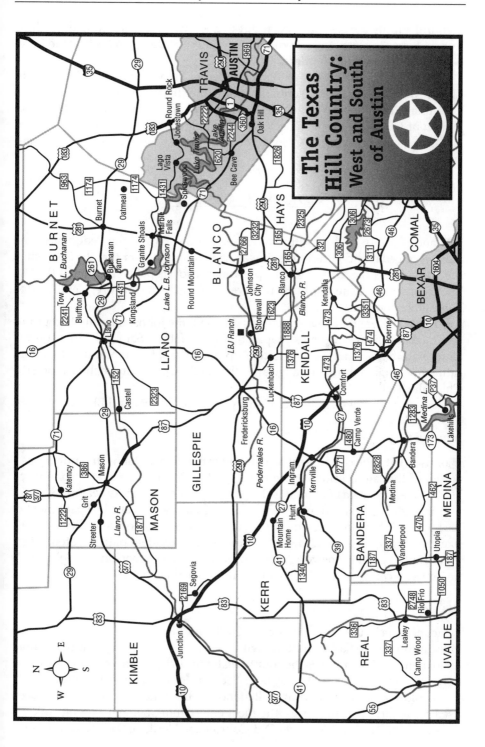

plentiful supply of rock, have been put to good use in constructing everything from cottages to courthouses, with many of these buildings reflecting the European style of immigrant settlers.

Worth noting: The towns of Blanco, Boerne, Fredericksburg, Johnson City, Llano, Marble Falls, and Wimberley form the Texas Hill Country Regional Christmas Lighting Trail from Nov. 29 to the end of December yearly. For information on all the festivities, check with the Regional Headquarters Office, 703 N. Llano, Fredericksburg, TX 78624, 866-TEX-FEST, www.fredericksburg-texas-events.com.

BLANCO COUNTY

Blanco County is hilly, with two rivers, the Blanco and the Pedernales, and lots of cedar and Pecan trees. It was named for the river that the Spanish in the 1700s called *blanco*, or "white," presumably for its pale reflection of the sky. The county was created in 1858 and owes its fame to the late president Lyndon Baines Johnson.

But even before that country boy made good, the Johnson family had put its name on the Blanco County map. LBJ's grandfather, Sam Ealy Johnson Sr., along with his brother Tom, rounded up mavericks, the unbranded longhorn cattle that roamed the open range after the Civil War, and drove them along the Chisholm Trail.

The two main towns in Blanco County are Johnson City and Blanco.

Johnson City

Johnson City, the county seat, is named for the pioneer Johnson family, ancestors of the late president. The town, on the Pedernales River (pronounced "PURD-in-alice") was founded in 1878 and became the county seat in 1891.

Although President Johnson was born in Gillespie County, he spent most of his boyhood years in Johnson City. If you ask a citizen of Johnson City what it's like growing up in a small town that produced a president of the United States, you're apt to get this answer: "I feel like it shows what a person can do. There's no limits. If you work hard, a small town is no handicap."

Blanco

Pioneer stockmen settled Blanco in 1853, and like most of the settlers in the Hill Country, they had to contend with Indians who naturally wanted to hold on to their land. Blanco was the county seat until 1891, when Johnson City to the north won the honor. But it took three elections for Johnson City to prevail.

The old courthouse building still stands in the center of town. It has been used for a variety of purposes, the most entertaining being a skating rink (on the second floor), but the active Old Courthouse Heritage Society is busy raising funds to restore it to its former glory. The town square is joined by a two-block city park, and the square features shops, the town library, and a bank.

BLANCO COUNTY LODGING

Johnson City has joined the trend for bed & breakfast accommodations; here you'll find a country inn and small two-room cottages. Both Johnson City and Blanco are quiet and relaxing places to spend the night.

Johnson City

THE EXOTIC RESORT RANCH
830-868-4357.
www.zooexotics.com.
235 Zoo Trail, Johnson City, TX 78636.
Price: Moderate.
Credit Cards: All.
Handicap Access: Yes.

The Exotic Zoo now has bed & breakfast cabins with cooking facilites, a swimming pool, hot tub, fishing, and even a huge fire pit for bonfires in the evening. Of the four cabins, two have kitchenettes, all have front porches overlooking a lake, and if you fish, you only have to pay for the fish you catch. The complimentary breakast is served in the kitchen, and there's a pool table in the game room.

WILDFLOWER INN
830-868-7499.
www.thewildflowerinn.com.
404B Hwy. 281 N., PO Box 38, Johnson City, TX 78636.
Price: Moderate.
Credit Cards: D, MC, V.
Handicap Access: Yes.

There's lots to do on this 224-acre property on the Pedernales River, even if you never go into town; endless hiking trails, a junior Olympic pool, miniature golf, a fitness and activity room; you can even do your laundry. Suites have whirlpool baths, rooms have king and queen baths, and a continental breakfast is included.

In town, there are several two-room houses in which to stay, each one offering privacy — you'll have the whole place to yourself — and the convenience of being right in the center of things. To book one, contact **Bed & Breakfasts — Johnson City** (830-868-4548; PO Box 913, 100 N. Nugent, Johnson City, TX 78636); descriptions of each follow. Prices are moderate, with continental breakfast included.

Boot Hill Guest House (830-868-8458; 207 Ranchview Dr., Johnson City, TX 78636) For a true western experience, the atmosphere here is bunkhouse but with comfort included. You'll find cedar bedposts, cowboy-print linens, a woodstove, Louis L'Amour western paperbacks, rocking chairs on the porch, and a barbecue grill, plus a modern kitchen with refrigerator, microwave, toaster, and coffeemaker.
Carolyne's Cottage B&B (830-868-4374; 103 Live Oak, Johnson City, TX 78636)

This stone cottage has lace curtains inside and flower-filled window boxes outside and is furnished with English country antiques.

Gingerbread House (507 W. Pecan Dr., Johnson City, TX 78636) This little house is nestled on a half acre of large oak trees, four blocks from the square. There are wicker rockers on the porch and a white picket fence in front.

Hoppe's Guest House (830-868-7359; 404 Ave. N, Johnson City, TX 78636) Another white picket fence encloses a yard full of century-old oaks. You'll find two bedrooms, one bath, and a wood-burning stove in the parlor; antique furniture adds to the quaintness.

Smith's Tin House (830-868-4870; 204 Ave. G, Johnson City, TX 78636) In describing this B&B, owner Cynthia Smith says, "Imagine driving up to Great-grandmother's house with its pressed-tin sides and front porch swing." The front sitting/sleeping room is furnished with antique wicker and an iron bed. An old iron bed is in the bedroom, too, plus there's a cozy country kitchen.

Motels: In Johnson City, accommodations are available at the **Save Inn Motel** (830-868-4044;107 Hwy. 281/290 S., PO Box 610, Johnson City, TX 78636) and the **Budget Motel** (830-868-7171; Hwy. 281/290, Johnson City, TX 78636). In Blanco, there's the **Swiss Lodge** (830-833-5528; 1206 N. Main St., Blanco, TX 78606) and the **Mobley Motel** (210-887-5866; 902 Main St., Blanco, TX 78606).

BLANCO COUNTY RESTAURANTS AND FOOD PURVEYORS

Hill Country dining is strongly influenced both by life on the range (chuck wagon cooking, frying, and barbecuing) and by Texas's neighbor south of the border, which has given rise to Tex-Mex, the style of Mexican food vastly preferred by the majority of Texans. A word of caution: neither "cuisine" (a rather fancy appellation to apply to the food you'll find outside big-city Austin and San Antonio) is for the fainthearted or the cholesterol-conscious.

Blanco

BLANCO BOWLING CLUB CAFE
830-833-4416.
310 4th St., Blanco, TX 78606.
Price: Inexpensive.
Cuisine: Down-home Tex-Mex.
Serving: B, L, D.
Credit Cards: None.
Handicap Access: Yes.

You may have to be a member to bowl here, but not to eat at the friendly roadside cafe fronting on the "exclusive" bowling alley. It's the sort of place where you get up and help yourself to more coffee if the staff is busy elsewhere, and where you can chat with cook Mary Mosby if she surfaces for a moment's respite at the counter.

The plate lunch is a real bargain. It might be a choice of two meats (roast beef or chicken) with mashed potatoes, peas, and carrots, and homemade cherry cobbler, tea, or coffee. Fridays and Saturdays it's an all-you-can-eat catfish fry, including salad bar. The pies — coconut, lemon, chocolate — are smothered in meringue, and Mary's doughnuts, twists, and cinnamon rolls are impossible to resist. So are the carne guisada breakfast tacos, little steaks-in-a-taco with brown gravy. For some authentic Hill Country ambiance, drop by early in the morning to catch some regulars at their daily domino game.

HARD SCRABBLE CAFE
830-833-4350.
323 Main St., Blanco, TX 78606.
On the Square, inside the Wagner & Chabot building.
Price: Inexpensive to Moderate.
Cuisine: Eclectic.
Serving: L daily except Mon., 11am–3pm; D Thurs.–Sat., 5:30pm–8:30pm.
Credit Cards: AE, D, MC, V.
Handicap Access: Yes.

This is a surprise, located inside an antiques and gift shop, with an innovative and imaginative menu. For lunch, there's a portabella mushroom sandwich with Swiss and Monterey Jack cheese, sautéed onions on grilled rye bread, or confetti sandwiches of cream cheese olive spread, red onions, lettuce, and tomato. Weekend meals include steak and quail, Adobe pork loin, and chicken Blanca on chili pasta. New specialties include quail dishes, the Thurdsay night tortilla soup "that everybody raves about" (Thursday night is Mexican night), and sautéed tilapia, a freshwater fish topped with a caper-dill sauce and served with lemon rice.

Bear figures in the front yard of Oso's Mexican Grill in Blanco. Oso is Spanish for bear.

Eleanor S. Morris

OSO'S MEXICAN GRILL & CANTINA
830-833-1304.
306 Pecan, Blanco, TX 78606.

Not only does Oso's serve enchiladas, tacos, chalupas, nachos, quesadillas, chimichangas, and burritos, but hamburgers, sandwiches, and Cobb salad are on the menu, too. Great margaritas as well, and if that isn't enough, newly opened

Price: Inexpensive.
Cuisine: "TexMex and Gringo."
Serving: L, D Mon.– Sat. 11am–9pm.
Credit Cards: AE, D, MC, V.
Handicap Access: Yes.

Oso's Bakery, just inside the door, offers "the most awesome kolaches I ever ate in my life," says a satisfied customer. The outside decor is attractive, with a white bear statue on the left (*oso* is Spanish for bear) and strawlike mariachi figures on the right.

REAL FOODS MARKET & CAFE
830-833-2483.
410 Fourth St., Blanco, TX 78606.
Price: Inexpensive.
Cuisine: Organic, Natural, Various Regional.
Serving: B, L, 10am–6 pm.
Credit Cards: AE, D, MC, V.
Handicap Access: Yes.

"**I** can't believe I found this in Blanco, Texas," exclaimed one customer as she surveyed the huge array of health foods and vitamins and the varied menu of the cafe, which offers comfort food (as in meat loaf and mashed potatoes) as well as Italian, Thai, and much more, all eminently health-conscious.

In an old hardware store on the square, the walls lined with rainfall charts dating back to 1900, owner Sherri Stockman says, "People meet here; there's always somebody to talk to."

The chicken salad and the quiche are specials, but so is the organic salad bar, stocked with tabouli, hummus, chickpeas, and other healthy choices. You can make your own power shake or smoothie with fruit juices, adding your favorite supplement, or have a wheat grass julep of apple and wheatgrass juices and spearmint, or maybe Sherri's Special, made of bananas, apple and orange juices, protein powder, vitamins, minerals, enzymes, and nutritional yeast.

SUNSET RESTAURANT AND BAR
830-833-5776.
419 W. 3rd St., Blanco, TX 78606.
Price: Inexpensive to Moderate.
Cuisine: Home-style.
Serving: B, L, D; closed Tues.
Credit Cards: AE, D, MC, V.
Handicap Access: Yes.

In this indoor/outdoor restaurant on the square, the warm family atmosphere and delicious home-cooked meals advertised are a fact, thanks to Kimberly and Kenneth Chapman, joint owner-chefs. The main course — a dinner special of chicken pot pie (a quarter of a whole!) — might be preceded by a delicious spicy vegetable soup with rice and accompanied by a vegetable (in season) and a baked potato. The bread is homemade, and so are the desserts — pecan pie, or chocolate shortcake with ice cream, topped with chocolate syrup and whipped cream.

A table out on the cool open porch led to a friendly conversation with two Frenchwomen visiting Houston, who had come to see the Hill Country. The women were thankful for the friendliness they encountered: "French people don't know how to do this, be like Texans," they said.

Johnson City

FEED MILL CAFE
830-868-7771.
103 W. Main St., PO Box
  1208, Johnson City, TX
  78636.
Price: Moderate.
Cuisine: Home Cooking.
Serving: L, D.
Credit Cards: AE, MC, V.
Handicap Access: No.

Here's the atmosphere of an old roadhouse saloon in historic Crofts Mill, an 1880s feed mill. Enter via an iron-railed concrete ramp partially covered with scattered red rugs (the red carpet treatment?). Inside, the cavernous place, with its high open beams and rafters, is filled with tables surrounded by an assortment of old bentwood chairs and picnic tables. The long wooden front and back walls are completely obscured by a huge collection of old beer signs (Lone Star occupying pride of place) and other roadhouse memorabilia.

The Feed Mill burger comes in either quarter- or half-pound size, decked out with all the fixin's. The King Kong burger "serves one hungry cowboy or two city slickers." If you're there for dinner, the house chicken-fried steak is crusty outside, juicy inside, and served with potatoes and gravy. The fried green tomatoes are served with a tangy homemade ranch dressing. Also popular are the chicken-fried steak sandwich and the cilantro catfish. The Feed Mill is a friendly family place — like a Texas dance hall without the dancing.

**HILL COUNTRY
  CUPBOARD**
830-868-4625.
www.hillcountrycupboard
  .com.
101 Hwy. 281/290 S,
  Johnson City, TX 78636.
Price: Inexpensive.
Cuisine: Contemporary
  Texan.
Serving: L, D daily
  6am–9pm, 6am–midnight
  Fridays; closed
  Thanksgiving, Christmas,
  and New Year's.
Credit Cards: AE, D, MC, V.
Handicap Access: Yes.
Special Features: See
  "Shopping."

The extensive menu here is pasted on both sides of a paper grocery sack — you can see how pretentious the Hill Country Kitchen is. They claim to serve the "world's best" chicken-fried steak, and we didn't dispute it. While we waited to be seated, we watched the bakers fill loaf pan after loaf pan with the most delicious-smelling bread dough. All the baked goods, from bread to hamburger buns to fantastic blackberry and peach cobblers, are made on the premises. Some are health-conscious, too, like the sugar-free apple, peach, coconut, and lemon pies.

**PASQUALES' MEXICAN
  RESTAURANT**
830-868-7682.
502 Hwy. 281/290 S,
  Johnson City, TX 78636.
Price: Moderate.

With more than 70 items on the menu, you won't be limited to Mexican dishes unless you want to be. "We specialize in Mexican food — but with something for everyone," is their motto. Special are the chiles rellenos, black bean and cheese taquitos, and popcorn shrimp. Other special-

Cuisine: Mexican, Hill Country Fare.
Serving: L, D daily except Sun.
Credit Cards: AE, D, MC, V.
Handicap Access: Yes.

ties include Friday night catfish and Saturday night char-broiled steak, all delicious in this family-owned-and-operated eatery.

SILVER K CAFE
www.silverkcafe.com.
830-868-2911.
209 E. Main St., Johnson City, TX 88636.
Price: Inexpensive to Moderate.
Cuisine: Hill Country Cuisine.
Serving: L Mon.–Sat. 11am–2pm; D Fri.–Sat. 5pm–10 pm; Sun. all-day buffet 11am–8pm.
Credit cards: MC, V.
Handicap Access: Yes.

The Silver K Cafe has a mission: "To provide Texas-friendly service in an atmosphere of rustic elegance, while showcasing Hill Country cuisine and Texas singer/songwriters. "And it does both admirably. Tables are set with fresh linens, and a sprig of rosemary gently spices up the table. Such entrees as tilapia Vera Cruz, a fish fillet baked in a robust tomato sauce served with coconut rice and fresh vegetables, or roast pork tenderloin with orange and rosemary sauce and served with corn-bread dressing and fresh vegetables, are quite a change from chicken-fried steak and barbecue. As for the singer/songwriters, there's a roofed, open-air area out back called Estrella, with a stage and all the appointments for live music performances. Texas singer/songwriter Joe Pat Hennen books special musical events there for other Texas performers. The restaurant is in the Old Lumber Yard (see "Shopping"), with many original architectural features adding to the ambiance.

BLANCO COUNTY FOOD PURVEYORS

Real Foods Market & Cafe (see "Blanco County Restaurants").

Texas Hills Vineyard (830-868-2321; www.texashillsvineyard.com; 1 mile east of Johnson City on Pedernales Park Rd. 6026) specializes in Italian-style wines: pinot grigio, sangiovese, moscato, and more. Open: Mon.–Sat. 10am–5pm, Sun. noon–5pm.

Whittington's Jerky (830-868-5500, 877-868-5501; whittingtonsjerky.com; 604 Hwy. 281 S., Johnson City, TX 78636) has a new plant, offering free samples of the jerky they've been making since 1962. "As long as you like it, we'll make it," say Sam and Susan Whittington to their customers around the globe.

BLANCO COUNTY CULTURE

Johnson City is now the home of the official **Blanco County Courthouse,** on the square at 7th and Nugent. The Greek Revival building was constructed in 1916 to replace the original 1891 courthouse located on the southwest corner.

Visit the **Blanco County Jail,** built in 1894. Maps for a walking and/or driving tour of Johnson City's historic structures are available from the **Johnson City Chamber of Commerce** (830-868-7684; www.lbjcountry.com; 406 W. Main St., Johnson City, TX 78636).

In *Blanco,* the **Old Blanco County Courthouse** is a fine example of Second Empire architecture. Designed by Austin architect Frederick Ernst Ruffini, the limestone building was completed in 1886, and when the county seat moved to Johnson City, this courthouse was used variously as an office building, opera house, and even a hospital. It's been restored to its original façade, and there's talk of locating the **Blanco Chamber of Commerce** there (830-833-5101; www.blancotex.com; 315 Main St., Blanco, TX 78606).

The Captain Perry Texas Ranger Museum in Johnson City.

Eleanor S. Morris

CAPTAIN PERRY TEXAS RANGER MUSEUM
830-868-7684.
www.lbjcountry.com.
Hwy. 290 at 404 W. Main, PO Box 485, Johnson City, TX 78636.
Open: Mon.–Fri. 9am–5pm.
Admission: Free.

The museum, in a portion of the ranger's log home, was moved from its original site about 3 miles west in 1972. Over his lengthy career as a Ranger, Capt. Cicero Rufus Perry served the Republic of Texas, the State of Texas, the United States Army, and the Confederacy. The museum houses a collection of Perry memorabilia as well as items commonly found in such a dwelling in the early days of the Texas frontier.

LYNDON B. JOHNSON NATIONAL HISTORICAL PARK
830-868-7128.
www.nps.gov/lyjo.
100 10th St., PO Box 329, Johnson City, TX 78636.

In Johnson City's Lyndon B. Johnson National Historical Park (don't get this mixed up with the LBJ Ranch and state park 14 miles west in Stonewall, Gillespie County), the white frame, white-picket-fenced boyhood home of the president is a far cry from his birthplace in Stonewall. A block west is Johnson's Settlement, the old ranch complex

LBJ's boyhood home in Johnson City.

Eleanor S. Morris

Visitor Center: Daily except Christmas and New Year's; 8:45am–5pm; Boyhood Home: 9am–5pm; Johnson Settlement Exhibit Center: 9am–4:30pm. Admission: Free.

owned by the president's grandfather and great-uncle from 1867 to 1872, which was a gathering point for cattle drives from seven counties. The settlement also served as an aid station for those wounded in the Deer Creek Indian battle. An original "dog-run" cabin, barn, and other buildings have been restored and are part of the living-history program offered by the park.

NIGHTLIFE

Eleanor S. Morris

This sign on Hwy. 281 just south of Blanco marks the entrance for Twin Sisters Dance Hall.

The **Twin Sisters Dance Hall** (830-833-5625; Hwy. 281, about 7 miles south of Blanco) puts on a dance the first Saturday of the month, from 9pm to 1am. Country-western, of course, with both local bands and groups from Austin, San Antonio, San Marcos, and New Braunfels. Very family oriented, with people of all ages doing the Texas two-step. Beer, wine, coolers, sodas, setups, chips, and candy are available. Admission: $5.

SEASONAL EVENTS

For exact dates, check with the **Johnson City Chamber of Commerce** (830-868-7684) or the **Olde Blanco Merchants & Business Association** (830-833-2201). Or check the Blanco Web site, www.blancotex.com, and the Johnson City Web site, www.lbjcountry.com.

Johnson City

JANUARY hosts the **Johnson City Chili Cook-Off.**

From APRIL to OCTOBER, on third Saturdays and Sundays, **Johnson City Market Days** offer crafts, antiques, food, and entertainment (see "Shopping").

The third weekend of AUGUST features the **Blanco County Fair & Rodeo.**

In OCTOBER, in both Johnson City and LBJ National Park, there's the **Cowboy Song & Poetry** along with **Heritage Crafts Day.** In DECEMBER Johnson City participates in the regional **Christmas Lighting Trail.**

Blanco

From APRIL through NOVEMBER, **Olde Blanco Market Days** are held on the third Saturday of the month.

During MAY's **Market Day**, there's a **Classic Car Show** and a wildly popular **Motorcycle Poker Run** — with cyclists playing poker on the run!

In JULY, around the Fourth, there's a **Red, White, and Blue Celebration.**

In NOVEMBER there is the annual **Lighting of Town Square** and the **Merchants' Open House** on the third weekend, as well as the **Parade and Quilt Show** the Friday after Thanksgiving.

NOVEMBER and DECEMBER feature the annual **Lighting Tour Spectacular** — 100,000 lights on the Blanco County Courthouse and 500,000 in the community, plus special activities all through late November and December. Call Regional Christmas Headquarters at 830-997-8515.

On the second Saturday of DECEMBER, the **Merry Merchants Market & Christmas Parade**, including a crafts show, takes place.

BLANCO COUNTY RECREATION

Pedernales Falls State Park east of Johnson City and **Blanco State Park** along the Blanco River Valley are the places in Blanco County for camping, fishing, hiking, and various kinds of fun on the water. Other ideas for recreation are also noted.

CAMPING

Roadrunner RV Park (830-868-7449; Hwy. 281-290 S., Johnson City, TX 78636) has clean rest rooms, laundry, meeting room and library, recreation area, and fax service.

Texas Hill Country Scenic RV and Camp Sites (830-868-2096, 512-413-8674; www.somedayfarms.com/rvsite; 1712 Hwy. 3232, Johnson City, TX 78636) has full hookup, 30 and 40 AMP service, and cooking grills.

The Wildflower Inn (see "Lodging") has shaded, paved, pull-through RV sites.

FAMILY FUN

THE EXOTIC RESORT ZOO
830-868-4357.
www.zooexotics.com.
235 Zoo Trail, Johnson City, TX 78636.
Four miles north of Johnson City on Hwy. 281.
Admission: Free.

Designed for both wild animals (giraffes, zebras, and springbok antelope, among others) and the people who enjoy their company, this 137-acre zoo provides guided vehicle rides during which you can feed the animals, and a petting zoo with baby deer, llamas, and even a kangaroo. More than half the animals are on, or have been on, the endangered species list.

PARKS

BLANCO STATE PARK
830-833-4333.
www.tpwd.state.tx.us/park/blanco.
U.S. 281, PO Box 493, Blanco, TX 78606.
Admission: Day use fee $1 per person 13 and over. Call for camping fees.

The park lies within the city limits along scenic Blanco River Valley. The 110-acre park has 21 campsites with water and electricity plus ten others with water, electricity, and sewage for RVs. The park also offers screened shelters, rest rooms and showers, a group pavilion with kitchen, fishing, boating, picnicking, hiking, nature study, swimming, seasonal pedal boats and canoe rentals, and a children's play area.

PEDERNALES FALLS STATE PARK
830-868-7304 (Ranger

On the scenic stretches of the Pedernales River east of Johnson City, strikingly beautiful water-

---

Scenic Drive

Two miles south of Blanco take FM 32 off U.S. 281. Portions of the drive toward San Marcos (in Hays County) follow a ridge called the "Devil's Backbone," a wonderful taste of Hill Country landscape. White-tailed deer are often sighted, especially early or late in the day.

station), 800-792-1112 (state park info). www.tpwd.state.tx.us/park /pedernal. 2585 Park Rd. 6026, Johnson City, TX 78636. Open: 8am–10pm daily. Admission: Day use fee $1 per person 13 and over. Call for camping fees.

falls flow over tilted stairs of layered limestone. The 5,212-acre park, with 6 miles of river frontage, offers swimming, tubing, fishing, 20 miles of hiking and biking trails, and campsites with water, electricity, picnic tables, barbecue grills, and tent pads. Hike-in primitive campsites are also offered, located a minimum of 2 miles from the trailheads. For birders, over 150 species have been spotted in the park.

Fishing: Single pole or rod and reel only.

Hiking: The 7.5-mile Wolf Mountain Trail leads to primitive camping areas, historic sites, and the river. The primitive trail system is a challenge for adventuresome hikers and includes a short nature trail.

Swimming: The state park swimming area begins 2.5 miles below the falls. There's tubing on the river.

BLANCO COUNTY SHOPPING

Both Johnson City and Blanco offer an assortment of interesting shops and boutiques featuring antiques, collectibles, and regional products and crafts. And don't forget **Johnson City Market Days** in City Park from April to October on the second or third weekend of the month. You'll find vendors of food, arts and crafts, antiques, and collectibles, including interesting originals like fabric-covered ceramics or a whirling cage around a brilliantly painted parrot or lovebird. In Blanco, **Olde Blanco Market Days** are held on the third Saturday of the month, April through November.

ANTIQUES

Johnson City

Johnson City has no lack of antiques shops, including the following:

Johnson City Antique Emporium: 830-868-7800; 100 N. Nugent, PO Box 913, Johnson City, TX 78636.
Molly's on Main Antiques: At the Old Lumber Yard, 830-868-4440; 209 E. Main, Johnson City, TX 78636.
The Silver Deer: 830-868-4422; 205 E. Main, Johnson City, TX 78636.

Blanco

Cranberry's Antiques (830-833-5596; 400 3rd St., Blanco, TX 78606, at Arts & Collectibles on the Square) Antiques research, repair, and refinishing; items on consignment; pricing guidebooks.

CLOTHING, CRAFTS, AND GIFTS

Johnson City

Chantilly Lace (830-868-7450; 408 Hwy. 281 N., Johnson City, TX 78636) is both a shop and a cafe, serving lunch and dinner.

Hill Country Cupboard (830-868-4625; 101 Hwy. 281/290 S., Johnson City, TX 78636; see "Restaurants") A small boutique features hand-painted knits labeled "Treasures by Victoria," one of the restaurant's owners. Bright and glittery — and dressy — T-shirts, pants, and other items are for sale, along with jars of Texas salsa, jams, and jellies. (The jalapeño might be hot!)

The Old Lumber Yard (830-868-2381; 209 E. Main, Johnson City, TX 78636) is a retail mall with toy and book vendors, jewelry, clothing, and other goods inside the redbrick arch of an old lumber yard.

Blanco

Gandalf's Goldwerks (830-833-4560; 309 Main St., Blanco, TX 78606) Custom-designed fine gold and silver jewelry, as well as diamonds and gemstones. Two cases are filled with silver charms of every description, and there's a wonderful corner of old books. Proprietor Robert J. Cox II is cordial and helpful even if you just want directions around town.

Rainbird Gallery (830-833-4545; 109 Main St., Blanco, TX 78606) This gallery is in an old Baptist church, 400 square feet of art up to the vaulted ceiling. Owner-artist Janet Fisher quotes Thoreau — "Art is nothing more than the meaning of life" — and her gallery is filled with meaning: paintings, Native American and western art, pottery, and stone and wood sculptures, including a "Texas" totem pole.

On Courthouse Square in Blanco you can also browse in an authentic small-town market. Check out unique gifts in the **Sunflower** (830-833-5344; 317 Main St., Blanco, TX 78606) and antiques, fancy goods, and curiosities in **Wagner & Chabot's** (830-833-4350; 323 Main St., Blanco, TX 78606).

BURNET COUNTY

B urnet County — pronounce it "BURN-it" – was created from Bell, Travis, and Williamson Counties in 1852 and named for David G. Burnet, a provisional president of the Texas Republic. Burnet, who was a New Jersey native, came to Texas as early as 1815. He didn't stay, but he must have liked what he saw because he returned in 1826, this time for good.

Like Stephen F. Austin, he also obtained permission from the Mexican government to settle immigrants in southeast Texas. The Convention of 1836, writing the Texas Declaration of Independence at Washington-on-the-Brazos, named him interim president of the Republic, and he served until Sam Houston was elected president. He was an early agitator for independence from Mexico.

The county — full of hills, caves, and cedar trees — has frontage on five of the beautiful Highland Lakes, and is in one of the most ancient geological areas of the world. Every mineral in North and South America can be found in the Burnet County area — even if there's only a little bit of it.

The county's two main towns are **Burnet** and **Marble Falls**; **Springdale** is a small community south of Marble Falls, with a winery and an art colony.

In 1848 the Texas Rangers set up a small station about 3 miles south of what is now the town of Burnet. Then, early in 1849, the U.S. Army, which had begun establishing forts across Texas from Fort Worth south to Uvalde to protect early settlements from the Indians, replaced the Ranger station with Fort Croghan, and the Rangers moved on to other sites.

Burnet

In 1882 the railroad arrived in Burnet, and not long afterward a block of the regional marble from nearby Holland quarries was shipped from Burnet to Washington, D.C., as Texas's contribution to the building of the Washington Monument. Today the Hill Country Flyer, a historic narrow-gauge steam train, comes to Burnet from Cedar Park (just west of Austin), and the Burnet Gunfighters stage a pretty good performance for passengers when they arrive.

The historic square has some shops, boutiques, and a tearoom, and there's a pleasant walk down along Hamilton Creek, paved and landscaped with a fountain and picnic areas. Steps lead down from both sides of Hwy. 29 W. just west of the intersection of Hwy. 281. The Texas Legislature has officially declared Burnet the Bluebonnet Capital of Texas, and, of course, there's a big Bluebonnet Festival every spring.

For more information, contact the **Burnet Chamber of Commerce** (512-756-4297; www.burnetchamber.org; 703 Buchanan Dr., Burnet, TX 78611).

Marble Falls

Hwy. 281 into Marble Falls forms a causeway across the lake on one side and the Colorado River on the other, a pretty sight either entering or leaving on the south side of town. You can see why Adam R. Johnson, Marble Falls's founder, decided the area had potential. Dreaming of a large manufacturing city powered by the "Great Falls," which back then poured over a marble ledge in the Colorado River, he began to buy up property as early as 1850.

But the Civil War interrupted his plans. Johnson rose to the rank of general in the Confederate Army. Although he was blinded in the war, this did not interfere with his inner vision for the town, and by offering some of his land as a right-of-way for a railroad to haul the plentiful granite, he put Marble Falls on the map around 1887.

The waterfall was covered by the development of Max Starke and Wirtz

Dams; the "Great Falls" are hidden from view beneath Lake LBJ. But if you're curious to see what they looked like, there's a picture on the wall in the Blue Bonnet Cafe.

For more information, contact the **Marble Falls/Lake LBJ Chamber of Commerce** (830-693-4449, 800- 759-8178; www.marblefalls.org.; 801 Hwy. 281, Marble Falls, TX 78654).

BURNET COUNTY LODGING

The town of Burnet has several bed & breakfasts, and there is one in Marble Falls. Motels in Burnet include the **Howard Johnson Express Inn** (512-756-4747; 908 Hwy. 29 W., Burnet, TX 78611), the **Holiday Inn Express** (512-756-1789; 810 Water St., Burnet, TX 78611) and the **Sundown Motor Inn** (512-756-2171; 205 N. Water St., Burnet, TX 78611).

Motels in Marble Falls include a **Best Western** (830-693-5122, 800-578-1234; 1403 Hwy. 281 N., Marble Falls, TX 78654), a **Ramada Limited** (830-693-7351, 800-1-RAMADA; 1206 Hwy. 281, Marble Falls, TX 78654) and **Hampton Inn on the Lake** (830-798-1895, 800-HAMPTON; 704 First St., Marble Falls, TX 78654).

Burnet

1884 AIRY MOUNT INN
Hosts: Charles and Rosann Hayman.
512-756-4149.
www.airymount.com.
Rte. 3, Box 280, PO Box 351, Burnet, TX 78611.
Price: Moderate.
Credit Cards: MC, V.
Handicap Access: No.

The Airy Mount Inn is located on 6 acres inside a 150-acre tract of land. In a barn on the property, the hand-hewn walls of solid limestone were built by slaves brought to Texas by the original owner after the Civil War. Not only were they paid well for their work, they were freed and stayed on as caretakers, masons, and farmers.

Accommodations include the Josephine Room, the General's Room, and the Santa Fe Suite, all upstairs. The living and dining rooms downstairs are filled with fine bronzes, books, and antiques. Breakfast is a "Texas-size feast" served in the barn's dining room, with huevos rancheros, eggs Benedict, or Alsace quiche. Additional amenities include use of the full-size kitchen, outdoor barbecue pit, and a washer and dryer.

MAIN STREET BED & BREAKFAST
Hosts: Happy and Mike Matthews.
512-756-2861, 512-756-4256.
808 N. Main St., Burnet, TX 78611.

This house dates from the 1930s, when it was built by Dr. Sam Paschall, who practiced dentistry in Burnet for many years. He enlarged his home to include a great room, where guests now enjoy music and games. Happy and Mike Matthews purchased the home in 1994, and Dr. Matthews is

Price: Moderate, EP.
Credit Cards: None.
Handicap Access: No.

following in the footsteps of the original owner: He's a dentist, too. And Happy is as happy as her name. The three guest rooms, with private baths, are comfortable and uncluttered, furnished in what Happy calls "early traditional." The great room has a player piano, an old-timey jukebox, a slot machine — and a stuffed goose or two.

THUNDERBIRD RESORT
Owner/Manager: John Williams.
512-756-4878, 800-210-7202.
www.touringtexas.com/ tbird.
200 Greenwood Hills Trail, Burnet, TX 78611.
Price: Inexpensive to Very Expensive, depending on cottage size.
Credit Cards: D, MC, V.
Handicap Access: Partial.

This family-run resort on Lake Buchanan has 20 cottages, large and small, on 30 acres of land facing 1,100 feet of waterfront. There's fishing for bass, crappie, catfish, and perch; canoes for rent at the marina; swimming and sunning in the large pool with a shaded terrace; and hiking, jogging, and bird watching, especially in the winter when bald eagles come to nest along the lake.

THE VERANDAS GUEST HOUSE
Hosts: Wayne and Mary Brown.
512-715-0190.
www.highlandlakes.com/ verandas.
108 East League St., Burnet, TX 78611.
Price: Expensive.
Credit Cards: AE, D, MC, V.
Handicap Access: No.

This handsome historic building was constructed in 1856 as a stagecoach stop. The well on the veranda used to quench the thirst of both travelers and horses; now it supplies water for the inn's handsome water garden and koi pond. Upstairs, off the veranda that encircles the house, are three guest suites, each with private bath, telephone, and TV/VCR. All have queen-size beds and are decorated with antiques and art. Breakfast might be huevos poblanos, tomatoes with fresh basil, fresh rosemary-roasted potatoes, a breakfast sundae (yogurt with fresh fruit), and sweet rolls or apple bread. Through the large antique painted glass wall in the dining room and common area, there's a lovely view of the colorful koi and other goldfish in the water garden and of a Japanese-style bridge over the water.

Marble Falls

LIBERTY HALL GUEST HAUS
Host: Wilburn Wall.
830-693-4518, 800-232-4469.
www.marblefallstexas.com/ liberty.htm.

History buffs enjoy staying in the historic house that was home to Gen. Adam Johnson, founder of Marble Falls, on land awarded to the heirs of Capt. William Baker, hero of the Alamo. From 1919 to 1935 it was the home of George and

119 Ave. G, Marble Falls, TX 78654.
Price: Moderate to Expensive.
Credit Cards: AE, MC, V.
Handicap Access: No.

Birdie Harwood; she was America's first woman mayor, elected by an all-male voting population. Wilburn Wall maintains the inn as his parents did. The Victorian parlor is a shrine to American patriotism. American flags, JFK memorabilia, a DSC (Distinguished Service Cross) Award on the wall, and photos of Wall family members who have served their country fill the room

White-painted bedrooms have shiny wood floors, Oriental-patterned rugs, and bright brass bedsteads. Some beds are covered in white with lacy dust ruffles, others in colorful quilts.

The upstairs porch looks out over the lake and the lovely view beyond. Each of the seven guest suites is equipped with a coffeemaker, and a continental breakfast is served in your room.

BURNET COUNTY RESTAURANTS AND FOOD PURVEYORS

The Treaty Oak, a native American marker tree.

Eleanor S. Morris

Burnet

BURNET COUNTY BBQ
512-756-6468.
Hwy. 29 W., Burnet, TX 78611.
Price: Inexpensive.
Cuisine: Barbecue.
Serving: L, D; closed Tues.

"You have to go to the country to get country BBQ" is Pat McCall's motto, and it works, since this restaurant has been a Burnet institution for more years than Pat has owned it. Specials include Elgin hot sausage, tender brisket, and meaty ribs. Pit-cooked meats taste even more flavorful in the rustic log-cabin atmosphere. Wood floors, wood

Credit Cards: None.
Handicap Access: Partial.

walls, and a working wood-burning stove in the corner of the narrow room add to the authenticity. (The only modern note is the air-conditioning in the summer, but who's complaining?) With the barbecue you get the usual fixings: potato salad, coleslaw and beans, and, for dessert, a choice of chocolate, lemon, coconut, or pecan pie.

Diego's Mexican Food in Burnet.

Eleanor S. Morris

DIEGO'S MEXICAN FOOD
512-715-0343.
3401 S. Hwy 281, Burnet, TX 78611.
Price: Inexpensive.
Cuisine: Tex-Mex.
Serving: B, L, D.
Credit Cards: AE, DC, D, MC, V.
Handicap Access: Yes.

HIGHLANDER RESTAURANT AND STEAK HOUSE
512-756-7401.
401 W. Buchanan, Burnet, TX 78611.
Price: Moderate.
Cuisine: Steaks, Seafood, Pasta.
Serving: B, L, D.
Credit Cards: Yes.
Handicap Access: Yes.

This family affair in a bright, large, airy building offers not only every conceivable Tex-Mex dish, but also American food and a children's menu. The Diego Special (named for owner Dominic Hernandez's son and chef) is very popular. It includes one tamale, one cheese and onion enchilada with chili con carne, one crispy taco, and one tortilla, and with beans and rice you have an entire Mexican dinner, especially if you order sopapillas, dripping with honey, for dessert.

Right next to the historic Treaty Oak — used by native Americans to point the way to water, in this case Hamilton Creek Springs — this restaurant is pretty accommodating. "We offer a variety of hand-cut steaks as well as favorite southern dishes, and if it isn't on the menu, ask and see if we can make it for you!" From rib eye to porterhouse T-bone to sirloin to southern dishes like grilled chicken seasoned with Cajun blackening or farm-raised catfish, they try to please.

RIVERWALK CAFE
512-756-4100.
635 Hwy. 29 W., Burnet, TX
  78611.
Price: Inexpensive.
Cuisine: Country-style.
Serving: B, L, D.
Credit Cards: None.
Handicap Access: Yes.

You'd never guess this pleasantly decorated building once housed a fast-food store with gas pumps out front. Now booths line the wide windows, and there's an attractive salad bar along a wall. The seafood croquettes are a delicious mix of crab, shrimp, and fish. Try the Riverwalk chicken plate, a grilled chicken breast topped with sautéed mushrooms, onions, and Swiss cheese. The homemade desserts include tasty lemon, coconut cream, and butterscotch pies; apple crisp; and cheesecake.

TEA-LICIOUS
512-756-7636.
228 S. Main St., Burnet, TX
  78611.
Price: Inexpensive.
Cuisine: Light Lunches.
Serving: L.
Credit Cards: AE, D, MC, V.
Handicap Access: Yes.

With luncheon tables scattered around several roomfuls of giftware and clothing, it's not hard to be entertained as you eat next to, for instance, a collection of teapots in imaginative shapes, from rooster to frog to rabbit. Sandwiches are fresh and varied; the spinach garden wrap of guacamole, spinach, cucumbers, mushrooms, tomatoes, and provolone is topped with ranch dressing. Broccoli cheese soup is the most popular soup of the day, and salads and quiche are also on the menu. Desserts include classic pies such as chess, lime icebox, and Boston cream; specialties are French silk, pecan cream, and coconut cream. The peach iced tea is a treat on a hot Texas day.

Marble Falls

BLUE BONNET CAFE
830-693-2344.
www.highlandlakes.com
  /bluebonnet.
211 Hwy. 281, Marble Falls,
  TX 78654.
Price: Inexpensive.
Cuisine: Texas Homestyle.
Serving: B, L, D daily.
Credit Cards: None.
Handicap Access: Yes.

For more than 60 years the Blue Bonnet Cafe has been a haven for delicious and generous portions of down-home country cooking. Lunchtime brings such old favorites as pot roast, meat loaf, chicken and dumplings, rich cream of cauliflower soup, and a renowned roster of homemade pies — in addition to apple, peach, and lemon, our favorites are the peanut butter and German chocolate. The restaurant's motto is "Texas friendly spoken here," and you can believe it!

**BROADWAY GENERAL
  STORE**
830-798-0200.
617 Broadway, Marble Falls,
  TX 78654.
Price: Inexpensive.
Cuisine: Homestyle
  Upscale.

Don't be taken aback when you find that the Broadway General Store is housed in a small white house. Just march up the steps to the porch, open the front door, and walk right in. Be sure to notice the tastefully displayed antiques and gifts — this seems to be the trend in Burnet County nowadays. Tables in the bright rooms are covered with

Serving: L, D.
Credit Cards: AE, D, MC, V.
Handicap Access: No.

snowy white cloths, and the chairs are an eclectic mix. The lunch menu offers soups, salads, sandwiches, ham and Swiss cheese quiche, and homemade desserts. Unusual and delicious is the cowboy soup, made with steak, potatoes, green and kidney beans, and just a taste of salsa. Restaurateur Pam Peters aptly dubs her dinner menu "homestyle upscale"; it features such comfort food as meat loaf and stuffed pork chops to chicken Florentine and shrimp Alfredo. As for desserts, special among the specials daily are chocolate sin and peanut butter pie.

DOCK'S SEAFOOD, STEAKS, & MORE
830-693-2245.
austin.citysearch.com,
search: Dock's.
900 FM 1431, Marble Falls,
TX 78654.
Price: Inexpensive to
Expensive.
Cuisine: Steak, Seafood.
Serving: L, D daily.
Credit Cards: AE, D, MC, V.
Handicap Access: Yes.

In a warm atmosphere of polished wood, green vines, and green marbleized tables, and surrounded by such aquatic features as both seascapes and mounted fish, you can have anything from the fresh catch of the day, char-broiled or deep fried, to a rib-eye steak marinated overnight in Dock's special blend of herbs and spices. We began with "bloomers," a huge onion sliced and fried in seasoned batter and served with a delicious sauce. An excellent choice from the comprehensive menu is the seafood grill, a remarkable combination of fish, shrimp, lobster, scallops, and vegetables. For dessert, the homemade carrot cake, specialty of Belinda Kemper of the Blue Bonnet Cafe (they share), is a tasty choice.

WILD HORSE GRILLE
830-798-0717.
201 N. Main St., Marble
Falls, TX 78654.
Price: Moderate to
Expensive.
Cuisine: International.
Serving: D, closed Sun.
Credit Cards: AE, D, MC, V.
Handicap Access: No.

International is the word here; just glance through the menu. Tex-Mex (Wild Horse quesadillas and scallop nachos), Asian (lobster spring rolls and beef satay), Italian (seafood linguini), French (eggplant Napoleon), southwestern (southwest shrimp cocktail), and just regular prime rib, rib-eye and sirloin, and surf (petite signature steak) and turf (lobster tail), dubbed "Cowboy and a Mermaid." Fresh desserts are made daily.

BURNET COUNTY FOOD PURVEYORS

Gude's Bakery & Deli (512-715-9903; 307 W. Polk St., Burnet, TX 78611; Mon.–Fri. 5am–7pm, Sat. 5am–2:30 pm) Here's informal breakfast, lunch and dinner — fresh-baked doughnuts, sub sandwiches, kolaches, pizza, sausage and cheese biscuits, and BBQ, all made fresh daily.
Latta Java Cafe (830-693-7199; 1107 Hwy. 1431 W., Marble Falls, TX 78654; Mon.–Fri. 7am–5pm, Sat. 8am–5pm) Still going strong is this espresso in the

hinterlands! This coffeehouse popped up a while back in Marble Falls, population just a tad over 4,000. The owner, Bob Tuteur, greets folks by their first names, and what the regulars like is that the food and coffee are as delicious as any you'd find in, say, Austin, but the atmosphere is far cozier and more personal than in cafes in the big city. This is about the only place for quiche in all of Burnet County; the crispy Belgian waffle is also recommended. Open for breakfast and lunch.

Texas Star Eatery (512-756-1762; 302 S. Boundary, in the Mockingbird House Gift Store, Burnet, TX 78611; lunch Mon.–Fri. 11am–2pm; desserts served all day) This busy gift shop has tables scattered among its displays. As its name implies, the food is pretty much Tex-Mex. Country-western music plays in the background, and signs such as "Life is too short to dance with ugly men" and "Don't try to drown your sorrows if she can swim" are posted on the walls. Delicious desserts, served all day, include such sweet treats as pecan pie, praline cheesecake, and chocolate cream pie.

BURNET COUNTY CULTURE

ARCHITECTURE

In *Burnet*, the **Burnet County Courthouse** on the square, currently being restored, is an Art Deco building constructed in 1937. Many of the buildings facing the courthouse date from the 1870s. Not open to the public but worth a look is the **Adam R. Johnson House** at 404 S. Water, built by the Confederate general who is credited with settling Marble Falls. Its high windows and thick walls of hand-hewn stone and logs were designed to protect against hostile Indians.

The **Old Burnet County Jail** (Washington and S. Pierce) was designed by the Austin architect F. E. Ruffini, who also designed the old Blanco County Courthouse in Blanco. Constructed in 1884 of local limestone, the jail was in use until 1981.

Buildings of architectural interest in *Marble Falls* include the **Roper House**, 707 3rd St. on the east side, built in 1888. This hotel was home to early drummers — traveling salesmen, that is — as well as such Texas politicians as Gov. Stephen Hogg. Completely renovated, with its exterior restored to its original appearance, it's now an office building (not open to the public).

Michel's Drugstore, 216 Main St., dates from 1891 and was rebuilt in 1927. It still has an old-fashioned soda fountain.

The **Brandt Badger House**, S. 4th, is of interest because the two-story house was built from the rubble left from the shaping of the granite blocks used in building the Texas capitol. Brandt Badger was a Confederate veteran, and he formed a partnership with Adam Johnson to found the town.

The **Old Marble Falls Jail** on 2nd St. is not open to the public, but it's one of the oldest structures in town. You can peek through the barred slit-hole windows to see the two cells of the gray concrete blockhouse. The **Gov. Oral M. Roberts Cottage,** 819 7th, was the home of the governor of Texas from 1879 to 1883. He later taught law at the University of Texas and retired to this whitewashed cottage in 1893.

Don't miss the **Marble Falls Chamber of Commerce** on Hwy. 281 at Broadway — and not only because of the information potential: It's in a picturesque old railroad depot. Here the 5-mile Granite Mountain and Marble Falls Railroad connected the quarry with the rails in 1889.

LIBRARIES

HERMAN BROWN FREE LIBRARY
512-756-2328.
www.rootsweb.com/~tx
burnet/Libraries.html.
On the Square, Burnet, TX 78654.
Open: Mon.–Fri. 10am–6pm.

The library is a treasure trove of information about Burnet County history and the geology of the area. It also offers a guidebook to historical markers and cemeteries in the county.

MUSEUMS

The interior of the Fort Croghan Museum depicts army life in old Texas.

Eleanor S. Morris

FORT CROGHAN GROUNDS AND MUSEUM
512-756-8281.
www.fortcroghan.org.
703 Buchanan Dr. (Hwy. 29 W.), Burnet, TX 78654.

The museum is on the site of a U.S. Army post that was in service from 1849 to 1853, the third of four forts established to protect settlements from hostile Indians. It was named for Col. George Croghan, a hero of the War of 1812. One of the original fort buildings is still there today, along with the "Old Powder House" built during the Civil War

Open: Apr.–mid-Oct., Thurs.–Sat. 10am–5pm. Admission: Free.

and several other 19th-century stone and log buildings that have been moved to the site. The museum depicts frontier days at the fort in exhibits of restored carriages, guns, furniture, and the like.

HIGHLAND LAKES AIR MUSEUM
512-756-2226.
www.kdi.com/~caf.
Kate Craddock Field, Burnet Municipal Airport, Hwy. 281 S., PO Box 866, Burnet, TX 78611.
Open: Primarily on weekends; call ahead (hours vary).
Admission: Adults $3, seniors $2, children $1.

This museum is operated by the Highland Lakes Squadron of the Confederate Air Force, based in Midland, Texas, whose mission is to preserve, in flying condition, a complete collection of combat aircraft that were flown by all military services in World War II. The CAF provides museum buildings, of which the Burnet museum is one, for the permanent protection and display of these aircraft as a tribute to the thousands of men and women who built, serviced, and flew them.

LCRA NIGHTENGALE ARCHAEOLOGICAL CENTER
512-598-5261, 800-776-5272, ext. 6714.
www.lcra.org/community .nightengale.html.
PO Box 302, Kingsland, TX 78639.
Burnet Cty. Rd. 126 off Hwy. 1431, on Lake LBJ.
Open: 2nd and 4th Sat., 2–5pm; group tours can be arranged at other times.
Admission: Free.

This public archaeological site on the Colorado River is the property of the LCRA (Lower Colorado River Authority) and is operated by the Llano Uplift Archaeological Society. The museum/educational center displays artifacts from prehistoric times. For about 10,000 years, from the end of the Ice Age to pioneer times, various peoples have inhabited the site. An interpretive trail allows visitors to walk through time. (Note: The mailing address is in Kingsland, Llano County, but the center is located in Burnet County.)

SEASONAL EVENTS

In APRIL, *Burnet* joins in the **Highland Lakes Bluebonnet Trail**, with a parade, arts and crafts fair, street dance, and tours of the fields of bluebonnets, primroses, Indian paintbrush, and many other wildflowers surrounding the Highland Lakes. *Marble Falls* also sponsors the **Bluebonnet Arts and Crafts Trail**.

In MAY, *Marble Falls* offers the **Howdy Roo Chili Cook-off.**

JUNE brings the **Burnet County Fair and Rodeo**, with a parade, carnival, entertainment, dances, livestock competition, and, of course, a rodeo, in Burnet.

The **Marble Falls Rodeo and Parade** is in JULY.

AUGUST brings the **Lakefest Drag Boat Race.**

Fort Croghan Day is in OCTOBER in *Burnet*.

In DECEMBER, **Burnet Christmas Lighting** sets the downtown square aglow with a tall tree, deer, smaller animals, a train, and a Hill Country scene. Fort Croghan is decorated as it was for the soldiers' first Christmas in 1849. Carolers and choirs sing, shops are open evenings, and Santa arrives one morning. *Marble Falls* creates the **Walkway of Lights**: thousands of lights reflected in Lake Marble Falls all through the month.

Check with the local chambers of commerce for exact dates: Burnet (512-756-4297; www.burnetchamber.org) and Marble Falls (830-693-4449; www.marble falls.org).

BURNET COUNTY RECREATION

For camping, swimming, water sports, and other Burnet County outdoor fun, refer to information below under "Parks" and "Lakes."

FISHING

In addition to these sites, good fishing can be found at other Burnet County lakes and parks — refer to those sections below.

Burnet County Park (RR 2341 off Texas 29W) On the east shore of Lake Buchanan, this is an excellent fishing camp. It's open all day, every day; no fee; first come, first served.

LCRA Cottonwood Resource Area (512-473-4083; mailing address: LCRA, PO Box 220, Austin, TX 78767) The LCRA (Lower Colorado River Authority) has reserved this property as a primitive recreation area for fishing and picnicking. The 17-acre site has one public boat ramp on the southeast side of Lake LBJ; there are no rest rooms and no running water. Camping is permitted, but there are no sites or facilities. No fee.

GOLF

Burnet

Delaware Springs Municipal Golf Course (512-756-8951, golf course; 512-756-8471, pro shop; 127 E. Jackson, Burnet, TX 78611) The 18-hole course is open seven days a week from daylight to dark, with a head professional golfer and an assistant professional.

Marble Falls

Blue Lake Golf Club (830-598-5524; 214 Bluebonnet Dr., Marble Falls, TX 78654) 9-hole public course, 7:30am–5pm.

Meadowlakes Country Club (830-693-3300; 220 Meadowlake Dr., Marble Falls, TX 78654) 18-hole public course, 6:30am–7pm.

NATURE

Scenic Drives

Old Lampasas Road-Smithwick is one of the most scenic drives in Burnet County. From Burnet take RR 963 northeast to RR 1174 south to Bertram. There take RR 243 to Oatmeal, the second oldest community in the county (and scene of the annual Oatmeal Festival, Labor Day weekend). Go south and rejoin RR 1174, and continue south to RR 1431 (or north to Marble Falls and U.S. 281 to return to Burnet).

For a panoramic view of Marble Falls, Lake Marble Falls, and the surrounding Hill Country, stop at the roadside park on U.S. 281 south of the Colorado River. There are picnic tables here, too.

Granite Mountain, an 866-foot dome of solid pink granite on the south side of FM 1431, is the largest surface granite quarry in the world. In the late 1880s it furnished pink granite for the Texas State Capitol in Austin. Souvenirs such as bookends, paperweights and boot scrapers are for sale at the Granite Mountain Stone Design showroom at 2400 Hwy. 1431 (800-573-3534, 830-693-3116).

PARKS

INKS LAKE STATE PARK
512-793-2223, 512-389-8900, camping reservations; 800-792-1112, state park info.
www.tpwd.state.tx.us/park /inks/inks.htm.
3630 Park Rd. 4 West, Burnet, TX 78611.
Off Hwy. 29 on Park Rd. 4 past Longhorn Caverns.
Open: Year-round; reservations necessary for camping.
Admission: Day use fee $1 per person 13 and over. Call for camping fees.

This 1,200-acre park offers camping, hiking (7 miles of trails), swimming, fishing, and water sports — you can rent canoes and paddleboats — on 800-acre Inks Lake, considered one of the most beautiful lakes in Texas. There are RV sites with full hookups, screened shelters, rest rooms with showers, and a dump station. There's even a 9-hole golf course. Campsite reservations are a must.

LONGHORN CAVERN STATE PARK
512-756-4680, business office; 1-877-441-CAVE, tour schedule.

The cavern was once a camp for Indians, a hiding place for outlaws during frontier days, a secret gunpowder factory and storage facility during the Civil War, and a dance hall and speakeasy during the 1930s. The natural air-conditioning of the large

Eleanor S. Morris

An entrance to Longhorn Caverns.

www.tpwd.state.tx.us./park
/longhorn/longhorn.htm.
Box 23, Burnet, TX 78611.
Park Rd. 4 off U.S. 281
between Burnet and
Marble Falls.
Open: Year-round
8am–10pm, except
Christmas Eve and
Christmas; cave tours
start at 10am.
Admission: Adults $10.95,
teens 13–19 $9.95,
children 2–12 $5.95.

"Council Room" made it very popular during hot Texas summers. According to geologists, it took a million years of water flowing through to carve out the cave, the largest in Texas and the third largest in the world. Although the entire cave is 11 miles long, the tour — which takes about an hour and a half — covers 1.25 miles, and it's always 64 degrees down there, so you may want to bring a light sweater or jacket. Flat rubber-soled shoes are highly recommended. The rest of the 639-acre park offers nature and hiking trails, picnic tables, and a snack bar and gift shop.

Family Fun

Marble Theater on Main Street, Marble Falls (830-693-4965; pages.tstar.net/ ~movies) shows "modern films with old-time nostalgia" every evening seven days a week. Show time is 7:30 if just one film is shown, 6 to 8:30 pm or 7 to 9 pm if two are shown. Cost: $4 adult, $3.50 senior, $3 children under 10 (with an adult).

Recreation on Burnet County Lakes

A view of Inks Lake, named for its deep blue color.

Eleanor S. Morris

Lake Buchanan was the first, and is the highest, of the Highland Lakes. It also has the largest surface area: 23,060 acres. Although much of the 192-mile shoreline is privately owned, a number of public and commercial places give access to boating, fishing, swimming, and other water sports, as well as camping. Both Burnet County on the east and Llano County on the west have a park on the lake.

There is excellent fishing for striped bass in Lake Buchanan. Numerous guides on the lake are eager to take visitors out for a fishing adventure. They provide all the bait and tackle you'll need, and they'll even fillet the fish for you on the dock. Call 512-793-2803 for these fishing charters.

Canyon of the Eagles (512-756-8787, 800-977-0081; www.canyonoftheeagles.com; 16942 RR 2341, Burnet, TX 78611) is a lodge and 940-acre nature park at Lake Buchanan. There are camping and RV facilities, a bird and butterfly trail and other nature trails, canoeing, kayaking, sailboating, fishing, and a lake cruise, as well as miles of lakeside beach. There's also a 64-room lodge and conference center.

A boat tour can offer a new perspective on sight-seeing and nature observation. **Vanishing Texas River Cruise** (512-756-6986, 800-474-8374; www.vtrc.com; PO Box 901, Burnet, TX 78611), at the Canyon of the Eagles on Lake Buchanan, provides guided tours up the Colorado River to see wildlife (especially birds), waterfalls, and towering cliffs. In summer there are dinner and sunset cruises; in winter the cruise offers a chance to view American bald eagles nesting on the banks of the river. Rates: adults $15, seniors and ages 13 and older $13, ages 2–12 $10.

Inks Lake covers 803 acres and is a reservoir used primarily for maintaining heads to produce electric power from the overflow from Lake Buchanan. Inks Lake offers year-round fishing, boating, and water sports; there are lakeside docks and marinas.

Lake LBJ and **Lake Marble Falls** are two constant-level lakes below Buchanan and Inks Lakes in the Highland Lakes chain. These two clear lakes offer fishing, skiing, and water recreation. At Lake LBJ, Granite Beach (830-693-9172; www.lakelbjmarina.com) offers family fun at the LBJ Yacht Club and Marina, the Cabins at Granite Beach, Boulder Water Slides, Granite Beach Grill, the Ship Store, and Aloha Rentals. For information, contact the Marble Falls Chamber of Commerce (830-693-4449; www.marblefalls.org; 801 Hwy. 281, Marble Falls, TX 78654). See "Parks" for more information.

BURNET COUNTY SHOPPING

The historic square in Burnet is one block east of Hwy. 281 at Jackson St. and is a pleasant place to stroll; it's lined with a large variety of gift and novelty shops, and there are several historic buildings on or near the square.

Burnet Antique Mall (512-756-7783; 206 S. Main St., PO Box 838, Burnet, TX 78611, on the square) Friendly Fannie Shepperd of Rocky Rest Inn is in charge of this enormous collection of everything and anything. The huge mall leads the shopper back and farther back, from one cubbyhole to the next. Furniture, lots of china, glassware, books, light fixtures, collectibles, and who knows what-all are to be had seven days a week.

Cobblestone Cottage (512-756-7407; www.cscgifts.com; 212 E. Jackson St., Burnet, TX 78611) is the place to go for plush bears, aromatherapy candles and oils, garden theme accessories and birdhouses, and Texas souvenirs.

Our Li'l Bit of Texas (512-756-7522; 117 E. Jackson St., Burnet, TX 78611, on the square) Charlene Miller has a shop chock-full of souvenirs as well as figurines, glassware, china, and bridal gifts. Texas ware abounds, too: books, placemats, rugs, candleholders, quilt racks, western and Christmas ornaments; Texas jam, jellies, and potpourri; and a lovely collection of T-shirts, mailboxes, and baskets hand-painted with Texas wildflowers.

The *Marble Falls* Chamber of Commerce offers a list of local shops selling everything from antiques, clothing, and gifts to pecans (at **Texas Hill Country Pecans,** 1009 N. Main, Marble Falls, TX 78654). Marble Falls favorites include the following:

Antiques Plus (830-693-3301; 1000 W. Hwy. 1431, Marble Falls, TX 78654) has, as the name implies, more than just antiques. They also have new and used furniture, collectibles, and gifts.

The Wood Shed (830-693-2024; 112 Hwy. 281 N., Marble Falls, TX 78654) It would be hard to miss this low, rambling building on the west side of the highway — a gift shop that grew over more than 25 years into "the woodshed that was," says owner Carol Collier. The huge interior stocks all sorts of Texas mem-

---

Dead Man's Hole

Some 140 years after becoming part of Texas's sometimes violent, colorful past, Dead Man's Hole has been dedicated as a historical site. Seventeen bodies, forerunners of some of today's Burnet County residents, were dumped here during a period of terror between secessionist and unionist sympathizers during the Civil War and the Reconstruction that followed. Located 3 miles southwest of Marble Falls, the site has a historical marker.

orabilia, Texana books and jams and jellies, clothing "geared to the Texas look," Indian turquoise and designer silver jewelry, hunting and fishing equipment, and even leather luggage.

GILLESPIE COUNTY

The 180 German immigrants with the sixteen ox-drawn wagons who trekked from New Braunfels to the Pedernales River were either a brave bunch or seriously misinformed, because they ended up in the heart of Comanche country despite the efforts of Prince Carl of Solms-Braunfels to make sure his German colonists were settling in safe territory. It was May of 1846 when they arrived on the banks of the Pedernales, and by 1847 stronger measures had to be taken for their protection or they would have been swept away by the powerful Indians. Thanks to Baron von Meusebach — who, unlike Prince Solms, renounced his title to become plain John O. Meusebach, citizen of Texas — the colonists were saved.

Meusebach, evidently a genius at diplomacy, crafted such a successful treaty with the Indians that the tiny town of Fredericksburg was left in peace. This scenic county of plateaus and hills broken by spring-fed streams was organized in 1848 from Bexar and Travis Counties and named for Texas Ranger captain R. A. Gillespie. Although Blanco County revels in the fact that President Lyndon B. Johnson grew up within its boundaries, Gillespie County can boast that he was born here, in the small town of Stonewall.

Gillespie County can also claim another famous American, Fleet Adm. Chester W. Nimitz, born in Fredericksburg.

Fredericksburg

For a taste of still-living Texas history, visit Fredericksburg, where many natives still speak German and live in quaint gingerbread-trimmed houses. Fredericksburg is so friendly that even its street signs spell out a welcome. The first letters of the streets running north and south across Main spell out "All Welcome"; traveling west from the courthouse square, the first letters spell "Come Back." (All Gillespie County listings are in Fredericksburg unless otherwise noted.)

The **Fredericksburg Convention and Visitors Bureau** (830-997-6523; www. fredericksburg-texas.com, now in their new headquarters at 302 E. Austin) offers a walking-tour map of the historic district, with more than 80 points of interest, including the Sunday houses.

Stonewall

Stonewall — founded in 1870 and named for Confederate general Stonewall Jackson — is so small it doesn't have an organized downtown, just what's along the highway: gas station, motel, restaurant. But it's famed equally for delicious

Gillespie County peaches (the Peach Jamboree is usually the middle weekend in June) and the LBJ Ranch, Lyndon B. Johnson's home.

GILLESPIE COUNTY LODGING

Fredericksburg has a dizzying array of bed & breakfast inns and guest houses — over 300! — if you want to spend the night and see even more of this historic spot. Below are five pleasant B&Bs. **Be My Guest** (830-997-7227, 800-364-8555) and **Gästehaus Schmidt Reservation Service** (830-997-5612, 866-427-8374; www.fbglodging.com) are reservation services listing many more country inns and B&Bs, historic homes, and secluded guest cottages. (For additional reservation services as well as other area information, log on to the **Fredericksburg Chamber of Commerce** Web site, www.fredericksburg-texas.com.) There are also several motels, among them **Sunday House Inn and Suites** (830-997-4484, 800-274-3762; 501 E. Main St., Fredericksburg, TX 78624) and other chains such as **Comfort Inn** (830-997- 9811, 800-228-5150; 908 S. Adams St., Fredericksburg, TX 78624), **Days Inn Suites** (830-997-1086, 800-320-1430; 808 S. Adams St., Fredericksburg, TX 78624), **Econo Lodge** (830-997-3437, 888-919-3437; 810 S. Adams St., Fredericksburg, TX 78624), and **Budget Host DeLuxe Inn** (830-997-3344, 800-BUD-HOST; 901 E. Main, Fredericksburg, TX 78624), among others.

BED & BREAKFAST INNS

Fredericksburg

DAS COLLEGE HAUS
Hosts: Bitsy and Bob
 Neuser.
830-997-9047, 800-654-2802.
www.dascollegehaus.com.
106 College St.,
 Fredericksburg, TX 78624.
Price: Moderate to
 Expensive.
Credit Cards: MC, V.

Built in 1916, this lovely home is a fine example of Greek Revival architecture. Hosts Bitsy and Bob have kept the wonderful assortment of old furniture assembled by previous owners. "It's been a love affair between us and two previous owners who are good friends," Bitsy says. This makes for an interesting change from the more usual German furniture of Fredericksburg, home of the first group of settlers brought to Texas by the Society for the Protection of German Immigrants in Texas. Downstairs, the Victorian Rose Suite has a paisley and rose-patterned wallpaper in both the king-size bedroom and the sitting room (with fireplace and gas log), complementing the pretty flowered quilt and the sheer canopy of lace over the bed. The Arbor Suite has hardwood floors, cedar walls, and a beamed ceiling plus a large bathroom with a skylight and stained-glass windows. Upstairs, off the L-shaped porch, the Victorian Green Suite can sleep six; the sitting room contains a sofa bed. The Country Cream Room, across the hall, features a charming queen-size white-

and-brass bed. Breakfast might be apple-pecan pancakes with crisp bacon, maple syrup, and oat-bran muffins. "We're health-conscious," says Bitsy. "The pancakes are fat-free. But the amount of syrup is up to you!"

This historic house, originally built in 1898, is now home to The Delforge Place B&B.

Eleanor S. Morris

THE DELFORGE PLACE
Hosts: Sandy and Lee Selig.
830-997-6212, 800-997-0462.
www.delforgeplace.com.
710 Ettie St., Fredericksburg, TX 78624.
Price: Moderate, EP.
Credit Cards: AE, D, MC, V.
Handicap Access: No.

Built in 1898, this historic house was moved to its present location in 1975 and considerably enlarged. Now that there are four guest rooms and suites – each with full private bath and mini-refrigerator plus "coffee corner" — in the main house (plus two suites next door in the also-historic Rabke-Weber House), it's hard to believe that this comfortable inn was once a one-room Sunday house. Sandy is following in the footsteps of the previous owners, the Delforges, who were famous for their breakfasts, and she offers a "world class" breakfast (featured in *Gourmet* and *Bon Appétit* magazines). You might have German sour cream twists, Belgian pastries, and homemade jams and jellies, as well as seasonal foods. Guests can play horseshoes, croquet, and archery on the inn's grounds.

MAGNOLIA HOUSE
Hosts: David and Dee Lawford.
830-997-0306, 800-880-4374.
www.magnolia-house.com.
101 E. Hackberry, Fredericksburg, TX 78624.
Price: Moderate, EP.
Credit Cards: AE, D, MC, V.
Handicap Access: No.

Innkeepers David and Dee took over this historic home in November 1999, and everything has remained the same — from the gourmet southern-style breakfasts of fresh fruit, homemade muffins and juice, waffles and crêpes, bacon and sausage, an egg entrée, sweet rolls, and biscuits and gravy to the antique china and silver the meals are served on. The stately home was built in 1923 for the Stein family: Edward Stein was the architect of the Gillespie

County Courthouse. The two suites, the Magnolia and the Bluebonnet, and the three guest rooms, the American Beauty, the Peach Blossom, and the Lilli Marleen, are all luxurious, with HBO and Encore premium channels, fresh flowers, and terry robes. The stone patio and fish pond make the outdoors inviting, too.

ORCHARD INN
Hosts: Annette and Mark Wieser.
830-990-0257, 800-439-4320.
www.orchard-inn.com.
1364 S. Hwy. 87, Rt. 3, Box 115, Fredericksburg, TX 78624.
Price: Expensive.
Credit Cards: All.
Handicap Access: No.

You'll really feel out in the country on these 60 acres, yet the inn is practically right in town. The property has a lake with paddleboats and fish ("and hungry ducks," says Annette), and the 1904 Victorian farmhouse has been enlarged into an elegant country inn. There are three suites in the north wing of the house, one of them in the older portion. A fourth room is located nearby in an 1870 log cabin, decorated in a hunting and fishing theme. Your gourmet breakfast might include mountain cherry frappé, glazed pork tenderloin, a cheddar cheese soufflé, rosemary potatoes, and homemade bread with homemade amaretto peach preserves. So bring a hearty appetite along with your luggage!

Rose Hill Manor in Stonewall is like the country inns one finds in the East. It has a superb restaurant as well.

Eleanor S. Morris

ROSE HILL MANOR
Hosts: Patricia and Robert Vander Lyn.
830-644-5541, 877-ROSEHIL.
www.rose-hill.com.
2614 Upper Albert Rd., Stonewall, TX 78671.
Price: Expensive.
Credit Cards: All.

Rose Hill Manor is in the tradition of a country inn, much like those found on the East Coast. Not only will you get a bed in a lovely guest room and a gourmet breakfast, but the restaurant, which is open to the public as well as inn guests, serves meals created by chefs Dean and Kimberly Brumm. The inn also has wine tastings every Saturday and Sunday from 1pm to 5pm. The large white house, with a cupola on the roof, is surrounded by a veranda upstairs and down, giving each of the four guest rooms a porch with a sweeping Hill Country view. Both the rooms in the main house and the four country cottages have king-size four-poster beds. The cottages also are equipped with refrigerators, microwaves, coffeemakers, and fireplace, and each has a screened porch with heat or air-conditioning. Breakfast might be fresh strawberries with cream, banana walnut waffles, and Opa's sausage (a well-known Fredericksburg delicacy).

GILLESPIE COUNTY RESTAURANTS AND FOOD PURVEYORS

Fredericksburg

ALTDORF GERMAN BIERGARTEN AND DINING ROOM
830-997-7865.
301 W. Main St.,
  Fredericksburg, TX 78624.
Price: Moderate.
Cuisine: German.
Serving: L, D Weds.–Mon.
Credit Cards: MC, D, V.
Handicap Access: Yes.

Indoors or out in the biergarten behind this restaurant, the food is delicious. Tourists appreciate good German food, proprietor Cameron Baird says, and local people who eat German food at home come for the restaurant's Tex-Mex fare. From the Hans and Fritz sandwich to the dinners of bratwurst, knockwurst, bockwurst, and schnitzel, or the Tex-Mex *comidas* (dinners) of enchilada, taco, and chalupa plates, everybody enjoys Altdorf — there's often a waiting line. The oldest part of the restaurant, the indoor dining room, was built in 1846 by German settler Conrad Wissemann. The room has big windows, lace curtains, a pine floor, and paintings and prints of Fredericksburg on the walls. But in good weather (which it almost always is in the Hill Country) most folks prefer to sit out under the big old trees in the biergarten.

ANDY'S DINER
830-997-3744.
413 S. Washington,
  Fredericksburg, TX 78624.
Price: Inexpensive.
Cuisine: Central Texas.
Serving: B, L, D.
Credit Cards: All but
  Discover.
Handicap Access: Yes.

Know that you'll appreciate Andy's brag that their chicken-fried steaks have been featured in the *Chicago Tribune*, the *Arizona Daily Star*, and the *Philadelphia Enquirer*. In addition, this friendly place is open seven days a week for three meals a day — and has been since 1957. The large main room has a model train riding on a track around the room, just below the ceiling, which you can watch while enjoying steaks, seafood, Mexican dishes, even German cuisine. Friday night there's an all-you-can-eat seafood buffet.

FRIEDHELM'S BAVARIAN INN AND BAR
830-997-6300.
905 W. Main St.,
Fredericksburg, TX 78624.
Price: Expensive.
Cuisine: German, Steaks, Seafood.
Serving: L, D Tues.–Sun.
Credit Cards: AE, D, MC, V.
Handicap Access: Yes.

There's often a wait at this bar and restaurant, a huge building with the ambiance of a Black Forest hunting lodge — fallow deer, moose, mule deer, elk, and boar heads are mounted on the wall — or a Bavarian *Bierstube* — there are old beer signs decorating the walls, along with a tall mirrored bar with columns, classic beer steins, and friendly if busy service. Sauerbraten nach bayrischer Art — Bavarian-style roast beef imbued with aromatic spices, herbs, and wine — is a good choice, as is the house version of Holstein schnitzel, breaded and topped with jäger mushroom sauce and, surprisingly, two sunny-side-up eggs. The whole-wheat bread is made with molasses and millet seeds, and apple strudel tops it all off. There's beer from a barrel, premium domestic beer, and imported beers; wines from both German and Hill Country cellars; margaritas, coladas, and daiquiris; and warmth and *Gemütlichkeit* everywhere. Three large dining rooms seat 300, and everything runs smoothly in spite of the crowd.

OLD GERMAN BAKERY AND CAFE
830-997-9084.
225 W. Main St.,
Fredericksburg, TX 78624.
Price: Moderate.
Cuisine: German.
Serving: B, L, D
Thurs.–Mon.
Credit Cards: None.
Handicap Access: Yes.

For authentic German food, from schnitzels to rouladen, this is a perfect place. And since it's also a bakery, you can choose your dessert right from the display case of fresh-baked goodies. The storefront restaurant is bright and friendly, and you can be sure you're dining in good company, since it's a popular spot for the locals — including the sheriff and his men.

WHEELER'S
830-990-8180.
204 E. Main St.,
Fredericksburg, TX 78624.
Price: Inexpensive.
Cuisine: Texan, German.
Serving: L.
Credit Cards: MC, V.
Handicap Access: Yes.

This family-owned-and-operated restaurant has a bright, clean look, with its fresh blue-and-white color scheme and white stucco walls. The motif reflects the mix of the menu, with a giant steer hide on one wall and Indian and other western art on the others, while outside, the restaurant is decorated with flower boxes and scalloped gingerbread trim. The corner room with its wide window walls is great for people-watching as you dig into your Texas chili and corn bread and beans, or the German plate of grilled bratwurst or knockwurst, red cabbage, sauerkraut, and hot German potato salad.

GILLESPIE COUNTY FOOD PURVEYORS

BAKERIES

Along with the Old German Bakery and Cafe (see "Restaurants"), try:

Dietz Bakery (830-997-3250; 218 E. Main St., Fredericksburg, TX 78624; 8am until sold out) Fredericksburg's oldest bakery (founded 1876) is famous for its bread — whole wheat, white, rye, and French. They're open only until they're sold out, so don't wait too long, since they're usually emptied out by noon. The pastries and cookies are delicious, too.

Fredericksburg Bakery (830-997-3254; 141 E. Main St., Fredericksburg, TX 78624; Mon.–Sat. 8am–5:30pm, Sun. 8am–5pm) This bakery prides itself on authentic German goods from its German baker — from apple strudel that's "made and tastes just like in Germany" to the popular sweet pretzels and breads made from high-fiber grains imported from Germany. Authentic, historic recipes date from 1917.

MARKETS

Fredericksburg

Das Peach Haus (830-997-7194; 1406 Hwy. 87 S., Fredericksburg, TX 78624; open May 15–Aug. 15) This fresh-fruit stand also stocks jams and jellies in its country store.

Stonewall

Grape Creek Country Market (830-990-4021; www.grapecreekmarket.com; 10618 Hwy. 290, 10.5 miles east of Fredericksburg) A long, low building crammed with unique gifts, Texas foodstuffs, fresh fruits, a garden shop with antique roses, and a restaurant with both eat-in and take-out barbecue and other foods such as cheeses and beef jerky.

WINERIES

Gillespie County is home to four award-winning wineries and a brewery.

Fredericksburg

Bell Mountain Oberhellmann Vineyards (830-685-3297; 463 Bell Mountain Rd., Fredericksburg, TX 78624; off Hwy. 16, 14 miles north of Fredericksburg; tasting room open Mar.–mid-Dec., Sat. only, 10am–5pm; call a day in advance for tour) After winemaking was revived in Texas, Bell Mountain was founded in 1976, establishing the first appellation in the state. Wines are estate bottled:

chardonnay, sauvignon blanc, semillon, Johannesburg riesling, cabernet sauvignon, pinot noir, and gewürztraminer.

Fredericksburg Brewing Company (830-997-1646; www.yourbrewery.com; E. Main St., Fredericksburg, TX 78624) 7,000 gallons of cold German lagers, ales, and wheat brews are offered here. Check out the restaurant, featuring excellent kolaches, and a bar amid a stone fireplace, bright copper vessels, and an enclosed biergarten. You can even spend the night in one of 12 "bed & brew" accommodations above the brewery — it's an adults-only retreat — and in the morning enjoy the Kolache Kafé for fresh baked goods and gourmet coffee.

Fredericksburg wines are available only at the winery.

Eleanor S. Morris

Fredericksburg Winery (830-990-8747; www.fbgwinery.com; 247 W. Main St., Fredericksburg, TX 78624) Just one block west of the courthouse, this winery boasts 14 to 16 releases tasted daily. It's won three medals in world wine championships conducted by the Beverage Tasting Institute in Chicago, so you might want to taste some of the many offerings. These wines are sold only in the winery. Open: Mon.–Thurs. 10am–6pm; Fri.–Sat. 10am–8pm; Sun. 12pm–6pm.

Stonewall

Becker Vineyards (830-644-2681; www.beckervineyards.com; Jenschke Ln. off U.S. Hwy. 290, Stonewall, TX 78671, 10 miles east of Fredericksburg; open daily with tours and tastings, picnic facilities) Bordeaux, viognier and other Rhône-style wines are the specialty here.

Grape Creek Vineyard (830-644-2710; www.grapecreek.com; PO Box 102, Stonewall, TX 78671; Hwy. 290, 10 miles east of Fredericksburg; tours Mon.–Sat. 10am–5pm, Sun. 12–5pm) This Hill Country winery is unique in that it has an underground cellar. In the tasting room, sample cabernet sauvignon, chardonnay, and sauvignon blanc under the Texas Hill Country appellation. Gift shop, too.

GILLESPIE COUNTY CULTURE

ARCHITECTURE

Special Fredericksburg attractions are the **Sunday houses,** little jewels of homes built in the 1880s by farmers and ranchers to be used on weekends when they came to town to shop, visit, attend Saturday night "oompah" (polka) dances and church on Sunday. They would arrive on a Saturday morning to sell their butter and eggs, shop for staples, and that evening they'd go visiting or dancing. Then after church on Sunday it was back to the farm.

Many of the houses have only two rooms, one above the other, with the stairway outside. There are all sorts of entertaining conjectures why. Were the children put upstairs and out of the way? Or were the women and children downstairs so the men could creep upstairs late at night without disturbing them?

Speaking of quaint, the Vereins Kirche Museum (http://www.pioneermuseum .com/ourmuseums.htm) is an eight-sided structure that looks just like a giant coffee mill. It was the first public building in the town, serving as a house of worship, school, and meeting hall. Now it holds city archives, a local history collection, and archaeological items. Admission is $1. Open: Mon.–Sat. 10am– 4pm, Sun. 1pm–4pm.

The "Coffee Mill" Vereins Kirche Museum, a replica of the original structure, the community church.

Eleanor S. Morris

MUSEUMS

Fredericksburg

FORT MARTIN SCOTT
830-997-9895.
www.fortmartinscott.com.

The fort was an active U.S. Army outpost for five years, from 1848 to 1853. It housed and trained supply soldiers working on scouting missions in

2.4 miles east of
   Fredericksburg on Hwy.
   290 E.
Open: Tues.–Sun.
   10am–5pm.
Admission: Free.

**GISH'S OLD WEST
MUSEUM**
830-997-2794.
502 N. Milam,
   Fredericksburg, TX
   78624.

the area. After it was abandoned by the Army, it was used by the Texas Rangers.

This museum is a treat for Old West buffs — if you can catch Joe Gish when he's there. "No regular hours," says Joe. "Museum is open when I'm here." This collection, gathered over 40 years, includes saddles, rifles and pistols, hats, chaps, spurs, lawmen's badges, and handcuffs, most used or worn by Old West cowboys and lawmen, as well as Old West photographs and art, all housed in a log cabin.

Eleanor S. Morris

The National Museum of the Pacific War, formerly known as the Admiral Nimitz Museum, is housed in what was the Steamboat Hotel during Nimitz's youth.

**NATIONAL MUSEUM OF
THE PACIFIC WAR**
830-997-4379.
www.tpwd.state.tx.us/park
   /nimitz.
340 E. Main St., PO Box 777,
   Fredericksburg, TX 78624.
Open: 10am–5pm daily
   except Christmas.
Admission: Adults $5,
   students and children
   6–12 $3, under 6 free.
Handicap Access: Partial.

Formerly the Admiral Nimitz Museum, the museum's main building, the Steamboat Hotel, was built by the grandparents of Fleet Adm. Chester M. Nimitz, last of the U.S. five-star admirals and a native son of Fredericksburg. His grandparents were among the first settlers in the community in 1846. The museum's three floors have exhibits about the war in the Pacific that are dedicated to all who served under the admiral. Behind the hotel, the serene Japanese Garden of Peace is a gift from the people of Japan. The History Walk, one block from the garden, displays guns, boats, and planes from World War II along the pathways. Also in the rear of the museum, the George Bush Gallery of the Pacific

War has been added, in an existing building that has been expanded. New is the Pacific War Combat Zone. "Americans can't visit World War II battlefields in the Pacific as easily as they can see similar combat sites in the U.S. and Europe," says museum director Joe Cavanaugh. "Here they can see how land, naval, and air forces worked together to win the war."

PIONEER MUSEUM COMPLEX
830-990-8441.
www.pioneermuseum.com.
309 W. Main.,
Fredericksburg, TX 78624.
Open: Mon.–Sat.
10am–5pm, Sun.
1pm–5pm.
Admission: Ages 11 and up
$4, under 11 free.
Handicap Access: No.

The complex consists of a house, store, stone smokehouse, barn, another old home, and a Sunday house. The main building is the Kammlah House, originally the home of the Kammlah family, keepers of the first general store.

Stonewall

LYNDON B. JOHNSON STATE PARK AND HISTORIC SITE
830-644-2252.
www.tpwd.state.tx.us/park/lbj.
PO Box 238, Stonewall, TX 78671.
Located 2 miles east of Stonewall on Hwy. 290.
Open: Daily 8am–5pm.
Admission: Bus tours ($3; children 6 and under free) leave from the visitor center 10am–4pm daily. Abbreviated self-guided tours allowed 5pm–dusk.

Laughing crowds listen to recordings of LBJ's jokes before boarding a small tour bus to see his birthplace, one-room schoolhouse, and other historic sights. The 700-plus-acre state park includes a visitor center, a "dogtrot" cabin from the 1840s, an outdoor amphitheater, a nature trail, and the Sauer Beckmann Living History Farmstead, which depicts the life of a traditional German family in the early 1900s. The tour includes the Old Junction schoolhouse, the Texas White House, LBJ Ranchlands, LBJ's birthplace, and the Johnson family cemetery. A new exhibit, "A Texas Hill Country Heritage: The Land and People that Inspired a President and First Lady," opened in August 2002. Hand-painted murals, interactive games, eyewitness quotes, and audio clips help visitors explore the diverse cultures of the Texas Hill Country and the landscape that shaped the values and character of one of America's most controversial and charismatic leaders.

SEASONAL EVENTS

Fredericksburg has an almost endless variety of festivals, every month of the year. Some are listed here, but check with the **Fredericksburg Chamber of**

Commerce (830-997-6523; www. fredericksburg-texas.com/events.htm) for details and dates.

MARCH is the beginning of Fredericksburg's **wildflower season** (which varies with the rainfall, sunshine, and temperature).

APRIL brings more wildflowers and the **Easter Fires Pageant**. One of Fredericksburg's biggest celebrations is the Easter Fires, commemorating Baron von Meusebach's peace talks. While the Indians and settlers were sitting around fires awaiting the outcome of the peace talks, a pioneer mother quieted her children's fears by telling them a charming tale of the rabbit who lit and tended those hillside fires to boil Easter eggs. Today, hillside fires glow each Easter eve while a pageant retells the story.

On the first or second weekend in MAY is the **Founder's Festival** and **Spring Tour of Homes**.

JUNE brings the **Stonewall Peach Jamboree & Rodeo**; the **Country Peddler Show** is on the second or third weekend.

In JULY there are the **Fourth of July Race Meet**; the **Night in Old Fredericksburg Festival**, midmonth; and the **Pari-Mutuel Horseracing Meet**, which takes place twice a month.

AUGUST is the month for the **Gillespie County Fair**, the oldest continuous county fair in Texas (since 1888). In addition to the fair, the **Pari-Mutuel Horseracing Trials Race Meet** occurs midmonth, and the **Pari-Mutuel Horseracing Meet** is on the fourth weekend.

In SEPTEMBER the **Country Peddler Show** comes around again at the beginning of the month.

OCTOBER is busy with the **Oktoberfest** on the first weekend; the **Mesquite Art Festival**, second weekend; and the **Food & Wine Fest**, fourth weekend.

In NOVEMBER the **Country Peddler Show** is held again around Thanksgiving, along with the **Turkey Trot**. The **Christmas Lighting Tour** starts on the fourth weekend.

Through DECEMBER the **Christmas Lighting Trail** lights up historic Main St. and residential areas (a map is available at the **Convention and Visitors Bureau**; 803-997-6523; 106 N. Adams, Fredericksburg, TX 78624). **Kristkindl Market** and **Candlelight Tour of Homes** are on the second weekend.

GILLESPIE COUNTY RECREATION

CAMPING

This section describes park and hiking trails as well as camping facilities. (See also www.fredicksburg-texas.com/camping.htm.)

Enchanted Rock State Natural Area (915-247-3903, 800-792-1112; reservations 512-389-9900; www.tpwd.state.tx.us/park/enchantd; 16710 RR 965, Fredericksburg, TX 78624; 18 miles north of Fredericksburg) Over 1,600 acres on Big Sandy Creek feature 46 tent sites and 60 primitive campsites, hiking trails, picnic area, barbecue grills, and group facilities. (For more information, see "Parks" under Llano County Recreation.)

Fredericksburg KOA (830-997-4796; www.touringtexas.com/koa; 5681 Hwy. 290 E., Fredericksburg, TX 78624; 5 miles from Fredericksburg) Facilities here include 90 RV and tent sites, Kamping Kabins (AC/heat), rec room, grocery, laundry facilities, cable TV, pool.

Hill Country RV Park (830-997-5365; 1589 E. Main St., Fredericksburg, TX 78624) The 43 sites here are level, full-hookup, pull-through sites. Cable TV, shower, laundry facilities, rec room.

Lady Bird Johnson Municipal Park (830-997-4202; Hwy. 16 S., Fredericksburg, TX 78624; 3 miles from Fredericksburg) This 340-acre park has 113 sites, all with full hookups, 50 tent sites, sports facilities, an 18-hole championship golf course (see "Golf"), and group facilities at the park. New is the nature trail along Live Oak Creek of different ecosystems.

Oakwood RV Resort (830-997-9817, 800-366-9396; Rt. 21, Box 218-B; Fredericksburg, TX 78624; 2 miles south on Hwy. 16 S. at Tivydale Rd.) 132 sites, full hookups, cable TV, paved roads, pool, laundry facilities.

Luckenbach, Texas

There's always music in this Luckenbach bar, where "everybody is somebody."

Eleanor S. Morris

Between Stonewall and Fredericksburg, take a little detour south on FM 1376, 4 miles to Luckenbach, famed in song and story. The spot was founded in 1849, but it never amounted to anything and was a ghost town by the 1970s. Nobody would have heard of Luckenbach if the late storyteller of Texas folklore, Hondo Crouch, hadn't purchased the town in 1970. It was brought to further notoriety by country-western music stars Willie Nelson and Waylon Jennings, who sang the song "Luckenbach, Texas." Jerry Jeff Walker got into the act by recording "Viva Terlingua " there.

The bend in the road is marked but is rather easy to miss, so be alert. There's a post office in downtown Luckenbach, which is a little way down the road on the north bank of Big Creek, but Fredericksburg has taken over the privilege of postmarking the town's mail. However, you can buy a Luckenbach postcard here, and they'll give it an extra postmark. Under the trees along the creek there's a dance hall. There's usually a lot of fun and music going on in the bar at the back of the souvenir shop/post office (except on Wednesdays and Sundays) as well as all sorts of activities in the dance hall. The motto here is "Everybody's somebody in Luckenbach." (For more information, call 830-997-3224 or 888-311-8990, or see the Luckenbach Inn's Web site for links to events in the area: www.luckenbachtx.com.) Luckenbach also has a famous festival, Willie Nelson's Fourth of July Picnic.

A bed & breakfast, the Full Moon Inn, is just off the road within half a mile of Luckenbach and just 10 minutes from Fredericksburg.

THE FULL MOON INN
Host: Capt. Matt Carinhas.
830-997-2205, 800-997-1124.
www.fullmooninn.com.
3234 Luckenbach Rd.,
   Fredericksburg, TX 78624.
Price: Moderate to
   Expensive.
Credit Cards: AE, D, MC, V.
Handicap Access: No.

Located on 12 acres along the banks of South Grape Creek, with an abundance of wildlife, you'll feel far from even the business of Fredericksburg if it's peace and quiet you prefer, but you can easily visit the surrounding attractions of Luckenbach Dance Hall, Fredericksburg shopping, L.B.J. State Park, and three great wineries. The two-bedroom 1800s Log Cabin is rustic and filled with antiques, the Coral and Cypress Rooms have a whirlpool tub and a fireplace, the Grape Suite has a full kitchen, and the Old Smokehouse is a charming cottage behind the Log Cabin. The Peach Room has a king-size bed and is handicap-accessible. A rock fireplace warms the main house, "and we do use our fireplace!" says Matt Carinhas. Well-behaved children and pets are welcome. Breakfast might be fresh fruit, French toast or sweet potato pancakes, pepperwurst sausage, and an egg mix of French-fried onions, cream, and Tabasco sauce. Lacy is the resident dog, and guinea fowl run all around the place. But the big surprise is Rooter Boy, the potbellied pig, curled up by the fireplace. The Full Moon Grill serves dinner Tues.–Fri. 5pm–9pm.

FAMILY FUN

Scenic carriage rides through Fredericksburg's historic district, with history narration, are offered by the **Fredericksburg Carriage Company** (830-868-4144; W. Main & Orange, Fredericksburg, TX 78624; reservations recommended).

GOLF

Lady Bird Johnson Municipal Golf Course (830-997-4010, 800-950-8147; Hwy. 16 S., Fredericksburg, TX 78624) Three miles southeast of town, this par-72 course is considered the finest 18-hole championship course in the Hill Country.

HORSE RACING

June, July, and August are racing months in Gillespie County. Since 1888 the folks in Fredericksburg have been enjoying pari-mutuel horse races, first on the abandoned grounds of Fort Martin Scott, where the parade grounds were dragged by logs to make the first racetrack. The second racetrack was two blocks along E. Travis St. In 1892 a third site was chosen, the 400 block between S. Adams and S. Lincoln. Now the fairgrounds and racetrack are next to the Lady Bird Johnson Municipal Park on Hwy. 16 S., 3 miles from Fredericksburg. The track is 5/8 mile long, with a covered grandstand as well as bleachers, plus 10 window ticket offices with full facilities. For racing schedules, contact the Gillespie County Fair Association, 830-997-2359; PO Box 526, Fredericksburg, TX 78624.

NATURE

Visit **Wildseed Farms** (830-990-1393, 800-848-0078; www.wildseedfarms.com; 100 Legacy Dr., Fredericksburg, TX 78624; 7 miles east of Fredericksburg on Hwy. 290; open 9:30am–6pm daily) for a tour of the Hill Country's famous wildflowers. Although you can see them by the roadside every spring, this is a year-round flowering. It's a 200-acre working wildflower farm, with bluebonnets, poppies, and other colorful Texas wildflowers grown and harvested for seed. There's a self-guided walking trail, a market center, and the Brew-bonnet Biergarten (with, of course, beer, plus boxed lunches and such snacks as peach sundaes). Be sure to bring your camera.

ROCK CLIMBING

There are no fewer than 45 listed climbs in Enchanted Rock State Natural Area, from the hand-crack Raw Hand Climb, with a good protection rating, to the face-climbing boulder of Sanders Traverse, with no protection. The climbs are rated according to the Yosemite Decimal System and range from 5.0 to 5.11, with higher ratings indicating increasing difficulty. Free climbing is permitted, but not the placement of bolts, pitons, or other devices that deface the rock in any way. Needless to say, you climb at your own risk. It's necessary to sign a climbing and rappelling release form before you begin.

TENNIS

FISD Tennis Center (Fredericksburg High School, Hwy. 16, Fredericksburg, TX 78624) The high school campus has eight courts, four lit for night play.

GILLESPIE COUNTY SHOPPING

Fredericksburg's Main Street is lined for blocks with shops, restaurants, and galleries.

Eleanor S. Morris

Fredericksburg is a tourist town, and eight blocks of the Main St. historic district, from Washington St. east to Bowie west, are lined on both sides with every sort of shop and boutique imaginable. Walking up the west side of the street you'll find the following:

Alley Annex Antiques (830-997-4448; 305 W. Main St., Fredericksburg, TX 78624) Texas and Southwest primitives as well as American oak and "ranch relics."

Ambeance Antiques, Etc. (830-990-8912; 215 W. Main St., Fredericksburg, TX 78624) Tucked behind the Back Porch down a secluded brick walkway are eight rooms where you can browse forever. "Everyone just loves to come here and spend an hour," owner Betty Bass says. "They say I'm not too touristy!"

The Back Porch (830-997-2757; 211 W. Main, Fredericksburg, TX 78624) A delightful shop full of one-of-a-kind folk art pieces, much of it made by Pam Brunet and proudly displayed by her father Tom. Lamps, clocks, birdhouses, lamp bases, and signs like "God Bless Texas" and "Grow Dammit" — all one of a kind.

Dodd's Family Tree Nursery (830-997-9571, 800-284-0352; 515 W. Main St., Fredericksburg, TX 78624) A garden and patio shop with native plants for xeriscape gardening. The nursery and flower shop also include a Christmas store with all sorts of things for the holidays.

Walking up as far as Bowie and crossing over to the east side of Main, you'll find:

Der Küchen Laden (830-997-4937; www.littlechef.com; 258 E. Main St., Fredericksburg, TX 78624) A complete kitchen shop full of cookware, baskets, spices, coffee beans, teas, and kitchen accessories.

The Epicurean Shop (830-997-0124; 315 E. Main St., Fredericksburg, TX 78624) Specializing in self-indulgence, this shop offers jams, jellies, specialty foods from around the world, and bath and body luxuries.

The Grasshopper and Wild Honey (830-997-5012; www.grasshopperfbg.com; 113 E. Main St., Fredericksburg, TX 78624) German nutcrackers and beer steins, Swarovski crystal, Chilmark pewter, and other collectibles.

Jabberwocky (830-997-7071; 105 N. Llano St., Fredericksburg, TX 78624) Quilts, clothing, bed and table linens, a nice selection of Spode ware, and other gift items.

Jeep Collins, Jewelry Maker (830-997-5490; 148A E. Main St., Fredericksburg, TX 78624) Handcrafted jewelry and leather products.

The Main Book Shop (830-997-2375, 800-225-2375; www.main-book-shop.com; 143 E. Main St., Fredericksburg, TX 78624) Lots of Texas guidebooks; Texas cookbooks; Texas gardening, fishing, and nature tomes. The shop also features an entire side wall of children's books, along with period paper dolls and such. Souvenirs, too, like Texas dominoes, cards, and Lone Star mugs.

Remember Me, Too (830-997-6444; 203 E. Main St., Fredericksburg, TX 78624) "Antiques and other whimsies," such as one-of-a-kind birdhouses, Santas, and shopkeepers Pam and Terry's very own creation, "Prairie Santas," which they carve from wood and clothe in old fabrics.

The Seasons (830-997-9180; 116 E. Main St., Fredericksburg, TX 78624) A shopful of gifts and decorative accessories.

Showcase Antiques (830-997-5505; 119 E. Main, Fredericksburg, TX 78624) A fine selection of cut glass, porcelain, art glass, maps, and prints, as well as furniture.

The Southwest Images Gallery (830-997-8688; 123 E. Main St., Fredericksburg, TX 78624) Antler and horn chandeliers, copper lighting fixtures and furniture, and other western decorative accessories.

Sweet Annie (830-997-0852; 219 W. Main St., Fredericksburg, TX 78624) The home of American country antiques along with potpourri, books, gifts, and lots of candy: candy sticks and old-fashioned bulk candy (horehound, rock, sour cherry, sour apple) by the pound and weighed on an old-fashioned scale.

Fredericksburg is also attracting art galleries, among them: **Charles Beckendorf** (830-997-5955; 519 E. Main St., Fredericksburg, TX 78624), **Fredericksburg Art Gallery** (830-990-2707; 425 E. Main St., Fredericksburg, TX 78624), **Thomas Kinkade Gallery** (830-990-2335; 131 E. Main St., Fredericksburg, TX 78624), and **Whistle Pik Gallery** (830-990-8151, 800-999-0820; www.whistle pik.com; 425 E. Main St., Fredericksburg, TX 78624).

HAYS COUNTY

The Balcones Escarpment, running right through the center of the town of San Marcos, is what gives Hays County its hills and the canyons, caves, and spring-fed streams. It is also what makes Hays County, on the eastern edge of the Hill Country, such an attraction. The Balcones created the freshwater springs that millions of years ago produced the San Marcos River — springs that are the source of more than 150 million gallons daily of some of the purest water in Texas. This crystalline water flows through 175 miles of the honeycomb limestone of the Edwards Aquifer before filling Spring Lake at Aquarena Springs.

The Spanish missions of San Francisco Xavier de los Dolores, San Ildefonso, and Nuestra Señora de la Candelaria remained here only for two years, between 1755 and 1757, before Apache and Comanche raids discouraged them. At the turn of the century several Spanish families arrived from Mexico, establishing a settlement they called San Marcos de Neve. But the Indian raids discouraged them, too, and by 1812 they had returned to Mexico.

Along came Texas Ranger John Coffee (Captain Jack) Hays, one of Stephen F. Austin's Rangers. Part of Hays's job was to protect the pioneers who had begun to trickle into the county and into Comanche territory around the end of the 1820s. However, in the time it took a Ranger to reload his single-shot sidearm, a Comanche warrior could charge and shoot half a dozen arrows, which put the Rangers at a disadvantage.

Samuel Colt had just invented his new five-shot repeater pistol. The Army scoffed at it, but Hays was clever enough to recognize the gun's potential when pitted against Comanche raiders. The weapon was put to the test in 1840, when a party of 70 Comanches surprised Hays and 14 other Rangers along the Pedernales River. In the past, in order to hold the Indians at bay with their rifles, the Rangers had run for cover. Now Hays led his men in a charge, their Colt pistols blazing. Expecting that the Rangers' guns would be empty after one round, the Comanches were baffled by these inexhaustible guns and driven off. After this display, the Comanches soon gave up on this part of Texas.

In 1843 the county was created and named for Hays, who had been so instrumental in making the land safe for settlers. By the time Texas became a state in 1848, settlers had established the river crossing. Soon the little town of San Marcos became a regular stopping point on the Old San Antonio Road (also known as the Camino Real) on the three-day stagecoach trip between Austin and San Antonio.

San Marcos

San Marcos, the county seat, is the home of Southwest Texas State University, opened in 1903 as a teachers' college (and the alma mater of President Lyndon B. Johnson). Now a liberal arts university, it contributes much to the town's cultural and entertainment activities. There's more nightlife here than in other Hill Country towns, thanks to the university; it centers mostly around the town square, with music, billiards, and beer for the college crowd.

With support from the Texas Dept. of Agriculture, San Marcos developed a program that has established the town as a marketplace for Texas-grown, Texas-produced, and Texas-designed goods. Look for the "Texas Natural" logo in the window of shops and restaurants.

For more information, contact the **San Marcos Convention and Visitors Bureau** (512-396-2495, 800-782-7653; www.sanmarcostexas.com; 202 North C. M. Allen Pkwy., PO Box 2310, San Marcos, TX 78667).

Wimberley

Little Wimberley, on the Blanco River and Cypress Creek, is a year-round summer resort and retirement area. It was settled in 1848 by a miller named William Calvin Winters. He built a mill on the Blanco River that was bought by Pleasant Wimberley in 1872. The town took his name when a post office was established in 1880.

Picturesque Wimberley bustles busily on the Lions' Market Days (first Saturday of the month, April to December), and it's the place to shop for antiques, collectibles, and crafts. The town is quaint, pretty, friendly, and crowded only on market days!

For more information, contact the **Wimberley Chamber of Commerce and Visitor Center** (512-847-2201; www.wimberley.org; PO Box 12, Wimberley, TX 78676).

HAYS COUNTY LODGING

San Marcos has a bed & breakfast, a resort, and a number of motels, described below. Besides the places listed here, Wimberley has a large number of other overnight lodging places. Contact **Wimberley Lodging** (512-847-3909, 800-460-4909; PO Box 1807, Wimberley, TX 78676).

San Marcos

CRYSTAL RIVER INN
Hosts: Cathy and Mike
  Dillon.
512-396-3739, 888-396-3739.
www.crystalriverinn.com.
326 W. Hopkins, San
  Marcos, TX 78666.
Price: Moderate.
Credit Cards: AE, D, MC, V.
Handicap Access: No.

There are nine rooms, three suites, and one two-bedroom apartment in this 1883 Victorian bed & breakfast in the historic district. Guest rooms in the Greek Revival home are named for Hill Country rivers, and a full breakfast, including eggs Benedict and raspberry French toast, is served — even in your canopy bed if you wish.

MOTELS

Just about every major motel chain is represented on the interstate as you enter town, including the **Comfort Inn** (512-396-5665, 800-228-5150; 1611 IH 35 N., San Marcos, TX 78666), **Days Inn** (800-DAYS INN; 1005 IH 35 N., San

Marcos, TX 78666), **La Quinta Inn** (800-531-5900; 1619 IH 35 N., San Marcos, TX 78666), **Motel 6** (512-396-8705; 1321 IH 35 N., San Marcos, TX 78666), **Rodeway Inn** (512-353-1303; 801 IH 35 N., San Marcos, TX 78666), and **Super 8** (512-396-0400; 1429 IH 35 N., San Marcos, TX 78666).

Wimberley

BLAIR HOUSE
Host: Jonnie Stansbury.
512-847-1111, 877-549-5450.
www.blairhouseinn.com.
100 Spoke Hill Rd.,
Wimberley, TX 78676.
Price: Expensive.
Credit Cards: AE, D, MC, V.
Handicap Access: Yes.

This lovely eight-room inn is nestled on 85 acres of privacy. The guest rooms all have private baths, four with Jacuzzi tubs and all with CD players. The library is stocked with books, videos, CDs, and periodicals, the walls are virtually a gallery of art, and outdoors you can hike in the hills, then go shopping in Wimberley.

And you'll need that exercise, because Jonnie is an excellent chef. A full-scale gourmet breakfast here began with fresh red raspberries, blueberries, and bananas, accompanied by a refreshing frozen orange juice/cranberry slush. Poached eggs were served in a ramekin over broccoli and covered with hollandaise sauce. On the side were tomatoes stuffed with fresh herbed bread crumbs, and scones with butter and homemade raspberry jam.

Another breakfast to die for is soufflé of French toast with toasted pecans and blueberries and real maple syrup. And Jonnie is generous with recipes: "We feel that food is a gift and an art, and, like love, it's no good unless you give it away." Each evening a dessert and complimentary tea or coffee are delivered to your room, and Saturday evenings feature five-course dinners. (Two-night minimum stay on weekends.)

INN ABOVE ONION CREEK
Host: Janie Orr.
512-268-1617, 800-579-7686.
www.bbonline.com/tx/onioncreek.
4444 Hwy. 150 W., Kyle, TX 78640.
Price: Expensive to Very Expensive (MAP).
Credit Cards: AE, MC, V.
Handicap Access: Yes.

This lovely rural inn, with a total of nine rooms and suites, serves guests both breakfast and dinner and will also provide a lunch basket if requested. Amenities include a swimming pool, 5 miles of trails on 500 acres in the Hill Country, and cooking, art, and musical weekends. All rooms have stone fireplaces and sitting areas, balconies with a view, and extra feather mattresses. Six of the rooms have whirlpool tubs.

Breakfast might begin with smoked salmon, continue with quiche and rosemary potatoes, include a fruit medley (a banana split dish covered with a mélange of apples, grapes, and pears in a vanilla yogurt sauce), and end with cinnamon coffee cake. Then it's time for a relaxing rock on the porch overlooking a gorgeous view of the hills. Children over 12 are welcome.

Grounds of the Lodge at Creekside in Wimberly.

Eleanor S. Morris

THE LODGE AT CREEKSIDE
Hosts: Merry, Sally, and Ashley Gibson.
512-847-8922, 800-267-3925.
www.acountryinn.com.
310 Mill Race Ln.,
  Wimberley, TX 78676.
Price: Expensive.
Credit cards: AE, D, MC, V.
Handicap Access: Yes.

Six private cabins and two luxury suites on 6 acres of land along tranquil Cypress Creek — all within walking distance of bustling Wimberley Square — are what this friendly family-owed lodge has to offer. Each cabin has a porch and a private entrance, a wood-burning stove, and a king- or queen-size bed. Each bath has a whirlpool — some even have their own little private sauna! Not to mention an almost-kitchen, with coffeemaker, microwave, and refrigerator. Phones are equipped with dataports, and of course there's cable TV and VCRs. As for the full gourmet breakfast, you can be served in the dining room or have it delivered to your door. Delicious dining by reservation on Saturdays; Champagne brunch every Sunday.

The lodge also has facilities for meetings and events, with all-inclusive conference rates available. No smoking, no pets, and the inn is not an appropriate place for children under eight.

HAYS COUNTY RESTAURANTS AND FOOD PURVEYORS

In addition to the eateries of San Marcos and Wimberley, we've included the popular Salt Lick in Driftwood, out in the country northwest of Wimberley.

The courtyard at Palmer's Restaurant in San Marcos is a favorite spot to dine al fresco.

Eleanor S. Morris

San Marcos

**CAFE ON THE SQUARE &
BREW PUB**
512-353-9289.
126 N. LBJ Dr., San Marcos,
TX 78666.
On the square.
Price: Moderate.
Cuisine: American,
Mexican, Game.
Serving: B, L, D; closes early
sometimes on Sun. &
Mon.
Credit Cards: AE, D, MC, V.
Handicap Access: No.

There's nothing "square" about this lively place, especially on weekends, even early in the morn. The loud and lively clientele is all ages, although there are plenty of college students.

The restaurant is in the historic T. A. Talbot Building, built in 1897. On the National Register of Historic Places, the building is charmingly old and worn. Long and narrow, it still has the original pressed-tin ceiling, wooden floors, and a skylight brightening up the cafe. Big old fans with huge glass petal globes hang low from the high ceiling. Wooden barstools are lined up at the black-and-white tile-top bar. Well-scrubbed wooden drop-leaf tables mix with iron-legged ice-cream parlor seats. Art by well-known Southwest artist Amado Pena decorates the walls, along with framed old magazine and sheet music covers.

Eggs Benedict are served on Saturdays and Sundays only, but the migas (eggs scrambled with tomatoes, onion, peppers, corn tortillas, and cheddar cheese, served with hashed browns and beans, a choice of pinto or black) are special all week. Also special are the wild game dishes: wild boar chops, fried quail, chicken-fried venison, buffalo burgers, and buffalo fajitas, all served with fries.

CENTERPOINT STATION
512-392-1103.
www.cypac.com/
centerpoint.
3946 IH-35 S., San Marcos,
TX 78666.

Boasting "the best malts on IH-35," this restaurant offers a wild mix of soda fountain, burgers, and memorabilia all packed into a brand-new building weathered to look as old as the hills. The old-fashioned soda bar and grill doesn't have ice-cream sodas, but there are sundaes, malts, and

Price: Inexpensive.
Cuisine: American.
Serving: L, D.
Credit Cards: AE, D, MC, V.
Handicap Access: A ramp alongside the rear.

floats made with Texas's own Blue Bell ice cream. Also available are sandwiches, some Mexican food, and homemade fudge filled with Texas-grown pecans — hold out your hand for a free sample. (See "Shopping" for what-all else is crammed into this busy market.)

GORDO'S BURGERS & STUFF
512-392-1874.
120 E. San Antonio, San Marcos, TX 78666.
On the square.
Price: Inexpensive.
Cuisine: Burgers, Sandwiches, Steak.
Serving: L, D.
Credit Cards: AE, D, MC, V.
Handicap Access: Yes.

Another San Marcos boast, this time it's "the best burgers in San Marcos." One of these "best burgers" is the Ultimate Gordo Burger, with two patties, extra cheese, bacon, chili, mushrooms, and jalapeños. "Does anyone actually eat a whole one?" we asked. The answer was a rousing affirmative.

Gordo's is a treat because it's in the town's old movie theater, with outside marquee and all. The lobby now has a large mirrored bar all along the right side, and the stage in back is all set for the live music Thursday through Saturday nights (see "Nightlife").

PALMER'S RESTAURANT, BAR AND COURTYARD
512-353-3500.
www.palmerstexas.com.
216 W. Moore (Ranch Road 12 and Hutchison), San Marcos, TX 78666.
Price: Inexpensive.
Cuisine: Hill Country.
Serving: L, D.
Credit Cards: AE, MC, V.
Handicap Access: Yes.

Walking into Palmer's through the lovely tree-shaded courtyard, past the fountain, you may decide to eat al fresco instead of indoors. Or savor the view from inside; the restaurant is in a beautifully renovated 1920s house, with stone fireplaces and casement windows. Special is chicken Palmer, sautéed breast topped with avocado and tomato and melted Swiss cheese, all with a brown herb sauce. There are beef and pork specials, as well as the catch of the day (no, not from the Blanco River nearby). Palmer's key lime pie, chocolate satin pie, and carrot cake are so rich that you can order just a sliver, not a whole piece.

Wimberley

CYPRESS CREEK CAFE & CLUB
512-847-2515.
PO Box 76, Wimberley, TX 78776.
On the square.
Price: Inexpensive.
Cuisine: Southwest, Mexican, Vegetarian.
Serving: B, L, D.

Friendly family atmosphere reigns here in this old stone building on the square. Vegetarian dishes like tofu sandwiches, veggie burgers, and vegetable plates vie with old favorites like fried catfish or country-fried steak "just like Mom used to make it." A Cypress Creek tradition is the black bean taco: a huge Texas-size flour tortilla filled with beans, sour cream, chunky salsa, and jack cheese garnished with diced tomatoes, onion, and lettuce.

Credit Cards: AE, D, MC, V.
Handicap Access: Yes.

We split it in half, it was so big. Pies are from the Wimberley Pie Company down the road, and the choices are legion — such as Dutch cherry pie, brownie pie, coconut pie, and Kentucky Derby pie, and cheesecake, too. Newest thing on the menu is ostrich (a red-meat ostrich burger has 40 percent less fat than beef, according to Texas A&M University). There's a dance hall in the rear (see "Nightlife").

THE FORK CAFE
512-847-0116.
201-B Stillwater Dr., Ste. 7, Winberley, TX 78666.
At S. River Center off RR 12 (just south of the Blanco River Bridge).
Price: Inexpensive.
Cuisine: Southwest, Steaks, Seafood.
Serving: L, D.
Credit Cards: MC, V.
Handicap Access: Yes.

The restaurant's motto, "Bringing you quality one fork at a time since the turn of the century," goes well with the copy of Grant Wood's *American Gothic* hanging on the wall — only the faces of the two farmers in the painting are portraits of owners Tom and Cali Kayser, and they're holding a large fork. It's clever; the door handle into the restaurant is also a large fork. The "Outta Here" menu includes snacks and starters, soups and salads, sandwiches, beef, chicken, pork, and seafood platters, as well as specialty dinners of fajitas, Alfredo penne pasta, and chicken Parmesan. Popular are the margarita pork chops and the garlic shrimp. Desserts include cream brulee (sic) and yummy hot cobblers — peach, blackberry, cherry.

JITAS AND RITAS
512-847-2674.
104 Wimberley Square, Wimberley, TX 78686.
Price: Inexpensive.
Cuisine: Caribbean, Brazilian, Louisiana.
Serving: L, D.
Credit Cards: AE, D, MC, V.
Handicap Access: Yes.

The delightful mixed cuisine results from the restaurateurs' backgrounds. Anja hails from Barbados and Frank from Texas. The chicken and beef fajitas are Barbados-style, marinated in a special sauce and threaded on skewers. The munchy, crunchy flying fish cakes are definitely Barbados, while the blackened chicken wrap is served with Barbados Bajar sauce. The shrimp burger, though, is definitely USA. Try the Barbados fruit punch on a hot day — and the tres leches cake is a cool treat, too.

Driftwood

THE SALT LICK
512-858-4959.
www.saltlickbbq.com.
18001 FM 1826, Driftwood, TX.
Price: Inexpensive.
Cuisine: Barbecue.

If you want to be one among a crowd of Texans, visit the Salt Lick on a weekend, where (off-duty) Hays County sheriff's deputies are needed to keep the parking lot in order. This rustic place under the cedar and mesquite is out in the country northwest of Wimberley. The windows of the sprawling cedar and limestone building look out onto hummingbird

The Salt Lick barbecue restaurant in Driftwood.

Eleanor S. Morris

Serving: L, D, daily
11am–10pm.
Credit Cards: None; cash
only.

feeders hanging just outside on the oak trees, and if you have to wait for a table, you'll be entertained by a guitar player.

As you enter, take a look at the giant circular open stone barbecue pit and the clumps of hanging sausages. A typical Saturday night crowd puts away 1,800 pounds of brisket, 800 rings of sausage, 500 racks of pork ribs, and 560 chickens, all smoked over oak, mesquite, and pecan for at least 24 hours — and only the owners know the recipe for the sauce.

You'll dine on bare wooden picnic tables and benches indoors — but you will eat on a plate. Barbecued beef, ribs, and sausage come with beans and coleslaw, and the barbecue sandwiches are delicious, too. Don't be fooled by the menu: Chicken "in season" is something you can order anytime.

Absolutely do not miss the daily fresh peach and blackberry cobblers. There's also homemade pecan pie. Notice, too, the sign declaring WE RESERVE THE RIGHT TO SERVE ANYBODY, and you'll know you're deep in the heart of Texas. One note: BYOB; Hays County is dry.

HAYS COUNTY FOOD PURVEYORS

Wimberley

The Old Mill Store (512-847-6128; PO Box 708, Wimberley, TX 78676; on the square; Sun.–Thurs. 10am–6pm, Fri. & Sat. 10am–8pm) Coffee shop, candy store — delicious odors of both fancy blends and homemade candy assail you as you push open the door. Steve Klepfer's place is down a brick walkway, past a garden, and into a shop made from an old house that was on the site waiting to be pulled down. The rare long-leaf pine and square nails have been preserved; even the marble counters were rescued from an old bank building. And the fudge is delicious.

Town Square Deli & Ice Cream Parlor (512-847-3333; on the square; open daily 7am–5pm for breakfast and lunch) This place is popular for eating both inside and out, and you'll also see happy visitors licking their ice cream cones as they walk around the square. Both hot and cold foods are available, along with daily specials, and only pure Texas Blue Bell ice cream is served, they say with pride.

Wimberley Pie Company (512-847-9462; www.wimberleypie.com; 13619 RR 12, Wimberley, TX 78676; Mon.–Fri. 8am–5:30pm, Sat. 10am–5pm, Sun. noon–4pm) Twenty-three varieties of pie, freshly baked, are for sale here, and once in a while the baker invents yet another one. Some unusual ones are sour cream peach, peanut butter, Toll House, and chocolate satin (with or without chocolate curls). If you're not a pie person, there's cheesecake — eight different kinds — cakes, muffins, and, for your four-legged friends, doggie treats.

Dripping Springs

New Canaan Farms (800-727-JAMS; www.newcanaanfarms.com; PO Box 386, Dripping Springs, TX 78620; 7 miles west of Dripping Springs on Hwy. 290) offers 40 delicious, unique Hill Country jams, jellies, salsas, dips, and sauces like jalapeño shrimp sauce or garlic onion jelly. But there are traditional flavors as well: to name a few, East Texas blueberry jam, cherry preserves, and old-fashioned peach butter.

HAYS COUNTY CULTURE

ARCHITECTURE AND HISTORIC SITES

The **Heritage Association of San Marcos** (512-393-3735; www.sanmarcos texas.com/tourism; PO Box 1806, San Marcos, TX 78667) has a "Tours of Old San Marcos" brochure. In the town park you'll find a marker on the site of **Camp Henry McCulloch**, located here during the Mexican-American War. Past the gazebo in the park, the path leads down to the 2-mile scenic **San Marcos River Walkway**, which links three small parks along the river.

In the 100 block along **Courthouse Square** are several brick and stone buildings built in the 1880s and 1890s when San Marcos was a busy cotton-raising center. The **Belvin Street Historic District** has several homes along a tranquil, shady street. The **Robert Hixon Belvin** home, **Crookwood**, and the **Herbert Yarbrough** home are open for tours.

Also of interest is the **Charles S. Cock** home, the only stone building of this style remaining in San Marcos. Don't miss the **Merriman Cabin**, built in 1848. Dr. Merriman, along with General Burleson, was responsible for laying out the town. One of the most interesting historic buildings, and possibly the largest log house remaining in Texas, is the **Claiborne Kyle Log House**, on the Old Austin Stagecoach Road. The nearby town of Kyle is named for a son, Fergus Kyle.

NIGHTLIFE

San Marcos

San Marcos is one of only a few exceptions to the dearth of a nightlife scene out in the Hill Country. After all, this is a college town, so of course there's life after dark. The following San Marcos venues all have a cover charge.

Like many of the town eateries, **Gordo's** (see "Restaurants") is both a restaurant and a nightclub, catering to the college crowd. Set on the square in the town's old movie theater, the lobby is the spot for a large mirrored bar, and the stage in the back room is all set for the nightly entertainment of live alternative, country, heavy metal, and Tejano music Thursday through Saturday. Then there's the huge projection TV for those important football games.

The **Green Parrot Bar** (512-353-9354; 124 N. LBJ, San Marcos, TX 78776; on the square; 4pm–midnight weeknights, 4pm–1am Sat.) Bands play periodically on Tuesday and Wednesday nights, "usually either Texas or rock."

Wimberley

The **Cypress Creek Cafe & Club** (512-847-2515; PO Box 76, Wimberley, TX 78676) comes alive every Friday and Saturday night with country music. Everybody's happy, everybody's dancing, and some folks even come down from Austin for the fun. Phone the cafe for information.

SEASONAL EVENTS

San Marcos

FEBRUARY brings **Carnaval**, a Mexican-style Mardi Gras with music, food, and merriment the weekend before Ash Wednesday.

In APRIL it's bluebonnet time in Texas, and in San Marcos the state flower is celebrated the second weekend with the **Bluebonnet Kite Festival** for food, fun, games, and a serious kite-flying competition.

The focus in MAY is on **Texas Natural and Western Swing Weekend** (512-393-8930), held in historic downtown San Marcos and featuring merchandise made in Texas by Texans. The festival offers food, music, crafts, cowboy poets, and a mini chili cook-off. Don't miss the annual **Tours of Distinction**, also held in May — tours of the old homes of San Marcos, sponsored by the Heritage Society.

JUNE is the month for the **Texas Water Safari**. The world's toughest canoe race takes off from Spring Lake at the headwaters of the San Marcos River. Canoers and kayakers come from all over the nation to see who can race the 267 miles down to the Gulf Coast and the town of Seadrift.

In JULY there's an old-fashioned patriotic **Summerfest,** held on the fourth in Sewell Park. Live music, food booths, children's activities, and, of course, fireworks.

The **Gathering of Memories** in AUGUST or SEPTEMBER brings the Confederate

Air Force and thousands of followers to San Marcos with an air show, old World War II aircraft, a dinner dance, and an auction.

Republic of Texas Chilympiad, the men's chili cook-off in SEPTEMBER, features chili teams from all over the country, beauty pageants, arts and crafts, food booths, live music, dancing, and lots of fun for the whole family.

The **Sights and Sounds of Christmas** come early in DECEMBER, a community festival on the banks of the San Marcos River. Children's activities, community choirs, arts and crafts booths, and a food court all help to make the season merry. Check with the San Marcos Convention and Visitors Bureau (512-396-2495, 888-200-5620; www.sanmarcostexas.com/tourism) for exact dates.

Wimberley

Market Day, the first Saturday of every month from MAY to OCTOBER, draws shoppers to check out work created by local artists and craftsmen along with antiques and flea markets. Check with the Chamber of Commerce (512-847-2201) for exact dates.

HAYS COUNTY RECREATION

CAMPING

United RV Park (512-353-5959, 800-344-9906; 1610 IH-35 N., San Marcos, TX 78666) Swimming pool, playground, and 100 sites shaded by large trees, each with full hookups 30/50 AMPS. Pets allowed.

FAMILY FUN

A glass-bottom boat at Aquarena Springs provides an educational view of an underwater archaeological site on the riverbed.

Eleanor S. Morris

AQUARENA CENTER
512-245-7570.
www.aquarenacenter.com.
921 Aquarena Springs Dr.,
San Marcos, TX 78666.
Open: Daily 9:30am–5pm,
with extended hours
between Memorial Day
and Labor Day. Closed
Christmas week and first
week of the New Year.
Admission: Free; glass-
bottom-boat rides $6
adults, $5 seniors, $4
children.

Even since Southwest Texas State University purchased Aquarena Springs in 1994, the focus of
the 90-acre theme park has been changing from entertainment to nature tourism, conservation, and
education. While gliding across Spring Lake in a
glass-bottom boat, view the springs that bubble up
from the Edwards Aquifer and from the headwaters
of the San Marcos River, the freshwater springs that
created the river millions of years ago in the Balcones Fault, a fracture in the earth's crust. The water
flows through 175 miles of the honeycomb limestone of the Edwards Aquifer before filling Spring
Lake. Glass-bottom-boat rides on Spring Lake view
an underwater archaeological site on the bottom
and the remains of Clovis Man, who lived on the
San Marcos River more than 12,000 years ago.

The lake is also the home of more than a hundred varieties of aquatic life,
some of them endangered species found nowhere else on earth. At the Aquar-
ium/Endangered Species Exhibit, see the Texas blind salamander, gambusia,
fountain darter, and San Marcos salamander, among other species.

WONDER WORLD PARK
512-392-3760.
www.wonderworldpark
.com.
Wonder World Dr., San
Marcos, TX 78667.
Off IH-35 at Exit 202.
Open: Summer 8am–8pm,
winter 9am–5pm.
Admission: Adults $15.95,
seniors $11.95, children
4–11 $11.95, under 4 free.

When a huge earthquake rocked this area 30
million years ago, it created an enormous
cave underground along the 1,800-mile-long Balcones Fault. You can observe the fault line 160 feet
below the earth's surface or above it from the Tejas
Observation Tower. Adding to the fun are a wildlife
petting zoo, a miniature train ride, and a mysterious
Gravity House, where you'll be challenged to keep
your balance.

"The Devil's Backbone" Scenic Drive

Take FM 32 just south of Wimberley to the ridge called "The Devil's Backbone" for
a trip through classic Hill Country landscape. Glimpse white-tailed deer on this
winding, razor-backed ridge along the 24 miles west to Blanco (Blanco County).

GOLF

SWT Golf Course (512-245-7593; Aquarena Springs Dr., San Marcos, TX 78666)
has a 9-hole par 35 course; **Quail Valley Country Club** (512-353-1644; 2701

Airport Hwy. 21, San Marcos, TX 78666) has an 18-hole course. Both are open to the public.

WATER SPORTS

CANOEING: Rapids, twisting channels, and constant flow levels make San Marcos one of Texas's premier canoeing streams. The **Texas Water Safari**, billed "the toughest boat race in the world," is on the second weekend in June; beginning from City Park it runs nonstop the 267 miles south to Seadrift on the Texas coast. Canoes can be rented from **TG Canoe Livery** (512-353-3946; 2000 Hwy. 80 #160, San Marcos, TX 78666) and **Spencer Canoes** (512-357-6113; 9515 FM1979, Martindale, TX 78655).

TUBING: About 23.5 miles of the San Marcos River are suitable for tubing, beginning at City Park and ending at the County Road 199 crossing west of Stairtown on Hwy. 80. **Lions Club Tube Rental** (512-396-LION; PO Box 994, San Marcos, TX 78667) rents tubes in City Park. Tube down the river and then ride the **Breakfast Lions River Taxi** back to the tube rental building. There you'll find soft drinks, Sno-Kones, and snacks along with San Marcos River souvenirs. Free parking, lockers available.

HAYS COUNTY SHOPPING

San Marcos has a nice assortment of shops around the square and on the streets leading away from it. Little Wimberley is a hotbed of shops, most clustered around the small, wedge-shaped square.

ANTIQUES AND GIFTS

San Marcos

Centerpoint Station (512-392-1103; www.cypac.com/centerpoint; 3946 IH 35 S., San Marcos, TX 78666, at exit 200) Decorated with old store fixtures and antique advertising signs, Centerpoint Station calls itself "a general mercantile, offering you and your family a nostalgic experience." From the front porch to the old house tacked on at the rear, you'll find all sorts of stuff, old and new — country and western antiques, hand-dipped candles, old dishpans and baskets, handmade birdhouses, Texas gourmet foods, thousands of old tin signs, even a lamp with a base made of welded horseshoes. (See also "Restaurants.")

Heartworks Co. Paper Bear (512-396-2283; 214 N. LBJ Dr., San Marcos, TX 78666, on the square) A Texas-size 8,000-square-foot former Western Auto store crammed with gifts, toys, candy, games, beads, fake jewels — a wonderful place just to browse and marvel.

Two P's in a Pod (512-392-8967; 306 N. Edward Gary, San Marcos, TX 78666) The two P's in the name of this boutique/gift shop are the owners, Pam and Phyllis. The shop features the work of Texas artists, including jewelry, tole-painted furniture, and designer clothes, plus antiques and other "heartwarming necessities."

Wimberley

Betsy's Hanger (512-847-3405; 13801 RR 12, Suite 101, Wimberley, TX 78676, half a block south of the square) "Naturally comfortable" clothing with both a Southwestern and an ethnic flair. Jewelry and other accessories, too.
Woodshed Treasures (512-847-9466; 100 Oak Dr., Wimberley, TX 78676, on the square) Antiques, crafts, unique jewelry, collectibles. Visit with local craftsmen on site.

ART AND CRAFTS

Wimberley

The Old Mill Store (512-847-3068; PO Box 708, Wimberley, TX 78676, on the square) Rugs, furniture, wall hangings, hammocks, antiques, jewelry by local artists, and gourmet foods.
Rancho Deluxe (512-847-9570; 14010 RR 12, Wimberley, TX 78676, on the square) Rustic and eclectic home furnishings. Limestone from deep in the heart of Texas is carved by Hill Country artists into bookends, lamps, candleholders, vases. Also custom furniture and cedar beds, wrought-iron lamps, and tables. A best-seller is a children's swing made from a small saddle.
Sable V (512-847-8975; PO Box 1772, Wimberley, TX 78676, on the square) The gallery features special shows throughout the year of original works by artists in ceramics, glass, sculpture, paintings, and jewelry.
Wimberley Glass Works (512-847-9348; www.wimberley.org/index, click on "name"; PO Box 1724, Wimberley, TX 78676, 1.6 miles south of the square off RR 12; open daily 10am–5pm) Entertaining glass-blowing demonstrations as well as glassware for sale.

SHOPPING MALLS AND OUTLETS

Prime Outlets San Marcos (512-396-2200, 800-628-9465; www.sanmarcostexas .com/tourism, click: Your Shopping Outlet; 3939 IH-35 S., San Marcos, TX 78666; Mon.–Sat. 10am–9pm, Sun. 11am–6pm) More than 115 of the top names in merchandising are gathered in this open-air hacienda-style mall, with 10 eateries in the food court and a children's playground.
Tanger Outlet Center (512-396-7446, 800-408-8424; www.sanmarcostexas.com/ tourism; I-35, exit 200, San Marcos, TX 78666; Mon.–Sat. 9am–9pm, Sun. 11am–6pm) A smaller outlet mall across Center Point Rd. from the above mall, with a good but smaller selection of brand-name outlets.

KIMBLE COUNTY

Eleanor S. Morris

Goats along the highway in mohair-producing Kimble County.

This was Apache land when the Spanish came through here in the 1700s, and they didn't even try to stay. By the time Anglo settlers appeared in the 1850s, some 150 years later, the Apaches had been run off by Comanches, who swooped down from the Great Plains on their fast horses. The legislature went ahead anyway and created Kimble County from Bexar County in 1858, naming it for George C. Kimble (also spelled "Kimbell" and "Kimbel"), who led the "Immortal 32" from Gonzales to the Alamo, coming to the aid of beleaguered Texans and dying with them on March 6, 1836. Hostilities between the Comanches and the settlers went on for about 20 more years; the last Indian incidents were reported in 1876.

By then outlaws, not Indians, were the settlers' problem. Horse thieves, cattle rustlers, and gunmen needed to be brought to justice, but they threatened to prevent any court meetings in the county. The presiding judge asked the Texas Rangers for help, and three companies of Rangers scoured the canyons of the Llano River. When the judge arrived at the oak grove where court was held, he found 40 outlaws chained to the trees. He handed out the necessary sentences, thereby considerably reducing the power of the outlaws in the new county.

Kimble County is a leading producer of wool and mohair. Angora goats were brought to Texas in 1849, and since the 1920s Texas has produced the most mo-hair in the country. There are also more flowing streams here than in any other Texas county.

Junction

In the far northwest corner of the Hill Country, Junction (pop. 2,800), the county seat, was originally in the settlement of Kimbleville. It was moved to the junction of the North and South Llano Rivers, which is how it got the name of Junction. The first courthouse was built in 1878, and when it burned, all the county's early records burned with it. The present courthouse was built in 1929.

Although the town admits to being "quite a ways" from most of the Hill Country, it calls itself "The Jewel of the Hill Country." (But it also likes to be known as "The Front Porch to the West.") Junction is the place for hunting, fishing, camping, and canoeing on the clear flowing waters of the Llano River. And though all of Texas is friendly, you'll find Junction extra friendly!

KIMBLE COUNTY LODGING

Junction has no bed & breakfasts at this writing. There is a relatively large selection of motels for such a small town. Two are described below; contact the Chamber of Commerce of Kimble County (915-446-3190; www.junctiontexas.net; 402 Main St., Junction, TX 76849) for additional information and a complete list.

DAYS INN
915-446-3730, 800-325-2525.
I-10 exit 457, 111 Martinez,
Junction, TX 76849.
Price: Inexpensive.
Credit Cards: AE, CB, D,
DC, MC, V.
Handicap Access: Two
rooms.

The motel has 50 comfortable rooms and sits on a rise overlooking the Llano River. Amenities include a pool, hot tub/spa, videos, VCR rental, and a continental breakfast served from 6am to 10:30am. It's very popular during the deer and dove hunting season Nov.–Dec.

SLUMBER INN
915-446-4588.
2341 N. Main, Junction, TX
76849.
On IH-10.
Price: Inexpensive.
Credit Cards: AE, D, MC, V.
Handicap Access: Yes.

This motel has 31 nice clean rooms in pastel colors and with light, modern furniture. Amenities include a swimming pool, cable TV, and a family restaurant (see "Restaurants") nearby. The Honeymoon Suite has a king-size bed, refrigerator, microwave, wet bar, and Jacuzzi.

KIMBLE COUNTY RESTAURANTS AND FOOD PURVEYORS

COME 'N' GIT IT
915-446-4357.
2341 N. Main St., Junction, TX 76849.
Price: Inexpensive.
Cuisine: American, Hill Country.
Serving: B, L, D.
Credit Cards: AE, D, DC, MC, V.
Handicap Access: Yes.

This big wide barn of a room, with high ceilings and wood paneling, soothes and relaxes with soft background music. Tables are spread out in the center of the room, and bushel-basket lampshades shade the blue booths that line walls decorated with beer signs and shiny copper pans. Simply delicious here are the chicken quesadillas, one to a serving but huge. A large tortilla, toasted and stuffed with sautéed chicken, green pepper and onion strips, and cheddar cheese, with shredded lettuce and tomato, makes a delicious taste treat. The salad bar is fresh, too; especially tasty is the chickeny chicken salad with red grapes and pecans. You enter the restaurant by way of a convenience store, which seems to be a Junction custom. And you know what the main entertainment is this far west in the Hill Country when you see this sign on the back wall: "I love when the seasons change — from huntin' to fishin'."

ISAACK'S RESTAURANT
915-446-2629.
1606 Main St., Junction, TX 76849.
Price: Inexpensive.
Cuisine: Home-style, Cafe, Steak.
Serving: B, L, D.
Credit Cards: AE, DC, MC, V.
Handicap Access: Yes.

Everything is homemade in this busy diner that dates from the 1950s. It sports a classic counter with stools as well as tables and booths, and the daily lunch special might be all-you-can-eat catfish with potato salad, beans, and coleslaw. The huge and tender 12-inch chicken-fried steak is a specialty, as are the mozzarella cheese sticks, fried and served with a red horseradish or white ranch dressing. Homemade vegetable soup and sirloin steak are on the menu daily. "We stick with one soup; we're good at it," says the friendly waitperson. "And we'll substitute anything for anything." The restaurant motto is "Hunt in the hills, fish in the Llano, but eat with us!"

LA FAMILIA RESTAURANT
915-446-2688.
1927 Main St., Junction, TX 76849.
Price: Inexpensive.
Cuisine: Mexican.

Artemisa Lozano knows authentic Mexican food — she and her clan (her sister, sister-in-law, three nieces) in this family restaurant all hail from Chihuahua in northern Mexico. The menu offers steak tampequena, carne asada, and steak à la Mexican, along with such usual fare as chimichangas.

Serving: L, D.
Credit Cards: AE, D, DC,
  MC, V.
Handicap Access: No.

The warm, welcoming decor of red walls and wood and the friendly ambiance make this a pleasant dining place.

LUM'S
915-446-3541.
2031 Main St., Junction, TX
  76849.
Price: Inexpensive.
Cuisine: Barbecue.
Serving: L, D until
  midnight.
Credit Cards: MC, V.
Handicap Access: Yes,
  except for rest rooms.

"Our customers come for our ribs; we're known on the interstate," manager Rick Lumbley says, busy with customers in the family convenience store/self-serve restaurant. Sure enough, a traveling couple sitting comfortably in the dining room, pleasant with stone walls, a fireplace, and picnic tables, said, "We plan our trips from Lubbock to Uvalde so we can stop here." The aroma is mouthwatering the moment you step in the door, and folks line up for platefuls of barbecue ribs, brisket, sausage, and deli food, all where it can be seen and chosen from behind glass counters. Not to mention the pies: buttermilk, key lime, coconut, chocolate. There's outdoor patio dining, too.

KIMBLE COUNTY FOOD PURVEYORS

Donuts and More (915-446-2749; 1907 Main St., Junction, TX 76849; Tues.–Sat. 4am–2pm) If ever there was a misnomer, this is it. This is a bakery, coffee shop, lunch room, meeting place, and only incidentally a "donut" shop. Oh, they bake doughnuts: glazed, jellied, twists, chocolate, cheese pockets, even doughnut holes. And they are good. The Meltons begin before dawn, cheerfully, with the breakfast pizza and the breakfast tacos, Larry rolling the tortillas. Customers in the know come from all over — Dallas, Houston, Austin — for the pecan caramel rolls, the apple-raisin strudel, the hamburgers — gigantic light and fluffy homemade buns covering half a pound of ground chuck. "They're pretty big; sometimes [two] people each eat half," Larry confesses. The small shop is bright with red-checked tablecloths and green ivy.
Sutton Pecan Company (915-446-4533; 415 Main St., Junction, TX 76849; open late Oct.– mid-Jan., Mon.–Fri. 9am–5pm, Sat. 9am–3pm) Diane and Ron Sutton sell lots more than pecans in the shop they occupy in an old filling station. Not only pecans in every form imaginable — pralines, pecan brittle, pecan clusters, chocolate-covered pecans, turtles — but also just about every kind of nut and every kind of bean, including speckled anasazi beans from Colorado. And it's a treat to sample all the chocolate-covered nuts while making up your mind.

KIMBLE COUNTY CULTURE

HISTORIC BUILDINGS AND MUSEUMS

The Kimble County Historical Museum, in Junction, has displays of Hill Country pioneer life.

Eleanor S. Morris

Still in use, the stone **Kimble County Jail** (N. 5th St. and Pecan) in Junction was built in 1892. The **old Pepper home,** the first two-story house in Kimble County and the childhood home of the wife of Gov. Coke Stevenson (1941), is about 5 miles south of Junction on U.S. 377. The limestone building was built in 1877.

The **Kimble County Library** (915-446-2342; 208 N. 10th) contains the O. C. Fisher Museum, a duplicate of the Washington office of this longtime congressman from the district. Librarian Jerry Fairchild is very helpful.

The **Kimble County Historical Museum** (915-446-4219; 4th and College Sts.) displays pioneer artifacts, documents, clothing, tools, and other relics of early settlers. There is some World War II paraphernalia, too. Longtime resident Frederica Wyatt knows all about it and is happy to share. Open Mon.–Fri. 9:30am–noon, 2pm–5pm. Weekends by appointment.

SEASONAL EVENTS

Check with the **Junction Chamber of Commerce** (915-446-3190) for exact dates. Popular in Junction is the flea market on the courthouse lawn on fifth Saturdays (the months vary from year to year).

APRIL in Junction brings the annual **Easter Pageant,** the Saturday before Easter.

In MAY comes **Bad Company Rodeo & Dances**.

In **July,** on the fourth, there are **Fireworks in the Park**.

AUGUST offers the **Summer Classic Rodeo & Parade, Goat Sale, and Dance.**

In SEPTEMBER the annual **Kimble County Kow Kick** (arts and crafts) takes place on Labor Day.
OCTOBER, there's the **Kimble County Health Fair.**
In DECEMBER, it's **Christmas in Junction.**

KIMBLE COUNTY RECREATION

CAMPING

Fox Hollow Cabins (915-446-3055; 8315 Box 236, Junction, TX 76849, on the South Llano River) Two cabins with kitchen, dishes, linens are completely furnished.
KOA Kampgrounds (915-446-3138, 800-562-7506; www.koakampgrounds.com/ where/tx, click: Junction; 2145 N. Main St., Junction, TX 76849; on the North Llano River) Four one-bedroom cabins, 48 RV sites (39 with full hookups), picnic tables, and barbecue pits located on a quarter-mile of river frontage. Hot showers and rest rooms in the main building along with game room, laundry room, convenience store, swimming pool, and playground.

CANOE RENTALS

KOA Kampgrounds (915-446-3138, 800-562-7506; 2145 N. Main St., Junction, TX 76849) Rentals for canoeing on the North Llano River.
Sonny's Canoes (915-446-2112; 214 Patricia Dr., Junction, TX 76849; near the South Llano River at Flat Rock Crossing).
South Llano River Canoes (915-446-2220; HC 15, Box 214F, Junction, TX 76849; 6 miles south of Junction off Hwy. 377 on the river) Day trips and weekly rates; drop off and pick up.

GOLF

Junction Golf Association (915-446-2968; FM 2169, Junction, TX 76849) A 9-hole, 2,800-yard course, a challenging one for the size. The irrigated course nestles in the shadows of Lovers Leap and winds along the bottomlands of Cedar Creek and the South Llano River. No reservations needed for individuals.

PARKS

The best places for swimming and other water sports, as well as other activities, are at Kimble County parks.

Schreiner Park (915-446-3880; on the South Llano River) Boat ramp, swimming, picnic tables and barbecue grills, and a small covered pavilion.

South Llano River State Park (915-446-3994; www.tpwd.state.tx.us/park/slano/ slano.htm; 5 miles south of Junction off U.S. 377 on Park Rd. 73) The 2,657-acre park lies along the winding South Llano River and is considered one of the best canoeing and tubing rivers in Texas. The wooded park is the home to white-tailed deer, armadillo, fox squirrels, javelina (wild boar), wood ducks, and turkeys. (River frontage and bottomlands are closed from October to April to protect the winter roosting areas of the Rio Grande turkey.) Facilities include campsites with water and electricity, 4 miles of hiking trails, wildlife observation, and picnicking.

Walter Buck Wildlife Management Area (915-446-3994; www.tpwd.state.tx.us /wma/wmarea/walterbuck.htm; PO Box 392, Junction, TX 76849) On the south fork of the Llano River, adjoining the South Llano River State Park, this park has 2,155 acres with several hiking and mountain bike trails. No camping is permitted.

KIMBLE COUNTY SHOPPING

Conchos and Crosses (915-446-8558; 1409 Main St., Junction, TX 76849) offers unique jewelry, fashionable clothing, and gifts.

City Pharmacy (915-446-2511; 602 Main St., Junction, TX 76849) carries small gift items.

Cowboy Cottage (915-446-3394; 310 Main St., Junction, TX 76849) has unique accessories and gifts as well as home furnishings.

The General Store in Junction has just about everything you could want.

Eleanor S. Morris

The General Store (915-446-2514; 406 Main St., Junction, TX 76849) is just that, an old-fashioned general store with just about everything you'd want out in the Hill Country. Ladies love the clothing, bath and beauty products, Texas-grown gourmet foods, and specialty items; guys go for the hunting and fishing supplies; ranchers come in for livestock and deer feed, hats, and boots. And everything else.

Generations III (915-446-2663; 911 Main St., Junction, TX 76849) is the work of three generations of women, just like it says: owner Carolyn Trimble, daughter Kathy, and granddaughter Lisa. You'll find attractive and stylish women's clothes and jewelry here.

LLANO COUNTY

The word *llano* is Spanish for plains, and it's hard to understand why such a name was chosen for this spectacularly scenic part of the Hill Country when the county was created from the Bexar District of Gillespie County in 1856.

Originally Llano County was part of the tract purchased by a group of German noblemen, who made a treaty with the Comanche and opened up the Fisher-Miller land for settlement. A hill called Packsaddle Mountain was the scene of a famous 1873 battle between the settlers and the Apaches. A war party of about 20 Apaches had been harassing the settlers, stealing horses, cows, and even clothing. Eight settlers trailed the Indians to their camp on top of the hill and attacked them. Taken by surprise, three Indians were killed, and the others ran away. A granite marker was placed to mark the spot in 1938. There's also a state marker about 14 miles southeast of Llano on Hwy. 71. Actually, the real Texas Packsaddle Mountain is in Big Bend in West Texas, but this Hill Country hill has been called a mountain ever since the battle.

Today ranching is the main business of the county, with deer hunting in season a good second. The area, part of the Llano Uplift, has also attracted gold and silver prospectors from the Spaniards to today's rock hounds. Amethyst, dolomite, garnet, quartz, and tourmaline also abound. The most unusual mineral here, however, is llanite, a rare brown granite embedded with crystals of pink and blue feldspar found nowhere else in the world. Rock hounds can enjoy hunting for this and other minerals (see "Rock Hunting" below), but please note that landowners no longer permit rock hunting on their land because of the threat of lawsuits. Possibly the best place to find llanite is the bar in the Badu House lounge — one long slab of it.

Llano County has several towns, of which the largest is Llano (pop. 2,990) on the clear waters of spring-fed Llano River. Kingsland, the next largest (pop. 2,646), was founded in 1855 as Kingsville and was a popular spot for fishing even before the rivers were dammed to make lakes. Tow (pronounced to rhyme with "now") is famous for its vineyard. Last but not least, Buchanan Dam (pronounced "buck-an-an," pop. 1,109) is the name not only of the dam but also of this small resort and retirement community, which grew at the construction site of the dam.

For more information, contact the **Llano Chamber of Commerce** (915-247-5354; 700 Bessemer Ave., Llano, TX 78643).

Kingsland

Nothing much happened to Kingsland until the railroad — and a general store — came in 1892. Then the railroad began to bring fishermen and vacationers from Austin to the town. In 1951 the construction of the Granite Shoals Dam (now Wirtz Dam) at the junction of the Colorado and Llano Rivers created Inks Lake and Granite Shoals Lake. (The latter was later renamed in honor of Lyndon B. Johnson.) Today Kingsland is both a resort and a retirement haven. FM 1431 through Kingsland is lined with cafes, convenience stores, and outlets for fishing and boating supplies.

Llano

The town was settled around 1855 and became the county seat a year later. By 1860 it was well established, with stores, saloons, and a hotel. When iron was discovered in the late 1800s, this small town became a boomtown: Llano hoped to become "the Pittsburgh of the West." But there was none of the coal needed to turn the iron into steel, so the boom went bust, and it was back to the granite business as usual. Today the streets named Bessemer and Pittsburgh remain as reminders of Llano's ambitious dream.

A fire destroyed much of the city north of the Llano River, where most of the action took place. All that was left was the sturdy First National Bank, now the Badu House Inn, and Bruhl Drugstore, now restored to house the Llano County Museum. Today most of Llano lies south of the river.

LLANO COUNTY LODGING

Kingsland

THE ANTLERS HOTEL
Hosts: Lori and Anthony
    Mayfield.
915-388-4411, 800-383-0007.
www.theantlers.com.
1001 King St., Kingsland, TX
    78639.
Off Hwy 1431 at the railroad
    crossing.
Price: Expensive.
Credit Cards: All.
Handicap Access: Yes.

Accommodations include the historic adults-only Antlers Hotel, one- or two-bedroom cabins and cottages with kitchens in the woods and around the orchard, a train car named the McKinley Coach, and no fewer than three cabooses: imagine spending the night in a real train caboose! Each caboose offers a living and dining area, bath with shower, queen-size bed, and two child-size bunks, efficiency kitchen, and TV/VCR. Enjoy morning coffee or watch the sunset up in the cupola.

For meals, the Antlers has opened the Kingsland Old Town Grill on the property, across the road from the hotel (see "Restaurants").

Llano

There are three motels: a **Best Western** (915-247-4101, 800-346-1578; 901 W. Young, Llano, TX 78643), a **Travelodge** (915-247-4111, 800-578-7878; 700 W. Young, Llano, TX 78643), and the **Hill Country Suites** (915-247-1141; 609 Bessemer Ave., Llano, TX 78643). There are also two hotel/bed and breakfasts:

BADU HOUSE
Host: Sharon Taylor.
915-247-1207.
www.baduhouse.com.
601 Bessemer Ave., Llano,
　TX 78643.
Price: Moderate, EP.
Credit Cards: AE, MC, V.
Handicap Access: No.

Here's a chance to sleep in marble halls that once held a lot of money — the Badu House began life as a bank. Now it's an inn, with a restaurant and lounge. Be sure to check out the latter, the Llano Badu Club, where the bar is topped with a huge slab of Texas's famous llanite, found nowhere else in the world. The six guest rooms are not large, but they are filled with antiques, and each has a private bath with Victorian brass fixtures, including pull-chain commodes, pedestal sinks, and claw-foot tubs. There's also a two-bedroom suite with views of Packsaddle Mountain and Sandstone Mountain to the east.

DABBS RAILROAD
　HOTEL
Host: Gary Smith.
915-247-7905.
www.only-zuul.com/dabbs.
112 E. Burnet St., Llano, TX
　78643.
Price: Inexpensive, EP.
Credit Cards: None.
Handicap Access: Yes.

This old hotel has become something of a cult place for the young and adventurous. The hotel was recreated following the original floor plan, service, and menus as they were in 1907, when the hotel served as overnight lodging for the men who worked on the railroad. Like those railroad men of long ago, guests can lounge on the front porch in rockers or sit on throw-covered wooden benches in the small lobby. Don't look for luxury — the railroaders didn't have it back then, and you won't have it now. As stark and sparsely furnished as it was for the railroad men, the bare bones of the place are compensated for by the warmth and enthusiasm of the host. Nine rooms contain simple white iron double beds, and guests share two baths, one upstairs and one down. All-you-can-eat breakfasts and Saturday-night dinner are cooked by Gary and are served family style, paper plates and all, on a long picnic table in the kitchen. Campers are permitted to pitch their tents below the rolling lawns down to the river. Guests play games and stroll along the Llano River behind the hotel, in general enjoying the kids-away-at-summer-camp atmosphere of this unusual getaway. (For more information see "Culture" below.)

LLANO COUNTY RESTAURANTS AND FOOD PURVEYORS

U nless you plan to head out to Buchanan Lake, where there are some informal (and not highly recommended) eateries on the shore, expect to dine in town, either in Llano or Kingsland. Llano is known for the exceptional flavor of the local barbecue, and included below are two examples of this Texas specialty, along with the innovative Badu House. Kingsland now has the Kingsland Old Town Grill.

Kingsland

KINGSLAND OLD TOWN GRILL
915-388-2681.
1010 King St., Kingsland, TX 78639.
Price: Inexpensive to Moderate.
Cuisine: Texas Hill Country, Steak.
Serving: L, D, closed Mon. and Tues.
Credit Cards: Yes.
Handicap Access: No.

S teaks are the specialty here, but there's plenty of everyday hamburgers, cheeseburgers, chicken-fried steak, etc., with lunch specials Wednesday through Sunday, 11am to 2pm.

Llano

BADU HOUSE RESTAURANT
915-247-4304.
601 Bessemer Ave., Llano, TX 78643.
Price: Moderate to Expensive.
Cuisine: Continental, American, Game.
Serving: D.
Credit Cards: AE, MC, V.
Handicap Access: No.

B adu House, with its marble halls, was once a bank (see "Lodging"). The menu is innovative and sophisticated for such a small town. Try the quail, or the New Zealand rack of lamb, marinated in lemon garlic and served with a pesto sauce. The filet of beef is grilled with forest mushrooms, flamed in Scotch, and served with espagnole sauce. For dessert try either the wickedly chocolate Llano river bottom pie with a cream filling or the yellow jacket pie of coconut, lemon custard, and cream, topped with toasted coconut.

COOPER'S OLD TIME PIT BAR-B-CUE
915-247-5713.
www.coopersbbq.com.

E verything is authentic country barbecue here, from the outdoor pits filled with mesquite, which smoke the brisket, ribs, chicken, pork, and goat, to the butcher paper on which your choice is

604 W. Young St., Llano, TX
78643.
Price: Inexpensive.
Cuisine: Barbecue.
Serving: L, D.
Open: Daily.
Credit Cards: AE, D, MC, V.
Handicap Access: Yes.

served. Choose your own particular morsels directly from the aromatic pit. It's all priced by the pound, including your potato salad and pinto beans.

INMAN'S KITCHEN
915-247-5257.
809 W. Young St., Llano, TX
78643.
Hwy. 29 W.
Price: Inexpensive.
Cuisine: Smoked Meats.
Serving: L, D.
Credit Cards: AE, MC, V.
Handicap Access: Yes.

Inman's is famous all over the state for its turkey sausage. Barbecued beef, ham, and turkey are also delicious, along with homemade breads and pies.

The Llaneaux Seafood House.

Eleanor S. Morris

LLANEAUX SEAFOOD HOUSE
915-247-3663.
102 Legion Dr., Llano, TX
78643.
Price:Moderate.
Cuisine: Seafood.
Serving: D, SB.
Credit Cards: AE, D, MC, V.
Handicap Access: Yes.

The seafood here is seasoned with a complex blend of Cajun spices, as in crawfish or shrimp étouffée, red beans and rice with andouille sausage, or catfish, crawfish, or oyster po' boys. There's even an appetizer of fried alligator. But the menu also offers steak and chicken and includes an extensive wine list.

LLANO COUNTY FOOD PURVEYORS

Kingsland

Sweet Things Donut and Bake Shop (915-388-3460; RR 1431 N., Kingsland, TX 78639) Delicious baked treats for breakfast, lunch, and snacking. Try the crunchy apple cobbler.

Tow

Fall Creek Vineyards (512-476-4477; www.fcv.com; FM 2241 2.2 miles north of Tow on Lake Buchanan; also 1111 Guadalupe St., Austin, TX 78701; tastings and tours Mon.–Fri. 11am–3pm, Sat. noon–5pm; also Sun. noon–4pm Mar.–Nov.) An interesting detour for wine buffs is a visit to this vineyard north of Buchanan Dam. Texas is earning a fine reputation as a wine-producing state, and the winery, with European-style buildings on the lakeshore, produces chardonnay, chenin blanc, sauvignon blanc, riesling, and zinfandel. Complimentary tours and tastings, plus in August there's a Grapestomp Celebration, where the public is invited to "Kick off your shoes & stomp some grapes!!!" — along with river cruises and orchard hayrides.

The entrance to award-winning Fall Creek Vineyards in Tow.

Eleanor S. Morris

LLANO COUNTY CULTURE

ARCHITECTURE AND HISTORIC BUILDINGS

In *Llano*, the **Downtown National Historic District** includes many sites of historical interest, such as the **Corner Drug**, 1898, **Buttery's Storage**, 1880, and, more recently, the **Lan-Tex** movie theater. A walking-tour brochure of the district is available from the **Llano Chamber of Commerce** (915-247-5354; 700 Bessemer Ave., Llano, TX 78643), or you can take the tour virtually at www .llanochamber.org/walk.htm.

Start with the **County Courthouse**, which was built in 1892; it's the 39th oldest courthouse in Texas, and one of only three that have had no additions. The forbidding **Old Llano Jail**, of gray granite quarried in the county, still has bars covering the arched entrance and all the windows. The original red metal roof of this Romanesque Revival building gave the jail a nickname — prisoners actually spoke fondly of "staying over at the Red Top." The ground floor was the jailer's office and living quarters; the only jailbirds today are the pigeons who come to roost through the broken upper windows and the gallows opening in the roof.

The **Dabbs Railroad Hotel**, a 1907 hotel (see "Lodging"), is the last remaining example of a group of such hotels on the Llano River at the end of the railroad tracks. It was famous as a "home away from home" for train crews when they parked their locomotive in front of the hotel and stayed the night. The walls are hung with old photographs, and hotelkeeper Gary Smith has many tales to tell of the old days. For example, in the 1930s the hotel was a favorite hideaway for the Barrow gang of Bonnie and Clyde fame.

The **Llano County Museum** (915-247-3026; 310 Bessemer Ave.) is housed in the old Bruhl Drugstore, built in 1922. Displays illustrate Llano's boomtown days with collections of numerous Indian artifacts, rocks, and gems. There's also an exhibit about the days when polo was part of Llano, thanks to "the world's greatest polo player," Llano's own Cecil Smith.

The **Hill Country Wildlife Museum** (915-247-2568; 826 Ford St.) is the repository of the Campbell Collection, the third largest collection of taxidermy mounts in the world.

The **Llano County Library** on Ford St. and the river is in what were three one-story buildings, all built in 1904 and once home to a variety of businesses, from furniture and liquor to a pharmacy and a domino parlor.

In _Kingsland_, the **Antlers Hotel**, built in 1901 by the Austin & Northwestern Railroad as a resort, was once a popular destination, especially for Austinites who came to vacation on the Colorado River. It's now back in business and popular once more (see "Lodging").

SEASONAL EVENTS

In JANUARY, the **Llano County Junior Livestock Show** takes place.

In APRIL, the **Bluebonnet Arts and Crafts Trail** is a must stop in both Llano and Kingsland. A juried art show with original works by 75 visiting artists and artisans is held at the Kingsland House of Arts and Crafts. Local artists join with exhibitors from across Texas and neighboring states. Llano also hosts the **Old Time Fiddle Fest**, a **Crawfish Boil**, and a **Golf Open**.

In JUNE in Kingsland the annual **Aqua-Boom Festival** begins, offering a scholarship pageant, a golf tournament (at the Packsaddle Country Club), a music fest on the grounds of the chamber of commerce, a boat parade, and much more. The festival continues in JULY with a pageant, parades, a fish fry, arts and crafts fair, races on the lake, and fireworks. About 10,000 visitors are drawn to this small town of about 3,500.

In Llano there's the annual **July 4th Party**. For music lovers, in AUGUST, there's the **Grapestomp** out at **Fall Creek Vineyards**.

SEPTEMBER brings the **Llano Chamber Garage Sale**.

OCTOBER offers a **Heritage Day Festival** in Llano and a **Gem and Mineral Show** in Kingsland, which also sponsors a **Halloween Carnival** on the last weekend.

NOVEMBER brings a **Fall Arts and Crafts Show** on the second weekend to both Llano and Kingsland. In Llano, in addition to **Santa's Big Night**, there's both the **Courthouse Lighting** (10 miles of lights!) and the **Hill Country Lighting Trail**.

DECEMBER is busy with more Santa Land and the **Hill Country Christmas Lighting Tour**, plus the **Parade of Lights**. Kingsland celebrates with its **Christmas Tree Lighting** and **Merchants' Christmas Open House**. Check with the chambers of commerce (Llano: 915-247-5354; Kingsland: 915-388-6211) for exact dates.

LLANO COUNTY RECREATION

A diversity of outdoor recreation can be found in Llano County, be it on land or on water. The county's camping sites and hiking trails are described here under "Parks."

FISHING

There's year-round fishing on the picturesque, spring-fed **Llano River**, which runs through the city, and in **Lake Buchanan**, too, which forms part of the eastern border of Llano County (see below, along with other lakes in the Highland chain). Additional fishing spots are described in "Parks."

GOLF

Llano Municipal Golf Course (915-247-5100; Old Castell Rd., Llano, TX 78643)
Two miles west of the Llano courthouse, this challenging 18-hole course is on the banks of the Llano River, adjacent to Robinson City Park. A fully equipped pro shop, golf carts. The course has a new clubhouse that serves beer and wine.

HUNTING

The Llano Basin has the highest concentration of deer in the United States, which is why Llano boasts of being the Deer Capital of Texas. It's also considered one of the best areas in the state for bow hunting. There's the chance of bagging other game, too, such as dove, turkey, and quail. For a license, contact the **Llano Chamber of Commerce** (915-247-5354; www.llanochamber.org; 700 Bessemer Ave., Llano, TX 78643).

Packsaddle Mountain and Other Scenic Routes

Viewed from Highway 71, long, low Packsaddle Mountain is of interest not only to historians, thanks to the famous battle of August 5, 1873, but also to geologists. It consists of 600-million-year-old sandstone in horizontal layers, resting on even more ancient Packsaddle schist. This in turn is exposed in Honey Creek at the foot of the mountain. Tempting traces of gold, silver, and other minerals have been found in the sands of the creek, but most geologists agree that whatever might have been there eroded eons ago.

PARKS

Robinson City Park (Main St., Llano, 2.5 miles west of courthouse) This park on the Llano River offers picnicking, a swimming pool, and a challenging golf course (see "Golf"). Campgrounds are next to the park, and the 100 RV camping sites with electricity and water, the community center, and the rodeo grounds are operated by the Llano County Community Center. (Call 915-247-5354 for information on camping.)

Buchanan Dam and Lake Buchanan

Buchanan (pronounced "buck-an-an") Dam was completed in 1937 and at that time was the longest multiple-arched dam in the U.S. It's a popular place for many outdoor and water-related activities around Lake Buchanan. (For more information about the Highland Lakes, see www.highlandlakes.com.)

For BOATING, try **Alexander Boat Dock** (915-379-2721; RR 1, Box 16, Tow, TX 78672) on the lake, a complete marina with boat rentals, fuel, and oil.

When FAMILY FUN is the order of the day, try the **Buchanan Dam Visitor Center** (512-793-2803; Hwy. 29, Buchanan Dam, TX 78609). From here there are spectacular views of Buchanan Lake, the largest of the Highland Lakes, and telescopes to view with. The museum tells of the construction of the dam in 1937. Exhibits include photographs, area history, a living-history videotape, and a xeriscape garden. It's fun to feed the fish that gather below the observation deck, waiting for handouts.

FISHING enthusiasts will find plenty of opportunities on Lake Buchanan — which covers 23,000 surface acres — with white bass, striped bass, largemouth bass, catfish,

The Falls River Falls, seen along the route of the Vanishing Texas River Cruise, were formed more than 400,000 years ago when volcanic activity created the Llano Uplift

Eleanor S. Morris

spotted bass, crappie, and walleye lurking beneath the surface. Numerous guides on the lake can take visitors out for a fishing adventure, provide tackle and bait, and even fillet the fish for you back on the dock. For fishing charters on Lake Buchanan call 512-793-2803. Two fishing docks on Lake Buchanan are **Cottonwood Cove** (915-379-2641; RR 2241, Tow, TX 78672) and **Eagle's Nest Lodge** (915-379-3131; 16746 RR 2241, Tow, TX 78672).

On the HIGHLAND LAKES: **Lake Buchanan** was the first created and is the highest of the Highland Lakes, and it also has the largest surface area. Although much of the 124-mile shoreline is privately owned, there are a number of public and commercial access points for boating, fishing, swimming, and other water sports, as well as camping. Both Burnet County, on the east, and Llano County, on the west, have parks on the lake.

Inks Lake, at a constant level, covers 803 acres and is a reservoir used primarily for maintaining heads to produce electric power from the overflow from Lake Buchanan. This lake offers excellent year-round fishing, boating, and water sports; there are lakeside docks and marinas.

Lake LBJ is a constant-level lake below Buchanan and Inks Lakes. The clear lakes offer good fishing, skiing, and water recreation. For more information, contact the **Kingsland Chamber of Commerce** (915-388-6211; 1341 Hwy. 1431, Kingsland, TX 78639).

Other camping and RV sites include **Cedar Lodge Waterfront Resort** (512-793-2820; www.highlandlakes.com/cedar; 1400 RR 261, Buchanan Dam, TX 78609), **Pelican Point Resort** (915-379-2373; PO Box 148, Tow, TX 78672; Hwy. 2241), and **Sunrise Beach Marina & Lodge** (915-388-9393; www.highland-lakes.com/marina; 667 Sandy Mtn. Dr., Llano, TX 78643).

Black Rock Park (512-473-4083, 800-776-5272, ext. 4083; www.lcra.org/com munity/blackrock.html; State Hwy. 251 between Hwy. 29 and Bluffton) Black

Rock Park on Lake Buchanan is under the aegis of the LCRA, and the 10-acre park on the 23,000-acre lake offers fishing, camping, picnicking, boating, wading, hiking, and water sports. Campers can choose one of 30 designated campsites equipped with table and grill. Water is available, and there are two rest rooms plus an outdoor wash-off cold shower.

For wading and swimming, be advised that the areas are not designated and lifeguards are not provided. For boating, a free single-lane public boat ramp in neighboring Llano County Park accommodates motorboats and sailboats.

Many anglers consider the park a "hot spot" for bank fishing; others enjoy casting from a boat.

Enchanted Rock State Natural Area (915-247-3903; www.tpwd.state.tx.us/park/enchantd/enchantd.htm; 16710 RR 965, Fredericksburg, TX 78624) Even though the mailing address is Fredericksburg (see Gillespie County), this fantastic hunk of rock is located primarily in Llano County, 22 miles south of Llano. One of three exfoliated rock domes in the world (the others are Stone Mountain in Georgia and Ayers Rock in Australia), this massive 500-foot-high mound of solid granite covers almost 650 acres. It's also considered among the oldest (1 billion years) exposed rocks in North America, rising like a huge bald pate above the 1,643-acre park.

Myriad tales and legends have contributed to the name "enchanted." Some Indian tribes feared to set foot upon it; they believed it was the site of human sacrifices. Others fancied that ghost fires flickered on the crest on moonlit nights. Others may have used it as a rallying point, but they all held it in awe and reverence.

The diversity of the rock face provides challenging face climbs and numerous crack climbs to those adventurers who make it to the cave on top. And the 4-mile hike around the base can yield great wildlife sightings: One recent hiker reported seeing a large turtle, two armadillos, four cows, twelve deer, a big black snake eating a lizard, and "a lot of rock squirrels" all on one walk. There are several other designated trails in Enchanted Rock Natural Area so visitors can explore the more remote areas of the park.

ROCK HUNTING

L lano County considers itself the central mineral region of Texas; the abundance and diversity of minerals here are unequaled anywhere else in the state. Rock hunters can search below Buchanan Dam for quartz, granite, gneiss, flint, schist, feldspar, and limestone. As for llanite, you might be lucky and find some at the **Llanite Outcropping**, a highway cut on Hwy. 16 at the intersection of Hwy. 29, about 10 miles north of Llano, that's a favorite stopping place for rock hunters wanting to get a sample.

LLANO COUNTY SHOPPING

In Llano, the streets around Courthouse Square — Main, Berry, Sandstone, and Ford — offer everything from antiques to gifts to clothing and accessories for every occasion and every age. For a real nostalgia trip, the choice is **Acme Dry Goods** (915-247-4457; 109 W. Main St., Llano, TX 78643), an old-fashioned dry goods emporium with the original fittings, including a polished-brass cash register to ring up sales of today's merchandise. The **Llano Fine Arts Gallery** (915-247-4839; 503 Bessemer Ave., PO Box 8, Llano, TX 78643) is sponsored by the Llano Fine Arts Guild and exhibits more than 200 framed paintings, as well as photographs, prints, sculpture, ceramics, pottery, stained glass, enamels, and an assortment of crafts. Special courtyard exhibits are organized in the spring and fall.

MASON COUNTY

This statue on the lawn in front of the Mason County Courthouse memorializes the cattlemen, drovers, and cowboys of old Texas.

Eleanor S. Morris

Mason County, created from Bexar and Gillespie Counties in 1858, is an almost undiscovered secret, placed as it is up at the far northwest edge of the Hill Country. Yet it is only 40 miles north of that popular tourist destination, Fredericksburg. German settlers, spreading north from Fredericksburg as early as 1848, were some of the county's earliest Anglo residents.

Fort Mason, named for Lt. George T. Mason, who lost his life in the war with Mexico, was established to guard against Comanche and Apache raids on Texas settlements to the east. The town developed from a trading post alongside the fort, and both town and county took the fort's name. The town was designated the county seat in 1861, shortly after U.S. soldiers left when Texas seceded from the Union. That was the year that Col. Robert E. Lee was commanding officer at the fort. Since Virginia had not as yet left the Union, Lee did not shed his U.S. uniform until he arrived home to take over the Army of Northern Virginia.

The vacant fort was irresistible to the people of Mason, and they began to build their town from its stones. Now a replica stands on the site, a hill south of the courthouse.

After the Civil War, Mason became cattle country. In the 1870s cattle rustling led to bloody feuds between ranchers and rustlers, called both the Mason County War and the Hoo Doo War. Texas Rangers soon arrived to restore law and order.

Much of the country was settled before the invention of barbed wire, and so Mason County abounds in rock fences that meander up hillsides, along creek beds, and through live-oak groves, built by Germans settlers who used the most plentiful resource they had to fence in their cattle.

Mason County claims that more deer roam here than in any other place in Texas, a claim that Llano — which calls itself the "Deer Capital of Texas" — must certainly dispute. Topaz, the state gem of Texas, is found only in Mason County, near the communities of Streeter, Grit, and Katemcy.

Mason (pop. 2,160) is about the only town in the county large enough to have something to offer visitors, but you'll find more here than perhaps you bargained for. For more information, contact the **Mason County Chamber of Commerce** (915-347-5758; www.masontxcoc.com; 108 Ft. McKavitt St., PO Box 156, Mason, TX 76856).

MASON COUNTY LODGING

In Mason there's no mail delivery; everybody picks up mail at the post office. That means that many of the sites have no street address — you have to go by their location. There are two motels, the **Hill Country Inn** (915-347-6317; 454 Ft. McKavitt St., Mason, TX 76856; on Hwy. 87 S.) and **Fort Mason Inn** (915-347-0052; 866 San Antonio, PO Box 1138, Mason, TX 76856; on Hwy. 87 S.), and several small bed & breakfasts. Here are three of the latter, conveniently near all the sights.

BRIDGES HOUSE BED & BREAKFAST
Hosts: Mary Hemphill.
915-347-6440.
305 Broad St., PO Box 264, Mason, TX 76856.
Two blocks north of the courthouse on the corner of Broad & Olmos.
Price: Moderate.
Credit Cards: None.
Handicap Access: Yes.

This little house is part of the National Register Historic District. The 1884 stone house is complete with old-fashioned gingerbread trim and 17-inch-thick stone walls. Bright, hand-painted wall and cupboard decorations by Mary, an artist, are everywhere. Colorful birdhouses are painted on the wall of the entry, and grapevines trail along the walls of the bathroom. Both guest rooms share the bath and the sitting room. A Christmas Room has a tree up in a corner year-round, hung with old-fashioned decorations. There's a small refrigerator and coffeemaker for guests' convenience, and a continental breakfast is served in the sitting room.

MASON SQUARE BED & BREAKFAST
Hosts: Monica and Brent Hinkley.
915-347-6398/6824, 800-369-0405.
134 Ft. McKavitt St., Mason, TX 76856.
North side of the square.
Price: Inexpensive to Moderate.
Credit Cards: MC, V.
Handicap Access: No.

Monica (whose full name is Monica Maria Teresa Veronica Bastidas Valenzuela Hinkley) and Brent totally gutted this upstairs hostelry atop several of the square's businesses. From what was once a rooming house, then apartments, they created three lovely, brand-new guest rooms, each with a private bath. A comfortable common room has a dining table and chairs and a TV and VCR. Tall French doors open onto the front balcony, giving a wide view of the courthouse in the center of Mason's town square. A food center is set up along one wall of the wide hall, with refrigerator, dishwasher, microwave, dishes, and whatever is needed for the continental breakfast that is included, or your own provisions. The Hinkleys also run the Red Door B&B just up the street at #234.

OMA'S & OPA'S HAUS
Hosts: Julia and Merton Pepper.
915-347-6477, 800-508-5101 (in Texas only).
617 El Paso St., PO Box 1158, Mason, TX 76856.
Price: Moderate.
Credit Cards: None (cash and checks only).
Handicap Access: No.

This large Victorian stone house reflects the German pioneer influence — not only in its name, but the home itself looks like a big Sunday house. Painted sparkling white with Dutch blue trim, it's as spic and span inside as out. The four guest rooms are the Green and Pink Room, with a genuine Amish quilt for a coverlet; the Twin Bed Room; the Blue Room, with a four-poster bed; and the TV Room, which has a sitting room for its namesake. Bathrooms are shared. Both the Green and Pink Room and the TV Room open onto the large upstairs wraparound porch, but everyone has access to the porch just below. There's a swing downstairs, and a nice side yard with a birdbath. Julia will feed you pancakes and bacon for breakfast, or just cereal and bananas if you prefer.

MASON COUNTY RESTAURANTS

COOPER'S PIT BARBECUE
915-347-6897.
Hwy. 87 S., Mason, TX 76856.

As in its twin restaurant in Llano, everything is authentic country barbecue here, from the outdoor smoking black pits of mesquite that cook the brisket, ribs, chicken, pork, and goat to the butcher paper on which your choice is served. You pick it

Price: Inexpensive.
Cuisine: Barbecue.
Serving: L, D.
Credit Cards: MC, V.
Handicap Access: Yes.

out directly from the pit, and it's priced by the pound. Same with the potato salad and pinto beans. If you eat it on the premises, on the picnic tables inside, there's an additional small charge for bread, onions, and jalapeño peppers.

KELLER'S RIVERSIDE STORE
915-347-0055.
9760 Hwy. 87 S., Mason, TX 76856.
Price: Inexpensive to Moderate.
Cuisine: Steak, Seafood, Mexican.
Serving: L, D, Thurs.–Sun.
Credit Cards: MC, V.
Handicap Access: No.

Although Keller's is a little out of town (about 11 miles south), it's interesting both for good food and history. Crockett Keller's great-grandfather opened a store right here in 1862. The land was also the site of one of the Hoo Doo War gunfights (see "Mason County") and although over the years the Kellers lost the land, in 1968 Crockett got it back, and he and wife Diane opened the restaurant in May 2001. "We have not opened a can!" Crockett says with emphasis. Everything is fresh, from vegetables to fish and oysters. Stuffed pork loin comes with your choice of either sausage or guacamole stuffing, stuffed beef tenderloin can be ordered with a portabella mushroom on top, you can have a portabella burger or quiche of the day, among other items on the extensive menu. The setting might be rustic, but there are white tablecloths and napkins on every table.

SANTOS TAQUERIA
915-347-6140.
1025 San Antonio, PO Box 1246, Mason, TX 76856.
On the southeast corner of the square.
Price: Inexpensive.
Cuisine: Mexican.
Serving: B, L Mon.–Sat. 6:30am–2pm.
Credit Cards: None.
Handicap Access: No.

"From the heart of Mexico to the heart of Texas" is Santos's motto, and you can really believe it when you eat to the sound of tortillas being patted by hand in the open kitchen in the center of the restaurant. Gorditas, chalupas, taquitos, quesadillas, all authentic south-of-the-border — no Tex-Mex here. And a bonus is that everyone who enters will look at you, a stranger, smile, and say, "Howdy."

WILLOW CREEK CAFE
915-347-6124.
102 Ft. McKavitt St., Mason, TX 76856.
North side of the square.
Price: Inexpensive to Moderate.
Cuisine: Sandwiches, Pizza.
Serving: L, D Thurs.–Sun.
Credit Cards: None.

The original thick rock walls from 1904 and high ceilings provide an interesting contrast to the modern wood tables and chairs that furnish this large, light restaurant. Interesting features include the cashier's stand, a tall ledger desk from an old train station, and a big old table seating six or eight. (The place was once a Ford dealership; it still has a drive-up ramp and bi-fold doors.) House special pizzas are unusual. The Southwestern is topped

Handicap Access: Yes, except rest rooms.

with black beans, grilled chicken, onions, and mild green chilies; the Greek Veggie has spinach, sun-dried tomatoes, feta cheese, artichoke hearts, and red onions. A special drink is the prickly pear tea. Or BYOB.

ZAVALA'S CAFE
915-347-5365.
PO Box 1612, Mason, TX 76856.
On Hwy. 87 N.
Price: Inexpensive.
Cuisine: Mexican, American.
Serving: B, L, D; closed Christmas.
Credit Cards: MC, V.
Handicap Access: Yes.

Fajitas, huge burritos, cinco cinco, nachos (corn chips topped with refried beans, taco meat, cheese, lettuce, tomato, sour cream, and gua-camole), and some of the biggest and best chicken-fried steaks are served in this pleasant restaurant with its warm wood wainscoting, arched mirrors, Mexican village mural, and Tiffany-style lamps. Everything is made from scratch and is delicious, from the chicken breast Portuguesa to the chopped steak à la Mexicana. Fresh homemade pies include pecan, coconut, lemon, and chocolate.

MASON COUNTY CULTURE

ARCHITECTURE

The **Mason County Courthouse**, a Classical Revival building from 1909, is made of native sandstone and has been repainted in its original colors. In-side, almost every room has a fireplace trimmed with ornate pressed metal. Newly restored is the small stone building alongside the courthouse, containing a wonderfully welcome old-fashioned convenience: public toilets.

The **Seaquist House**, a large three-story Victorian mansion at 400 Broad St., is one of the most beautiful homes of early Texas. It was built in the 1880s and 1890s for a local banker. He maintained an office in the house, and you can still see his name, E. M. Reynolds, etched into the glass of the door. Now completely restored, the house is the home of the Garner Seaquist family, descendants of Oscar Seaquist, a Swedish boot maker who bought the home in 1919. The house has 22 rooms, 15 fireplaces, and a shower room in the three-story water tower. It was the first house in Mason to have indoor plumbing, and the third-floor ball-room, 30 by 60 feet, is enlarged by two spacious porches; there's a billiards room, too. The home is open for tours by appointment only (call 915-347-5413 for tour information).

HISTORIC BUILDINGS AND DISTRICTS

Much of Mason has been designated a National Historic District, and you can begin to cover it by taking a walking tour of Mason Courthouse

Square. The pecan trees were planted in the 1930s. Other buildings of interest on the square are the **Mason National Bank,** the **Mason County Jail** (still in use!), and the **Bill Martin House.** According to town historians, the occupants of this house once kept Nubian goats out back; it seems that a goat named Opal liked to jump on top of her fence. City crew workers would yell at her to get back in the pen, and she obeyed. She became so well trained that soon anyone driving by who saw her would yell, "Opal, get back in your pen," and she would.

The Mason County Jail

The Mason County Jail was built in 1894 and is still in use when needed — which is very rarely.

Eleanor S. Morris

Although cattle rustling and general lawlessness took place all over the Texas frontier, the situation came to a head in Mason County in 1875 with the Hoo Doo War. Several rustlers were apprehended and put in the Mason County Jail. But they were soon out on bail, and the sheriff found it impossible to find them to bring them to justice. Other arrests were made, and one man was killed while in the custody of the deputy sheriff. Finally a rancher was shot from ambush and a county official was killed on a street in Mason, the last straw. The county split into three factions, one trying to stay neutral and keep the peace while the other two continued to fight with each other.

The last act of the Hoo Doo War was the burning of the Mason County Courthouse on January 27, 1877. But by that time the leaders of both factions were either dead or in jail or had disappeared.

Today Mason invites visitors to "Come see where one of the ten famous Texas feuds took place. Walk the streets that once knew lawmen, outlaws, desperados . . ."

City Hall is in a renovated 1923 Mission-style building at 124 Moody St., and next door at 118 Moody is the **Odeon Theater,** in continuous operation since 1928. The theater was the site of the premiere of the Disney film *Old Yeller* —

Mason native Fred Gipson was the author of the book. A preservation society has been formed for its renovation and claims that the Odeon is "the oldest continuous running theater in Texas." Nowadays not only new releases but also vintage movies and live theater with local thespians provide the drama.

Fort Mason, about five blocks south of the courthouse, is high on Post Hill above the town, commanding a wide view. Original building materials were used to re-create the one reconstructed building, which rests on the original foundation. The double fireplace foundations are also original. Crumbling foundations of 23 buildings include barracks, officers' quarters, and stables.

LIBRARIES

Mason County M. Beven Eckert Memorial Library (915-347-5446; 410 Post Hill, Mason, TX 76856) An exhibit here details the career of Fred Gipson, author of *Old Yeller*, the book that became a Walt Disney movie.

MUSEUMS

The Mason County Museum (915-347-6242; 300 Moody St., Mason, TX 76856) A general collection of Mason County historical items and artifacts. The museum is housed in an old schoolhouse built in the 1870s of materials gathered from Fort Mason buildings. An old spring that supplied the fort with water flows just east of the museum. Admission is free. Museum hours are variable; check with the Chamber of Commerce (915-347-5758).

SEASONAL EVENTS

For information contact the **Mason County Chamber of Commerce** (915-347-5758; www.masontxcoc.com; 108 Ft. McKavitt St., Mason, TX 76856).

In JANUARY a **Livestock Show** is scheduled.

APRIL and MAY bring riotous fields of **wildflowers**, and the Mason County Chamber of Commerce offers a map of three spectacular drives through the county.

In JUNE is a **Catfish Fry.** JULY brings the **Roundup Rodeo** and **Arts and Crafts Show**.

In NOVEMBER Mason really lights up for the **Tannenbaum Arts and Crafts Show**: the courthouse, historic homes, and churches are all brilliantly aglow with holiday lights. Also in November, the second Saturday, the city puts on a **Wild Game Dinner** — after all, this is huntin' country. Dinner is donated venison, wild hog, rattlesnake, elk, and exotic game.

Come DECEMBER there's a **Christmas Lighting Tour** through all the lighted sights, and a **Christmas Home Tour.**

MASON COUNTY RECREATION

CAMPING

You can camp in Mason County at **Garner Seaquist Ranch** (see "Topaz Hunting") and at **Fort Mason City Park** (915-347-4669), which has shaded RV spots on the edge of the park's golf course (see "Parks").

Dos Rios RV Park (915-347-1713; 8221 RR 2389) is located on the Llano River, quiet, scenic, offering fishing, canoeing, nature trails.

For additional camping choices, contact the **Mason County Chamber of Commerce** (915-347-5758; PO Box 156, Mason, TX 76856).

FISHING

Catfish and bass abound on the Llano River, and you can put into the river at river crossings where access is made simple by the low-water bridges. **Luther Simon** (915-347-6221, HC 60 Box 17, Mason, TX 76856) runs a fishing camp on the Llano River 8 miles southwest of Mason on RR 1871.

NATURE

The **Eckert James River Bat Preserve** (512-263-8878, directions and information; off RR 2389, southwest of Mason) is home to one of the largest free-tailed bat colonies. Wintering in Mexico, the bats arrive in Mason County in the spring, remaining until fall in a "maternity" cave, where female bats bear and rear their young. Each evening the bats leave the cave for dinner, an exodus of perhaps 4 to 6 million bats.

Both the exodus flight and the return are spectacular, with the bats streaking caveward like dive bombers. The preserve, 12 miles from town, is open to the public May through October, Thurs.–Sun. evenings, 6–9pm. Arrange a tour by calling 915-347-5970 during the season or 915-347-9472 during off-season (www.sig.net/~masoncoc/batcave.htm).

PARKS

Fort Mason City Park (915-347-6449; U.S. 87, 1 mile south of town) This 125-acre park has picnicking facilities under large pecan trees, fully equipped RV hookups, primitive campsites, a 9-hole golf course (**Comanche Creek Golf Course**, 915-347-5798), a rodeo arena, walking trails, and a playscape.

TOPAZ HUNTING

Garner Seaquist Ranch (915-347-5413; PO Box 35, Mason, TX 76856) charges $10 per person per day to hunt topaz, the Texas state gem, and you keep what you find. You'll need a pick and shovel and a ¼" mesh wire screen; small pieces of topaz can sometimes be found by sifting dirt through the screen. Camping charges are $5 per day for primitive camping and $10 per day for hookups to water and electricity and the use of showers.

MASON COUNTY SHOPPING

Most shopping in Mason County is around Mason's main square, where you'll find antiques, crafts, gifts, and specialty items. **Antiques and Crafts** (915-347-6440; 201 Westmoreland, Mason, TX 76856; on the south side of the square) was once a combined old lumberyard and funeral parlor. Now it's packed with antiques from early German settlers and later residents, too. Treasures include quilts, pottery, vintage clothes, old sheet music, and furniture. **Underwood Antique Mall** (915-347-5258; 100 N. Live Oak, PO Box 752, Mason, TX 76856; on the east side of the square) offers antiques and country treasures; and more antiques are at **P. V. Antiques** (915-347-5496; 1102 El Paso, Mason, TX 76856).

Also (mostly) on the main square:

Market Square (915-347-5516; 105 Ft. McKavitt St., Mason, TX 76856; on the north side of the square) offers gifts for all occasions made by area cottage industries and artisans, including iron creations and leather goods. As a bonus, there's a soda fountain in the rear of the shop.

Texas topaz is available uncut, cut, and mounted at the following locations in Mason: **Benjie's Books and Gifts** (915-347-6323; 203 Ft. McKavitt St., PO Box 915, Mason, TX 76856), **Market Square** (see above), and **Country Collectibles** (915-347-5249; 320 Ft. McKavitt St., Mason, TX 76856; out on U.S. Hwy. 87N., 2 blocks from the courthouse square).

Beyond the main square are these two recommended shops:

Glenn Marshall Custom Knives are justly famous. You can order one in your own design or his. Visitors are invited to see Glenn at work at his shop, sharpening and honing blades as he has done since he made his first knife in 1930 (915-347-6207; 305 Hoffman St., Mason, TX 76856).

Ramona's Gallery of Arts (915-347-6635; 120 Moody St., Mason, TX 76856) specializes in original art. You'll find paintings, bronzes, oils, pastels, and watercolors, plus crafts and art supplies.

CHAPTER FIVE
Along the River
SAN ANTONIO AND BEXAR COUNTY

Eleanor S. Morris

Sight-seers float on a barge on the San Antonio River along the River Walk.

The history of Bexar (pronounced "bear") County is that of its principal city, San Antonio. No written records of the history of the Indian tribes exist before the Spanish came in the 17th century to find Yanaguana, a Payaya-Coahuiltecan Indian village on the San Antonio River. (The story of the coming of the Spanish and the establishment of the missions that formed the nucleus of what is Texas's third largest city can be found in Chapter One.)

Bexar County was created in 1836. Its name derived from the original 17th-century Spanish name for San Antonio: San Antonio de Béjar. The viceroy of New Spain at that time was one Baltazar de Zúñiga, Marqués de Valero, and the town's name honored his brother, the Duque de Béjar, who had died in 1686 defending Budapest against the Turks. San Antonio de Béjar soon became just Béjar — or Bexar, an alternate spelling. Eventually that name was applied to the county, and the principal population center came to be known simply as San Antonio.

The terrain of Bexar County is hilly, its rich black to thin limestone soil dotted with mesquite and other brush. Deer and wild turkey abound, and, like the rest of the Hill Country, there are spring-fed streams and underground water supplies. The San Antonio River flowing through the center of town is spring-fed.

San Antonio is the county seat and includes several small incorporated towns, such as Castle Hills, Balcones Heights, Alamo Heights, Olmos Park, and Terrell Hills. Outside the city, little Leon Springs, just about the only community in the county outside of San Antonio, has a popular barbecue restaurant and a dance hall.

The city's growth was limited to the central area until after Texas won independence from Mexico in 1836. But even with expansion, the early plan of the city, laid out in 1767, was respected: Alamo Plaza became a major commercial site, and Commerce Street was the main banking and financial district. The 20th century brought major changes in the form of skyscrapers and ornate architecture, such as the Smith-Young Tower, built in 1929. But the Depression called a halt to such growth. Not until construction of the Paseo del Rio in the 1940s, the city's great urban project along the San Antonio River, was all of downtown San Antonio brought together as one entity. The river flows 20 feet below street level, right through the heart of downtown. Lined with restaurants and shops and traveled by barges full of sightseers, the River Walk is surely the city's main attraction.

While San Antonio has an abundance of different cultures and cherishes them all, more than half of its population is of Hispanic origin, and Spanish is spoken most everywhere. But native American, Anglo, German, African-American, and Latin American cultures all contribute to the flavor that makes San Antonio such an exciting place to visit. It's often called a "party town," and its many fiestas (at least two a month, usually more) certainly warrant that appellation. Anything and everything is cause for celebration in this happy, friendly town, which even created a Mud Festival to "celebrate" the chore of cleaning out the San Antonio River each spring.

SAN ANTONIO LODGING

Like any large city, San Antonio has its share of large hotels, part of national chains such as the **Hilton Palacio Del Rio** (210-222-1400, 800-445-8667; www.hilton.com; 200 S. Alamo St., San Antonio, TX 78205), the **Hyatt Regency** (210-222-1234, 800-233-1234; www.hyatt.com; 123 Losoya St., San Antonio, TX 78205), and the **Marriott Rivercenter** (210-223-1000, 800-648-4462; www.MarriottHotels.com; 101 Bowie St., San Antonio, TX 78205). New is the **Westin Riverwalk** (210-224-6500, 800-WESTIN-1; www.westin.com; 420 W. Market St., San Antonio, TX 78205). Several of the city's historic hotels have become affiliated with national chains, such as the **Sheraton Gunter Hotel** (210-227-3241, 888-999-2089; www.gunterhotel.com; 205 E. Houston St., San Antonio, TX 78205), the **Wyndham St. Anthony Hotel** (210-227-4392, 800-227-6963; www

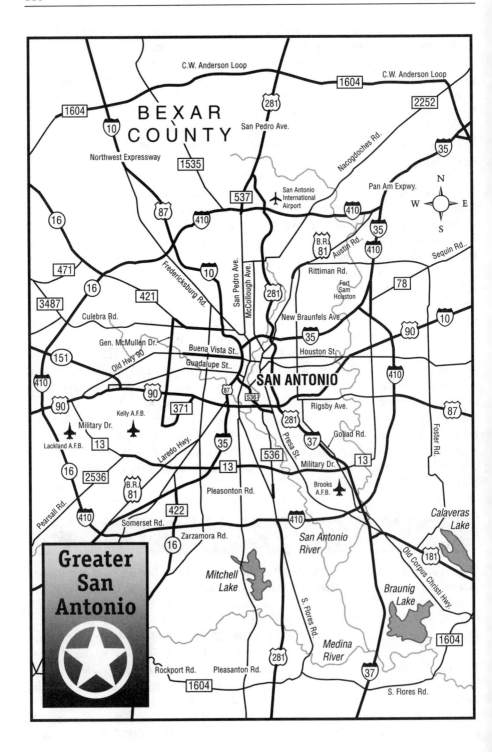

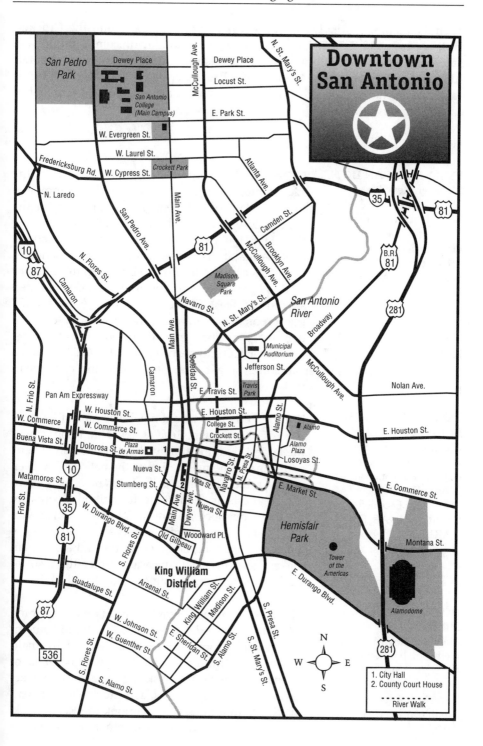

Downtown San Antonio

San Pedro Park

Dewey Place

McCullough Ave.

Dewey Place

Locust St.

N. St. Mary's St.

San Antonio College (Main Campus)

E. Park St.

W. Evergreen St.

W. Laurel St.

Fredericksburg Rd.

W. Cypress St.

Crockett Park

Atlanta Ave.

N. Laredo

San Pedro Ave.

Main Ave.

Camden St.

35

81

10

81

N. Flores St.

Brooklyn Ave.

McCullough Ave.

B.R. 81

87

Camaron

Madison Square Park

Navarro St.

N. St. Mary's St.

San Antonio River

Broadway

281

N. Frio St.

Main Ave.

Camaron

Soledad St.

Municipal Auditorium

Jefferson St.

McCullough Ave.

Nolan Ave.

Pan Am Expressway

E. Travis St.

Travis Park

W. Houston St.

E. Houston St.

Alamo St.

W. Commerce

W. Commerce St.

College St.

Crockett St.

Alamo

E. Houston St.

Buena Vista St.

Dolorosa St.

Plaza de Armas

1

Alamo Plaza

Losoyas St.

Matamoros St.

Nueva St.

Navarro St.

N. Presa St.

E. Commerce St.

10

Stumberg St.

Villita St.

E. Market St.

Frio St.

35

W. Durango Blvd.

Main Ave.

Dwyer Ave.

Nueva St.

81

S. Flores St.

Old Gilbeau

Woodward Pl.

Hemisfair Park

Montana St.

Guadalupe St.

King William District

Arsenal St.

King William St.

Madison St.

Tower of the Americas

E. Durango Blvd.

S. Presa St.

Alamodome

87

W. Johnson St.

E. Sheridan St.

S. Alamo St.

536

S. Flores St.

W. Guenther St.

S. Alamo St.

S. St. Mary's St.

N

W   E

S

1. City Hall
2. County Court House

River Walk

.wyndham.com; 300 E. Travis St., San Antonio, TX 78205), and the **Crockett Holiday Inn** (210-225-6500, 800-292-1050; www.holidayinn.com; 320 Bonham, San Antonio, TX 78205). But San Antonio also has independent historic hotels such as the **Menger** and the **Mansion del Rio**, described below. Also well represented, particularly in the historic area of town, are a number of bed & breakfast establishments.

HOTELS

EMILY MORGAN HOTEL
Manager: Rene Uresti.
210-225-8486.
705 E. Houston, San
   Antonio, TX 78205.
Price: Expensive to Very
   Expensive.
Credit Cards: AE, D, MC, V.
Handicap Access: Yes.

The Emily Morgan is right next door to the Alamo, and the hotel is named for a heroine of the Texas War of Independence: Emily Morgan, the Yellow Rose of Texas. She is credited with assisting Sam Houston in the routing of Mexican general Santa Anna at the Battle of San Jacinto. Opened in the 1920s as a medical office building, the 13-story Gothic Revival structure was the first documented skyscraper west of the Mississippi. Now its 177 guest rooms, lobby, and meeting rooms have all undergone a major renovation. Down feathertops, bathrobes, snack bar and coffeemaker, CD and stereo system, Jacuzzi tubs and a fitness center, among other amenities, make it a comfortable and convenient place to stay.

FAIRMOUNT HOTEL
Manager: Beth Acker.
210-224-8800, 800-996-3426.
www.wyndham.com.
401 S. Alamo St., San
   Antonio, TX 78205.
Price: Very Expensive.
Credit Cards: AE, D, DC,
   MC, V.
Handicap Access: Yes.

In 1985 this 79-year-old hotel was moved halfway across downtown. True to Texas tradition, it was the largest building to have been moved anywhere, and it made the news all over the nation. However, service rather than size is the focus here, as is attention to guests, in the European tradition. Rooms are not large, but such features as 24-hour room service and valet parking, complimentary shoe shines, twice-a-day maid service, and a concierge and a doorman make a stay here very pleasant. Amenities also include a fine restaurant, lounge, and a health club.

HOTEL VALENCIA
210-227-9700.
Manager: Roy Kretshmer.
www.hotelvalencia.com.
405 N. St. Mary's, San
   Antonio, TX 78205.
Price: Very Expensive.
Credit Cards: AE, DC, D,
   MC, V.

This new hotel specializes in luxury, beginning with custom-designed beds in the 214 contemporary guest rooms and suites, twice-daily maid service and turndown, cordless two-line speaker phones at bedside and desk, high-speed Internet access, in-room spa services, and much else. The Citrus Restaurant and a bar overlook the River Walk, and a terrace offers access down to the river. Special

Handicap Access: Yes.

attention has been given to such amenities as bed and bath linens, bath scales, hair dryers, other bath amentities, and much more.

LA MANSION DEL RIO
Manager: Michael Bazar.
210-225-2581, 800-292-7300.
www.lamansion.com.
112 College St., San Antonio, TX 78205.
Price: Expensive.
Credit Cards: AE, D, DC, MC, V.
Handicap Access: Yes.

La Mansion reflects the Hispanic heritage of San Antonio with its architecture and its atmosphere. Although the hotel is on the River Walk, it's a few blocks away from the traffic both downtown and on the river, so it presents a quiet, relaxed place to stay. Built as a school in the late 1880s by the French-speaking Brothers of Saint Mary, the original structure grew from two stories to four. In 1966 the school moved to other quarters, and the rehabilitated building became the luxurious 337-room Mansion del Rio; amenities include room service and a swimming pool. Restaurant Las Canarias (named not after birds but the first civilian settlers, who came from the Canary Islands in 1731) is noted for its fine meals and, recently, all renovated rooms.

MENGER HOTEL
Manager: Hector Venegas.
210-223-4361, 800-345-9285.
www.historicmenger.com.
204 Alamo Plaza, San Antonio, TX 78205.
Price: Expensive to Very Expensive.
Credit Cards: AE, D, DC, MC, V.
Handicap Access: Yes.

The Menger was built in 1859 as a two-story, 50-room hotel, but it quickly became so popular that a three-story addition was added shortly thereafter. "Staying at the Menger" is still a byword. There have been many additions and embellishments since; in 1909, marble floors, Corinthian columns, and filigreed balustrades were added to the original lobby by noted architect Alfred Giles, making it an opulent showcase. But just as splendid as the hotel is its colorful history: General Robert E. Lee rode his horse into the lobby; Teddy Roosevelt recruited his Rough Riders for the Spanish-American War in the hotel bar; and Sarah Bernhardt, Lilly Langtry, and Mae West called the Menger home when they were in town. The historic rooms in the 19th-century wing have more charm than luxury; the newer rooms are more spacious and up to date. Amenities include a health club, restaurants, room service, swimming pool (in a garden just beyond a large glass wall of the lobby), and some kitchenettes.

BED & BREAKFASTS

In San Antonio, the bed & breakfast scene includes Victorian mansions with either Texas or European accents, and even a log cabin.

BECKMANN INN AND CARRIAGE HOUSE

On the National Register of Historic Places, as well as within the King William Historic Dis-

Innkeepers: Betty Jo and
  Don Schwartz.
210-229-1449, 800-945-1449.
www.beckmanninn.com.
222 E. Guenther St., San
  Antonio, TX 78204.
Five blocks from
  downtown, in King
  William Historic District.
Price: Moderate to
  Expensive.
Credit Cards: AE, D, DC,
  MC, V.
Handicap Access: No.

trict, Beckmann Inn is justifiably proud of its listing: Exceptional. The house was built in 1886 by Albert Beckmann for his bride, Marie Dorothea, daughter of the San Antonio Guenther flour mill family. Around 1913 the home's Victorian style was converted to Greek Revival, and the porch was extended.

The parquet living room floor has an unusual decorative border, brought all the way from France. The yesteryear ambiance of the inn does not extend to its kitchen, however, where breakfast preparation includes glazed cranberry pear with mint and cranberry bread, and cinnamon-pecan French toast with an apricot glaze topped with strawberries and cream.

THE OGÉ HOUSE
Innkeepers: Sharrie and
  Patrick Magatagan.
210-223-2353, 800-242-2770.
www.ogeinn.com.
209 Washington St., San
  Antonio, TX 78204.
Edge of downtown, in King
  William Historic District.
Price: Expensive to Very
  Expensive.
Credit Cards: AE, CB, D,
  DC, MC, V.
Handicap Access: No.

The Ogé House (pronounced oh-jhay), a three-story building squared off by a set of porches top and bottom, is one of the most magnificent homes to be found in San Antonio's King William Historic District of fine houses. Built in 1857 for Louis Ogé, a pioneer cattle rancher and a Texas Ranger, the mansion boasts 11 stairs up to the front door and a central lobby with two guest rooms opening off it. Upstairs, the Giles and Mathis suites both open onto the porch across the front of the house, while Riverview, off the landing by the back stairs, is especially private, with its own porch and view of the river. On the main level, the Mitchell Suite has a platform canopy bed and a daybed. The Bluebonnet Room is done in Texas antiques, with a four-poster rolling pin bed and the desk of a Texas judge.

But that's all you'll find of Texas. Sharrie and Patrick prefer to think of their inn as more of a small European hotel. A deluxe continental breakfast begins with poached pears and goes on to such delicacies as pecan log roll, apple torte, cherry cheesecake, and fruit pastries. The library at the rear of the house is relaxing, with soft yellow walls, white woodwork, and satin striped sofas. A brass bucket there is filled with menus from all of the city's many fine eating places.

RIVERWALK INN
Innkeepers: Johnny
  Halpenny and Tammy
  Hill.
210-212-8300, 800-254-4440.
www.riverwalkinn.com.
329 Old Guilbeau St., San
  Antonio, TX 78204.

This group of log homes was transported log by log from Tennessee, where the inn's owners, Jan and Tracy Hammer, found them in a state of ruin. Originally built in 1842, the restored cabins represent the inn's philosophy: "We hope that our guests relive the history of old San Antonio through the lifestyles of Texas heroes Davy Crockett and James

On the River Walk at the beginning of King William Historic District.
Price: Expensive.
Credit Cards: AE, D, MC, V.
Handicap Access: No.

Bowie, who were from Tennessee," says innkeeper Halpenny. "Of course," he adds, "with all of today's amenities — the feel of the old with the technology of the new." Every Sunday morning at breakfast, a storyteller makes an appearance to entertain guests while they tuck into Johnny's baked French toast with spiced apples, along with ham and cheese ko-lachkes (a legacy of the ethnic pioneers of central Texas, these are wonderful Czech pastries).

The eleven rooms are named in honor of the heroes of the Alamo; each is dec-orated with country antique furniture, and nine of them have views of the river from outside porches or balconies. Fireplaces are of stone, and in many of the rooms you can see the cabin's log layers. Tall pine four-poster beds, homey quilts, old chests, and comfy armchairs make each room a relaxing and com-fortable haven.

A YELLOW ROSE
Innkeepers: Deb Field-Walker and Kit Walker.
210-229-9903, 800-950-9903.
www.ayellowrose.com.
229 Madison St., San Antonio, TX 78204.
Five blocks from downtown San Antonio.
Price: Expensive to Very Expensive.
Credit Cards: AE, D, MC, V.
Handicap Access: No.

The yellow-painted brick Yellow Rose B&B is a fine example of the many homes that were built in San Antonio's King William Historic District more than a century ago. Built in 1878 by Charles Mueller, a German immigrant house painter, the house, like many in the neighborhood, was a Victo-rian beauty. The large entry hall and other rooms still contain some of the English antiques that Deb and Kit purchased along with the inn from the pre-vious owners. It was a turnkey operation, Deb ex-plains, as she serves a breakfast of her famous country French toast, made of French bread oozing with caramel and pecans. The homemade oat bran and pecan muffins are mouthwatering, too.

Both new innkeepers are experienced at making guests happy: They were in charge of food and beverage concessions in the golf industry in their native Al-buquerque, New Mexico. Like their predecessors, Deb and Kit believe that innkeeping is all about relaxing and having a good time.

SAN ANTONIO RESTAURANTS AND FOOD PURVEYORS

For such a large and busy city, hosting countless tours, tourists, conventions, meetings, and festivals, many of San Antonio's huge selection of restaurants are surprisingly inexpensive. And the choices are legion — you'll find excellent American, Western, Southwestern, Mexican, French, Italian, Spanish, Chinese,

Japanese, Taiwanese, Korean, Indian, Greek, Indonesian, Indian, and Middle Eastern cuisine, and more. The eateries on the River Walk alone range from innovative Southwestern through Cajun to barbecue and, of course, Mexican.

Clothing is casual chic in most places except along the River Walk, where many visitors wear shorts and sandals, and the dining is outdoors. Chez Ardid is an exception, where men are expected to wear jackets.

Following is a representative sample of the many great places to enjoy San Antonio dining.

BIGA ON THE BANKS
210-225-0722.
203 S. St. Mary's, San Antonio, TX 78205.
Price: Moderate to Expensive.
Cuisine: Continental, American.
Serving: D Mon.–Sat.
Credit Cards: AE, D, DC, MC, V.
Handicap Access: Yes.

Biga has been named "one of America's best restaurants" by *Gourmet* magazine. The restaurant features such delicacies as antelope and quail with chestnuts and currant sauce, although lamb, veal, scallops, and salmon are also recommended. Such side dishes as sweet potato noodles, served with lamb and rice noodles on Thai salad, add to the flavor.

BOUDRO'S
210-224-8484.
www.boudros.com.
421 E. Commerce St., San Antonio, TX 78205.
On the River Walk.
Price: Inexpensive to Moderate.
Cuisine: Texas Bistro, Steak, Seafood.
Serving: L, D.
Credit Cards: AE, CB, D, DC, MC, V.
Handicap Access: Yes, elevator from street level.

The wonderful innovative mixture of Louisiana Cajun and Tex-Mex at Boudro's has won an award from the Texas Hill Country Food and Wine Festival. The herb-cured salmon tacos with marinated cucumbers, red onions, jicama, and slaw on fresh flour tortillas may be a starter, but it's worthy of an entire meal. Other offerings include smoked chicken or crab enchiladas, duck-and-sausage gumbo, blackened fish fillets or prime rib, and mesquite-grilled bobwhite quail. Enjoy your feast under yellow awnings on bright red chairs as the river and the barges float by. Or better yet, with reservations for two or more, dine on a barge.

CASA RIO
210-225-6718.
430 E. Commerce St., San Antonio, TX 78205.
On the River Walk.
Price: Inexpensive.
Cuisine: Mexican.
Serving: L, D.
Credit Cards: AE, D, DC, MC, V.
Handicap Access: Yes.

Casa Rio celebrated its 57th anniversary in 2003. It's the oldest and largest Mexican restaurant on the river, and the very first one to appear on this world-famous waterway. Dine under colorful umbrellas — or barge in (by reservation), enjoying San Antonio-style Mexican food.

COUNTY LINE SMOKEHOUSE AND GRILL
210-229-1941.
www.countyline.com.
111 W. Crockett St., San Antonio, TX 78205.
On the River Walk.
Price: Inexpensive.
Cuisine: Barbecue.
Serving: L, D.
Credit Cards: AE, CB, D, DC, MC, V.
Handicap Access: Yes.

For far more than 10 years the County Line has served up some of the best barbecue in town. And if you don't want barbecue, well, there are grilled steaks, kabobs, chicken, fish, salads, great margaritas, and ice-cold beer. While there is another location at 10101 IH-10W (210-641-1998), this spot boasts party barges. Call to reserve if you'd like to cruise the river while enjoying your barbecue.

EARL ABEL'S FAMILY RESTAURANT
210-822-3358.
4200 Broadway, San Antonio, TX 78205.
Price: Inexpensive.
Cuisine: American.
Serving: B, L, D.
Credit Cards: AE, D, MC, V.
Handicap Access: Yes.

This San Antonio tradition has been around since 1933. The red-patterned carpet, the captain's chairs, and the wood paneling make a restful atmosphere for enjoying the comfort-food dinner of the day, such as a New England boiled dinner (Monday), flaky turkey turnovers with giblet gravy (Tuesday), and smothered Swiss-style Salisbury steak with mashed potatoes (Wednesday). But of course there are enchiladas, tacos, and chili on the menu as well as other chicken, steak, and seafood choices.

Eleanor S. Morris

El Mercado, the city's Mexican marketplace, has many shops and restaurants, including El Mirador Cafe.

EL MIRADOR
210-225-9444.
722 S. St. Mary's St., San
  Antonio, TX 78205.
King William Historic
  District.
Price: Inexpensive.
Cuisine: Mexican.
Serving: B, L, D
  Tues.–Thurs. and Sat.; SB.
Credit Cards: AE, MC, V.
Handicap Access: Yes
  (restaurant), no
  (bathrooms).

For more than 35 years the Trevino family has been serving delicious food made from Mexican family recipes. El Mirador's cantina decor, with its saltillo tile floor, arches, and hanging baskets, plus the artwork of Frida Kahlo, reflects the adventure of authentic Mexican cuisine, such as sautéed shrimp in mole sauce, fiesta chicken quesadillas, nachos del golfo (sautéed lobster and crab with ancho relish, avocado salsa, and a spinach-radicchio salad), and other unusual dishes. Or try their renowned sopa Azteca, which always draws crowds.

FIG TREE RESTAURANT
210-224-1976.
www.figtreerestaurant.com.
515 Villita St., San Antonio,
  TX 78205.
At La Villita and the River
  Walk.
Price: Very Expensive.
Cuisine: Continental.
Serving: D.
Credit Cards: AE, D, DC,
  MC, V.
Handicap Access: No.
Special Features:
  Reservations
  recommended.

The Fig Tree offers fine continental dining and a romantic atmosphere, with a patio view over the River Walk. The menu lists such long-standing favorites as beef Wellington, chateaubriand, and fresh salmon and lobster.

**GUENTHER HOUSE
  RESTAURANT**
210-227-1061.
www.guentherhouse.com.
205 E. Guenther St., San
  Antonio, TX 78204.
South of King William
  Historic District.
Price: Inexpensive.
Cuisine: American.
Serving: B, L Mon.–Sat.
  7am–3pm, Sun.
  8am–2pm.
Credit Cards: AE, D, MC, V.
Handicap Access: No.

For an early breakfast in a historic setting, the Guenther House can't be beat. The Guenther name is an old San Antonio one: The restaurant is in the historic Guenther House, surrounded by a garden; next door is the historic Guenther flour mill (now Pioneer Flour Mills). While the place is famed for fluffy biscuits smothered in cream gravy, the breakfast tacos are special, too. When you enter the restaurant, cast an eye at the baked goods in the case to your left so you'll know what to order to sweeten your breakfast — or to have for dessert after lunch (soups and salads).

HOUSTON STREET BISTRO
210-476-8600.
204 E. Houston St., San
  Antonio, TX 78205.
Price: Inexpensive.
Cuisine: European Casual.
Serving: L daily, D when
  there's a performance
  next door in the Majestic
  Theater.
Credit Cards: All.
Handicap Access: Yes.

This storefront cafe is pretty chic, modeled on European bistros. Fine food in a relaxed, casual atmosphere is the scene, and the only non-French touch is a huge curved American flag covering the ceiling. International specialties like Tuscan white-bean soup, Greek pasta salad, chicken Gorgonzola, and portabella mushroom sandwich dot the menu. Before you're even served your order, out comes a delicious loaf of fresh bread and olive oil dip to keep you going until the food arrives.

The restaurant offers lunch boxes to go if you want to eat somewhere al fresco.

IBIZA
210-270-0786.
715 E. River Walk, San
  Antonio, TX 78205.
Price: Moderate.
Cuisine: Mediterranean.
Serving: B, L, D.
Credit Cards: AE, D, DC,
  MC, V.
Handicap Access: Yes.

Dining in the open air along the river, watching the barges float by, is a relaxing way to enjoy a full breakfast, lunch, or dinner at Ibiza, named for one of Spain's Balearic Islands. White chairs, blue-topped tables, and colorful napkins provide a pleasant setting for tapas (Spanish appetizers), specialty coffee drinks, and homemade desserts, too. Live entertainment Friday and Saturday evenings.

LA FOGATA
210-340-1337.
www.lafogata.com.
2427 Vance Jackson, San
  Antonio, TX 78205.
Price: Inexpensive to
  Moderate.
Cuisine: Mexican.
Serving: L, D Sun.–Thurs.
  11am–10pm, Fri. & Sat.
  11am–11pm; B Sat. & Sun.
Credit Cards: AE, CB, D, DC,
  MC, V.
Handicap Access: Yes.

Authentic and traditional foods of northern Mexico are on the menu here. Tacos al carbon (charcoal-broiled meat), frijoles borrachos (drunken beans), flour tortillas, quesadillas (melted cheese in corn tortillas), simple but filling, are a treat — so much so that the restaurant is often quite crowded. But the food is worth it.

LA MARGARITA MEXICAN RESTAURANT & OYSTER BAR
210-227-7140.
120 Produce Row, San
  Antonio, TX 78205.
Market Square (El Mercado).
Price: Inexpensive.

La Margarita may be a Mexican restaurant, but it's housed in a two-story building straight out of New Orleans, with lacy balconies and a wrought-iron-fenced patio. With dining both inside and out, La Margarita is the "home of the sizzling fajitas," claiming to be the first to bring that dish to San Antonio. Louisiana oysters and jumbo shrimp served Acapulco style are also on the menu here, and chicken en-

Cuisine: Mexican, Oyster Bar.
Serving: L, D, SB.
Credit Cards: AE, CB, D, DC, MC, V.
Handicap Access: Yes.

chiladas topped with tangy green tomatillo sauce and Monterey Jack cheese, served with guacamole, Spanish rice, and beans, keep La Margarita honest as a Mexican restaurant as well as a seafood bar. So does the nightly mariachi music. And the delicious tequila margaritas live up to the restaurant's name.

LIBERTY BAR
210-227-1187.
sanantonio.citysearch.com, search: Liberty Bar.
328 E. Josephine St., San Antonio, TX 78205.
Price: Inexpensive.
Cuisine: American.
Serving: L, D.
Credit Cards: AE, MC, V.
Handicap Access: Yes.

Don't be put off by the rather run-down exterior here. The decor is aged 19th century, set in what used to be Boehler's Gardens, a venerated San Antonio spot. The menu, printed daily, offers fresh breads, fresh vegetable salads, hearty steaks cooked on a mesquite grill, and specials like linguini, grilled bluefish, and even such a homey thing as a grilled cheese sandwich (but made special with Muenster cheese and chipotle peppers).

LITTLE RHEIN STEAK HOUSE
210-225-2111.
www.littlerheinsteakhouse.com.
231 S. Alamo St., San Antonio, TX 78205.
On the River Walk.
Price: Expensive.
Cuisine: Steak.
Serving: D.
Credit Cards: AE, D, DC, MC, V.
Handicap Access: Yes.
Special Features: Reservations recommended.

Dining here is either in the historic stone building up on the street level or on several levels of the River Walk patio — stairs lead from river to street level. Little Rhein boasts USDA choice steaks as well as fresh seafood, chops, and delicious appetizers and cocktails.

LONE STAR CAFE
210-223-9374.
sanantonio.citysearch.com, search: Lone Star Cafe.
237 Losoya St., San Antonio, TX 78205.
On the River Walk.
Price: Inexpensive to Moderate.
Cuisine: Texas.
Serving: L, D.
Credit Cards: AE, MC, V.
Handicap Access: Yes.

Here's a great taste of Texas on the River Walk in a restaurant that's on the street level indoors, but with a second-story view of the goings-on along the river. Although the Texas-sized steaks, chicken-fried steak, catfish, baked potatoes, and onion rings served with Texas beer and wine are delicious inside, they're even tastier if you climb the stairs from the river up to the porch way up under the leafy branches of the trees overhanging the river. Live country music Thursday and Friday nights.

Mariachi musicians at El Mercado's famous Mi Tierra Cafe & Bakery pose for the camera.

Eleanor S. Morris

MI TIERRA CAFE & BAKERY
210-225-1262.
www.mitierracafe.com.
218 Produce Row, San Antonio, TX 78207.
On Market Square.
Price: Inexpensive to Moderate.
Cuisine: Mexican.
Serving: Open 24 hours daily.
Credit Cards: AE, D, DC, MC, V.
Handicap Access: Yes.

Mi Tierra is where all visitors go sooner or later — it's another San Antonio classic. Huge colorful murals cover the walls of the — what else? — Mural Room, and the lobby boasts the "world-famous" Mariachi Bar. Mexican dishes, such as chiles rellenos, cabrito alhorno, and gallina en mole are relished to the sound of soulful mariachi music nightly. Take a number and join the lineup in front of the bakery counters at the entrance to purchase fresh Mexican pastries: empanadas (fruit turnovers), pan dulce (sweet rolls), and that creamy Mexican sweet, dulce de leche (condensed milk candy).

THE ORIGINAL MEXICAN RESTAURANT
210-224-9951.
528 River Walk, San Antonio, TX 78205.
Price: Inexpensive to Moderate.
Cuisine: Mexican.
Serving: L, D.
Credit Cards: AE, D, DC, MC, V.
Handicap Access: Yes.

You're certain to get a combination of authentic Mexican food and authentic San Antonio history here, both paying tribute to the restaurant's origins in 1899, when it defined Mexican food for San Antonio. A "new" site overlooking the river was dug out in 1960 from beneath D. Heye & Company Saddlery (famous for outfitting Teddy Roosevelt's Rough Riders). Saturday and Sunday evenings from 6 to 9 you'll enjoy strolling mariachi musicians.

REPUBLIC OF TEXAS
210-226-6256.

Although the Republic of Texas is long gone, this restaurant keeps the memory alive and well.

sanantoniocitysearch.com, search: Republic of Texas.
526 River Walk, San Antonio, TX 78205.
Price: Moderate.
Cuisine: American, Tex-Mex.
Serving: L, D.
Credit Cards: AE, D, MC, V.
Handicap Access: Yes.

Outdoors along the river, you'll dine under red, white, and blue Lone Star–decorated umbrellas. The margaritas are Texas-sized — all the food is, actually, so bring an appetite.

Tortilla soup with tomato, tortilla chips, and melted cheese for a starter; enchiladas — rojo, chicken, cheese — smothered in delicious sauce that enhances the beans and crispy Spanish rice; scoops of guacamole atop shredded lettuce and chopped tomato . . . it's pretty much all typical Tex-Mex, but especially flavorful and well done. And you can have the likes of grilled chicken in a special sauce if that's your choice, and that will be very flavorful too.

TOMATILLOS CAFE Y CANTINA
210-824-3005.
3210 Broadway, San Antonio, TX 78209.
Price: Inexpensive.
Cuisine: Mexican.
Serving: L, D.
Credit Cards: AE, D, MC, V.
Handicap Access: Yes.

Award-winning margaritas, served with big smiles, and a fiesta party atmosphere characterize Tomatillos Cafe y Cantina. The food is Tex-Mex and good, beginning with their quesadilla appetizers and on to the enchiladas, tamales, and burritos.

TOWER OF THE AMERICAS RESTAURANT
210-223-3101.
www.toweroftheamericas.com.
222 HemisFair Plaza, San Antonio, TX 78205.
Price: Expensive.
Cuisine: American, Southwestern.
Serving: L, D daily.
Credit Cards: All.
Handicap Access: Yes.

Take an elevator ride into the clouds for some fine dining. Tables for four to six line the wide glass observation windows in the revolving dining room (with others on a tier above), providing quite a view of San Antonio from 750 feet in the air. Dishes like the sky-high shrimp and Brie bisque, grilled asparagus, lobster tail, and prime rib are a treat. (If you make a reservation in advance, a shuttle will pick you up and return you to your downtown hotel.)

Enjoy live jazz piano in the High in the Sky Lounge on Friday and Saturday nights.

ZUNI GRILL
210-227-0864.
www.joesfood.com.
511 River Walk, San Antonio, TX 78205.
Price: Expensive.
Cuisine: Southwestern, New Mexican.

Attractive wrought-iron chairs and bright tile-topped tables make this an attractive place to eat and people-watch. The restaurant is opposite one of the high arched bridges that cross the river, and there's a small garden between the river and the restaurant. Zuni's adventurous menu includes fresh anchovy bread, applewood-smoked salmon,

Serving: B, L, D.
Credit Cards: AE, DC, MC, V.
Handicap Access: Yes, elevator at Hyatt Hotel next door.

blue corn enchiladas, black bean soup with white cheddar cheese, and spinach or duck quesadillas.

SAN ANTONIO FOOD PURVEYORS

This sampling of San Antonio food purveyors focuses on the downtown and River Walk areas.

Marble Slab Creamery has several locations. Try the one at Rivercenter Mall on the river level (849 E. Commerce St., San Antonio, TX 78203) or the one at North Star Mall (Loop 410 and San Pedro, San Antonio, TX 78212). In both you can enjoy fresh homemade ice cream with a choice of more than 30 mix-ins.

Mi Tierra Cafe & Bakery (210-225-1262; www.mitierracafe.com; 218 Produce Row, San Antonio, TX 78207, on Market Square) is good for Mexican pastries and other specialties (see "Restaurants" for more information).

Pecan Street Delicatessen (210-227-3226; 152 E. Pecan St., San Antonio, TX 78205, corner of St. Mary's) The name may not match this deli, which calls itself an "exotic Mediterranean deli," but the menu does. Try a Greek gyro of beef and lamb on handmade pita bread, or a "Pita the Great," a whole-wheat pita pocket filled with hummus, tabouli, tomatoes, feta cheese, and kalamata olives. Then there's the muffaletta, herb-and-cheese-crusted focaccia bread topped with smoked ham, Genoa salami, provolone, and its own olive mix. This is a busy place, packed with small round tables and bentwood chairs all crammed together, and everyone's friendly. Come for breakfast or lunch, Mon.–Fri. 7:30am–3pm, Sat. 10am–3pm.

Schilo's Delicatessen (210-223-6692; 424 E. Commerce St., San Antonio, TX 78205; B, L, D, closed Sun.) Here's another San Antonio classic, from 1917 no less, consistently voted the best German restaurant for miles around. Not at all fancy, the large storefront restaurant's decor consists of an acrylic tile floor of many colors, old wooden tables and booths, and high ceilings, highlighted by three flags — American, Mexican, and Austrian — and lots of beer signs. The mustard and horseradish is homemade, as is the root beer in a barrel in the rear. Split pea soup and potato pancakes are a specialty, along with bratwurst, wiener schnitzel, and cheesecake. Come Saturday night the place resounds with the music of Terry Cavanaugh.

COFFEEHOUSES

Of coffeehouses there are dozens, all over town. The San Antonio visitor on the River Walk in need of a caffeine (or decaf) lift might try **Starbucks** of the national chain (210-229-4445; 111 W. Crockett St. W., San Antonio, TX 78205).

**CANDLELIGHT
COFFEEHOUSE**
210-738-0099.
3011 N. St. Mary's St., San
Antonio, TX 78210.

This aptly named coffeehouse keeps late hours. It's open from 4pm until midnight on week nights and from 4pm to 1am on Friday and Saturday. The coffee is rich but not too strong, and you can design your own sandwich from a variety of gourmet breads and fillings. Also offered are soups, pastas, desserts, and wine.

**ESPUMA COFFEE AND
TEA EMPORIUM**
210-226-1912.
928 S. Alamo St., San
Antonio, TX 78210.

Folks come from all over the city to this popular coffeehouse in the King William Historic District. Local artists' works grace the brightly painted walls, and along with coffee you can enjoy light fare such as soups and sandwiches. Live music, too, on most Friday nights.

SAN ANTONIO CULTURE

Eleanor S. Morris

The Alamo, former Spanish mission and the site of a storied battle for Texas independence.

As a service of San Antonio's **Office of Cultural Affairs**, recorded information on music and theater performances, literary events, dance, museums, and visual arts is available by calling 210-222-ARTS, visiting their Web site at www.sanantonio.gov/art/website, or writing them at PO Box 839966, San Antonio, TX 78283.

ARCHITECTURE

San Antonio is variously described as picturesque, charming, even quaint. All of these terms can be used to describe the city's architecture because the buildings don't reflect any one influence. When the city was founded in 1718 by Spanish soldiers and settlers, they brought with them a strong Baroque style. Next came Anglo, German, and French immigrants, bringing their own architectural styles. Art Deco had its day, too, in the 1920s and '30s.

The climate also exerted an influence; to many of these various styles were added the thick walls, covered walks, and broad overhangs that provide protection from the heat, creating a style of architecture that became uniquely San Antonio. The Spanish influence is best seen in the missions and the architecture of such buildings as **La Mansion del Rio** (see "Lodging"). The post–Civil War homes of the **King William Historic District** are a mixture of Greek Revival, Romanesque, Palladian, and other styles, and many are the work of English-born architect Albert Giles, who designed numerous other structures in the Hill Country. The **Kress Building** (315 E. Houston) has an Art Deco storefront in shades of pink, yellow, green, and copper terra-cotta; the tall **Casino Club Building,** on a triangular lot (102 E. Crockett), crowns its Art Deco style with an eye-catching blue dome.

But it's the **Paseo del Rio,** the River Walk, that makes San Antonio unique. The San Antonio River, below street level, winds its way through the downtown and is lined with lush gardens, restaurants, nightclubs, and shops. Arched bridges provide access to each side of the river, and barges float down the center, filled with sight-seers enjoying both the ride and the view.

DANCE

San Antonio is host to a variety of dance events, from ballet to cloggers to ethnic to visiting companies. For information on dance activities, which take place at performance spaces throughout the city, contact **San Antonio Dance Umbrella** (210-212-7775; 825 S. St. Mary's St., San Antonio, TX 78205).

GALLERIES

San Antonio's abundance of ethnic cultures — Native American, Anglo, Spanish, Mexican, German, African-American, and Latin American — all contribute to an array of sophisticated art galleries displaying a wide variety of international and regional art. Here is a sampling:

Blue Star Art Space (210-227-6960; 116 Blue Star St., San Antonio, TX 78204) An 11,000-square-foot showcase in the King William Historic District, housing art by regional, national, and international artists. The complex is run by the artists themselves.

Chamade Jewelers (210-224-7753; www.lavillita.com/chamade.html; 504 Villita St., San Antonio, TX 78205) Made-to-order jewelry as well as pieces imported from France and Italy; platinum, silver, and precious stones.

Galeria Ortiz (210-225-0731; www.galeriaortiz.com; 248 Losoya St., San Antonio, TX 78205; also at 102 Concho St., San Antonio, TX 78207) The gallery specializes in contemporary Southwestern art. Paintings, sculpture, folk art, silver jewelry, and gift items are collected in two locations: Losoya St. is in the Alamo Historic District downtown, and Concho St. is in Market Square.

Harry Halff Fine Art (210-822-0713; www.harryhalff.com; 7726 Broadway, San Antonio, TX 78209) European, American, and early Texas paintings and works on paper are the specialty here.

Little Studio Gallery of La Villita (210-227-8893; 103 King Phillip V St., San Antonio, TX 78205) Here you'll find local artists displaying their oil paintings, watercolors, acrylics, and other works, all for sale.

Monte Wade Fine Arts (210-222-8838; 514 Paseo de la Villita St., San Antonio, TX 78205) Spirit warriors, star travelers, raku ceramics, and other diverse styles and flavors of the Southwest are captured here, in both contemporary and classic works.

Southwest School of Art and Craft (210-224-1848; www.swschool.org; 300 Augusta St., San Antonio, TX 78205) This former convent has been put to work as an art center, with galleries, studios, and classrooms. Commissioned in 1848 by the French Catholic order, today within the old walls the Ursuline Gallery sells contemporary crafts from all over the United States in addition to the works of the craft center's teachers, students, and other local artists. You'll find art accessories, ceramics, glass and textiles, jewelry, and other wearable art.

GUIDED TOURS

Gray Line Tours San Antonio (210-226-1706, 800-472-9546; www.grayline.com; 217 Alamo Plaza, Suite B, San Antonio, TX 78205) A selection of tours, among them Alamo and the Mission Trail, San Antonio Sampler, and Texas Hill Country Escape.

Lone Star Trolley Company (210-226-1706; 217 Alamo Plaza, PO Box 2508, San Antonio, TX 78299) Tickets and boarding only at the corner of Crockett and Alamo Sts. across Alamo Plaza from the Alamo.

San Antonio City Tours (210-247-0238; www.sanantoniocitytours.com; Alamo Visitor Center, 216 Alamo Plaza, San Antonio, TX 78205) Professionally narrated tours on air-conditioned buses of the Alamo, the missions, Market Square, King William Historic District, and other local attractions.

Texas Trolley (210-227-0238; Alamo Visitor Center, 216 E. Crockett St, San Antonio, TX 78205, at the Alamo Plaza) The trolley makes seven stops so passengers can get off and explore at their leisure, then hop back on at their own convenience. Trolley stops include the Alamo, Market Square, Mission Concepcion, IMAX Theater, HemisFair, and more.

HISTORIC SITES AND DISTRICTS

The Alamo Cenotaph on Alamo Plaza, memorial to the heroes of the Alamo.

Eleanor S. Morris

THE ALAMO
210-225-1391.
www.thealamo.org.
PO Box 2599, San Antonio, TX 78299.
Alamo Plaza, bet. Houston and Commerce Sts.
Open: Mon.–Sat.
   9am–5:30pm, Sun.
   10am–5:30pm; closed
   Christmas Eve and
   Christmas Day.
Admission: Free. Donations accepted.

Established in 1716 as the Misión San Antonio de Valero, the building was abandoned as a mission long before the events that earned its place in history: On February 23, 1836, a handful of men, defending the building against the Mexican forces led by Gen. Santa Anna, died to the last one. "Remember the Alamo!" became a cry that inspired the final victory that won Texas its independence from Mexico. The Daughters of the Republic of Texas have established both a shrine and exhibits about the battle and the defenders of the fort. The shrine is simple, a dignified memorial to those who are considered the state's first heroes — although they came from many states, even other countries. The atmosphere is hushed and reverential as visitors move through the old stone building.

The Alamo cenotaph on Alamo Plaza in front of the Alamo is a tribute to the Texas heroes who lost their lives defending the Alamo. The sculpture, by Pompeo Coppini, was dedicated during the Texas Centennial of 1936.

SPANISH GOVERNOR'S PALACE
210-224-0601.

Built in 1749 — and dubbed by the National Geographic Society "the most beautiful building in San Antonio" — this national historic landmark

105 Plaza de Armas, San Antonio, TX 78205.
Open: Mon.–Sat. 9am–5pm, Sun. 10am–5pm.
Admission: Adults $1, children 7–13 50¢, under 7 free.

housed the officials of what was then the Spanish province of Texas. It's claimed to be the only remaining early aristocratic home in all of Texas.

King William Historic District, a 25-block neighborhood of restored early Texas homes, begins at the corner of King William and South St. Mary's Sts., on the south bank of the San Antonio River. It was the city's most elegant residential neighborhood in the 1800s, and it's once again a fashionable area, with many of the old homes remodeled and restored. The San Antonio Conservation Society (210-224-6163; 107 King William St., San Antonio, TX 78204) provides a walking tour brochure, or visit their Web site at www.saconservation.org to take a virtual tour.

La Villita means "little village," and this walled square block in the heart of downtown was the original settlement of old San Antonio; it's on the National Register of Historic Places as a historic district. The houses have been restored and are now occupied by artists' and artisans' studios, shops, and restaurants open daily (210-207-8610; www.lavillita.com for a virtual tour; 418 Villita, San Antonio, TX 78205, at Presa St.).

Sunset Station (210-222-9481; 1174 E. Commerce St., San Antonio, TX 78205), set in the 1902 Southern Pacific railroad depot in the heart of the St. Paul Square Historical District, is designed to be an urban entertainment center. Here you'll find all the facets of San Antonio's rich and diverse culture. The complex consists of indoor venues, with an outdoor pavilion and amphitheater.

MUSEUMS

BUCKHORN SALOON AND MUSEUM
210-247-4000.
www.buckhornsaloon.com.
318 E. Houston St., San Antonio, TX 78205.
Open: 10am–5pm daily.
Admission: Adults $9.99, seniors $9, children 3–12 $7.50.

Before you take in this wild place with more than 3,500 specimens of game animals either stuffed in their entirety or mounted on the walls, be sure to "belly up to the bar." In this, its new home, the museum has included a virtual recreation of an 118-year-old saloon, where you can step up to the same bar or sit at the same tables where cowboys and cattlemen have enjoyed themselves for ages. And sometimes gunfights take place out front at high noon (of course!), usually on Saturday and Sunday.

INSTITUTE OF TEXAN CULTURES
210-458-2300.
www.texancultures.utsa.edu.

The museum was founded for the interpretation and assimilation of Texas history and folk culture; every ethnic group that helped to form Texas is represented in depth. Many of the entertaining and

The Missions

Eleanor S. Morris

The Mission San José was founded in 1720.

San Antonio has four missions established in the 18th century by Spanish priests: San José, Concepción, Espada, and San Juan. Operated by the San Antonio Missions National Historical Park (210-534-8833), they are still active as parish churches. All are open to the public daily 9–5; admission is free.

Mission Concepción (210-534-1540; 807 Mission Rd., San Antonio, TX 78210) Built in 1731, this is considered the oldest unrestored stone church in the country. Remaining are the church, sacristy, and several convent rooms.

Mission San Francisco de la Espada (210-627-2021; 10040 Espada Rd., San Antonio, TX 78214) This is the smallest mission, known for its unique archway and nearby stone aqueduct. It was established in 1731, and the Indian quarters are still there, but they have not been restored. Guided tours are available.

Mission San José (210-932-1001; 6701 San José Dr., San Antonio, TX 78214) Called "the Queen of the Missions," San José, built in 1720, is noted for its beautiful rose window. The mission is set in a large walled compound, and, in addition to the church, a granary and Indian quarters have been restored. It's still a working church: masses are held Mon.–Fri. 8am; Sat. 5:30pm; Sun. 7:45am (Spanish), 9am, and 10:30am, and at noon there is a mariachi mass. Guided tours are available.

Mission San Juan Capistrano (210-534-0749; 9101 Graf Rd., San Antonio, TX 78214) Nestled in a rural setting, with rare statues, this, too, is still an active church, with masses Tues.–Fri. 8am (Spanish); Sat. 6pm; Sun. 9am, 10:30am (Spanish), and noon.

801 S. Bowie St., San Antonio, TX 78205. At Durango Blvd.
Open: Tues.–Sun. 9am–5pm; closed Mon., Thanksgiving, Christmas.
Admission: Adults $5, seniors $3, children 3–12 $2, under 3 free.

instructive displays and discussions of Texas history and culture are geared to the younger set.

INSTITUTO CULTURAL MEXICANO
210-227-0123.
600 HemisFair Plaza Way, San Antonio, TX 78205.
Open: Tues.–Fri. 10am–5pm., Sat. & Sun. 11am–5pm.
Admission: Free.

Lectures, exhibits, films, and visual and performing arts are presented for an understanding and appreciation of the Hispanic culture so much a part of San Antonio. The gift shop features quality Mexican folk art as well as books and art posters.

McNAY ART MUSEUM
210-824-5368.
www.mcnayart.org.
6000 N. New Braunfels, San Antonio, TX 78209.
At U.S. 81 Business Hwy.
Open: Tues.–Sat. 10am–5pm, Sun. noon–5pm.
Admission: Free except for some special exhibitions and events; donations accepted.

The museum is housed in a 24-room mansion once belonging to artist and art collector Marion Koogler McNay, who was "steadfast in her commitment to the advancement and enjoyment of modern art." Here you'll find not only changing exhibits and a fine collection of 19th- and 20th-century art but also collections of post-Impressionist paintings, early New Mexican arts and crafts, and medieval and Gothic art.

PIONEER TRAIL DRIVERS AND TEXAS RANGERS MEMORIAL MUSEUM
210-822-9011.
3805 Broadway, San Antonio, TX 78205.
Memorial Mall in Brackenridge Park, next to Witte Museum.
Open: May–Aug. 9am–4pm daily; Sept.–Apr. 11am–4pm daily.
Admission: Adults $3, seniors $2, children 6–12 $1.

A combined effort of the Texas Trail Drivers Association and the Texas Rangers Association, this museum celebrates the history of "Old Texas," with memorabilia from early cattle ranching and trail drive days.

SAN ANTONIO MUSEUM OF ART & NELSON A. ROCKEFELLER CENTER FOR LATIN AMERICAN ART
210-978-8100.
www.sa-museum.org.
200 W. Jones Ave., San Antonio, TX 78215.
Open: Tues. 10am–9pm, Weds.–Sat. 10am–5pm, Sun. noon–5pm; closed Thanksgiving and Christmas.
Admission: Adults $6, seniors and students with ID $5, children 4–11 $4, under 3 free. Free Tues. 3–9pm.

Housed in a restored 1884 brewery, the building has glass elevators, skylights, and a skywalk. The collection of Asian art and Latin American folk art is considered the most comprehensive in the southern United States. There are also exhibits of Greek and Roman antiquities and contemporary art; in 1998 the museum opened the country's first center for the study and appreciation of Latin American art.

WITTE MUSEUM
210-357-1900.
www.wittemuseum.org.
3801 Broadway, San Antonio, TX 78209.
Open: Mon., Weds.–Sat. 10am–5pm, Tues. 10am–9pm; Sun. noon–5pm; closed Thanksgiving, Christmas Eve, and Christmas Day.
Admission: Adults $5.95, seniors $4.95, children 4–11 $3.95. Free Tues. 3–9pm.

In this museum of natural history and science, exhibits include native American and Texas natural and social history, such as "Dinosaurs: Vanished Texas," and natural science. Exhibits include discoveries and hands-on experiences. Don't miss the H-E-B Science Treehouse, a four-level hands-on exhibit space with, yes, a real tree house — plus outdoor water exhibits on the San Antonio River.

MUSIC AND NIGHTLIFE

Most of San Antonio's nightlife centers around the River Walk.

Durty Nelly's Irish Pub (210-222-1400; 200 South Alamo St., San Antonio, TX 78205) is as authentic an Irish pub as you're likely to find this side of Erin. Frosty beer helps the old-time sing-alongs along; professional entertainment nightly as well.

Howl at the Moon Saloon (210-212-4695; 111 W. Crockett St., San Antonio, TX 78205, overlooking the River Walk) has been voted the "town's best piano bar" in a local poll. The original Dueling Pianos pound out high-energy, all-request, rock 'n' roll sing-along fun nightly until 2am. Cover charge; entertainment.

Jim Cullum's Landing (210-223-7266; www.landing.com; 123 Losoya St., San Antonio, TX 78205) is the place for exciting nonstop jazz from high noon until the wee hours of the morning. Food, too: the lunch and dinner menus feature southern-style Cajun dishes.

Rivercenter Comedy Club (210-229-1420; 849 E. Commerce St., San Antonio, TX 78205, fourth level of Rivercenter Mall) features stand-up comedy entertainment at the far end of the River Walk. Optional is the dinner-show package.

The **San Antonio Symphony** (210-554-1010; www.sasymphony.org; 222 E. Houston St., San Antonio, TX 78205) performs in the Majestic Performing Arts Center, also the place to see other concerts and touring Broadway shows.

Sunset Station (see "Historic Sites and Districts") is an entertainment complex consisting of five indoor music venues, as well as an outdoor amphitheater and pavilion, with live music and casual theme restaurants.

SEASONAL EVENTS

This happy party town has so many festivals it's impossible to list them all. Contact the **San Antonio Convention & Visitors Bureau** (210-207-6700, 800-447-3372; www.sanantoniocvb.com; Visitor Information Center, 317 Alamo Plaza, San Antonio, TX 78205) for a full list. Meanwhile, here are some highlights:

JANUARY comes in with a bang with a **Cowboy Breakfast**. More than 35,000 cups of coffee, 15,000 breakfast tacos, and 10,000 sausage biscuits are served up free at Sunset Station along with live entertainment (210-287-6110). Also in January, the **Martin Luther King Jr. Rally**. And in either January or February, depending on when the work is done, there's the **River Walk Mud Festival** in honor of the annual river cleanup, with a king and queen elected for the occasion.

FEBRUARY brings the excitement of the **San Antonio Stock Show & Rodeo**, with 16 days of livestock judging, rodeo action, carnival fun, and country-western stars at SBC Center (210-225-5851; www.sarodeo.com). Events include an Arts and Crafts Festival (210-227-4262).

MARCH brings **St. Patrick's Day**, with a variety of events. There's an Irish Festival at La Villita and the Arneson River Theater; a 5K run; a golf tournament; a street parade and a river parade on the River Walk, which follows the Dyeing o' the River Green; and solemn ceremonies at the Alamo to honor the fallen heroes.

In APRIL the annual **Tejano Music Awards** is such a big and important event for the artists and fans of Tejano music that it's held at the Alamodome (210-222-8862, 300-500-8470). There's also the annual **Starving Artist Art Show** (210-226-3593), with about a thousand artists exhibiting and selling their work to support the Little Church of La Villita's program to aid the less fortunate. Later in the month comes the biggest celebration of the year, **Fiesta San Antonio** — nine days of parades, carnivals, sporting events, band concerts, art shows, and elegant balls are among the more than 100 events to attend (877-SA-FIESTA; www.fiesta-sa.org).

MAY has a number of festivals, too. Among them, the **Tejano Conjunto Festival** is a six-day celebration of the music born in South Texas, a mixture of Mexican and German. It's celebrated, studied, and performed at the Guadalupe Cultural Arts Center (210-271-3151; www.guadalupeculturalarts.org). **Cinco de Mayo** commemorates the Battle of Puebla between Mexican and French forces. May also is **Dance Month,** in various locations around the city (210-222-5787; www.sanantonio.gov/art). The Memorial Day weekend is marked by the annual **Return of the Chili Queens** (210-207-8601) to celebrate chili at Market Square. What began as the concoction of the women who set up their stands in the plazas at night in old San Antonio became known as chili.

JUNE celebrates **Juneteenth**, with observances throughout the city honoring the date in 1865 that Texas slaves received word of the Emancipation Proclamation. The annual **Texas Folklife Festival** is a four-day celebration of some 30 cultures and ethnic groups whose traditions have shaped Texas. Enjoy ethnic entertainment, food, dances, games, and craft demonstrations at the Institute of Texan Cultures (210-458-2300; www.texancultures.utsa.edu).

One of the festivals in JULY lasts the entire month. The annual **Contemporary Art Month** features dozens of events involving scores of artists, performers, and musicians in a celebration of San Antonio's creative community (210-222-2787; www.sanantonio.gov/art). Right at the start of the month, of course, comes the **July 4th Celebration**, which San Antonio celebrates with festivals, concerts, and fireworks all across the city (800-447-3372 for details and schedule).

AUGUST sees the start of Class 1 Thoroughbred horse racing at the **Thoroughbred Meet**, held all month (and through October 29) at Retama Park Racetrack (210-651-7000; www.retamapark.com). Also this month, watch the **Annual Scout Canoe Challenge** at the SBC/IBC Plaza (210-227-4262; River Walk Association, 213 Broadway St., San Antonio, TX 78205). Also, jumping the gun, is the **Labor Day Arts & Crafts Fair** on the River Walk (210-227-4262).

Come SEPTEMBER San Antonio helps our neighbors south of the border celebrate Mexican independence during the annual **Diez y Seis de Septiembre**. The Mexican Consul General's office honors Mexico's independence with an enactment of "El Grito," the cry by Father Hidalgo on September 16, 1810, that launched Mexico's rebellion against Spain. This is the signal for music and dance all over the city: La Villita, the Arneson River Theater, Market Square, Guadalupe Plaza, and Plaza Mexico at HemisFair Park (210-223-3151).

Also in September, the annual **Jazz's Alive** features jazz bands from New Orleans and San Antonio, sponsored by the San Antonio Parks and Recreation Department at Travis Park downtown (210-207-8480; www.ci.sat.tx.us/sapar).

In OCTOBER , **Oktoberfest San Antonio** takes place on two successive weekends, bringing authentic German food and drink along with brass bands (210-222-1521). Midmonth see the annual **Cojunto Shootout**, a battle of the bands Cojunto style, free in Market Square (210-207-8000). Also this month are the **Halloween** and **Día de los Muertos** (the Day of the Dead) celebrations, held in Market Square (210-207-8600).

The beginning of NOVEMBER sees **Los Altares del Mercado,** many altars created by local communities also honoring the dead, at Market Square (210-207-8601). In this tradition of the Mexican Amerindians, families decorate graves and make marigold altars, pan de muerto, candles, and food offerings for the dead (210-434-6711, ext. 240 or 254). In late November Santa Claus arrives by river — the San Antonio River, of course — in a floating procession ushering in the **Holiday River Parade and Lighting Ceremony**. Some 70,000 Christmas lights on trees and bridges make a fairyland of the Paseo del Rio (210-227-4262).

Following closely, at the beginning of DECEMBER , thousands of candles illuminate the River Walk in the **Fiesta de las Luminarias**. In the middle of the month, the San Antonio Preservation Society presents its annual recreation of **Las Posadas**, a 16th-century religious pageant. Citizens, choirs, mariachis, and visitors join in a candlelit procession from La Mansion del Rio to the Arneson River Theater, reenacting the search for shelter by Mary and Joseph (210-224-6163; www.saconservation.org).

THEATER

One of the many delightful adornments of the River Walk in San Antonio is the Arneson River Theater.

Eleanor S. Morris

Recorded information about theater and other San Antonio performances is provided by the **City of San Antonio Office of Cultural Affairs** at 210-207-8483 or 800-894-3819 and at its Web site, www.ci.sat.tx.us/DACA.

Alamo Street Restaurant and Theater (210-271-7791; 1150 S. Alamo St., San Antonio, TX 78210) Housed in a building listed on the National Register of Historic Places, the restaurant/theater serves home-style cooking seasoned with Texas playwrights.

Arneson River Theater (210-227-4262; 418 La Villita, San Antonio, TX 78205, on the River Walk) A 1939 WPA project, the theater has an open stage on one side of the river and audience seating on the other side. Drama and dance performances are offered here monthly.

Guadalupe Cultural Arts Center (210-271-3151; 1300 Guadalupe St., San Antonio, TX 78207) With performances fusing theater, music, and dance, this group has become a pacesetter in the country for Hispanic theater. Original plays are performed in both English and Spanish at the beautifully restored Guadalupe Theater, and many have been produced by Hispanic companies in other cities.

Harlequin Dinner Theater (210-222-9694; 2652 Harney Rd., San Antonio, TX 78234) Dinner here, out on the Fort Sam Houston Military Base, is a somewhat formal affair. Cocktails are served in the lounge, and there's a salad bar and a choice of three or four home-style dinner entrées. The shows are on the light side, usually such enduring musicals, mysteries, and comedies as *Arsenic and Old Lace*.

IMAX Theater Rivercenter (210-225-4629; 849 E. Commerce St., San Antonio, TX 78205, Rivercenter Mall, second level) A good way to get into the spirit of Texas and the Alamo is to take in *The Alamo* . . . *The Price of Freedom*, a 45-minute documentary that's larger than life on the six-story screen, with a six-track stereo sound system. *The Alamo* is always on, but in addition there are other offerings; call for titles and show times. Admission: adults $8.95, seniors and youth $7.95, children 3–11 $5.50.

Magik Children's Theatre of San Antonio (210-227-2751; www.magiktheatre.org; 420 S. Alamo St. in Hemisphere Park, San Antonio, TX 78205) A daytime and evening series of professional performances for children.

Majestic Theatre (210-226-3333; 226 E. Houston St., San Antonio, TX 78205) This refurbished 1928 movie house is an attraction on its own, performances or not. This ornate fantasy of design features the towers and arches of a Moorish palace lining the walls and reaching up to the twinkling stars in the sky, and cherubs with musical instruments perched on the proscenium arch. Call for more information about performances, which include film, dance, Broadway shows, and music.

San Pedro Playhouse (210-733-7258; 800 E. Ashby Pl., San Antonio, TX 78205, in San Pedro Park) The San Pedro opened in 1929 as the home of the oldest civic company in San Antonio, the San Antonio Little Theater. The Doric columns supporting the imposing Greek edifice come from an older structure known as Old Market House.

SAN ANTONIO RECREATION

THE ALAMODOME
210-554-7700, 800-884-3663.
www.nba.com/spurs/.
100 Montana St., San
Antonio, TX 78205.

Flexibility is the key to the multipurpose Alamodome, with architectural and design elements combined to provide an ideal setting for expositions, trade shows, annual conventions, sports events, and entertainment venues. Past events include NBA All-Star Games, Big 12 Conference Games, Campbell Soups Champions on Ice, and concerts by such performing artists as KISS, George Strait, and Elton John. The NBA San Antonio Spurs also call the Alamodome home. Phone or visit the Alamodome Web site to see what's on when you're in town.

BICYCLING

For bicycling, boating, and other water sports, and for horseback riding, Brackenridge Park (see "Parks") is the place.

CAMPING

Alamo KOA Kampgrounds (210-224-9296; 602 Gembler Rd., San Antonio, TX 78219) Less than 10 minutes from downtown. Complete facilities for campers, tenters, and trailers in a parklike setting with 400 modern spaces, a pool and spa, supplies, and propane — and on a city bus line to boot.
Blazing Star Luxury RV Resort, Camping, Parks and Beaches (877-387-5777; 1120 W. Loop 1604, San Antonio, TX 78219) 260 sites with full hookups, water, electricity, sewer, and basic cable. Pull-through sites with trees and lush native Texas vegetation; three bathhouses with individual bathrooms; 8,000-square-foot clubhouse, general store, video game arcade, laundry room, and one- and two-bedroom cottages.

FAMILY FUN

San Antonio offers plenty of activities for children. In addition to those listed below, see the Magik Children's Theatre and the IMAX Theater Rivercenter (under "Theater") and several of the museums listed in "Museums."

SAN ANTONIO CHILDREN'S MUSEUM
210-212-4453.
www.sakids.org.
305 E. Houston St., San Antonio, TX 78205.
Open: Tues.–Fri. 9am–5pm, Sat. 9am–6pm, Sun. noon–5pm.
Admission: $4.

Hands-on and minds-open are the bywords for this museum. More than 80 exhibits are designed for children ages two to ten.

SAN ANTONIO ZOOLOGICAL GARDENS AND AQUARIUM
210-734-7183.
3903 N. St. Mary's St., San Antonio, TX 78212.
Brackenridge Park.
Open: Labor Day–Mem. Day, 9am–5pm daily; Mem. Day–Labor Day until 6pm.
Admission: Adults $7, seniors & kids 3–11 $5, under 3 free.

Widely acclaimed as an outstanding zoo, here are more than 50 acres tucked away in an abandoned rock quarry on the edge of Brackenridge Park, housing one of the largest collections of animals in the country: 3,400 specimens and 700 species. Particularly special is the African animal group, one of the largest and most varied in the world.

SEA WORLD OF TEXAS
210-523-3611.
www.seaworld.com.
10500 Sea World Dr., San Antonio, TX 78251.
Ellison Dr. and Westover Hills Blvd., off Hwy. 151 16 miles northwest of downtown San Antonio.
Open: Mar.–Oct. (weekends and some days in spring, daily in summer, weekends in fall). Call 210-523-3611 or see their Web site for latest schedules.
Admission: Adults $39.99 + tax, children 3–11 $29.99 + tax; 10 percent off adult price for seniors.

The world's largest marine adventure park, with more than 25 shows, exhibits, and rides. The park has the world's largest zoological population of Pacific white-sided dolphin, including the only two born in captivity.

Besides the "Great White," an inverted (upside-down) roller coaster, still going strong, there's the "Steel Eel," a hypercoaster with a 15-story drop and speeds of 70 mph, and the fast and furious "Rico Loco." There are also various water rides, a water park (Lost Lagoon), and the Texas Walk sculpture garden.

Now there's also the Sea Star Theater, a 4-D venue showing family-friendly films like *R. L. Stine's Haunted Lighthouse*, by the author of those popular children's books.

SIX FLAGS FIESTA TEXAS
210-697-5050.
www.sixflags.com.
PO Box 690290, San Antonio, TX 78264.
I-10 W. at La Cantera Pkwy.
Open: Hours vary. Call for info.
Admission: Adults $36.99, guests under 48 inches tall $22.99, seniors $24.99.

Exciting rides and spectacular shows promise fun for the whole family at this Texas park. The wild rides are roller-coasters Poltergeist and Boomerang; the Screamin' Skycoaster, a freefall adventure; and the Superman Krypton Coaster, billed "the only floorless coaster in the Southwest." And now you can be properly chilled and thrilled by "Scooby-Doo Ghostblasters — the Mystery of the Haunted Mansion."

TOWER OF THE AMERICAS
210-207-8615.
www.towerof the americas.com.
600 HemisFair Park, San Antonio, TX 78205.
Open: Observation deck 9am–10pm, Fri.–Sat. to 11pm.
Elevator Fees: Adults $4, seniors $2.50, children 4–11 $1.50.

Ride up the elevator inside this 750-foot tower and, if the wind is strong enough, you can feel the tower sway. At the summit, the observation deck presents a windy 360-degree view of all of San Antonio, and the restaurant (see "Restaurants") at the summit is a revolving one.

On the River and Around the City

It's fun to take a leisurely clip-clop drive in a horse-drawn carriage along San Antonio's historic streets. **Lone Star Carriage** (210-533-3977; 302 Iowa St., San Antonio, TX 78210) and **Yellow Rose Carriage** (210-337-6495; 100 S. Alamo St., San Antonio, TX 78219) provide this mode of seeing the city sights.

A river tour along the Paseo de Rio is offered by **Yanaguana Cruise Inc.** (210-244-5700, 800-417-4139; www.sarivercruise.com; 345 E. Commerce St., Ste. 202, San Antonio, TX 78205). A 35- to 40-minute narrated historic tour is $5.25 for adults, $3.65 for seniors, $1 for children 5 and under.

GOLF

San Antonio has 10 municipal and public golf courses — plus more than 300 days of sunshine per year. Call individual courses for greens fees and tee times. A San Antonio golfing guide is also available (call 800-447-3372 to ask for a copy, or log on to www.SanAntonioVisit.com).

Brackenridge Park (210-226-5612; 2800 N. Broadway, San Antonio, TX 78209) The oldest 18-hole public course in Texas. "Old Brack" opened in 1916 and in 1922 hosted the first Texas Open. With 6,185 yards, it is still a challenge.

Cedar Creek (210-695-5050; 8250 Vista Colina, San Antonio, TX 78255) In northwest San Antonio, this course is set on the picturesque southern border of the Hill Country, with steep elevation changes, several waterfalls, and other challenges.

Fair Oaks Ranch Golf & Country Club (830-981-9604; 7900 Fair Oaks Pkwy., San Antonio, TX 78006) Acreage in the hills, with two 18-hole courses in a beautiful Hill Country country-club atmosphere.

La Cantera Golf Club (210-558-4653; 16641 La Cantera Pkwy., San Antonio, TX 78256) Carved from the walls of a limestone quarry, this course includes a tee shot from atop an 80-foot quarry wall, aiming at Fiesta Texas's famous "Rattler" roller-coaster.

Mission del Lago Golf Club (210-627-2522; 1250 Mission Grande Rd., San Antonio, TX 78221) Built at the same time as Cedar Creek, but here the land is flatter and golfers contend with a Texas wind.

Olmos Basin Golf Course (210-826-4041; 7022 McCullough, San Antonio, TX 78216) One of the city's most popular courses, having hosted the men's city championship 27 times.

Pecan Valley Golf Course (210-333-9018, 800-336-3418; 4700 Pecan Valley Dr., San Antonio, TX 78223) Only minutes from downtown, this course was the site of the 50th PGA championship in 1968. Rated in *Golf Digest's* "Top 50 Public Courses."

Quarry Golf Club (210-824-4500; 444 E. Basse Rd., San Antonio, TX 78209; call for directions) Built on the 85-acre site of the former Alamo Cement Quarry in northeast San Antonio. Rated "#4 Best Course in Texas" by *Golf Digest* in 1995.

Riverside Golf Course (210-533-8371; 203 McDonald, San Antonio, TX 78210) Right on the land where Teddy Roosevelt trained his Rough Riders. Opened in 1929 as a 9-hole course; 11 more were added in 1961, all par 3s. A full-size 18-hole championship course offers "6,729 yards of fun."

Silverhorn Golf Club of Texas (210-545-5300; 1100 W. Bitters Rd., San Antonio, TX 78216) On a 262-acre tract at Blanco and Bitters in North San Antonio, the city's newest course may be one of its finest, with a classic 7,000-yard layout.

Six driving ranges are also located around the city: **Alamo Country Club** (210-696-4000; 9700 Rochelle Rd., San Antonio, TX 78240) is an 18-holer, with discount pro shop, concessions, and PGA professional instructors. **Allgolf at Panther Springs** (210-492-7888; 16900 Blanco Rd., San Antonio, TX 78232) has a putting and chipping green, club repair, and weekly putting contests. **Blossom Golf Center** (210-494-0002; 13800 Jones Maltsberger Rd., San Antonio, TX 78247) is a practice and teaching center, with a full staff of PGA professionals offering clinics and private instruction; club rental available, plus a snack bar. The hitting area of **Polo Field Driving and Practice Range** (210-736-9592; 915 E. Mulberry, San Antonio, TX 78212) accommodates 60 people, with a driving range of 450 yards, separate putting and chipping greens, and a sand trap. **San Pedro Driving Range and Par 3** (210-349-5113; 6102 San Pedro Ave., San Antonio, TX 78216) accommodates 50 people in the hitting area and offers lessons and many junior golf activities.

PARKS

Brackenridge Park (210-207-3000, 210-207-8590; 2800 N. Broadway, San Antonio, TX 78209) In the center of town are some 443 acres of wooded parkland, with a playground and picnic area and the nationally recognized San Antonio Zoo; Japanese tea gardens, with outstanding floral displays and ponds; the Witte Museum; a golf course and polo field; a miniature railroad, carousel, skyride, paddleboats, and horse and bike trails.

HemisFair Park/Tower of the Americas (210-207-8610; 200 S. Alamo, San Antonio, TX 78205, bounded by S. Alamo and Durango, next to Convention Center) This city park, with cascading water gardens, children's playground, and museums, is on the site of the 1968 World's Fair and includes the Institute of Texas Cultures and the Mexican Cultural Institute.

Paseo del Rio: The River Walk (210-227-4262; Paseo del Rio Association, 213 Broadway St., San Antonio, TX 78205) It may come as a surprise to learn that the famous Paseo del Rio, the River Walk, is operated as a city park. Nestled 20 feet below street level, the cobblestone and flagstone paths border both sides of the San Antonio River as it winds through the very heart of downtown, the center of the business district. Stretching for about 2.5 miles, from the Municipal Auditorium and Conference Center on the north end to the King William Historic District on the south, most of the walkways, arched bridges, and entrance steps were completed between 1939 and 1941. It remained a park until 1968, when San Antonio hosted the HemisFair World's Fair. Now the banks are lined with restaurants and shops, with a few quiet, parklike stretches in between. The area is partially accessible to the handicapped.

SAN ANTONIO BOTANICAL GARDENS AND LUCILE HALSELL CONSERVATORY
210-207-3250.
www.sabot.org.
555 Funston Pl., San Antonio, TX 78209.
Open: Mar.–Oct. 9am–5pm daily; Nov.–Feb. 8am–5pm; closed Christmas and New Year's Day.
Admission: Adults $4, seniors $2, children 3–13 $1.

Of the garden's 33 acres, about half are dedicated to native Texas vegetation, where there are three gardens, each devoted to a specific ecological region of Texas: the Edwards Plateau (Hill Country), the east Texas Piney Woods, and the south Texas scrub country. Each garden also features a cabin characteristic of its region: a reconstructed stone house from the Hill Country, a log cabin from the Piney Woods, and an adobe structure typical of the scrub country.

The rest of the acreage is devoted to formal gardens, plus a conservatory complex of five buildings displaying plants from various climatic regions around the world. There is also a small Japanese garden, donated and built by residents of Kunamoto (San Antonio's Japanese sister city), and a garden for the blind featuring plants of unusual texture and scent, in elevated beds and with signs in Braille.

HORSE RACING

Horse-racing fans can visit **Retama Park Racetrack** (210-651-7000; www.retamapark.com; Retama Pkwy., I-35 at Loop 1604, Schertz, TX 78154), a Class 1 Thoroughbred and quarter horse track about 15 minutes north of downtown San Antonio. The track is open summer and fall for live racing; open daily year-round for simulcast racing. Admission: general $2.50; clubhouse $3.50).

TENNIS

San Antonio Parks and Recreation Dept. (210-207-PARK; www.co.tx.us/sapar) operates tennis courts throughout the city at 35 neighborhood parks.

McFarlin Tennis Center (210-732-1223; 1503 San Pedro Ave., San Antonio, TX 78212) A municipal center with 22 outdoor lighted courts at $1.50 per hour per person. After 5pm $2.50 per hour per person.

SAN ANTONIO SHOPPING

Uniquely San Antonio is **Market Square,** often referred to by the locals as El Mercado, Spanish for "market," after the large air-conditioned indoor mall within the square (210-207-8600; 514 W. Commerce St., San Antonio, TX 78207). On the square, historic buildings contain dozens of stores, galleries, gift and fashion stores, and restaurants. As for El Mercado itself, once you enter it's hard to remember that you're not actually south of the border: here you'll find the largest Mexican market outside of Mexico. El Mercado houses more than 32 specialty shops of Mexican curios, arts and crafts, glassware, ceramics, leather goods, clothing and accessories (such as serapes and sombreros), toys, gifts, and games.

ANTIQUES AND ART

Antiques at 115 Broadway (210-222-1265; 115 Broadway, San Antonio, TX 78205) This group of stores offers an assortment of jewelry, art, and furniture that, if not antique, are certainly collectible.

Galleria II (210-227-0527; 218 S. Presa, San Antonio, TX 78205) This artists' co-operative is housed in a Victorian building, circa 1873, in La Villita. Artists are at work here creating stained glass, pottery, and watercolors.

J. Adelman Antiques (210-225-5914; 202 Alamo Plaza, San Antonio, TX 78205) Located in the Menger Hotel (with another shop at 7601 Broadway). Here you'll find top-notch items, with jewelry, silver, etc. from estate sales and fine furniture imported from France and England.

River Square Antiques, Collectibles & Gifts (210-224-0900; 514 River Walk, San Antonio, TX 78205) Antique and contemporary fine jewelry, art, porcelain, glass, silver, toy soldiers, and smoking and political collectibles.

CLOTHING AND GIFTS

Angelita I (210-224-8362; 208 N. Presa St., San Antonio, TX 78205) Clothing, silver jewelry, and accessories. The shop is housed in one of the historic homes of La Villita; while shopping, take a look at the original fireplace and 200-year-old beams in the adobe house.

Heritage Gift Shop (210-225-4629; 849 E. Commerce St., San Antonio, TX 78205, at the IMAX in Rivercenter Mall) Texas gifts and souvenirs, with a large collection of Alamo and Texas history books, maps, prints, historical reproductions; clothing; and Southwest and Texas jewelry.

Village Weavers (210-222-0776; 418 Villita St., San Antonio, TX 78205) Hand-woven clothing, blankets, skirts, sweaters, rugs, and other textile items are woven in this shop, also in La Villita. You'll find the work of artists from San Antonio and many Latin America countries here.

OUTLETS

North Star Mall (210-340-6627; 7400 San Pedro Ave., San Antonio, TX 78216) San Antonio's largest shopping mall has more than 200 specialty stores, such as Saks Fifth Avenue, Marshall Field's, and Abercrombie & Fitch. You can pick up a complimentary shopping bag and coupon booklet for shops in the mall at the information booth, or give them a call.

Rivercenter Mall (210-225-0000; 849 E. Commerce St., San Antonio, TX 78205) The San Antonio River was extended so that an arm of it flows into this horse-shoe-shaped three-story mall with a view. More than 110 specialty shops, Foley's and Dillard's department stores, restaurants, and IMAX and other movie theaters have taken root here.

BEXAR COUNTY

Leon Springs

This small community of about 500 residents on Interstate 10 west of San Antonio began as a stagecoach stop back in the 1840s, and today San Antonians still enjoy stopping here for great barbecue and a lively dance hall.

LEON SPRINGS DANCE HALL
210-698-7072.
www.leonspringsdancehall.com.
24135 IH-10 W., Leon Springs, TX 78257.
Open: Fri.–Sat. 7pm–2am, year-round.

Barely 25 minutes from downtown San Antonio, the Leon Springs Dance Hall has had a colorful history, from stagecoach stop to brothel to popular dance hall. There's a cover charge — from $2 to $6 or more, depending on who's playing — but both local South Texas bands like Jay and Eric and nationally known performers like Asleep at the Wheel make it well worthwhile. If you're in town for a holiday, you might catch the likes of the Labor Day Luau, with hula skirts and whole roasted pig, the St. Patrick's Day party, or the New Year's Eve bash. But the hall is open all year (Friday and Saturday evenings), and there's always a live band and often specialty shows.

RUDY'S COUNTRY STORE AND BAR-B-Q
210-698-2141.
www.rudysbbq.com.
24152 IH-10, Leon Springs, TX 78257.
Cuisine: Barbecue.
Serving: L, D.
Price: Inexpensive.
Handicap Access: Yes.

"Ilaid the bricks, designed the pits, the recipes — they're all mine," says Doc Holiday, who has been the owner and operator of Rudy's since 1989. The barbecue sales got so great that the groceries were moved back and back again, he says, and now long picnic tables fill the place both inside and out. You order outside and get your barbecue handed to you on butcher paper, and you make your own sandwich. The turkey is what Rudy's is most famous for, but the brisket and the ribs — oh, my.

CHAPTER SIX
Old West and Old Country
HILL COUNTRY WEST AND NORTH OF SAN ANTONIO
BANDERA, COMAL, KENDALL, KERR, MEDINA, REAL, & UVALDE COUNTIES

Eleanor S. Morris

View down Main Street of Bandera, the "Cowboy Capital of the World."

O ut in the counties west and north of San Antonio, you'll find an interesting mix of cultures. The Old West cowboy atmosphere of Bandera contrasts with European Old Country quaintness in Castroville and Comal County. What doesn't change is the beauty of the Hill Country landscape and the relaxed friendliness of its residents.

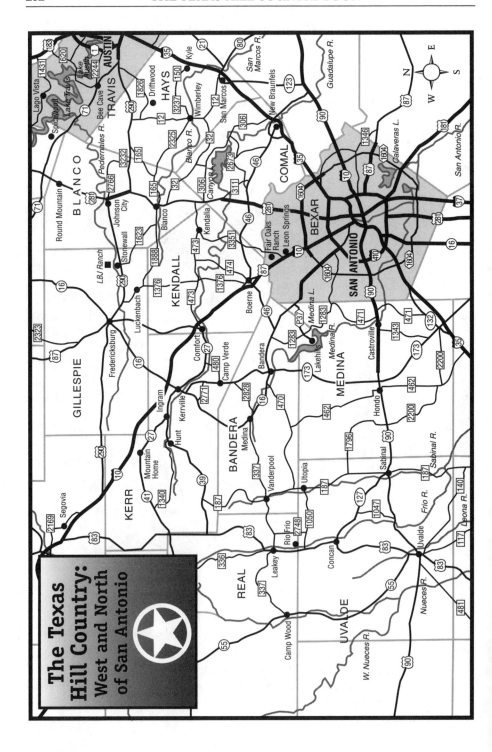

The Texas Hill Country: West and North of San Antonio

BANDERA COUNTY

Bandera, city and county, calls itself "The Cowboy Capital of the World," and with pretty good reason, thanks to the dude and resort ranches (as well as some working ones) concentrated here. It's true horse country, with endless opportunities for horseback riding on supervised trail rides at most dude ranches, and for more independent riding at others. The limestone cliffs towering over the Medina River and the meandering creeks make for spectacular trails. Oak, walnut, native cherry, and Uvalde maple grow bounteously among the mesquite and cacti. The Sabinal River, in extreme western Bandera County, also adds to the scenic beauty.

The county was created in 1856 from surrounding Bexar and Uvalde Counties, but nobody is sure how it got the name. In the 1730s there were several Indian battles in what is now called Bandera Pass; a General Bandera was sent to take care of the situation. The question is: Were Bandera and Bandera Pass named for him, or for the banner (*bandera* is Spanish for "flag") that was raised in 1732 as a reminder of the Spanish/Apache Treaty of that year?

Bandera is the only incorporated town in the county. Tiny Medina calls itself the "Apple Capital of Texas." Tinier Vanderpool's claim to a place on the map is the state natural area of Lost Maples, a surprise in the Hill Country.

For more information about Bandera County, contact the **Bandera Convention and Visitors Bureau** (830-796-3045, 800-364-3833; www.banderacowboy capital.com; 1206 Hackberry, PO Box 171, Bandera, TX 78003).

Bandera

The town began in 1852 when settlers came to make shingles from the many cypress trees along the river. The town was also the site of a Mormon colony. At last count, Bandera had eleven dude ranches, five motels, seven one- or two-room bed & breakfasts, and nine RV parks, cabins, and campgrounds, in addition to a nice selection of restaurants, shops, and honky-tonks, where Saturday night dances offer popular country-western tunes for Texas two-stepping.

BANDERA COUNTY LODGING

Bandera has several motels, such as **Bandera Lodge** (830-796-3191, 800-796-3514; 1900 Hwy. 16 S., PO Box 2609, Bandera, TX 78003) and the **River Front Motel** (830-460-3690, 800-870-5671; PO Box 875, Bandera, TX 78003), but most people come here for the dude ranches. Bandera dude ranch prices include either the full American plan for meals (breakfast, lunch, and dinner) or the modified (breakfast and dinner). Price ranges at this writing are listed here, but ask before making reservations in case of change.

**CASAS DE AMIGOS
BB&D**
Hosts: J. Pat and Cindy
   Breedlove.
830-460-7479.
446 Live Oak Ridge,
   Bandera, TX 78003.
Price: Moderate.
Credit Cards: No.
Handicap Access: No.

At this BB&D (bed, breakfast, and dinner) you not only get great lodging and breakfast, you also get dinner! You can have breakfast any time, and you might get one of the Breedloves' (they both cook) famous omelets — like one of cream cheese, spinach, and green chilies — served with fresh fruit and homemade bread. As for dinner, J. Pat is great on the grill, with steaks and seafood or chicken cordon bleu or Kiev.

Reservations are required in this hacienda since there are only two guest houses (casitas) across the courtyard from the Breedloves' home. But both have living rooms, fully equipped kitchens, and Jacuzzis and sleep four to five people. The courtyard has a cascading fountain, and the rooftop deck, where breakfast is served, offers spectacular sunset views. All enjoyed with a margarita — "or your choice of beverage," says Cindy. Complimentary beverages await in the fridge, and the cookie jar is always full of homemade cookies.

DIXIE DUDE RANCH
Hosts: Clay and Diane
   Conoly.
830-796-4481, 800-375-9255.
www.dixieduderanch.com.
PO Box 548, Bandera, TX
   78003.
FM 1077 9 miles southwest
   of Bandera.
Serving: Full American
   Plan.
Price: Inexpensive.
Credit Cards: AE, D, MC, V.
Handicap Access: Yes.

The Dixie Dude Ranch, a 725-acre working stock ranch breeding longhorn cattle, is the oldest dude ranch in Bandera, dating from 1937. The ranch has 19 guest rooms in cabins and offers horseback riding, swimming, fishing, and a playground, entertaining families with bonfires, cookouts, hayrides, rodeos, trick ropers, and other activities. Hike the trails and hunt for fossils and arrowheads, and then come back and chow down on barbecue and fried chicken.

FLYING L GUEST RANCH
Ranch Manager: John
   Junker.
830-460-3001, 800-292-5134.
www.flyingl.com.
PO Box 1959, Bandera, TX
   78003.
Off Hwy. 173 at Wharton's
   Dock Rd., 1.5 miles south
   of Bandera.
Serving: Modified American
   Plan.
Price: Inexpensive to
   Moderate.
Credit Cards: AE, D, MC, V.
Handicap Access: Partial.

More of a resort than a dude ranch, the Flying L has 542 acres on San Julian Creek, with 40 suites, some with fireplaces and Jacuzzis, in 25 villas on the property. In addition to the usual dude ranch activities of horseback riding, hayrides, and cookouts, the resort has an 18-hole championship golf course, with some of the villas overlooking the 9th fairway. The course has a driving range and a pro shop. Facilities also include a swimming pool, lighted tennis courts, basketball court, and volleyball. There's a general store, too, and a program of children's activities during holidays, spring break, and summer.

MANSION IN BANDERA
Hosts: Cooper and Nancy Barnett.
830-796-4590.
www.mansioninbandera.com.
1005 Hackberry, Bandera, TX 78003.
Price: Moderate to Expensive.
Credit Cards: AE, D, MC, V.
Handicap Access: Yes.

Just off Main Street, on a lovely wooded corner, the Mansion is an 1880 limestone home. The main house features four large one- or two-room suites with private entrances, the carriage house has a Spanish suite and a honeymoon suite, and the guest quarters feature three separate suites.

Chef Cooper serves up delicious eggs Benedict as one of his specialties down in the Country Kitchen, and fine dining is available to the public on Fri. and Sat. evenings (by reservation only).

A wrangler saddles up the horses for a trail ride at the Mayan Ranch near Bandera.

Eleanor S. Morris

MAYAN RANCH
Hosts: the Hicks family.
830-796-3312, 830-460-3036.
www.mayanranch.com.
PO Box 577, Bandera, TX 78003.
0.5 mile from center of Bandera.
Serving: Full American Plan.
Price: Moderate.
Credit Cards: AE, DC, MC, V.
Handicap Access: Yes.

Very popular, especially with European visitors, this large dude ranch goes all out, western-style, for its guests. It's a family affair, with three generations of Hickses making sure that dudes of all ages have a wonderful time. There are 68 guest rooms on this 324-acre spread, some in stone cottages, others in lodges. The Medina River winds around the property, sparkling and cool for swimming, tubing, and fishing. The Hicks family has owned this ranch for more than 40 years, and they put on a real Texas spread: Barbecues, steak fries, and cowboy breakfasts cooked on the trail all contribute to a Wild West experience. Trail rides, a Texas-size swimming pool, volleyball, a general store, and a saloon are also part of the fun. Children's activities are offered during the summer.

TWIN ELM GUEST RANCH
Hosts: Kerry and Bridgitte Hearnberger.
830-796-3628, 888-567-3049.
www.twinelmranch.com.
PO Box 117, Bandera, TX 78003.
On FM 470 off Hwy. 16, 4 miles from downtown Bandera.
Serving: Full American Plan.
Price: Inexpensive.
Credit Cards: AE, MC, V.
Handicap Access: No.

Twin Elm was established in 1939 and, with 200 beautiful acres on the Medina River, is still going strong. Twenty-one clean rustic rooms, all air-conditioned, are just right for singles, couples, families, and youth groups. Barbecue, country breakfasts with hot biscuits, and home-style meals served both indoors and out keep guests fortified for horseback riding, rodeos in the summer, swimming in the pool, or riding the rapids in the Medina River. There are campfires and hayrides, and a game room with TV — but no TV in the guest rooms, or telephone, either, so this is a real getaway.

Vanderpool

TEXAS STAGECOACH INN
Hosts: Karen and David Camp.
830-966-6272, 888-965-6272.
www.bbonline.com/tx/stagecoach.
HC 02, Box 166, Vanderpool, TX 78885.
Five miles south of Vanderpool on Hwy. 187.
Price: Moderate.
Credit Cards: None.
Handicap Access: No.

This stately white ranch house with black shutters and lots of porches stands on the foundation of the original house of 1885. Karen Camp has realized her dream of being the innkeeper of a Texas stagecoach stop where in bygone days horse and wagon drivers tied up at the large iron ring in the massive oak out in front. She and David have remodeled the 6,000-square-foot "mansion" into common rooms, five guest rooms, and a gift shop and gallery (with paintings by David, cowboy turned artist, among the offerings). The two "Christmas" trees in the large common room are always up because they're decorated by season. There are no telephones or television "within reach" (although, of course, there are phones for emergencies), says Karen, who encourages guests to take advantage of both contemplating and boating on pretty Sabinal River right down at the bottom of the lawn. (The fishing of bass and catfish is "catch and release.") There's also excellent bird watching and other nature experiences on these 3 acres along the river, way out in the county, with a lot more to be had at the Lost Maples Natural Area nearby. There's horseback riding nearby at Wagon Wheel Stables in Utopia (Billy Fisher, 830-966-2391, $12 for about a 2-hour ride).

BANDERA COUNTY RESTAURANTS AND FOOD PURVEYORS

BANDERA ICEHOUSE
830-796-4737.
202 W. Hwy. 16, Bandera,
TX 78003.
One block off Main St.
Price: Inexpensive.
Cuisine: Pizza, American.
Serving: B, L, D.
Credit Cards: AE, D, MC, V.
Handicap Access: Yes.

This is the place for quick, light dining, especially if you're hungry, say, at 5am, which is when the Bandera Icehouse opens. The bakery also serves "hot stuff pizza" and fried chicken, as well as made-to-order submarine sandwiches, salads, and ice cream.

BILLY GENE'S RESTAURANT
830-460-3200.
1205 Main St., Bandera, TX 78003.
Price: Inexpensive.
Cuisine: American, Tex-Mex, Seafood, Steak.
Credit Cards: AE, D, MC, V.
Handicap Access: Yes.

Billy Gene's is situated behind the River Front Motel, with a wonderful view of the Medina River. The restaurant is large and bright, with tall ceilings and glass walls. There's a covered patio out back overlooking a small waterfall. Serving certified Angus beef along with chicken-fried steak, the restaurant also offers a seafood specialty every evening, such as coconut shrimp or stuffed crab. Top it all off with sinful raspberry chocolate cheesecake.

BUSBEE'S BAR-B-Q
830-796-3153.
319 Main St., Bandera, TX 78003.
Price: Inexpensive.
Cuisine: Barbecue.
Serving: L, D daily.
Credit Cards: None.
Handicap Access: Yes.

This rustic restaurant claims it's the cowboy's choice. They offer delicious barbecued beef, ribs, sausage, ham, and chicken — until they run out. Their specialty salads are delicious, too: mesquite-grilled chicken salad, brisket salad, and a combo salad. Draft beer.

CABARET CAFE & DANCE HALL
830-796-8166.
801 Main St., Bandera, TX 78003.
Price: Moderate.
Cuisine: Seafood, Steak, Family-style.
Serving: L, D Tues.–Sun.
Credit Cards: AE, MC, V.
Handicap Access: Yes.

Enjoy top regional country-western bands while you dine on steak, baby back ribs, and other family-style offerings. Desserts include an apple and cranberry cobbler and freshly made puff pastry filled with fruit or cheese. The help is friendly, the diners laid back.

**FOOL MOON CAFE AND
  COFFEE HOUSE**
830-460-8434.
204 Main St., Bandera, TX
  78003.
Price: Inexpensive.
Cuisine: Southwestern.
Serving: B, L, D.
Credit Cards: No.
Handicap Access: Yes.

The Southwestern-style food here offers a change from everyone else in town. No chicken-fried steak or barbecue; instead, homemade soup, blue-corn chips, chicken salad, muffins, and carrot cake are on the menu along with espresso, cappuccino, and all the usual favorites offered by a coffeehouse. And you can sit outdoors in the little park alongside if you wish.

OST RESTAURANT
830-796-3836.
305 Main St., Bandera, TX
  78003.
Price: Inexpensive to
  Moderate.
Cuisine: Mexican, Texan.
Serving: B, L, D.
Credit Cards: D, MC, V.
Handicap Access: Yes.

OST stands for Old Spanish Trail, which passed through Bandera once upon a time. The restaurant specializes in chicken-fried steak and Mexican dishes like enchiladas in chili as well as down-home food like soup, biscuits, pies, and cakes, all homemade. OST also specializes in "breakfast anytime," and the chuck wagon is ready for the daily buffet.

FOOD PURVEYORS

*The soda fountain at the
General Store on Main
Street.*

Eleanor S. Morris

Bandera General Store (210-796-4925; 306 Main St., Bandera, TX 78003) boasts that it is the best ice cream shop, serving Texas's finest, Promised Land Ice Cream, in more than a dozen flavors and in every way: old-fashioned sodas, shakes, floats, malts, cones, banana splits. . . . There's also a gift shop; see "Shopping."

BANDERA COUNTY CULTURE

HISTORIC BUILDINGS AND MUSEUMS

Take a look at the **Bandera County Courthouse** on Main St. between Pecan and Hackberry. The Renaissance Revival structure was built in 1890 of locally quarried limestone with massive cypress trusses; its cupola dominates Bandera's skyline. The bronze monument on the courthouse lawn, dedicated to the champion cowboys of the county, backs up the town's claim that it's the "Cowboy Capital of the World."

Eleanor S. Morris

Discover how the West — and Bandera — were won at the Frontier Times Museum.

**FRONTIER TIMES
 MUSEUM**
830-796-3864.
www.texasguides.com/
 frontiertimes.html.
510 Main St., Bandera, TX
 78003.
Corner of 13th, one block
 north of the Bandera
 County Courthouse.
Hours: Mon.–Sat. 10am–
 4:30pm, Sun. 1–4:30pm.
Admission: Adults $2,
 under 18 25¢; children
 under 6 free.

Within the stone walls of the museum you'll find a collection of 33,000 "pieces of history" — everything Bandera considers memorable, from bells and bullets to bottles and branding irons, including an entire room of cowboy lore. Great souvenirs, too. The museum was founded in 1927 by J. Marvin Hunter, who for 60 years collected data and artifacts about Texas (and elsewhere).

LIBRARIES

BANDERA COUNTY LIBRARY
830-796-4213.
515 Main St., Bandera, TX 78003.
Across from the courthouse.
Hours: Mon., Tues., Fri. 8am–5pm; Thurs. 8am–8pm; Sat. 9am–1pm. Closed Weds.

Visitors can obtain temporary check-out privileges for a refundable $20 deposit. The library houses an extensive genealogical research and Texana collection, and there is a paperback book exchange.

NIGHTLIFE

Eleanor S. Morris

The Blue Cowboys performing in Arkey Blue's Silver Dollar honky-tonk on Main Street, Bandera.

What's a western cowboy town without a honky-tonk, the whang of a steel guitar, and the wail of a fiddle backing up a forlorn country-western singer? Add a wall full of neon beer signs, a pool table, and the sliding of boots on a sawdust-covered floor and you have pure Texas.

One of the most famous honky-tonks is **Arkey Blue's Silver Dollar Bar** (830-796-8826; 308 Main St., Bandera, TX 78003), where Arkey and the Blue Cowboys set boots to hopping on the sawdust floor. There's a bar and long tables where you can sip a cool beer in between numbers. So head on down the stairs for some boot-scootin' and listening to Arkey's ballads about cheatin' 'n' heartbreak, fast women, and slow horses.

For more than 50 years the **Cabaret Cafe and Dance Hall** (see "Bandera County — Restaurants") has been a big draw, featuring well-known country-western names on weekends like Clay Barker, Johnny Bush, and Kitty Wells. The restaurant/cabaret is open for boot-scootin' as well as food Fri. and Sat. until 2am, and Thurs., Sun., and Mon. until 11pm (closed Tues., Weds.). The **11th Street Cowboy Bar** (830-796-4849; 303 11th St., Bandera, TX 78003) has live music Weds., Fri., Sat., and Sun. **Cowboy Capital Hotel's Purple Cow** (703 Main St., Bandera, TX 78003; 830-796-4100) has live music Fri. and Sat. And there are others; call the Convention Bureau for upated information.

SEASONAL EVENTS

For information on events taking place in Bandera, contact the **Bandera Convention and Visitors Bureau** (830-796-3045, 800-364-3833; www.banderacowboycapital.com; PO Box 171, Bandera, TX 78003).

There are a lot of rodeos here, but it is cowboy country. The **Summer Rodeo Series** at Twin Elm Guest Ranch (see "Lodging") begins in April and continues through the Labor Day Weekend. And there's more:

JANUARY brings the **Bandera County Junior Livestock Show.**

At the end of FEBRUARY there's the annual **Winter Texas Appreciation Party** for all the Yankees and Canadians who come down to get out of the cold.

MARCH offers the **Lakehills American Legion Chili Cookoff** and **Lakehills United Methodist Church Fish Fry.**

In APRIL there's the **Bandera County Regional Foundation Art Show & Sale** and the **Cowboy Palace Spring Fling.**

MAY is a busy month, with the **Cowboy Capital Rodeo Association PRCA Rodeo** as well as **RiverFest**, the **Funtier Day Parade**, and the **Bandera County Artists Association Arts and Crafts**, among other events.

In July there's the **Fourth of July Parade and BBQ**. There's also a **Fourth of July Pet Parade**, featuring, among others, Best Matched Owner and Pet and Most Talented Pet.

Medina, the "Apple Capital of Texas," hosts the **Texas International Apple Festival** in AUGUST at Love Creek Orchards Cider Mill & Country Store (800-449-0882), which stocks everything relating to the apple, even apple trees on dwarfing rootstock suitable for growing in Texas.

On Labor Day Weekend in SEPTEMBER there's the **Cajun Festival & Great Gumbo Cookoff.**

OCTOBER brings the **Hill Country Gypsy Motorcycle Rally**, the **Professional Armed Forces Rodeo Association World Finals** in Mansfield Park, and the **Great Hill Country Pumpkin Patch** in Medina.

NOVEMBER celebrates the annual **Hunters Bar-B-Q and Outdoor Expo,** also in Mansfield Park. Call the Bandera Convention and Visitors Bureau (830-796-3055) for information.

The beginning of DECEMBER sees the start of a month-long **Cowboy Christmas** in Bandera. Call 830-796-3045 or 800-364-3833 for further information.

BANDERA COUNTY RECREATION

Opportunities for horseback riding are at the ranches described in "Lodging," above. Or contact the **Bandera Convention and Visitors Bureau** at 830-796-3045, or see their Web site, www.banderacowboycapital.com.

CAMPING

Bandera

Additional camping areas are mentioned under "Parks."

Bandera Beverage Barn and RV Park (830-796-8153; 1503 W. Main St., PO Box 435, Bandera, TX 78003) 5.5 acres on the Medina River; facilities include tent camping, 40 full RV hookups, a full-line convenience store, rest rooms, picnic tables, fishing, and tubing.

Skyline Ranch RV Park (830-796-4958; Hwy. 16, 1.5 miles west of Bandera, PO Box 1990, Bandera, TX 78003) Spacious pull-through sites and full hookups are provided here on 60 acres adjoining the Medina River. There's also a rec hall with full kitchen, showers and rest rooms, laundry facilities, pitch-putt green and shuffleboard, and free cable TV. Pets on leashes are welcome.

On and In the Water

Medina Lake in the southeast corner of the county, created by a dam completed in 1913, is a major reservoir with 254,000 acre-feet storage capacity. The lake is popular for boating, swimming, water skiing, and fishing.

The Medina River is considered one of the most scenic and exciting rivers in Texas. Tubes, canoes, and kayaks can be rented at **Fred Collins Workshop** (see "Shopping") half a mile north of Bandera. **Medina Kayaks and River Ranch** (see "Camping — Medina") also rents kayaks.

Medina

Medina Kayaks and River Ranch (830-589-7215; 761 Haley Ln., Medina, TX 78055) Private and primitive tent sites, kayak rental. For day use: swimming and picnicking along ½ mile of Medina River frontage. Tent sites are scattered among various species of shade trees and natural vegetation, affording privacy. Campers will also find a canoe awaiting their use.

FISHING

Medina Lake, Medina River, and the Sabinal River are good for fishing. Medina Lake is full of crappie, white bass, and black bass, and it's also the best place to catch huge yellow catfish. The Medina River, with its canopy of towering cypress trees, provides good fishing for spotted bass, Guadalupe bass, largemouth bass, perch, and catfish. (See "Parks" below for more fishing opportunities.)

GOLF

Flying L Guest Ranch (800-292-5134; see "Lodging") and **Lost Valley Resort Ranch** (830-460-8008) have 18-hole courses open to the public. Both have fully stocked pro shops and offer both individual and group lessons.

PARKS

Bandera County Park (Park Rd. 37 and Medina Lake) The park is open seven days a week, 8am–10pm. The only public boat ramp on the lake is here, and use of the ramp is free. Amenities include rest rooms, picnic tables, and barbecue pits. Fee: $4 per day per vehicle.

Hill Country State Natural Area (830-796-4413, camping reservations 512-389-8900; RR 1, Box 601, Bandera, TX 78003, FM 1077, 12 miles from Hwy. 173 intersection) Opened in 1984 primarily for equestrian use, this 5,400-acre park is also popular with hikers, backpackers, and all-terrain bicyclists who enjoy 36 miles of trails, 23 of those miles designated multiuse. Facilities include walk-in tent sites, backpacking camping areas, and fishing and swimming on a spring-fed creek. Mar. 1–Oct. 31, open daily; Nov. 1–Feb. 28, Fri. noon–Sun. 10pm.

Lost Maples State Natural Area (830-966-3413, reservations for camping 512-389-8900; HCR1, Box 156, Vanderpool, TX 78885, 5 miles north of Vanderpool on RR 187) Bigtooth maples, hidden deep in a remote Hill Country canyon, display fall colors that rival any in New England. What are they doing here in a land that has no such flora anywhere else in the big state of Texas? Evidently they are left over from a much earlier age, the Pleistocene Age, when the county was much wetter and cooler. Somehow they have survived, protected from high summer temperatures and dry winds by the high canyon walls along the Sabinal River. People come from miles around to marvel at the blaze of red, yellow, and orange in a sea of green Texas live oak. The 2,174-acre park, open all year, has other attractions: steep limestone canyons, nature trails, clear streams, and bubbling springs. Campsites with water and electricity are available, as are primitive camping areas. At the Interpretive Center, exhibits tell about local natural history, and bird watching is especially rewarding here in the springtime.

Mansfield Park (830-796-3168; PO Box 877, Bandera, TX 78003, 3 miles from Bandera on Hwy. 16 N) The park has 30 RV campsites, water, electricity, dump station, public rest rooms, hot showers, indoor recreation area, two softball fields, picnic tables, charcoal grills, shady tent sites, and — since this is the "Cowboy Capital of the World" — even a rodeo arena.

TENNIS

Tennis courts are at the **Flying L Guest Ranch** and the **Mayan Ranch** (see "Lodging").

BANDERA COUNTY SHOPPING

Folks come to Bandera mostly to enjoy the Old West ranches and cowboy atmosphere, so shopping is not on the fancy side. Here are a few shops, however, if you can't resist, and Main Street is lined with more:

American Indian Jewelry (830-796-4000; 311-B Main St., Bandera, TX 78003) A large selection of original jewelry designs from the Navajo, Zuni, Hopi, Pawnee, Sioux, and Cherokee tribes, in silver, turquoise, and onyx. Earrings, bolo ties, necklaces, pendants, bracelets, and rings; dreamcatchers, too.

Country Accents (830-535-4979; 8312 Hwy. 16 S., Bandera, TX 78003, bet. Bandera and Pipe Creek) The place for American antiques, furniture, glassware, stoneware, primitives, and quilts; they specialize in Blue Willow china.

Fred Collins Workshop (830-796-3553; Box 1869, Bandera, TX 78003, Hwy. 16 N., ½ mile north of Bandera) This fascinating shop features western-style woodcrafting, designing and creating rustic furniture to customer specifications. Based on your ideas, photographs, or sketches, the workshop creates the design, supplies the wood, and will either complete the project or leave it in any stage of completion for you to finish. Dining tables, benches, fireplace mantels, entertainment centers, freestanding bars, porch swings — just about anything that can be made of wood.

Gingerbread House (830-796-3616; 1110 Cedar St., Bandera, TX 78003) Antiques, original craft items, stuffed animal toys, jewelry, homemade candies, stained glass, floral items, beautiful dolls, and T-shirts, all here in abundance.

Love's Antique Mall (830-796-3838; 310 Main St., Bandera, TX 78003), in the historic Bandera Ranch Store, not only has antiques, but several folks have set up shop there to make furniture out of cedar and old barn wood, a growing industry in Bandera.

Old West Imports (830-796-7386; 206 Main St., Bandera, TX 78003) Right on the corner of Main and Hwy. 16, you'll find a great assortment of both Mexican and Indian art. Pottery, rocks, jewelry, serapes, Guadalajara glassware, Mayan figures, and even fountains for indoors and out.

COMAL COUNTY

In the early 1840s, the fledgling Texas government resolved to counter underpopulation in the Hill Country through the empresario system, borrowed from the previous Spanish and Mexican governments. Through this arrangement, German-born Henry Fisher had acquired a huge land grant northwest of Austin. Sam Houston, president of the Republic of Texas, commissioned him to represent the republic to the German states of the Rhine, which put Fisher in touch with a group headed by Prince Carl of Solms-Braunfels. This was the Adelsverein, the Society for the Protection of German Immigrants to Texas. The organization proposed to sponsor emigration to Texas and encourage the Germans, once in Texas, to stay together.

Meanwhile, Fisher had discovered that his piece of land was still held by the Comanche. In 1844 he convinced the unsuspecting Prince Carl to buy his 4 million acres and collected the princely sum of $9,000, his sales pitch being that the land was accessible, fertile, and perfectly suited for coastal commerce — never mind that it was teeming with hostile Comanches.

The first contingent of immigrants was to arrive that December; Prince Carl sailed ahead to the new land to prepare for them. Once there, he learned all too quickly how he had been taken advantage of. But with his immigrants on the way there was nothing to be done but to find another, safer site. He looked to the south of Fisher's land and, 50 miles southeast of Austin, found 9,000 acres on the Guadalupe River at the foot of the Balcones Escarpment. Before sailing for home he laid out the town, which he naturally named New Braunfels.

New Braunfels

New Braunfels was established in 1845 on the Comal River, the shortest river in the U.S. It rises from a cluster of springs in the northwest part of town and remains entirely within the city limits until it spills into the much longer Guadalupe River flowing south below Canyon Dam. New Braunfels became the county seat in 1846, and it has grown into a bustling, thriving town with much of historic interest; here you can dine in biergartens and dance to oompah music to your heart's content.

Gruene

On the north edge of town is the historic village of Gruene (pronounced "green"), now part of New Braunfels. Gruene began in the 1850s as a German village. Many of the historic buildings there have been restored (though some are still in ruins). You'll find old homes and stores, an inn, a restaurant in an old mill, and, best of all, Gruene Hall, claimed to be the oldest dance hall in Texas (see "Nightlife") and still going strong.

COMAL COUNTY LODGING

Comal County lodging centers around New Braunfels, where the **Greater New Braunfels Chamber of Commerce** (830-625-2385, 800-572-2626; www.nbcham.org; 390 S. Seguin St., PO Box 311417, New Braunfels, TX 78131) has installed information kiosks for museums and attractions, bed & breakfast establishments, resorts, condominiums, cabins, campgrounds, and motels, but there are also several places to stay in historic Gruene.

New Braunfels

The lobby of the historic Hotel Faust, with a 1929 Model-A Ford.

Eleanor S. Morris

HOTEL FAUST
Managers: Bob and Judy
  Abbey.
830-625-7791.
www.thehotelfaust.com.
240 S. Seguin St., New
  Braunfels, TX 78130.
Price: Moderate to
  Expensive.
Credit Cards: AE, D, DC,
  MC, V.
Handicap Access: Yes.

KARBACH HAUS
Hosts: Kathleen and Ben
  Jack Kinney.

The Faust Hotel opened in 1929 (just before the Crash), and it has been restored in the spirit of its times. The spacious lobby sports a bright yellow 1929 Model-A Ford in addition to pillars and posts and wainscoting as a backdrop for the antique sofas and chairs and Oriental rugs. The hotel supposedly has a ghost, that of Walter Faust, the original owner, who would be proud of the full-service dining facilities and other amenities. There's even a microbrewery now, producing handcrafted beers.

Kathleen Kinney grew up in this historic mansion, and the six spacious guest rooms are furnished with many antiques. Each room has a tile

830-625-2131, 800-972-5941.
www.bbhost.com/karbach.
487 West San Antonio St.,
New Braunfels, TX 78130.
Price: Expensive.
Credit Cards: AE, D, MC, V.
Handicap Access: No.

bath, some with Jacuzzis, TV/VCRs, king or queen beds with down quilts, and fluffy robes. The living room has a grand piano, a library, and an inviting fireplace. There's a guest refrigerator and an ice maker, and Kathy is not bragging when she says "the breakfasts are world class." You might have eggs Benedict along with pecan waffles and a fruit salad laced with Kahlúa. The multicourse breakfasts always include an egg dish, a meat dish, and a sweet.

LAMB'S REST INN
Hosts: George and Judy Rothell.
830-609-3932, 888-609-3932.
www.bbhost.com/lambsrest bb.
1385 Edwards Blvd., New Braunfels, TX 78132.
Price: Moderate to Expensive.
Credit Cards: D, MC, V.
Handicap Access: No.

This delightfully restful inn on the Guadalupe River has five guest rooms, one of them a two-room suite. All have private baths and sitting area, and two also have a Jacuzzi. Sit on the porch or a deck, and listen to the river as it cascades over those Hill Country rocks. Then maybe take a dip either in the clear cool river or the inn's pool.

Breakfast is Judy's delight, beginning perhaps with poached pears in raspberry sauce and topped with almond whipped cream, followed by French toast and homemade sausage, cinnamon-walnut bread, and perhaps a piña colada frappé. And in the afternoon enjoy refreshments reminiscent of high tea.

PRINCE SOLMS INN
Hosts: Bob and Pat Brent.
830-625-9169, 800-625-9169.
www.princesolmsinn.com.
295 E. San Antonio St., New Braunfels, TX 78130.
Price: Moderate to Expensive.
Credit Cards: AE, D, MC, V.
Handicap Access: No.

This famous Texas landmark has been in continuous operation as an inn since it was built in 1898 by immigrant German craftsmen. The eight guest rooms and two suites all have private baths, and all are furnished with lovely antiques. A separate one-bedroom cottage just behind the inn is ideal for honeymooners. The entry doors are 10 feet high, the ceilings are 14 feet high, and there's a courtyard in the rear.

Breakfast will be filling, whether it's quiche, banana pancakes, or scrambled eggs, all always served with either sausage or bacon, homemade breads and banana butter, and English muffins, toast, or bagels. The fine restaurant in the cellar, formerly Wolfgang's Keller, has been remodeled and is now the Uptown Piano & Wine Bar.

Gruene

GRUENE MANSION INN
Hosts: Cecil and Judy Eager.
830-629-2641.

Here's another historic place to spend the night right on the banks of the Guadalupe River. On the National Register of Historic Places, the inn is

www.gruenemansioninn
.com.
1275 Gruene Rd., New
Braunfels, TX 78130.
Price: Expensive.
Credit Cards: No.
Handicap Access: One
room.

located in the Historic District on the northern edge of New Braunfels's city limits. The Eagers treasure the history of the mansion and carry on the tradition of *gemütlich* ("easygoing") begun by Henry Gruene back in the mid-1800s. The cottages along the Guadalupe River have little porches that overhang the riverbank, each furnished with antiques and handmade quilts. The Sunday Haus contains eight rooms decorated in rustic Victoriana: king-size beds, fireplaces, old Victorian bathtubs, and yet more antiques.

MOTELS

A mong others, New Braunfels has a **Days Inn** (830-608-0004, 800-329-7466; 963 IH-35 N., New Braunfels, TX 78130); a **Holiday Inn** (830-625-8017, 800-465-4329; 1051 IH-35 E., New Braunfels, TX 78130); a **Rodeway Inn** (830-629-6991, 800-967-1168; 1209 IH-35 E., New Braunfels, TX 78130); and the **Bavarian Old Town Inn** (830-629-6888, 800-950-8528; 201 Loop 337, New Braunfels, TX 78130).

COMAL COUNTY RESTAURANTS AND FOOD PURVEYORS

You'd expect — correctly — to find such culinary specialties as German sausage and German pastry here. Several smokehouses provide such tasty meals; two of them are described below. New Braunfels also has several sophisticated eating spots that are a departure from more traditional fare.

New Braunfels

HUISACHE GRILL
830-620-9001.
www.huisache.com.
303 W. San Antonio St., New
Braunfels, TX 78130.
Price: Inexpensive.
Cuisine: New American,
Southwest.
Serving: L, D daily.
Credit Cards: AE, D, MC, V.
Handicap Access: Yes.

The restaurant is named for that scrubby tree (pronounced "wee-satch-ee") covering the Hill Country and on down into northern Mexico. The restaurateurs chose the name because they feel that the native vegetation "provides a thread between the many cultures of our rich regional heritage, just as our cuisine reflects varied influences." That it does — and deliciously, too, with innovative dishes like salmon niçoise, grilled spinach with lime garlic butter, Yucatán chicken, pecan-crusted ruby red trout, and grilled mahi mahi, among others.

NEW BRAUNFELS SMOKEHOUSE
830-625-2416.
www.nbsmokehouse.com.
146 Hwy. 46 S., New Braunfels, TX 78130.
Corner of Hwy. 46 and U.S. 81.
Price: Inexpensive.
Cuisine: German, Smoked Meats.
Serving: B, L, D.
Credit Cards: AE, D, MC, V.
Handicap Access: Yes.

This family-owned smokehouse is a 50-year-old Central Texas tradition, with delicious meats custom-smoked by Rocky Tays according to old German family recipes — with a touch of Mexican influence. Try the special turkey or sausage gumbo with corn bread and coleslaw for a satisfying lunch, or order a dinner plate of baby back ribs, beef brisket, and bratwurst served with German potato salad, pinto beans, and a tossed salad.

OMA'S HAUS
830-625-3280.
541 Hwy. 46 S., PO Box 310667, New Braunfels, TX 78130.
Price: Inexpensive.
Cuisine: German, American.
Serving: L, D.
Credit Cards: AE, D, DC, MC, V.
Handicap Access: Yes.

Oma is German for "grandma," and the cozy family atmosphere here is planned to be like Grandmother's house. The long, low wooden building off the highway offers delicious German dishes like jäger schnitzel and strudel — especially the peach strudel, a departure from the usual apple, and, of all things, a chocolate strudel!

Gruene

GRISTMILL RIVER RESTAURANT AND BAR
830-625-0684.
1287 Gruene Rd., New Braunfels, TX 78130.
Price: Inexpensive.
Cuisine: Seafood, Steak, American.
Serving: L, D.
Credit Cards: AE, D, MC, V.
Handicap Access: Yes.

H. D. Gruene built this mill in the 1800s to serve the cotton community. The setting, back behind Texas's oldest dance hall (see "Nightlife") and beneath Gruene's water tower, makes for an unusual place to dine. Although there are tables in front beyond the open double doors, try for a table out back overlooking the Guadalupe River or in the pleasant room to the right, with an enclosed view of the river.

Veggie lovers will appreciate the typical "Try These!" menu that includes fresh steamed broccoli, cauliflower, carrots, and green beans. But it's the tortilla soup, the chicken Caesar salad, the pork loin sandwich, the Guadalupe chopped steak, the bronze catfish — and the Jack Daniel's pecan pie, made with chocolate chips and a trace of whiskey — that make folks flock to the Gristmill. Often — especially on weekends — there's a wait, but sitting outdoors under the trees is hardly a hardship.

RUDY'S COUNTRY STORE AND BAR-B-Q
830-609-3337.

"The Wurst BBQ in Texas" is Rudy's motto. Actually, Rudy's is a meat market that sells cooked meat (sold by the pound) either to take home or eat

www.rudys.com.
936 Loop 337, New
  Braunfels, TX 78130.
Price: Inexpensive.
Cuisine: Barbecue.
Serving: B, L, D.
Credit Cards: All major.
Handicap Access: Yes.

on the spot. The barbecue comes out of the pit, is cut in front of you, and is served fresh to your order on white butcher paper, accompanied by slices of fresh bread. There's brisket, turkey breast, pork loin, prime rib, chopped beef, sausage, and pork spare ribs.

Along with the meat you can order side dishes like corn — creamed or on the cob — potato salad, coleslaw, pinto beans, green bean salad, new potatoes, and jumbo smoked potatoes.

COMAL COUNTY FOOD PURVEYORS

Cafe Fontana (830-608-9041; 489 Main Plaza, New Braunfels, TX 78130) Sandwiches, ice cream, yogurt, and pastries along with your cup of cappuccino.

Naegelin's Bakery in New Braunfels is the oldest bakery in Texas.

Eleanor S. Morris

Naegelin's Bakery (830-625-5722; 129 S. Seguin St., New Braunfels, TX 78130) The oldest bakery in Texas, baking German, French, and Danish breads and pastries since 1868. Indoors, around the corner from a bakery case crammed with temptations, is a small area with tables and chairs where you can consume the fresh strudel, bear claws, and pull-aparts on the spot. **Rudy's Country Store and Bar-B-Q** (see "Restaurants").

COMAL COUNTY CULTURE

ARCHITECTURE

New Braunfels has fine examples of German *Fachwerk* ("framework") construction, adapted to native cedar and limestone, throughout the town. This framework consists of heavy squared timbers with the spaces between the wood filled in with stone and brick. The entire surface is then plastered over.

HISTORIC BUILDINGS

Four of New Braunfels's historic buildings are listed on the National Register of Historic Places. The old **Plaza Hotel** on Main Plaza, built in 1851, is touted as the first hotel in Texas to have running water piped in. Others are the **Stephen Klein** house, built in 1846 (131 S. Seguin St.), and the **First Protestant Church**, established in 1845 (296 S. Seguin St.).

MUSEUMS

BAETGE HOUSE
830-629-2943.
1300 Church Hill Dr., New Braunfels, TX 78130.
Open: Tues.–Fri. 10am–2:30pm, Sat. and Sun. 2–5pm.
Admission: Adults $2, children 6–18 50¢, under 6 free.

This two-story house, built in 1852, is a good example of the German *Fachwerk* construction then prevalent in New Braunfels. On the second floor you can inspect the construction technique; on the first floor, admire the antique furnishings, which predate 1860.

CHILDREN'S MUSEUM
830-620-0939.
www.nbchildren.org.
386 W. San Antonio St., New Braunfels, TX 78130.
In the New Braunfels Marketplace.
Open: Mon.–Sat. 9am–5pm; Sun. noon–5pm.
Admission: Children and adults $3, seniors $2, under one year free.

The Children's Museum is a learning environment for children and families that seeks to stimulate thought and inspire imagination. Understanding is gained through hands-on educational exhibits and programs that focus on fine arts, culture, science, and technology.

MUSEUM OF TEXAS HANDMADE FURNITURE
830-629-6504.
1370 Church Hill Dr., New Braunfels, TX 78130.
Open: Feb.–Nov., Tues.–Sun. 1–4pm; closed Dec.–Jan., major holidays.
Admission: Adults $5, seniors $4, children 6–12 $1, under 6 free.

The historic Andreas Breustedt home is the perfect setting for this collection of handmade furniture — beds, tables, chairs, armoires — crafted during the 1800s. English ironstone and other artifacts from the 1700s are also on display. The one-room log cabin on the property features more furnishings and the tools used to make them.

SOPHIENBURG MUSEUM
830-629-1572.
www.nbtx.com/sophien burg/museum.htm.
401 W. Coll St., New Braunfels, TX 78130.
Open: Mon.–Sat. 10am–5pm; 1–5pm Sun.
Admission: Adults $5, students free.

The museum is on a small hill amid parklike grounds; it's the site where Prince Carl Solms-Braunfels built a log fortress to serve as administrative headquarters for his colony. You'll find many of his personal effects, a model of his castle in Braunfels, much historical genealogical information, and items from the colonists' households. There are native American artifacts as well.

NIGHTLIFE

The **Watering Hole** (830-625-0045; 1390 McQueeney Rd., New Braunfels, TX 78130) is the place for ice-cold beer, after-dinner cocktails, and a night of dancing in air-conditioned comfort. State-of-the-art lighting brightens up the dance hall, where there's dancing to DJ music Thurs., Fri., and Sat. nights, with karaoke on Weds. evenings.

The bar inside Gruene Dance Hall, the oldest dance hall in Texas.

Eleanor S. Morris

Take a look at the bar, made with a chainsaw by wood carver Terry Boguist. He's captured the spirit of New Braunfels with not only cowboys and long-horns but also tubers floating down the Guadalupe.

Gruene Hall (830-606-1281; 1281 Gruene Rd., New Braunfels, TX 78130), con-sidered the oldest dance hall in Texas and virtually untouched since 1878, has a large open-air dance floor festooned from the rafters with old advertisements, a huge outdoor garden, and even a wood-burning stove for cold evenings.

This dance hall is featured on the cover of George Strait's first album — he worked as a ticket taker at the hall. And Lyle Lovett launched his career here. The music includes the best in contemporary country, blues, and folk, and "bel-lying up to the bar" makes you feel like the real thing.

SEASONAL EVENTS

This marker celebrates Gruene Hall as the oldest dance hall in Texas.

Eleanor S. Morris

For additional information about events in New Braunfels, contact the **Greater New Braunfels Chamber of Commerce** (830-625-2385, 800-572-2626; www.nbcham.org; 390 S. Seguin St., PO Box 311417, New Braunfels, TX 78131).

Old Gruene Market Days (830-629-6441) take place the third Saturday and Sunday of each month, with more than a hundred vendors featuring craft items.

MARCH sees **Downtown Alive — Art in New Braunfels** (830-629-8022).

Come APRIL, the two-day annual **Folkfest** celebrates New Braunfels's her-itage and culture on the grounds of Conservation Plaza and the Texas Museum of Handmade Furniture, with food, furniture-making, demonstrations of old-style crafts, and tours of historic buildings (830-629-6504).

MAY brings more than a hundred artists and craftsmen together for the **New**

Braunfels Arts League Arts and Crafts Show, a two-day event held at the New Braunfels Civic Center (830-629-5959).

JUNE sees the two-day **Summer Juried Art Show** at the Hummel Museum & Art Gallery (830-625-5636).

In JULY take in the **Fourth of July Parade**. Enjoy the second two-day arts and crafts show put on at the New Braunfels Civic Center, the **Summer Showcase of Arts & Crafts.**

SEPTEMBER brings the **Comal County Fair**, one of Texas's oldest and largest fairs, at the fairgrounds (830-625-1505).

In OCTOBER there's the annual **Moving Waters Pow Wow** at Canyon Lake, featuring arts, crafts, intertribal competition dancing, food, and storytelling (830-964-3613).

NOVEMBER is the month for the famous **Wurstfest**, a sausage festival where phenomenal quantities of sausage and beer are consumed each year on the banks of the Comal River. Walk off some of what you've eaten in the 10K walk, then take in the arts and crafts sale. November also begins **Festtage in New Braunfels**, a half-month-long celebration to showcase New Braunfels as a major holiday mecca for visitors, with something going on every week. For information, contact the chamber of commerce.

COMAL COUNTY RECREATION

Much of Comal County's recreation is based on and around the lakes, rivers, and springs; see "On, In, and Along the Water" on the next page for camping, fishing, hiking, swimming, and various water sports.

FAMILY FUN

Children's Museum (see "Museums").

Landa Park Miniature Train (830-625-8285; 2107 Northcrest Dr., New Braunfels, TX 78130) For a mere $2 per person you can chug around the park's 196 acres, enjoying both the breeze and the view (summer 10am–8pm).

Natural Bridge Caverns (830-651-6101; www.tourtexas.com/caverns; 26495 Natural Bridge Caverns Rd./FM 3009, Natural Bridge Caverns, TX 78266) The caverns are named for a 60-foot natural limestone bridge that spans the entrance. The caverns were found in 1960 by students from St. Mary's University in San Antonio. The cave's sinkhole, with a tiny passage, had been known for a hundred years, but the students crawled down the 11-inch spiral into what many consider one of the great show caves of the world. In addition to wonderful stalagmites and stalactites and other formations, various minerals create colors comparable to melting rainbow sherbet. Open daily at 9am except Thanksgiving, Christmas, and New Year's Day; last tour 6pm. Admission: 13 and over $12, children 4–12 $7, seniors 65 and over $10.

On, In, and Along the Water

Tubing and swimming in Lands Park, just one of many places in Comal County to enjoy the water.

Eleanor S. Morris

Canyon Lake, about 30 minutes north of town on Hwy. 306, boasts 80 miles of scenic shoreline bordering deep blue water. Seven public parks with picnic areas, swimming beaches, and boat launches are around the lake. Camping, fishing, hiking, cycling, and boating are activities enjoyed here almost year-round. For more information, contact the Canyon Lake Chamber of Commerce, 830-964-2223.

Whitewater Sports (830-964-3800; 11860 FM 306, HC3/Box 22, New Braunfels, TX 78130) offers campgrounds, canoes, rafts and shelter, kayaks, and fishing, all under one facility close to Canyon Lake, where most of those activities take place.

Landa Park is the spot where Comal Springs bubble out of the ground to fill the giant pool with clear, fresh water. There's an Olympic-size pool, too, in the 196 acres right in downtown New Braunfels. The springs were discovered in 9000 B.C. — that's when native Americans found them, along with roaming buffalo, bears, and panthers. The park has picnic areas, a miniature train (see "Family Fun"), paddleboat and tube rentals, glass-bottom boat tours (830-608-2163), and a golf course (see "Golf"). Hikers enjoy the park's nature trail. The arboretum walking tour takes in more than 96 species of trees.

Prince Solms Park is east of Landa Park, along the Comal River. The tube chute here is popular as a launch pad to a relaxing float down the river.

Rafting the **Guadalupe River** from Canyon Lake through New Braunfels is very popular. There are falls with names like Devil's Playground Rapid, the Chute, and Slumber Falls; your river outfitter can advise you of their varying degrees of difficulty. Outfitters include **Jerry's Rentals** (830-625-2036; 4970 River Rd., New Braunfels, TX 78132), **Roy's Rentals** (830-964-3721; 6350 River Rd., New Braunfels, TX 78130), **Rockin R River Rides** (830-629-9999, 800-55-FLOAT; www.rockinr.com; 1405 Gruene Rd., New Braunfels, TX 78130), **Rio Raft Co.** (830-964-3613; PO Box 2030, New Braunfels, TX 78130), and **Gruene River Raft Co.** (830-625-2800; www.gruene.net/riverraftco; 1404 Gruene Rd., New Braunfels, TX 78130).

A scenic route to drive is FM 306 from New Braunfels to Satler along the Guadalupe River. Another exceptionally beautiful route is along the "Devil's Backbone" on FM 32, northwest of Canyon Reservoir.

Natural Bridge Wildlife Ranch (830-438-7400; www.nbwildliferanchtx.com; 26515 Natural Bridge Caverns Rd./FM 3009, Natural Bridge Caverns, TX 78266) Take an African safari on 200 acres of Texas Hill Country to see 500 animals, including giraffes, wallabies, rhinoceros, and zebras. Some of the exotic animals are pretty tame — the African ostrich, the yak, and the sable antelope, among others, will put their heads into your car window, looking for a treat. (Be sure to get a complimentary container of food before you climb aboard.)

There is a petting zoo, snack bar, and picnic area on the grounds. Open 9am–5pm daily; closed Thanksgiving, Christmas, New Year's Day. Admission: adults $11, children 3–11 $6.

Schlitterbahn Waterpark (830-625-2351; www.schlitterbahn.com; 305 W. Austin, New Braunfels, TX 78130) The name translates to "slippery road," and there are slippery spots galore in this exciting water park. The rides are color-coded for passive, moderate, agressive, and high thrill, so you know in advance what you're getting into. Tube shoots, wild slides from a German castle, bumper boats, a giant hot tub, a swimming lagoon and sand beach, and a children's play area make this heaven — especially on a hot Texas summer day. Open weekends in May and Sept., daily Mem. Day–Labor Day. All-day admission: adults $28.50, children 3–11 $23.85 + tax.

GOLF

Landa Park Golf Course (830-608-2174; www.golfsatx.com/courses/Landa _Park_Golf_Course; 340 Landa Park Dr., New Braunfels, TX 78130) An 18-hole municipal course. Greens fees weekdays are $14; weekends $16. Call for tee times. Miniature golf, too, for $2 per game per person (830-608-2169; 192 Landa Park Dr., New Braunfels, TX 78130).

Sundance Golf Club (830-629-3817; www.sundancegolf.com; 2294 Common St., New Braunfels, TX 78130) Challenging 18-hole course for the serious golfer. With four lakes on the course, water is a factor on seven of the holes. Signature hole #3 is a 337-yard par 4 dogleg over a large lake named appropriately No Guts, No Glory.

TENNIS

John Newcombe Tennis Ranch (830-625-9105, 800-444-6204; www.newktennis.com; PO Box 310469, 325 Mission Valley Rd., New Braunfels, TX 78131) A complete tennis facility with adult programs, junior summer camps, and all sorts of professional tennis training.

Prince Solms Park (830-608-2160), to the east of Landa Park, has tennis courts.

COMAL COUNTY SHOPPING

New Braunfels

The **Furniture & Antique Consignment Shop** (830-609-0004; 236 W. San Antonio) has "quality gently used furniture and antiques," as well as decorative items and collectibles. **Accents** (830-629-2414; 392 N. Seguin) offers decorative accessories and gifts as well as home furnishings. **Country Faire** (830-620-4382; 270 San Antonio) specializes in country furniture, handicrafts, collectibles, and antiques. **Henne Hardware** (830-606-6707; 246 W. San Antonio) has been in business since 1857, selling not only hardware but also unique gifts.

Gruene

Visit **Gruene Antique Co.** (830-629-7781; 1607 Hunter Rd., New Braunfels, TX 78130), housed in H. D. Gruene's Mercantile Building on the corner of Hunter and Gruene. **Dancing Bear** (830-629-2059; 1632 Hunter Rd., New Braunfels, TX 78130) is in a 1900 historic house. **Texas Homegrown** (830-629-3176; 1641 Hunter Rd., New Braunfels, TX 78130) specializes in denim skirts and jumpers. Try **Cactus Jack's Antiques** (830-620-9602; 1706 Hunter Rd., New Braunfels, TX 78130) and **Cotton Eyed Joe's** (830-606-1995; 1608 Hunter Rd.) for Texas- and Gruene-themed souvenirs and gifts. Fun is **Gruene General Mercantile** (830-629-6021; 1610 Hunter Rd. Gruene), doing business "the old-fashioned way" with a soda fountain, homemade fudge, Texas souvenirs, books, and lots more.

Gruene General Mercantile offers handmade furniture, pottery, and other handcrafts.

Eleanor S. Morris

KENDALL COUNTY

Kendall County was named for a man who was both a pioneer sheepman and an adventurous newspaperman. George Kendall was one of the founders of the *New Orleans Picayune*, in Louisiana, but he also raised sheep and goats in the Hill Country. After a calm spell on the ranch he liked to get out and cover the news himself. In between, he traveled back and forth to New Orleans, keeping an eye on both his newspaper interests and his sheep and goats. When the county was created in 1862 from Blanco and Kerr Counties, it was named after him. The terrain consists of a hilly plateau with spring-fed streams, caves, and scenic drives. Two small towns, Boerne (pronounced "burn-ee") and Comfort, are of interest.

Boerne

In 1851 a town named Tusculum, a commune for a group of German intellectuals, was moved 2 miles east from its original site and formally renamed Boerne after a German political writer and poet of the time, Ludwig Borne, whose criticism of the political order in Germany in the 1840s inspired the immigrants.

Comfort

This little town was established by German settlers from New Braunfels who were so worn out by their journey that when they found this pretty, picturesque site with its pure water, they settled right down and called it "Camp Comfort."

KENDALL COUNTY LODGING

A few miles out in the county from the town of Boerne are two resorts: Tapatio Springs and the Guadalupe River Ranch. But fine accommodations can be had in town, as well.

For further information, contact the **Greater Boerne Area Chamber of Commerce** (830-249-8000, 888-842-8080; www.boerne.org; 126 Rosewood Ave., Boerne, TX 78006). There is also a **Bed & Breakfast Reservations Service** (830-336-3809, 866-336-3809; www.BoerneReservations.com).

Boerne

**BOERNE VISTRO &
COUNTRY INN**
830-816-2470, 888-282-7722.
www.boernevistro.com.

Each of the 14 guest rooms of this inn is individually decorated, many with antique or vintage furniture. Set in the center of town, the inn is within easy walking distance of all Boerne's attractions.

911 S. Main St, Boerne, TX
78006.
Price: Moderate.
Credit Cards: AE, D, MC, V.
Handicap Access: No.

The Boerne Vistro (see "Restaurants") offers an extensive menu.

**GUADALUPE RIVER
RANCH**
Host: Amy Dolan.
830-537-4837, 800-460-2005.
www.guadaluperiverranch
.com.
PO Box 877, Boerne, TX
78006.
FM 474, about 8 miles
northwest of Boerne.
Price: Expensive to Very
Expensive.
Credit Cards: AE, D, MC, V.
Handicap Access: Yes, two
rooms.

This beautiful property — 46 guest rooms, 400 acres along the Guadalupe River — has quite a bit of celebrity status. Once it was the hideaway of movie star Olivia de Havilland, who wanted relief from her *Gone With the Wind* fame. The ranch offers a "complete plan" with breakfast, lunch, and dinner; a "sight-seer plan" with breakfast and dinner; and a "breakfast plan." Or indulge your senses at the ranch's spa, which offers its own packages.

What to do here? Tennis, hiking on nature trails, fishing, canoeing, tubing, horseback riding, mountain biking, and enjoying the exercise and game room, swimming pool, hot tub, and sauna — or just plain lazing the day away. The public as well as inn guests may use any of the ranch facilities as well as dine, but reservations are necessary.

TAPATIO SPRINGS
Manager: Jennifer Fierro.
830-537-4611, 800-999-3299.
www.tapatio.com.
PO Box 550, Boerne, TX
78006.
Deep Hollow Rd. off FM 46,
about 4 miles west of
Boerne.
Price: Expensive.
Credit Cards: AE, D, DC,
MC, V.
Handicap Access: Yes.
Special Features: Golf
packages.

This resort has been named one of the top 10 Texas golf resorts. The 18-hole par 72 course designed by Billy Johnston not only offers 6,500 yards of challenging play, but the resort has also recently added another 27-hole course. There are also four lit tennis courts, a heated swimming pool, Jacuzzi, saunas, and fully equipped exercise rooms. Stay in one of 112 rooms, including seven suites and 13 junior suites, in the Ridgeview Complex of one or two-bedroom suites. The Blue Heron Restaurant & Lounge offers gourmet dining in a casual yet elegant setting, or grab a quick bite in the Turn Cafe.

YE KENDALL INN
Host: Mike McClure.
830-249-2138, 800-364-2138.
www.yekendallinn.com.
128 W. Blanco, Boerne, TX
78006.
Price: Moderate to
Expensive.
Credit Cards: AE, D, MC, V.
Handicap Access: One room.

Here's an old stagecoach stop, built in 1859. This Texas landmark was a gathering place for lawmen, cattle drovers, army officers, and other characters of the frontier. Nowadays the inn's nine rooms and four suites all have private baths. The long, wide building fronts on the downtown plaza and houses the Limestone Grill Restaurant and a boutique with very attractive women's apparel. Restored buildings on the property are home to an-

Visitors at Ye Kendall Inn, Boerne.

Eleanor S. Morris

tique and gift shops collectively called The Village. The room rate includes a continental breakfast.

The inn is pretty quiet — "Hill Country quiet," says Mike, "unless there's something going on at the plaza, like the yearly Abendkonzert."

Comfort

THE COMFORT COMMON
Hosts: Jim Lord and Bobby Dent.
830-995-3030.
www.comfortcommon.com.
717 High St., Box 539, Comfort, TX 78013.
Price: Inexpensive to Moderate.
Credit Cards: AE, D, MC, V.
Handicap Access: No.

Six rooms and a suite of this historic hotel are in the original building, the Ingenhuett-Faust Hotel, built in 1880 from plans drawn up by Albert Giles, noted Hill Country architect. The other two, one a log cabin, are in the rear of the property, grouped with several picturesque shops and buildings around two large, open, grassy areas. Porches, swings, and a gazebo make this a relaxing spot. Mimi's Cafe just next door shares the green spaces, and it's where Comfort Common guests take their breakfast of scrambled eggs and sausage, biscuits and gravy, sweet breads and fruit (see "Restaurants"). This popular place gets reserved a year in advance for the Christmas holidays.

MEYER BED & BREAKFAST ON CYPRESS CREEK
Innkeeper: Shane Schleyer.
830-995-2304, 888-995-6100.
www.meyerbedandbreak fast.com.

This interesting collection of historic houses is gathered together around a stone-walled courtyard. The oldest building, dating from 1857, was the last stop for the stagecoach before crossing the Guadalupe River. The newest is a four-plex stucco building constructed in 1920 and operated as the

845 High St., Comfort, TX 78013.
Price: Moderate.
Credit Cards: AE, MC, V.
Handicap Access: Yes.

Meyer Hotel until 1956. Breakfast is served in the White House Hotel, built in 1887 when the railroad came to Comfort. You might start the day with a mushroom and black olive quiche or scrambled eggs and ham slices rolled into a croissant. Bite-size German potatoes seasoned and stir-fried, sausage in biscuits, rolls and fresh fruit, and lemon poppy seed cake are among the offerings.

Eleanor S. Morris

The Comfort Common bed & breakfast is a historic hotel built by a noted Hill Country architect.

KENDALL COUNTY RESTAURANTS AND FOOD PURVEYORS

Boerne

BOERNE VISTRO
830-249-9563.
911 S. Main St., Boerne, TX 78006.
Price: Inexpensive to Moderate.

The classic English country setting, along with an extensive menu, make this a pleasant dining experience. The back of the large room is open to 22-foot bookcases, and upstairs the sports bar has a view overlooking downtown Boerne. Specialties include jäger schnitzel, trout amandine, and grilled sal-

These well-stocked bookshelves are at the back of Boerne Vistro.

Eleanor S. Morris

Cuisine: Continental.
Serving: L, D weekly; B Sat.–Sun.
Credit Cards: AE, D, MC, V.
Handicap Access: Yes.

mon cilantro, among many others. On Fri. and Sat. nights, bananas Foster are served, and on the second or third Thurs. of the month there's a wine tasting, "Wines Around the World." And this friendly family place lets kids under 10 eat free on Thurs. nights.

FAMILY KORNER
210-249-3054.
1234 Main St., Boerne, TX 78006.
Price: Inexpensive.
Cuisine: Home-style.
Serving: B, L, lunch buffet, D (closes at 2pm Sun.).
Credit Cards: D, MC, V.
Handicap Access: Yes.

The lunch buffet yields up fried chicken and roast beef, carrots and green beans, creamed potatoes, cabbage cooked with chunks of ham, fresh pinto beans, fluffy biscuits, and apple cobbler to top it all off, all at bargain prices. Dinners come with potatoes, salad, and dinner rolls.

Restaurant decor is Hill Country German, with signs saying DANKE SCHÖN, AUF WIEDERSEHEN, and DIE KÜCHE WILKOM. Wooden booths sport tulip stencils, and there's a birdcage, pictures, and planters. A cocktail lounge, the Dutch Boy Club, is in the rear (closed Sun.), and there's live country music.

PEACH TREE KOUNTRY KITCHEN
830-249-8583.
448 S. Main St., Boerne, TX 78006.
Price: Inexpensive.
Cuisine: American Home-style.
Serving: L Tues.–Sat.
Credit Cards: AE, D, DC, MC, V.
Handicap Access: No.

Daily lunch specials include such old-time favorites as meat loaf, or more gourmet offerings such as crispy walnut chicken breast. There's always a delicious homemade soup of the day, plus a quiche of the day. If it should (rarely) happen to be a cold day, you might find Cajun shrimp gumbo on the menu. And you'll want to save room for such desserts as butternut maple or pecan fudge cake. The china is old and fine; the napkins are lace.

Comfort

CYPRESS CREEK CAFE
830-995-3977.
408 Hwy. 27 W., Comfort,
TX 78013.
Price: Inexpensive.
Cuisine: American Home-
style.
Serving: L, D Tues.–Sat., L
Sun.
Credit Cards: AE, CB, D,
DC, MC, V.
Handicap Access: Yes.

Although the Cypress Creek Cafe is no longer on Cypress Creek, it has moved only two and a half blocks away. Delicious liver and onions, chicken and dumplings, and baked meat loaf are popular here. The steaks, fish, seafood, sandwiches, and salads are all prepared from family recipes.

MIMI'S CAFE
830-995-3470.
814 High St., Comfort, TX
78013.
Price: Inexpensive.
Cuisine: Home-style.
Serving: L Thurs.–Mon.
Credit Cards: MC, V.
Handicap Access: No.

The restaurateurs here aren't fooling when they say they love to cook — and cook whatever strikes their fancy. The bookshelf crammed with cookbooks is testimony to their dedication (the books are not for sale, no matter how much the clients beg). The tiny stone building was the post office back in 1908, and you can elect to eat inside or on the rear patio, which shares lovely green space with Comfort Common next door. Try the baked potato soup, the green chili chicken spaghetti, and the bread pudding with bourbon sauce, and especially the famous German chocolate pie, a remarkable concoction of flaky crust, creamy caramel filling, and a rich and crunchy chocolate, coconut, and pecan topping.

KENDALL COUNTY FOOD PURVEYORS

Bear Moon Bakery (830-816-2327; 401 S. Main, Boerne, TX 78006) Housed in the Joe Voght Building, with a stone marker overhead dating it from 1912. Cinnamon rolls, pigs in a blanket, and assorted cookies, rolls, and cakes fill the bakery case. There is a breakfast buffet of these goodies as well as sandwiches, soups, and salads for lunch.

Sister Creek Vineyards (830-324-6704; www.sistercreekvineyards.com; 1142 Sisterdale Rd., Sisterdale, TX 78006, on FM 1376 12 miles north of Boerne) Chardonnay, pinot noir, and cabernet sauvignon are made here from traditional French techniques in a restored century-old cotton gin. Gracefully aged in French oak casks with a minimum of filtration and fining, the wines can be tasted daily 12–5pm, or by appointment. "Out of the way, but worth the trip," is the winery's boast.

KENDALL COUNTY CULTURE

ARCHITECTURE

In *Boerne*, almost every structure still standing was built of Hill Country limestone, beginning with the **Kendall County Courthouse,** one of the oldest in the state still in use. It was started in 1870 and finished in 1908. **City Hall,** a two-story limestone building, was originally built to house one of Boerne's first schools.

From 1876 to 1920, Alfred Giles was a prolific architect in South Texas, and *Comfort* boasts having more buildings of his design than anywhere else, with the exception of San Antonio.

HISTORIC SITES AND MUSEUMS

In both Boerne and Comfort, as well as much of the rest of the Hill Country, museums are often housed in historic buildings.

Boerne

KENDALL COUNTY AGRICULTURAL HERITAGE CENTER
830-537-4526.
PO Box 1076, Boerne, TX 78006.
Next to city park on Hwy. 46 E.
Open: Sat. and Sun. 1:30–4:30pm, closed mid-Dec.–mid-Jan.
Admission: Free.

Exhibits tell the tale of pioneer farm life, displaying items used to develop the frontier. A working blacksmith shop is described as the only one of its kind west of the Mississippi. There's also an 1896 threshing machine and other antique farm machinery, implements, and equipment.

KUHLMANN-KING HISTORICAL HOUSE AND HENRY J. GRAHAM BUILDING
830-249-2030.
402 E. Blanco St., Boerne, TX 78006.
Open: Sun. 1–4pm, and by appointment.
Admission: Free.

This complex of two historic buildings is staffed by knowledgeable volunteer docents who are well versed in Boerne's history. The changing museum exhibits in the Graham House showcase items donated by community members.

Comfort

All along the 800 block of High Street you'll find what may be the most complete 19th-century business district still standing. Many of the buildings were designed by Alfred Giles, and most are still in use today.

Goldbeck-Faltin Cabin (7th St., next to Faltin & Company) is Comfort's oldest building, built in 1854 as the first mercantile establishment. It was bought in 1856 by August Faltin and has been in the Faltin family ever since. Great-grandson August Faltin III is restoring the *Fachwerk* cabin. Some of the wood paneling in the house is rare longleaf pine, and August has also collected some fine furniture pieces of the same wood.

Eleanor S. Morris

The Goldbeck-Faltin Cabin is Comfort's oldest building, built in 1854 in the Fachwerk *style*

Faltin General Store (see "Shopping"), built in 1879, was the first two-story building in town and also the first to be designed by Alfred Giles. It served as a general store and warehouse, with the owners residing on the second floor.

The **Comfort Museum** is in Jacob Gass's blacksmith shop, circa 1891. The present owner has made it available as a museum, but it's open only on special occasions or by appointment. It's on the corner of 8th and High Street.

Comfort has the only memorial to Union soldiers in the state of Texas. Many of the German settlers, here only a few years, very naturally were opposed to secession. But being Union sympathizers didn't make them very popular, and in 1862, when 65 of them decided to head for Mexico, they were ambushed by a group of 94 Confederate cavalrymen. Nineteen of them fell in the battle on the west bank of the Nueces River over in Real County; nine more, wounded, were executed. Grieving friends and relatives erected the monument, with its touching inscription, TREUE DER UNION, on High Street.

LIBRARIES

The **Public Library** in _Boerne_, in the historic Dienger Building, is recognized as one of the finest for a city of this size. There's a historic research room and interesting exhibits like the 1614 Low German (Platte-Deutsch) version of Martin Luther's translation of the Bible, one of only 10 known to exist today.

SEASONAL EVENTS

In JANUARY there's the **Junior Livestock Show and Sale**.

FEBRUARY to DECEMBER are **Boerne Market Days**. FEBRUARY also sees the **St. Valentine's Day Motorcyle Massacre Rally**.

MARCH has the **Hill Country Optimist Antique Show** at the fairgrounds (830-995-3670).

APRIL hosts the two-day **Spring Art Walk** on Main Street (830-249-4635).

Father's Day in JUNE is the occasion for **Berges Fest**, the Festival of the Hills, with three days of food, fun, and festivities. The celebration is a rich portrayal of Boerne's German heritage, with lots of lederhosen and oompah music at Main Plaza (830-249-4635).

JUNE through **August** brings **Abendkonzerte**, free summer evening performances by the Boerne Village Band in Main Plaza.

In SEPTEMBER, the **Kendall County Fair** is Texas's second-longest-running county fair. That's when professional cowboys show off their riding and roping skills at the rodeo. More bronc-busting goes on Saturday and Sunday, while at the Exhibit Hall farmers, ranchers, cooks, and bakers vie for blue ribbons and cash prizes (830-995-4442).

In late OCTOBER visit the Boerne **Key to the Hills Fall Antique Show**, sponsored by the Chamber of Commerce and complementing Boerne's reputation as an antiques destination (830-249-8000).

In NOVEMBER, around Thanksgiving, enjoy **Dickens on Main**, a Victorian event (830-816-1796).

DECEMBER brings **Lighting of the Town, Weihnachts Fest Parade** (830-816-2176), and **Oma's Christmas Fair**.

KENDALL COUNTY RECREATION

Camping enthusiasts should head for **Cascade Caverns** and **Guadalupe River State Park**, described below. For fishing, try **Boerne City Lake**, yielding largemouth bass up to 10 pounds, or **Guadalupe River State Park**. For golfing, **Tapatio Springs**, described in "Lodging," is a good choice.

Places for swimming and other water sports are the parks listed below. Windsurfing is popular on Boerne City Lake, where no powerboats are permitted.

NATURE

The Hill Country has several deep, ancient living caverns that offer great hot weather escapes — if only for a moment.

CASCADE CAVERNS
830-755-8080.
226 Cascade Caverns Rd.,
Boerne, TX 78015.
Off I-10, 16 miles southeast of Boerne.
Open: Mon–Fri. 10am–5pm,
Sat.–Sun. 9am–5pm.
Admission: Adults $11.95,
children 3–11 $7.95,
children under 3 $1.

The caverns here are long and narrow, requiring some stooping under still-dripping ceilings, but this offers an intimate look at many formations not usually seen so closely. The grand finale is the Cathedral Room, with one of the largest waterfalls in Texas, plunging 100 feet down the cavern walls into a 20-foot-deep pool.

A slide presentation before the tour explains the cavern's formation by flowing water, which dissolved and absorbed the limestone to carve out the tunnel-like walls. Tours begin every half hour and last about an hour.

The 105-acre park and campground also offer picnic grounds, swimming pool (summers), gift shop, snack bar, dance pavilion, and meeting hall.

CAVE WITHOUT A NAME
830-537-4212.
325 Kreutzberg Rd., Boerne,
TX 78006.
6 miles north of Boerne on
FM 474, then follow signs.
Open: Daily (except
holidays) 10am–4:40 pm.
Admission: Adults $11,
children $6, under 5 free.

"Deepest, darkest secret in Texas," claims the Cave Without a Name. Why the odd name? When it was discovered, a contest for a name was held at local schools, and this is what won! Guided tours last an hour and a half, and rubber-soled shoes are recommended. Maybe even a light wrap: the caverns are 66 degrees year-round.

The **Cibola Wilderness Trail** along Cibola Creek is a great place for hiking, a 65-acre greenbelt divided into various ecosystems: marsh, prairie, cypress creek bottom, and upland woods. Trails vary in length from 0.25 mile to 2.6 miles. The Cibola Nature Center (830-249-4616; 140 City Park Rd., Boerne, TX 78006) offers environmental awareness programs.

PARKS

Boerne City Park (830-249-9511; Hwy. 46 E., Bourne, TX) This park offers an Olympic-size swimming pool, eight lit tennis courts, baseball, soccer and softball fields, and volleyball courts.

Comfort Park (bounded by Main and Broadway, 4th and 5th Sts., Comfort, TX) This city park was dedicated in 1854 by Comfort founder Ernest Altgelt. On the west side of the park there is a bust of Altgelt and a gazebo.

Guadalupe River State Park (830-438-2656, 512-389-8900 camping reservations; www.tpwd.state.tx.us./park; 3350 Park Rd. 31, Spring Branch, TX 78070, 13 miles east of Boerne on Hwy. 16) Here are over 1,900 acres of scenic Hill Country on the beautiful Guadalupe River. Across from the park, limestone cliffs line the river and cypress trees shade the picnic and camping areas. Natural rapids flow within the park, and all sorts of wildlife may be seen, such as white-tailed deer, coyote, fox, and armadillo. To the delight of birders, the park's juniper thickets provide a resting place for the rare golden-cheeked warbler. The park provides tent and RV camping, rest rooms, showers, picnic sites, fishing, canoeing, swimming, and hiking. There's also a Texas Park Store.

KENDALL COUNTY SHOPPING

B oerne has quite a few shops full of antiques and other necessities along the seven-block historic downtown district. The street signs say HAUPTSTRASSE (German for "High Street"), but the addresses are listed as on Main Street. In Comfort, the shopping highlight is the town's antiques stores.

Boerne

Alte Stadt Mall (830-249-8192; 265 S. Main St., Boerne, TX 78006) Here's a collection of small shops in a courtyard. **Humdinger's** (830-249-7067) has gifts, clothing, and collectibles; **Furniture Plus** (830-249-1821) has antiques, handmade furniture, and jewelry. **Boerne Clock Co.** (830-249-6080) is not only the shop for antique and new clocks, but it also offers service, repair, and restoration of timepieces. For a break, **Boerne Apple Company** (830-249-4706), right in the center of it all, offers homemade apple pie, apple crisp, and Cornish pasties.

Heartland Gifts (830-749-7869; 140 S. Main St., Boerne, TX 78006) has fine gifts, jewelry, and clothing.

HeyDay (830-249-4951; 615 S. Main St., Boerne, TX 78006) There's not only handcrafted furniture but also primitives, folk art, and decorative accessories.

Traditions at the Depot (830-816-2795; 518 S. Main St., Boerne, TX 78006) On the banks of Boerne's Cibola Creek, housed in a restored 1883 rural Texas railroad depot, you'll find not only women's clothing but also distressed pine furniture, hooked rugs, lamps, and even Spode china.

Comfort

Antiquities, Etc. (830-995-4190; 702 High St., Comfort, TX 78013, at 7th St.) American primitives, Victoriana, and old pillars, posts, and pediments fill this large shop set back from the corner by a grassy yard. Two sisters, Nancy Billingsley and Jane Braswell, run the establishment from behind a wonderful long wooden seed cabinet whose drawers are filled alternately with seed corn and hard candies. There's a huge, spectacular carved wooden gateway from India.

Faltin & Company (830-995-3279; 7th and Main St., Comfort, TX 78013) You'll find fine collectibles here as well as antiques and specialty gifts. August Faltin, whose great-grandfather built the German *Fachwerk* cabin next door, prides himself on displaying such fine and unusual items as Russian filigree jewelry.

Highbrow & Hicks Antiques (830-995-4192; 22 Hwy. 87, Comfort, TX 78013) Full of Hill Country treasures in a historic house, this 7,000-square-foot gallery features dealers of American and European fine furniture and accessories, as well as works by Texas artists.

KERR COUNTY

Historic Campe Verde General Store and Post Office.

Eleanor S. Morris

Another county named for a member of Stephen F. Austin's colony is Kerr County. Named for James Kerr, it was created in 1856 from the western part of Bexar (pronounced "bear") County. Hills, spring-fed streams, and Ingram Lake and Dam on the Guadalupe River make Kerr County yet another beautiful Hill Country county, but with a difference.

In 1921 the U.S. Department of Health announced that Kerrville was the healthiest spot in the nation. This brought a regular parade of consumptives here in the early part of the century. Nowadays this healthy reputation probably accounts for the many kids' summer camps up and down the river.

The U.S. Army frontier post Camp Verde was established in 1855 on the banks of Verde Creek, part of a string of forts built to protect pioneers. In 1856 the post had the dubious distinction of being the only camel base on the frontier. Jefferson Davis, secretary of war in 1855, had the bright idea of purchasing a herd of camels to study whether they would make better pack animals in the West than horses and mules. This interesting experiment was interrupted by the Civil War, and reports say that by the time the war was over, the camels were scattered all over. The experiment was not resumed — by then the railroads were beginning to replace pack animals of all kinds.

The army abandoned the camp in 1869, and the only thing you'll find in Camp Verde is the Camp Verde General Store. But it's a fine old-timey store, and the real friendly folks there enjoy telling the tale of the Texas camels. (See "Shopping.") Most of the action in Kerr County centers around the city of Kerrville; Ingram and Hunt are centers of summer camping on the river. All three towns are just a few miles apart along the Guadalupe River.

Kerrville

The man behind Kerrville was Charles Schreiner, who came from France in 1852, became a Texas Ranger, went off to the Civil War, and came back broke. Backed by a prosperous businessman, he opened a department store that is still in business today. A man of many parts, he also believed that sheep raising could be profitable and helped make Kerrville a mohair capital. Additionally, he was instrumental in bringing the railroad to Kerrville, and he established the Schreiner Institute, now Schreiner College.

Hunt

Hunt is on the cypress-laden banks of the Guadalupe River and is the site of many private summer camps for youngsters.

Ingram

Here the Old Spanish Trail crosses the Guadalupe River. Ingram is named for the man who built the first store and post office here.

KERR COUNTY LODGING

Kerr County lodging consists mainly of resorts and motels, the resorts taking advantage of lovely locations on the banks of the Guadalupe River. Bed & breakfast establishments are a smaller-scale alternative.

For more information, contact the **Kerrville Convention & Visitors Bureau** (830-792-3535, 800-221-7958; www.ktc.net/kerrcvb; 2108 Sidney Baker, Kerrville, TX 78028).

Kerrville

DAYS INN OF KERRVILLE
830-896-1000, 800-329-7466.
2000 Sidney Baker,
Kerrville, TX 78028.
On Hwy. 16.
Price: Moderate.
Credit Cards: AE, D, DC, MC, V.
Handicap Access: Yes.

One of the Hill Country's newest motels, Days Inn offers 40 rooms, each one with a microwave, refrigerator, coffeemaker, and hair dryer.

FLAGSTAFF INN
830-792-4449, 888-896-0397.
906 Junction Hwy.,
Kerrville, TX 78028.
Price: Moderate.
Credit Cards: AE, DC, MC, V.
Handicap Access: Yes.
Special Features: Small pets allowed.

Close to shopping, restaurants, and river recreation areas, this motel has 20 rooms as well as 19 apartments if you're planning to stay for a while. The courtyard has picnic tables and grills, and the motel offers cable TV and some kitchenettes.

INN OF THE HILLS RIVER RESORT
Manager: Richard Bill.
830-895-5000, 800-292-5690.
1001 Junction Hwy.,
Kerrville, TX 78028.
Price: Moderate to Very Expensive.
Credit Cards: AE, D, DC, MC, V.
Handicap Access: Yes.

The Inn of the Hills is a classic Kerrville resort on the Guadalupe River, where you can lounge by the river or practice your golf on the putting green. Enjoy swimming, fishing, and boating on the river, or work out at the adjacent Family Sports Center, which guests of the resort can enjoy free. There are beautiful gardens, and you can sail a small sailfish or paddle a boat right beneath the window walls of the River View Restaurant, the resort's dining room.

RIVER RUN BED & BREAKFAST INN
Hosts: Ron and Jean Williamson.
830-896-8353, 800-460-7170.
www.riverrunbb.com.
120 Francisco Lemos St.,
Kerrville, TX 78028.
Price: Moderate.
Credit Cards: AE, D, MC, V.
Handicap Access: Yes.

This pretty inn, built of native stone with a sloping tin roof, is a fine example of German-style Hill Country architecture. Containing four guest rooms and two suites furnished in warm country style, with iron bedsteads covered with pretty quilts, the inn is a relaxing spot where bird-watchers get their fill either sitting on a porch or browsing on the property. Check out the turn-of-the-century pharmacy counter in the living room, with a collection of early medicine.

The inn also boasts a wonderful cook: "I'm not a chef," protests innkeeper Ron. "I'm a cook. Never took formal training." We think you'll agree he doesn't need it after you down a breakfast of a mild Southwest quiche (with peppy salsa on the side), potatoes Prescott (hash browns wth ham, Monterey Jack and Colby cheeses, topped with hollandaise sauce à la eggs Benedict), homemade country oat bread, and a fruit bowl of four fruits, perhaps pineapple, peaches, strawberries, and apples. Ron has won a national award for one of his recipes — there's the proof of the pudding!

Y. O. RANCH RESORT
Manager: Virginia Barton.
830-257-4440, 877-967-3737.
www.yoresort.com.
2033 Sidney Baker,
  Kerrville, TX 78028.
Price: Expensive.
Credit Cards: D, DC, MC, V.
Handicap Access: Yes.

The covered wagon out front gives you a good idea what to expect inside: an interior dedicated to the spirit of the Texas ranch, filled with antiques, artifacts, and other remembrances of a century ago. The stone walls, high-beamed ceiling, mounted animal heads, tile floors, iron chandeliers, and wall sconces all hark back to the days of great ranches when countless cattle roamed endless acres. The Western-theme rooms are grand to stay in, too.

Hunt

RIVER INN RESORT
Manager: Chelsea
  Barrington.
830-238-4226, 800-841-0501.
www.riverinnresort.com.
HC 2, Box 269, Hunt, TX
  78024.
Price: Moderate to
  Expensive.
Credit Cards: MC, V.
Handicap Access: Yes.

This is a real getaway for fun, rest, and relaxation: 60 condominium units are equipped with all the basic necessities — but no telephones or television (though each unit has a cable connection, and portable televisions are available if you just can't stand all the nature here). It's much more fun, though, to enjoy all the activities on the beautiful Guadalupe River: a water chute, tubing, canoeing and paddleboating, fishing, playing tennis, volleyball, shuffleboard, and horseshoes, and a game and family room to gather in. A restaurant, Gallops on the River, is also here.

**SUNDOWN CARRIAGE
HOUSE BED &
BREAKFAST**
Host: Sandra Eyster.
830-238-4169.
Rte. 2, Box 263A, Hunt, TX
  78024.
Price: Moderate to
  Expensive.
Credit Cards: None.
Handicap Access: No.
Special Features: Two-night
  minimum.

Accommodations include one comfortable downstairs room with its own entrance, and a two-bedroom, kitchen, and living-room suite upstairs, all furnished in French provincial and antiques. Breakfast is served on a lovely terrace one level down from the house and overlooking the Guadalupe River, very quiet and private. No pets please, Sandy says. "We have enough for anyone!" — a Great Dane, golden retriever, and three cats.

KERR COUNTY RESTAURANTS AND FOOD PURVEYORS

Kerr County cuisine offers not only the traditional Hill Country menu of chicken-fried steak, tamales, and sauerbraten, but also some updated fare in Kerrville and Hunt — thanks to the influx of restaurant-goers from Houston and San Antonio, parents of the summer camp kids along the river.

Kerrville

BIGGARDI'S
830-895-1441.
843 Junction Hwy.,
  Kerrville, TX 78028.
Price: Moderate.
Cuisine: American.
Serving: L, D.
Credit Cards: AE, D, MC, V.
Handicap Access: Yes.

Local diners like Biggardi's because the big black-and-white tiled restaurant, with its shiny chrome tables and chairs, has the feel of the '50s. Owner Bill True confesses to liking old movies, and the restaurant is full of film-star nostalgia: posters and murals of the likes of Groucho Marx and Laurel and Hardy are interspersed with Walt Disney characters. It's informal, too, with people coming in wearing tuxedos or shorts and sandals. They come in for the no-microwaving, no-rewarming steak and shrimp, burgers and beer, the fresh salad bar, and the crisp and crunchy onion rings and fries piled high. The charbroiled chicken breast is tender, the burgers juicy, and it's all cooked out there right in the open, and you can watch if you want. Or you might prefer to watch major sporting events on the big-screen TV, while the kids in this family place run up and down the chrome-railed steps leading to the raised dining area. Beers are both domestic and imported, both old faithful and new trends. Of the latter, manager Ron Wynn says, "We try them, and if they stay popular we keep them; otherwise they go."

The juicy sweet/tart peach cobbler is cooked in a cast-iron stove over in a corner, and the chocolate suicide cake is called that because it's to die for. "We're the only Kerrville restaurant listed with the Texas Restaurant Association," Bill and Ron like to brag.

BILL'S BAR-B-QUE
830-895-5733.
1909-A Junction Hwy.,
  Kerrville, TX 78028.
Price: Inexpensive.
Cuisine: Barbecue.
Serving: L Tues.–Sat.; closed
  Sun. & Mon.
Credit Cards: None.
Handicap Access: Yes.

Don't be put off by the rustic look of the place, with its open-woodshed, tin-roof appearance on the edge of the highway to Ingram and Hunt. The locals know what's what, and Bill sells out fast, which sometimes results in even more abbreviated hours. But once you've tasted the succulent ribs, the tender fork-cutting brisket, the well-seasoned sausage, and the juicy chicken in Bill's barbecue sauce, you'll understand why this is a Kerrville-Ingram-Hunt classic, a must stop on the road for those in the know. If you think ahead, you can even have *cabrito* (kid) — but you have to order this in advance.

COWBOY STEAK HOUSE
830-896-5688.
416 Main St., Kerrville, TX 78028.
Price: Moderate to Expensive.
Cuisine: Steak, Seafood.
Serving: D; closed Sun.
Credit Cards: AE, D, MC, V.
Handicap Access: Yes.

We're talking serious steak here, in a family-owned-and-operated house considered one of the best places to eat in town. For years they've been cooking over oak and mesquite wood and flavoring everything they put on the open circular stone pit with their own secret seasonings — but not before making sure the patron is not on a special diet (like no salt or pepper). Whether it's a "Super Kicker" top sirloin, a "Cowboy" T-bone, or a "Cowgirl" strip, it's cooked to perfection any way it's ordered — from rare (cool-red center) to well done (cooked dry) or beyond (then you're on your own!). Ours were medium with a perfect hot pink center, the baked potato was soft and creamy, the salad crisp and fresh. It's not all steak, either. Succulent swordfish, catfish, lamb, quail, and buffalo steak are on the menu; Louisiana gumbo, too.

And it was all enjoyed in a mini-museum because we were surrounded by cowboy art. The bronze by Kerrville artist Don Hunt, the etched-glass room divider, the Jack Terry paintings on the walls — it all adds to the western ambiance of the restaurant. Of the pencil sketches framed on the walls, Linda Ferris, the manager, says, "We gave crayons or pencils to artists from the museum [Cowboy Artists of America Museum] and told them to draw whatever they wanted."

There are three dining rooms; in the middle room is an interesting collection of bottles of hot sauce belonging to owner Richard Lorrie Ferris. (His brand, RLF, is all over the restaurant, too.) "It's still a beginner collection at 250," says daughter Linda. The wine room at the end has floors of mesquite wood; some fine Texas wines are on offer from Llano Estacado, Cap Rock, Slaughter-Leftwich, and Fall Creek vineyards.

This restaurant is so popular you may have to wait anywhere from five minutes to an hour. "If they're willin' to wait, we're willin' to serve them," Linda says, and it's no hardship in the pleasant western-motif bar, with a circular open stone fireplace, mesquite floor, and live entertainment on Fridays and Saturdays.

DEL NORTE RESTAURANT
830-257-3337.
710 Junction Hwy., Kerrville, TX 78028.
Price: Inexpensive.
Cuisine: American, Mexican.
Serving: B, L.

Being voted the best breakfast in Kerrville has not gone to the heads of owners Carmen and Rudy Rosales; they've been doing this for more than 15 years. Even though an unending chain of customers pours through the door of this clean, bright roadside cafe, service remains prompt and cheerful.

Credit Cards: AE, D, MC, V.
Handicap Access: Yes.

The huevos rancheros are just spicy enough, topped with Rudy's special sauce and accompanied by ham, refried beans, and tortillas. Rudy is the main chef, and he serves some mean barbecued spare ribs, with tender meat falling off the bone. This comes with mashed potatoes, green beans, and pinto beans. The salad bar is fresh, with crisp greens and fixin's. There are also seafood entrées to be had most days. Dessert choices include homemade buttermilk and pecan pies, and carrot cake.

HILL COUNTRY CAFE
830-257-6665.
806 Main St., Kerrville, TX 78028.
Price: Inexpensive.
Cuisine: Home-style, Tex-Mex.
Serving: Mon.-Fri. 6am–2pm, Sat. 6am–11am; closed Sun.
Credit Cards: None.
Handicap Access: Yes.

This is where the home folks go for breakfast — and have been doing so for more than 80 years. What with all the meetin' and greetin' it's a wonder any eatin' gets done. Eggs and omelets are served with hash browns or grits, toast, or light and fluffy biscuits; eggs rancheros come with hash browns or beans, flour tortillas, and hot sauce; and the breakfast taco eggs can come with either potato, sausage, bacon, or ham. The daily lunch special is a bargain, with such delectable home-cooked choices as smothered pork chops, stuffed bell peppers, meat loaf, baked chicken, and even a Mexican plate. And of course there's chicken-fried steak and deep-fried catfish.

JOE'S JEFFERSON STREET CAFÉ
830-257-2929.
1001 Jefferson St., Kerrville, TX 78028.
Price: Moderate.
Cuisine: Southern Home-style.
Serving: L, D Mon.–Fri., D Sat., closed Sun.
Credit Cards: D, MC, V.
Handicap Access: Yes.

In a lovely old Victorian mansion built in 1890, Joe Sanders, who perfected his culinary art at Threadgill's in Austin, serves Southern-style home-cooked meals, choice steaks, and fresh seafood in the connecting rooms of the oldest home in Kerrville. The house has been virtually unchanged except for the closing of the open porches on the first and second floors, which gave Joe more rooms in which to serve his mouthwatering down-home dishes like chicken-fried steak and chicken-fried chicken, a delicious departure from the classic steak but with the same batter and homemade scratch gravy on the side. Vegetables are country style; there's usually a choice of broccoli and rice casserole, black-eyed peas, mashed or new potatoes, or carrots glazed with sugar, butter, and cloves.

The grilled filet of sirloin is cut from the heart of the sirloin and served with fresh sautéed mushrooms. Fresh gulf coast shrimp is always available, too, either hand breaded and fried to a golden brown or boiled and served with homemade cocktail sauce. If you like, you can have all one or the other, or half and half. Catfish might be blackened, Cajun style, or hand breaded and deep fried in pure cholesterol-free vegetable oil (a small concession to health in all this old-fashioned indulgence). Wines are from both California and Texas. "Tourists like Texas wines," Joe says, and he stocks the best from Bell Mountain, Baron Creek, and Pecan Street as well as Shiner and other popular beers.

KATHY'S ON THE RIVER
830-257-7811.
417 Water St., Kerrville, TX
  78028.
Price: Moderate.
Cuisine: International.
Serving: B, L, D Weds.–Sat.
Credit Cards: AE, D, MC, V;
  no personal checks.
Handicap Access: Yes.

Kathy calls her cuisine international because she's from Taiwan but learned to cook in America. A good example is the plate of crispy wontons served with salsa, placed in front of us as soon as we sat down on the lovely terrace overlooking the Guadalupe River. The restaurant has an indoor dining room as well as several terrace levels outdoors for viewing the calm river, the greenery of Tranquility Island, the overhanging cypress trees, and the mallard ducks — very relaxing. Wrought-iron chairs, tables covered in bright flower-printed vinyl tablecloths, and the fresh air complete the mood.

The teriyaki-grilled chicken breast was especially tender and tasty — the sauce is one of Kathy's secrets. And the coleslaw was a surprise: crispy and sweet with chunks of pineapple and raisins among the shredded cabbage and carrots. The chicken-fried steak, a Texas standby, was creditable, although perhaps it could have done with a little less generous portion of cream gravy. The wine list includes several from Texas's Ste. Genevieve, Llano Estacado, and Fall Creek vineyards. Special drinks from the bar are another of Kathy's fortes. Some she has gathered from different regions, while some — like her special frozen margaritas — are her own concoction.

PATRICK'S LODGE
830-895-4111.
2190 Junction Hwy.,
  Kerrville, TX 78028.
Price: Inexpensive.
Cuisine: Franco-American.
Serving: L, D.
Credit Cards: All.
Handicap Access: Yes.

Everyone walking in the door is greeted personally by Patrick, a transplanted Frenchman who makes a wonderful friendly Texan. He leads the way (letting you take a look at the delicious lunch buffet as you pass) to the dining area, a square wood-paneled room with large windows overlooking Goat Creek. Specialties are venison, veal, steak, and wild game. Also on the menu: fried mushrooms and stuffed mussels; filet mignon or chicken au poivre; medallions of venison Grand Veneur (sauce poivrade, red currant jelly, black pepper, brandy, and wine), as well as seafood and light choices for calorie counters.

Not unexpected is a lengthy wine list; the full bar offers sparkling wines, mixed drinks, imported and domestic beer, and nonalcoholic wine and beer.

TORTILLA FACTORY
830-257-4646.

This place is such a well-kept secret that it's almost impossible to find. It became a challenge

228 Jefferson St., Kerrville, TX 78028.
Corner of Rodriguez.
Price: Inexpensive.
Cuisine: Mexican.
Serving: L, early D
Mon.–Fri. 11am–6:30pm, Sat. 11am–6pm, closed Sun.
Credit Cards: None.
Handicap Access: No.

after several people whispered, "Romero's has the best Mexican food in town." Turned out to be in a small white building with only a sign pasted in the window saying Yes We're Open. Around to the side along Rodriguez, black paint on the wall announced Tortilla Factory, but there was no Romero anywhere. (As it turns out, Louis Romero is the owner.)

Inside, the regulars were all lined up by the window in the small space (with one table in the corner for take-out customers), and their instructions were to get in line at the small counter and place an order. They said, "When it comes you can go in and eat [in a small adjoining room] or take it with you." People kept coming in and doing both, and the place was humming. Tamales are made fresh every day in this mom-and-pop operation, and one happy customer told us they're like home cooking: you never know what to expect; sometimes they were hotter than others.

We tried the chalupa compuesta, a crisp tortilla with a layer of refried beans and cheddar cheese, a mound of lettuce, all topped with perfectly seasoned guacamole. The Mexican dinner, too, was as good as we've had anywhere, and better than many a Tex-Mex restaurant's offerings of enchilada, tamale, refried beans, rice, and chili, with corn tortillas. The small dining room has two pine-paneled walls and a third decorated with bullfighting murals, and the tables are simple Formica. The food was delicious; the experience, exhilarating.

Hunt

WAGON WHEEL CAFE
830-238-4095, 800-460-4401.
HC1 Box 158, Hunt, TX 78024.
Price: Moderate to Expensive.
Cuisine: Hill Country Contemporary.
Serving: L, D; closed Mon. and Jan.–Feb.
Credit Cards: D, MC, V.
Handicap Access: Yes.

A touch of California has come to the Hill Country in the form of chef Fred L. Raynaud, whose many credits include a listing in *Palm Springs Life* magazine as one of the "Great Chefs of the Desert" (1986). The restaurant, on the grounds of the Mo-Ranch Conference Center, is open to the public, and reservations are definitely in order. The restaurant's western decor of Hill Country stone and redwood decorated with horseshoes, Stetsons, and saddles is elegantly done; tables and chairs are Mexican ranch style, of cedar and pigskin, and tables are covered with long green runners. The glassware is thick-stemmed and handmade, and the china is heavy turquoise pottery.

The food served on those plates is robust and delicious, from the fried green tomato appetizers, crunchy and filled with creamy guacamole and cheese, to the champagne, lime, and herb-poached salmon tossed in a light mascarpone sauce with bow-tie pasta and vegetables. The West Texas rib eye was topped with ancho-chili sauce and Monterey Jack cheese, a tasty blend of flavors. The desserts are fantastic and clever; two must-tries are the mango-banana quesadillas — layered flour tortilla with mascarpone cheese and mango coulis — and the chocolate chimichanga, which is filled with melted chocolate, marshmallows, and pecans and served with a Kahlúa chocolate sauce.

KERR COUNTY FOOD PURVEYORS

the greengrocers deli & gourmet shop (sic) (830-257-3354; 225 W. Water St., Kerrville, TX 78028) is open Mon.–Fri. 10am–3pm for delicious sandwiches and desserts, as well as an impressive array of packaged gourmet items for sale. Almost the best part is entering the shop and inhaling the mouthwatering aromas therein. Breads — wheat, onion, rye, sourdough, pumpernickel, and white — are baked on the premises and make super sandwiches.

KERR COUNTY CULTURE

ARCHITECTURE AND HISTORIC DISTRICTS

Architect Albert Giles built Kerrville's Schreiner Mansion — now home of the Hill Country Museum — and he was the first builder to use the limestone that was everywhere for the taking. Craftsmen from Germany were imported to do the stonework, and the pink granite for the columns was imported from Italy.

Pick up a tour map of Kerrville's Downtown Historic District from any one of more than a dozen sponsors. You'll see 17 historic buildings, including homes, churches, shops, and the courthouse.

MUSEUMS

COWBOY ARTISTS OF AMERICA MUSEUM
830-896-2553.
1550 Bandera Hwy.,
Kerrville, TX 78028.
Open: Daily June–Aug.,
Tues.–Sat. Sept.–May;
9am–5pm, Sun. 1–5pm.
Admission: Adults $5,
seniors $3.50, children
6–18 $1.

The museum building is a work of art in itself, with an entrance ceiling composed of 18 domes made of a light brick and positioned without supporting forms. The gallery floors are of mesquite tree trunks cut into squared-off slices and highly polished, and the long galleries and rooms contain a large collection of paintings and sculpture by noted Western artists, many of whom actually lived the cowboy life. (According to the museum, all the artists are cowboys at heart.)

This sculpture, "Wind and Rain," stands at the entrance to the Cowboy Artists of America Museum in Kerrville.

Eleanor S. Morris

HILL COUNTRY MUSEUM
830-896-8633.
226 Earl Garrett St.,
Kerrville, TX 78028.
Open: Hours vary; call for times and admission.

Captain Charles Schreiner's mansion is the home of this museum filled with beautiful things from Schreiner's heyday: parquetry fashioned from 10 different woods, Oriental rugs, crystal chandeliers, and lovely furniture. German masons built the stone walls, the brass fixtures came from France, and the house contains a collection of both Schreiner family and Kerr County memorabilia.

THEATER AND CINEMA

Arcadia Theater (PO Box 1662, 701 Water St., Kerrville, TX 78029), in the old opera house building, runs films. A restoration committee, meanwhile, is raising funds for the theater's repair.

Smith-Ritch Point Theater of the Hill County Arts Foundation (830-367-5122, 800-459-HCAF; www.HCAF.com; PO Box 1169, Ingram, TX 78025) About eight performances take place Feb.–Nov. in an outdoor theater on the Guadalupe River, with the audience sitting under the stars. There's an indoor theater, too, for inclement weather.

SEASONAL EVENTS

Contact the Kerrville Convention & Visitors Bureau (830-792-3535, 800-221-7958) for further information.

The **Second Saturday Art Trail** (830-896-5530) takes place the second Saturday of each month, with more than a dozen galleries, all staying open until 8pm.

In JANUARY there's the **Junior Livestock Show**, with an auction.

FEBRUARY brings the **Hill Country Home and Garden Show** (830-895-5424) as well as a **Valentine's Weekend Celebration** (830-792-9830).

In MARCH, the **Spring Fest at the Point** (830-367-5121) includes a "white elephant" sale as well as food and drink, live entertainment, and more.

APRIL brings the annual **Easter Hill Country Bike Tour** (713-781-6052) and the **Easter Festival & Chili Cookoff** (830-864-4614).

MAY sees the annual **Kerrville Folk Festival** (800-435-8429), with songwriters and bands, concerts, arts and crafts, and more. Also the **Texas State Arts & Crafts Fair** (designated by the legislature as the official arts and crafts fair of Texas), with wine tasting, heritage craft demonstrations, live entertainment, and more. Paintings, pottery, sculpture, furniture, toys, leatherwork, clothing, and jewelry — it's all on exhibit and for sale (830-896-5711).

In JUNE there's a **Youth Rodeo** (830-216-5893) and a **Second Sunday Summer Serenade** in Louise Hays Park (830-257-0809).

JULY brings a **Community Patriotic Sing** and **4th of July on the River** (830-257-0809).

In AUGUST the **Kerrville Wine & Music Festival** (800-435-8429), a family outdoor music festival, celebates national songwriters and Texas wineries.

In SEPTEMBER the **Frontier Society of Austin** sponsors a college exhibit at the Hill Country Arts Foundation (830-367-5121), as well as a **Texas Gun and Knife Show** (830-257-5844). Buy and trade arrowheads, cowboy artifacts, etc.

OCTOBER brings the **Kerr County Fair** to the fairgrounds (830-257-8000).

In NOVEMBER there's both a **Christmas Bazaar** (830-367-5121) and a **Christmas Art Market** (830-895-2911).

In DECEMBER, join townsfolk for a **Community Messiah Sing** (830-257-0809).

KERR COUNTY RECREATION

The best places for boating, camping, fishing, hiking, and swimming in Kerr County are the parks described below.

BICYCLING

The **Hill Country Bicycle Works** (830-896-6864; 1412 Broadway, Kerrville, TX 78028) has just about everything human powered on wheels: bikes — mountain, road, cruiser, kids, tandems, low riders — in-line skates, and all sorts of accessories. They provide local route maps and sponsor weekly rides. Open Mon.–Fri. 10am–6pm, Sat. 10am–4pm.

FAMILY FUN

Zebras are among the exotic animals on the grounds of the Y. O. Ranch in Kerrville.

Eleanor S. Morris

Take the kids to the **Family Sports Center** (830-895-5555; 1107 Junction Hwy., Kerrville, TX 78028) for swimming, racquetball, and bowling, among other activities.

The whole family will enjoy viewing the exotic game on the **Y. O. Ranch**, where zebras, giraffes, and antelope are among the 36 species to be spotted on a guided tour of the historic Schreiner Ranch. The 50-square-mile ranch was established in 1880 by Capt. Charles Schreiner, and it's still a family-run working ranch, well known for registered quarter horses and longhorn cattle (830-640-3222, 800-YO-RANCH; Mountain Home, TX 78058). Tours: 10am daily; adults $28.95, children 12 and under half price.

GOLF

Golfland (830-896-4653; 199 Spur 100, Kerrville, TX 78028) A practice facility with night lighting, automatic and grass tees, target green, chipping and putting greens, sand bunkers, and a pro shop. Open Mon.–Sat. 9am–6pm, Sun. noon–6pm.

Scott Schreiner Municipal Golf Course (830-257-4982; Country Club Rd., Kerrville TX 78028, at Sidney Baker) This 18-hole course presents a refreshing challenge among rolling hills with great views — you'll want to take care not to be distracted. Pro shop, electric carts, putting greens, showers, and lockers are on the premises. Open year-round at 7:30am; no reservations.

HORSEBACK RIDING

If you've brought your boots and jeans, you can hit the trail in the Hill Country and feel like a real cowboy or cowgirl. **Lazy Hills Guest Ranch** (830-367-

5600; Hwy. 27 W., Henderson Branch, Ingram, TX 78025) offers trail rides and Texas cookouts.

PARKS

Kerrville-Schreiner State Park (830-257-5392, 830-257-CAMP for reservations; www.tpwd.state.tx.us/park; 2385 Bandera Hwy., Kerrville, TX 78028, on Hwy. 173) You'll find beautiful hills and the clear waters of the Guadalupe River in this 517-acre park. Wildlife enthusiasts will enjoy spotting white-tailed deer, turkeys, mallard ducks, raccoons, armadillos, and squirrels. There's swimming in the river, but no lifeguard on duty. Canoe and tube rentals are available. Fishing from the lit pier might net perch, bass, catfish, and crappie. Some 8 miles of hiking trails wind amid the live oak, juniper, and Spanish oak. Campsites for tent campers include water; other campsites provide water, electricity, and sanitary dump stations. There's also a Texas State Park Store. The park is open year-round, 8am–5pm daily, with a 2pm checkout for overnight guests. During the busy season, March–Thanksgiving, reservations for camping are recommended (Austin Central Reservations, 512-389-8900).

Louise Hays City Park (830-257-7300; Thompson Dr., Kerrville, TX 78028, west of Sidney Baker) A lovely park with the Guadalupe River running through it, right in the heart of downtown. There are shaded picnic tables, and a footbridge crosses the river to Tranquility Island, where the grassy riverbanks are shaded by cypress trees. Canoeing, paddleboating, and tubing 10am–dusk.

Riverside Nature Center (830-257-4837; 150 Francisco Lemos St., Kerrville, TX, 78029) is a small farm that has been transformed into an urban wildlife and native plant sanctuary, with more than 100 species represented: shrubs, cacti, wildflowers, and native trees and grasses. Open daily, dawn to dusk.

TENNIS

H. E. Butt Municipal Tennis Center (830-896-7955; 801 Tennis Dr., Kerrville, TX 78028, south of Tivy High School) Fourteen lit courts open to the public. Pro shop, lessons available. Open Mon.–Thurs. 9am–9pm, Fri.–Sat. 9am–5pm, Sun. 1–5pm.

KERR COUNTY SHOPPING

Browse through **Old Republic Square** (225 Junction Hwy., Kerrville, TX 78028), more of a courtyard than a square, lined with boutiques on either side. Shaded by pecan trees and cooled by fountains, 12 shops offer an assortment of goods and services. For instance, **Lynne's Treasure Chest** (830-257-2800) has unique ethnic ladies' apparel, while in **Little Bit of Texas** (830-896-

0300) you'll find gifts, souvenirs, T-shirts, caps, and lots of Texas books. And you can refresh yourself at the **Old Republic Inn** (830-896-7616), with great food, homemade desserts, and, of course, "friendly service."

Additional shopping places in the county are **James Avery, Craftsman** (830-895-6805; PO Box 290708, Kerrville, TX 78028, off FM 783 north of I-10); **Hill County Arts Foundation** (830-367-5121; PO Box 1169, Ingram, TX 78025, 507 TX Hwy. 39); **Kerr Arts & Cultural Center, Inc.** (830-895-2911; 228 Earl Garrett in the Old Post Office in downtown Kerrville, TX 78029); and the **National Center for American Western Art** (830-896-2553; 1550 Bandera Hwy., Kerrville, TX 78029). At **River Hills Mall** (830-896-0606; 200 Sydney Baker S., Kerrville, TX 78029, on Hwy. 27) you'll find department stores such as **Beall's** and **J C Penney,** among others.

On the outside walls of the **T. J. Moore Lumber Company**, at the intersection of TX 39 and TX 27 between Ingram and Kerrville, are the Kerr County Historical Murals: "History On A Wall." **Camp Verde General Store** (830-634-7722; at intersection of Hwys. 173 and 480, Camp Verde, TX 78010) is a unique mercantile offering, among other goods, camels in every shape, size, and material.

MEDINA COUNTY

The story of Medina County is a different Hill Country tale. It was settled not by Germans or Spaniards but by a small group of Alsatians from Alsace-Lorraine. Created from Bexar County in 1848, the county is named for the Medina River, which was probably named for Spanish engineer Pedro Medina. There are scenic hills in the north and fertile valleys to the south, with both Medina River and Medina Lake within the county's boundaries.

This land saw a lot of traffic right from the beginning. There was the Old Spanish Trail from Laredo to San Antonio, cutting across the southeast corner. And the stagecoach route from San Antonio to El Paso passed straight through from east to west. Today Hwy. 90 follows the exact same trail.

The county seat is Hondo, which has little of interest for the traveler, but the town of Castroville more than makes up for this as "The Little Alsace of America."

Castroville

Picturesque Castroville, on the banks of the Medina River, has the distinction of being the only Alsatian settlement in the United States. Many of the folks who live here can trace their ancestry back to Alsace-Lorraine, that tiny stretch of Rhineland that has bounced back and forth between France and Germany for years and years.

Castroville was colonized in 1844 by Henri Castro, who wasn't Alsatian, French, or German. He was of Portuguese descent, Jewish faith, and French citizenship, and is considered only second to Stephen F. Austin in the number of

St. Louis Catholic Church on the town square in Castroville.

Eleanor S. Morris

colonists that he recruited to Texas. A banker with a French company when the new Republic of Texas was looking for foreign loans, Castro struck up a friendship with Sam Houston, president of the republic. Houston appointed Castro the Texas Consul General in Paris, then awarded him a land grant in the Medina River valley.

Those first 2,134 Alsatians brought by Castro to the land beside the Medina River west of San Antonio were homesick enough to hang on to their heritage in an enduring way — they recreated a European hamlet, with many small whitewashed, peak-roofed stone cottages, small gardens, and Old World food and traditions. A traveler passing through in 1854 remarked: "The cottages are scattered prettily around a square, and there are two churches, the whole aspect being as far from Texas as possible. It might sit for a portrait of one of the poorer villages of the upper Rhône Valley."

As the town grew along the lovely banks of the Medina River west of San Antonio, it blossomed into an intriguing amalgam, derived from the Alsatian, French, German, Spanish, and English heritage of its early and subsequent settlers. But Castroville has never lost the ambiance created by those first Alsatians. Architects who made a survey of the city in the 1930s pronounced it to be absolutely unique in the United States. The town is recognized by the federal government as a National Historic District and by the state as a Texas Historic District.

For further information, contact the **Castroville Chamber of Commerce** (830-

538-3142, 800-778-6775; www.castroville.com; 802 London St., PO Box 572, Castroville, TX 78009).

MEDINA COUNTY LODGING

THE ALSATIAN COUNTRY INN
830-538-2262, 800-446-8528.
1651 Hwy. 90 W.,
Castroville, TX 78009.
Price: Inexpensive to
Moderate.
Credit Cards: AE, D, DC,
MC, V.
Handicap Access: One
room.

This motel up on a hill has 40 large, comfortable rooms and a wonderful panoramic view of the town just below, although the desk personnel say, "The best thing about this place is the people."

THE LANDMARK INN
Hosts: Park Rangers.
830-931-2133; prior
reservations:
512-389-8900, State Park
Reservation Center.
www.tpwd.state.tx.us/park
/landmark.
402 Florence St., Castroville,
TX 78009.
Price: Inexpensive.
Credit Cards: D, MC, V (if
reserved in advance; cash
or checks on the scene).
Handicap Access: One
room.
Special Features: Breakfast;
closed Mon., Tues.

The Landmark Inn on the Medina River has provided rest for weary travelers for more than a century. Now a State Historic Site, it's owned and operated by the Texas Parks and Wildlife Department (there's a $1 charge to tour the grounds). The inn's eight rooms (some with private bath) are furnished with authentic period pieces, and if you're lucky, you might get the room Robert E. Lee slept in. Or perhaps the upstairs or downstairs room of the tiny bathhouse: Before the Civil War the Landmark Inn was the only place to take a bath between San Antonio and Eagle Pass. It lost this valuable amenity when the lead lining the upstairs, which served as a cistern for water hauled from the river, was melted down into bullets for Confederate troops. You won't find televisions or telephones in the rooms, though they all have air-conditioning.

The L-shaped lobby of the inn serves as a museum, with artifacts and exhibits depicting the history of both the inn and the town. There's an old gristmill on the property, too.

LE PARC BED & BREAKFAST
1315 Lorenzo, Castroville,
TX 78009.
Price: Inexpensive.
Credit Cards: No.
Handicap Access: Yes.

As quaint as Castroville is Le Parc, nestled under shady pecan trees in the center of this charming town. The decor in the three guest rooms is French-German, and in addition to the bath, each room has a small refrigerator, TV, and VCR. The covered patio off to the side has a view of Houston

Le Parc Bed & Breakfast gives a traditional Texas welcome to visitors in Castroville.

Eleanor S. Morris

Square Park across the street. For breakfast you'll be treated to the likes of sour cream pancakes with lemon sauce and toasted almonds, eggs Florentine, Italian omelets, or Belgian waffles with real maple syrup, as well as fresh fruit, cappuccino, tea — and even a breakfast dessert. You might want to stay long enough to sample it all.

MEDINA COUNTY RESTAURANTS AND FOOD PURVEYORS

Thanks to the French and Alsatian influence here, the restaurant scene offers some gourmet variations on traditional Hill Country dining.

ALSATIAN RESTAURANT
830-931-3260.
403 Angelo St., Castroville, TX 78009.
On Houston Sq.
Price: Moderate.
Cuisine: Alsatian, Continental.
Serving: L daily, D Thurs.–Sun.
Credit Cards: AE, MC, V.
Handicap Access: Yes.

Housed in one of the charming Alsatian cottages of Castroville built between 1840 and 1845, the building retains its original look, the restaurant's focus being not on cosmetic updates but on good food.

Diners are offered a delectable menu of Alsatian, French, and Italian dishes, all preceded at the table by a cup of rich beef broth and a loaf of homemade whole-wheat bread with a dish of rich green pesto to dip it in. The comprehensive menu also suggests wines for each dish.

Eleanor S. Morris

The Alsatian Restaurant in Castroville reflects the French and Alsatian heritage of Medina County.

LA NORMANDIE
830-538-3070, 800-261-1731.
1302 Fiorella St., Castroville, TX 78009.
Price: Moderate to Expensive.
Cuisine: Traditional French.
Serving: L Sat. & Sun., Buffet L Tues.–Sat., D Weds.–Sun.
Credit Cards: No.
Handicap Access: Yes.

Here's another restaurant in a little stone cottage, just down the street from the Henri Castro House. Everything is prepared to order, and since good things take time, diners are invited to relax in the pleasant French country home surroundings "in joyful anticipation of the culinary delights to come." Soupe à l'oignon gratinée, escargots à la bourguignonne, filet mignon béarnaise, entrecôte maître d'hôtel — all are served with sauces on the side if you prefer. The menu continues with frog legs sautéed à la provençale, steak au poivre — seemingly a collection of every French dish you've ever dreamed of. Top off your meal with crêpes Normandie filled with apples flambé, crème anglaise, and crème Chantilly, and you almost believe you're in Paris or a little restaurant in Normandy.

LARRY'S RESTAURANT AND BAKERY
830-538-2595.
810 Hwy. 90 W., Castroville, TX 78009.
Price: Inexpensive.
Cuisine: American.
Serving: B, L, D.
Credit Cards: No.
Handicap Access: Yes.

For a casual, relaxed meal, this unpretentious storefront eatery is noted for steak, shrimp, chicken fingers, and old-fashioned hamburgers as well as hand-dipped ice cream — Texas's favorite, Blue Bell ice cream.

SAMMY'S RESTAURANT

830-931-2206, 830-528-2204.
202 Hwy. 90 E., Castroville,
TX 78009.
Price: Inexpensive.
Cuisine: Home-style.
Serving: B, L, D.
Credit Cards: D, MC, V.
Handicap Access: Yes.

Here's a restaurant with a story as old as Castroville — almost. Sammy Tschirhart's grandfather, August Tschirhart, bought the land in hopes that his sons would start their own business. He lived to see his grandsons Leon and Sammy operate a small icehouse in the 1940s, filling the iceboxes of those days before refrigeration. Soon Sammy began to sell hamburgers, and he eventually took over the business, offering curb service until 1969.

Now Sammy and Yvonne have a full-sized, full-service restaurant, serving steaks, seafood, and homemade pies and biscuits. A specialty is their Alsatian sausage, made with "seasonings that our family brought from Europe," Yvonne says. In Europe they used pork; here they use a mixture of beef, pork, and venison.

MEDINA COUNTY FOOD PURVEYORS

Haby's Alsatian Bakery (830-931-2118; 207 U.S. 290, Castroville, TX 78009) Here the aroma of honey buns, apple fritters, fruit stollen, and strudel is irresistible. The bakery is open six days a week; the doors open at 5am (for regulars who come in for coffee and streusel and other goodies on their way to work) and don't close until 7pm. The bakery is named for Nicklaus Haby, who came to Castroville in 1844 from Oberentzen, France. He was hired by Castro to hunt wild game to feed the colonists. Two years later he returned to France to collect his family and bring them to Texas. He served in the Mexican-American War of 1847 as a captain of the Texas Rangers.

R & R's Alsatian & Sausage Products (830-931-2430; 1034 Country Ln., Castroville, TX 78009) Market specialties here are Alsatian sausage and Parisa. Parisa, a local delicacy, is an appetizer of ground meat with cheese, onion, pepper, and salt, eaten with crackers.

MEDINA COUNTY CULTURE

Castroville was laid out in 1844 around a square, and with the plentiful stones of the Hill Country the Alsatians built sturdy houses with sloping roofs like those they had left behind in the Rhineland. The artisans who came over with Castro had to adapt to the material at hand and learned from the Mexicans in Texas to use native materials. Listed on the National Register of Historic Places, 97 of these buildings are still standing; it's interesting to see them scattered in among the contemporary ranch-style homes. Find them with the help of a map from the **Castroville Chamber of Commerce** (830-538-3142, 800-778-6775; www .castroville.com; 802 London St., PO Box 572, Castroville, TX 78009).

HISTORIC BUILDINGS AND SITES

There are quite a number of authentic Alsatian homes and buldings in Castroville, and a walking tour guide can be had at the Chamber of Commerce. Here are a few:

The **Bourquin House**, at the corner of Angelo and Petersburg, behind the Alsatian Restaurant, is considered one of the finest authentic restorations in Texas. It was built in 1849 and remained in the same family until it was sold to the present owners in 1974. It's a perfect little Alsatian cottage, painted a sort of dusty orange, and the stone wall at the rear, abutting the restaurant, was built from an original stone house that had been torn down long ago.

The Tschirhart name is an old Castroville one, too. The family home, known today as the **Cordier-Tschirhart-Seal Home**, is on Isabella between Paris and London Streets. It was built of native rock between 1844 and 1847.

The **Henri Castro Homestead** on Fiorella Street, off Hwy. 90 between London and Lafayette, is a small cottage that was recently restored and enlarged. It is now (surprisingly) a business office, but there's a marker out front telling all about it.

Henri Castro left no descendants in Castroville, but his wife, Amelia Castro, is buried here, in the St. Louis Cemetery at the foot of Cross Hill. In 1864, at the age of 78, he decided to return to France by way of Mexico. He fell ill in Monterrey, Mexico, and died there, but the whereabouts of his grave are unknown.

The restored Steinbach House in Castroville.

Eleanor S. Morris

The **Steinbach House** is an authentic 17th-century house relocated to the banks of the Medina River. The 1,232-square-foot two-and-a-half-story timber and brick *Fachwerk* house was originally built near Wahlbach, France, between

1618 and 1648 by the Steinbach family. It took five years of hard work, a joint effort on both sides of the Atlantic, to realize the dream of bolstering ties of the New World city to the Old World.

LIBRARIES

Castroville Public Library (830-931-4095; 802 London St., Castroville, TX 78009) Not only are there books and pamphlets about the town, there is also an extensive genealogy section in case you have some Alsatian ancestors to look up. An interesting addition is the Oral History Collection, where visitors can listen to tapes offering an invaluable source of unwritten history.

SEASONAL EVENTS

For specific dates and schedules, check with the Castroville Chamber of Commerce (see "Medina County Culture").

Market Trail Days on the second Saturday of each month from MARCH to DECEMBER are on Houston Square, where booths are packed with ceramics, needlework, wooden toys, painting, jewelry, produce — whatever anybody has to sell. Entertainment, besides shopping, includes music, dancing, an old car show, or whatever is timely, such as an Easter Egg contest or a Santa Claus visit.

The **Castroville Antique Show** is held twice a year, usually in MAY and SEPTEMBER, at Koenig Park on the scenic Medina River. In addition to wares for sale, there's an oompah band, a blacksmith, home tours, baked goods sales, and activities at the historic Landmark Inn. Also in May is **Medina County Trades Day**, which, notwithstanding the name, is a two-day event held in Castroville Regional Park (830-931-2525).

St. Louis Day in AUGUST is a big event, a day-long celebration and barbecue.

In DECEMBER Castroville has an **Old-Fashioned Christmas** in Houston Square, with 150 vendors, a free train ride, other entertainment, and a visit from Santa and Mrs. Claus (800-778-6775, 830-538-3142).

MEDINA COUNTY RECREATION

For tennis, hiking, fishing, and swimming and other water sports, refer to "Lakes" and "Parks" below.

GOLF

Alsatian Golf Club (830-931-3100; www.golfsatx.com/courses/Alsatian_Golf _Course; 1339 CR 4516, Ste. 120, Castroville, TX 78009, 2 miles west of downtown Castroville) The 18-hole, 72-par layout is about 6,800 yards in length and has five sets of tees. Fully stocked pro shop and clubhouse. Greens fees $26 weekdays, $35 weekends before noon, cart fee included.

LAKES

Medina Lake, about 20 miles north of Castroville on FM 471 to FM 1283, is 18 miles long and a favorite with water-skiers because of its calm waters both on the lake and in the many coves. Boat ramps are available for launching. Nine miles farther on FM 1283 will bring you to Medina Dam and a spectacular view if you walk across.

PARKS

Castroville Regional Park (830-931-4070; 1209 Fiorella St., Castroville, TX 78009) 126 acres of land on the Medina River. Recreational facilities include an Olympic-size pool; 35 RV camping sites with water, disposal, and electric hookups; two tennis courts and two volleyball courts; and fishing in the river.
(Joe Hoog, who provided the land for the park, used to recall his grandmother's tales of Indians coming down from the hills with wild game and turkey to exchange for sugar, salt, and coffee, and they would let her ride their ponies.)
Landmark Inn State Historical Park (830-931-2133; 402 Florence St., Castroville, TX 78009) In addition to beautiful landscaped grounds and historic structures (see "Lodging"), the park is a setting for many kinds of recreation. Fishing on the Medina River includes catfish, bass, and panfish (although the locals say it's not the fishing ground it's been in the past). For hikers, there is an interpretive trail and a river ford trail across the river. Swimming and wading in the river here are at your own risk.

MEDINA COUNTY SHOPPING

Alice's Antiques (830-931-9318; 1213 Fiorella, Castroville, TX 78009) is a collection of American oak, primitives, and kitchen and nostalgic collectibles.
Art Shop/Boutique (830-931-2428; 301 Lafayette, Castroville, TX 78009) is the place for ladies' fashions, as well as art and gifts.
Castroville Antique Mall (830-931-0604; 416 Paris St., Castroville, TX 78009) has furniture, primitives, glassware and more, in one of the town's historic commercial buildings.
Castroville Emporium (830-538-3115; 515 Madrid St., Castroville, TX 78009, on Houston Square) A selection of antiques, but Donald Belcher specializes mainly in antique lighting fixtures. The ceiling and walls of what was in 1866 a general store are now hung with fabulous fixtures. One or two are still gas

lamps, just for the heck of it, although most have been electrified. "Wasn't so long ago," says Donald, "both gas and electric fixtures were burning in Castroville homes."

Ima's Antiques (830-538-3312 or -2844; 509 Hwy. 90 W., Castroville, TX 78009) A beautifully preserved rose velvet Victorian settee and chairs are the first things we saw on entering this shop full of quality antiques. A second stunner: the Louis XV suite in the next room. New furniture, reproductions, and collectibles are also offered. (Owners Ima and LeRoy Seal live in the historic Cordier-Tschirhart-Seal Home.)

Landmark Inn Gift Shop (see "Lodging") Books, homemade soaps, note cards, jellies and preserves, and special pens handcrafted from local woods.

REAL COUNTY

R eal County (pronounced "ree-AL," with the accent on the second syllable) may be the most sparsely populated county in the Hill Country, but it is abundant in scenic beauty. Hunting, fishing, camping, and scenic drives are the attractions of this county on the western edge of the Hill Country, where the hills rise up majestically just before the land spreads out toward the plains to the west.

Organized in 1913 from surrounding Bandera, Edwards, and Kerr Counties and named for a legislator-rancher, Julius Real, the county has two small towns, Leakey (pronounced "lay-key"), population around 300, and Camp Wood, population 822.

The South Llano River wanders across the north edge of the county, but it's the sparkling clear Nueces River, beginning its journey to the Gulf of Mexico from beautiful Nueces Canyon, that gives Real County much of its charm. The hills are dotted with spring-fed streams, and canyons are thick with cedars, pecans, live oak, and walnut trees.

Real County has another claim to canyon beauty. In addition to Nueces Canyon, Rio Frio, a tributary of the Nueces River, forms Frio Canyon. This beautiful stretch of river flows south from Leakey to Concan down in Uvalde County. The river is popular for swimming, tubing, and fishing, and dozens of camps and lodges line its banks.

Leakey

Leakey was founded by early settlers Nancy and John Leakey, pioneers of Frio Canyon. The main activities for the visitor to Leakey include enjoying the lovely scenery and the outdoor recreation along Rio Frio.

Camp Wood

This town grew around a U.S. Army post established in 1857 on the site of a Spanish mission, San Lorenzo de la Cruz, which had been founded by Franciscan missionaries in 1762. Camp Wood is next to the beautiful Nueces Canyon, with the Nueces Lake and Nueces River to enjoy. There's a legend about the Nueces River: Whoever takes three drinks in three minutes from the river is bound to return for another drink before dying.

REAL COUNTY LODGING

There are only two motels in the little town of Leakey and in Camp Wood, but several lodges and lots of cabins and camping areas. A bed & breakfast and a resort are also described below. For more information, call the **Frio Canyon Chamber of Commerce** (830-232-5222; www.friocanyonchamber.com; PO Box 743, Leakey, TX 78873) or the **Nueces Canyon Chamber of Commerce** (830-597-6241; www.campwood.com; PO Box 369, Camp Wood, TX 78833). The town is popular in the summer for family reunions, among other things, and in the fall for hunting, so it's best to make reservations ahead of time.

Leakey

CLEARWATER RANCH
Hosts: Ruth Ann and Henry
Jones; Lisa and Tom
Teske.
830-232-6686.
www.frio.net.
PO Box 1101, RR 1120,
Leakey, TX 78873.
Price: Inexpensive
(bunkhouse); Moderate
(cabins).
Credit Cards: MC, V.
Handicap Access: Yes, one
cabin.

Imagine owning a mountain! Clearwater Ranch has 400 acres including Cooper Mountain, canyon, and pasturelands along half a mile of sparkling Rio Frio. Here in the great outdoors you can swim, fish, go tubing, hike, and take in the view — and the sunset — from Cooper Mountain. Cottages are air-conditioned, with king-size beds, microwave ovens, picnic tables on the large front porches, and barbecue pits at the ready. The ranch offers hayless rides (perfect for hay fever sufferers) through the working Brangus cattle ranch up to Cooper Mountain for a beautiful sunset.

FRIO CANYON LODGE
Hosts: Katherine and
Elizabeth Ross.
830-232-6800.
www.friocanyonlodge.com.
PO Box 508, Leakey, TX
78873.
Hwys. 83 & 337.
Price: Inexpensive.
Credit Cards: AE, D, MC, V.
Handicap Access: Yes.

The lodge is a wonderful mixture of old and new: The historic stone and cedar buildings were built back in 1941, but the spacious rooms are decidedly up to date, with modern decor, cable TV, and central heat and air-conditioning.

Located in the heart of downtown Leakey, the lodge is only ½ mile from the Frio River.

There's a swimming pool, a wooded courtyard, a picnic pavilion, and a restaurant. The restaurant serves lunch daily except Mon., and dinner Thurs., Fri., and Sat. evenings.

MOUNTAIN LAUREL INN
830-232-5246.
www.mtnlaurelinn.com.
PO Box 720, Leakey, TX 78873.
Hwy. 83 and 7th.
Price: Inexpensive to
  Moderate.
Credit Cards: AE, D, MC, V.
Handicap Access: Yes.

There are 20 rooms in this motel, counting the cabins. The motel rooms are lined up in the usual row, but the cabins are out under the trees.

**WHISKEY MOUNTAIN
  INN**
Hosts: Judy and Darrell
  Adams.
830-232-6797, 800-370-6797.
www.whiskeymountaininn
  .com.
HCR 1, Box 555, Leakey, TX
  78873.
Price: Inexpensive.
Credit Cards: D, MC, V.
Handicap Access: Yes.

This German farmhouse just south of town has a cypress plank exterior and a tin roof. The 50-foot porch, held up by huge cedar tree trunks, is the perfect spot to watch deer, rabbits, and raccoons while rocking away in a wicker rocker. "You might even sight an occasional bobcat," says Darrell. And of course there are birds galore. If you stay in one of the inn's two rooms (shared bath) you'll get a breakfast of juice and fruit and some of Judy's baking; if you're in one of the six cabins, you're on your own — but you'll have a kitchenette to cook in.

Camp Wood

HILL COUNTRY MOTEL
Manager: Lana Harper.
830-597-3278.
200 N. 4th St., PO Box 136,
  Camp Wood, TX 78833.
Price: Inexpensive.
Credit Cards: MC, V.
Handicap Access: No.

Owner Lana Gildart-Harper invites you for a "relaxed, refreshing getaway" at this clean, comfortable motel, with bath/shower combinations and color cable TV. There's a choice of three standard rooms and three with kitchenettes.

WOODBINE INN
Host: Sue Pryce.
830-597-2310.
PO Box 905, Camp Wood,
  TX 78833.
Hwy. 55.
Price: Inexpensive.
Credit Cards: AE, D, MC, V.
Handicap Access: Yes.

Named for the English word for honeysuckle, this nice new motel has two extra-long full-size beds in each room. The color-coordinated air-conditioned rooms are pretty and clean and have a coffeepot and coffee as well as cable TV.

REAL COUNTY RESTAURANTS AND FOOD PURVEYORS

Informality is the key to Real County restaurants, as the following descriptions prove.

A stuffed bear stands in the corner of the Frio Canyon Restaurant in Leakey.

Eleanor S. Morris

FRIO CANYON RESTAURANT
830-232-6810.
Hwy. 83, Leakey, TX 78873.
Price: Inexpensive.
Cuisine: American, Tex-Mex.
Serving: B, L, D.
Credit Cards: D, MC, V.
Handicap Access: Yes.

Window walls, wildlife stuffed and mounted — deer, bobcat, and such — are the decor here. Beware of the huge Kodiak grizzly bear rearing up in a corner! Formica tables and wooden chairs in a storefront building along Hwy. 83, the town's main street — a typical Hill Country cafe. And it's mighty friendly. Folks make themselves at home here, like the two men up from San Antonio for the weekend and enjoying a game of cards as they ate their meal.

The Frio Canyon salad was filling, even on the "Lite Side," with either grilled or fried chicken, chopped lettuce, tomatoes, hard-boiled egg, and cheese. The chef's salad, too, was topped with cheese and a boiled egg. For heartier dining, the pepper steak was spicy with jalapeños and cheese stuffed inside ground beef, with brown gravy on the side, baked potato or fries, and the vegetable of the day. Super nachos are topped with refried beans, taco meat, cheese, sliced jalapeños, and chopped tomato, with guacamole on the side, and you can order either eight or 16 of them. For dessert, among the fruit pies, cinnamon rolls, and doughnuts, the French silk pie was a pleasant surprise.

TJ'S COUNTRY KITCHEN
830-232-4347.
Hwy. 83 N., Leakey, TX 78873.
Price: Moderate.
Cuisine: Tex-Mex, American.
Serving: B, L, D.
Credit Cards: AE, D, MC, V.
Handicap Access: Yes.

If this restaurant looks like a Dairy Queen drive-in to you, you're not far wrong — that's what the building used to be. Now the brick walls and wide windows all around have gotten accustomed to Mexican platters of homemade enchiladas, tacos, and beans. But you'll also find the chicken-fried steak and catfish that are the haute cuisine of the Hill Country.

Camp Wood

CASA FALCON RESTAURANT
830-597-5111.
Hwy. 55, Box 152, Camp Wood, TX 78833.
Price: Inexpensive.
Cuisine: Mexican.
Serving: B, L, D; closed Weds.
Handicap Access: Yes.

The Falcon family, five sisters and four brothers, run this cheery Mexican cantina. Small and cozy under a low ceiling, with the usual pine paneling and Formica tables, the restaurant is made bright with striped Mexican curtains, hanging papier-mâché fruits and vegetables, and mounted game: a formidable set of horns, a beribboned deer head, even a large fish. The beef and chicken fajitas are tender and tasty; the carne guisada (chunks of beef in thick brown sauce) is tender. If you don't find what you want on the menu, "he'll make whatever you want," Mary says of the chef. "But . . . we have everything," she adds.

OLD TIMER RESTAURANT
830-597-2112.
Hwy. 55, Camp Wood, TX 78833.
Price: Inexpensive to Moderate.
Cuisine: American, Tex-Mex.
Serving: B, L, D.
Credit Cards: AE, D, MC, V.
Handicap Access: Yes.

This pine-paneled restaurant sports an encouraging sign: WELCOME. The picket-fence decoration along one wall is hung with mugs and pots. The menu offers breakfast egg plates or cowboy-sized pancake stacks; for lunch, deli sandwiches are spiced up out of the ordinary croissant or sub, with jalapeños added to the lettuce, tomatoes, onion, green peppers, mustard, and mayonnaise. Dinner steaks range from the ubiquitous chicken-fried to beef stew, rib eye, and T-bone; both fried catfish and whitefish are on offer, as are chicken and Mexican dishes.

PARKS PLACE
(No Phone)
101 N. Nueces (Hwy. 55), Camp Wood, TX 78833.
Price: Inexpensive.
Cuisine: Family-style, Country.
Serving: L, D.
Credit Cards: No.
Handicap Access: Yes.

If you're seized with a sudden hunger for a burger, this is the place. The meat patty is even bigger than the bun. The home-style cheeseburgers are delicious; steak and sirloin are also on the menu. On Friday night it's all the catfish you can eat. "We'll serve it, we'll fix it, if somebody wants it," is the motto here.

TONY'S TACO STAND
830-597-5190.
Hwy. 55, Camp Wood, TX 78833.
Price: Inexpensive.
Cuisine: Tex-Mex.
Serving: B, L, D.
Credit Cards: AE, D, MC, V.
Handicap Access: Yes.

Tony's is famous for breakfast tacos, but the enchilada plate — chicken, beef, or cheese — is abundant, and the friendly service is hard to beat.

REAL COUNTY FOOD PURVEYORS

Frio Pecan Farm (830-232-5294; PO Box 425, Leakey, TX 78873, on Hwy. 337 about a mile east of Hwy. 83) Not only can you buy fresh pecans, you can see how they're cracked professionally by taking a tour. Manager Harry Florence (who calls himself a "general flunky") says he'll show people the equipment and answer their questions. And, of course, he'll sell them bags of freshly cracked pecans.

REAL COUNTY CULTURE

HISTORIC BUILDINGS AND SITES

Leakey

Real County Courthouse, the **First State Bank** building, and **Leakey School**, all on Hwy. 83, are built of hand-cut native stone.

On the courthouse grounds, a marker commemorates the history of Leakey and its founders, Nancy and John Leakey. Six miles south of Leakey on Hwy. 336, a marker denotes the site of the McLauren Massacre, the last Indian massacre in the Southwest.

Camp Wood

There's a historic Spanish mission here, Mission San Lorenzo de la Santa Cruz, dating from 1762. Located not quite half a mile north of town on Hwy. 55, it's on the National Register of Historic Places. Restoration of the walls is currently under way, with the goal of restoring the mission to museum state.

MUSEUMS

REAL COUNTY HISTORICAL MUSEUM
830-232-5330.
Evergreen St., Leakey, TX 78873.
At Fourth St.
Open: Fri.–Sat. 10am–4pm.
Admission: Adults $1, children 25¢, under 6 free.

Exhibits here depict the pioneer days in Frio Canyon, with rooms set up just as they were many years ago. Pictures, clippings, and books tell of events in the 1880s and about the early settlers who came from all over the United States to begin new lives in this beautiful canyon.

WILDLIFE ART MUSEUM
830-232-5607.
PO Box 434, Leakey, TX 78873.
On Hwy. 337 E.

This privately owned museum features the art of taxidermy, along with sculpture, paintings, and carvings of wildlife, such as Texas white-tailed deer, buffalo, and birds. The taxidermist combines a

A room in the Real County Historical Museum, set up just as it was many years ago.

Eleanor S. Morris

Open: Mon.–Sat. 9am–5pm, closed Sun.
Admission: Donations.

knowledge of both zoology and sculpture, often spending years studying animals in their native habitats. The wildlife artist captures nature in wood, canvas, and bronze, all displayed in this unique small museum.

On the Rio Frio and in Nueces Canyon

Rio Frio yields catfish, perch, and bass to the anglers casting in its waters. Anywhere along the clear, cold river is also perfect for swimming, snorkeling, and tubing. Snorkelers can clearly see wonderful fish and plant life, and there are special underwater rocks for rock hounds.

Campers should contact the **Frio Canyon Chamber of Commerce** (830-232-5222; PO Box 743, Leakey, TX 78873) for a brochure listing the many cabins and campsites along the Frio River.

In **Nueces Canyon** the river and lake offer swimming, fishing, boating, and tubing year-round. (Adventurous snorkelers and scuba divers bring their own gear to plumb the crystal-clear river waters.) The Nueces River yields yellow and blue catfish and largemouth bass all year; Nueces Lake offers African perch and Guadalupe bass, as well. The lake, formed by a dam in the Nueces River, is 3 miles south of Camp Wood. Nueces Canyon is also the home of woodpeckers, hummingbirds, orioles, finches, doves, and many other bird species.

SEASONAL EVENTS

February in Leakey brings big-name bands from Del Rio, San Antonio, Austin, and even Oklahoma, for the **Blue Grass Festival**.

In **MAY** at the **Shrimp Boil** it's all you can eat for $10.

In **JULY**, the **July Jubilee** in Leakey is a big celebration on the weekend of the fourth, beginning with a parade on Hwy. 83 that marches to the corner of Hwy. 337. Floats and horses lead the way to all-day entertainment on the Courthouse Square, where 65 booths sell arts and crafts, food and drink. Square dancers, storytellers, cowboy poets, and fiddlers contribute to the merriment. Friday and Saturday there's a rodeo, and afterward on Saturday night there's a street dance (830-232-5222).

In Camp Wood in **AUGUST**, the **Old Settler's Reunion** is always the first weekend.

In Leakey there's all the excitement of a **Rubber Duck Race** in the Frio River over Labor Day in **SEPTEMBER**.

OCTOBER in Camp Wood means the **Fall Festival**, a combined hunters' and Halloween celebration.

In **NOVEMBER** in Leakey, the weekend after Thanksgiving, the **Hunters' Dinner and Dance** at the American Legion Hall swings to country-western music.

DECEMBER, there's **Christmas on the Square** in Leakey and **Christmas in the Canyon** in Camp Wood, with singing, Santa Claus, and parades.

REAL COUNTY RECREATION

Camping, boating, and many other activities that take advantage of Real County's scenic beauty are pursued at Wes Cooksey Park, on the Rio Frio, and in Nueces Canyon.

PARKS

Wes Cooksey Park (830-597-3223; Hwy. 55, Camp Wood, TX 78833) This park is technically in Uvalde County but is only 3 miles south of Camp Wood (and 37 miles north of Uvalde). Although park manager Bubba Hickman enjoys telling people to "bring your hammock and just rest under the shade of the beautiful oak trees," he's also quick to point out that the park is open year-round for swimming, boating, fishing, hiking, and camping. Campers will find 33 tent sites with electricity and water and 10 RV sites with full hookups. Facilities include two boat ramps, rest rooms with hot showers, public telephones, a dump station, grills, and campfires.

REAL COUNTY SHOPPING

Leakey isn't exactly the place to shop till you drop, but you may find a treasure or two or pick up some item that you forgot to pack. Camp Wood has

---

Scenic Drives

FM 337 between Leakey and Camp Wood is one of the most scenic roads in the Hill Country, passing through a land of massive timbered hills, steep cliffs, and numerous streams in secluded valleys, with roller-coaster dips and winding curves. A close runner-up is the same road from Leakey east to Vanderpool in Bandera County.

If you're interested in seeing the largest Texas live oak tree in the United States, travel 7 miles south of Leakey on Hwy. 1120 to Rio Frio, the county's first settlement, with the same name as the river it's located on.

---

just a few shops lining the main street along Hwy. 55, but one or two are well worth checking out.

Leakey

Canyon Charm (830-232-6102; Hwy. 83, Leakey, TX 78873) Antiques, collectibles, jewelry, and Texas decor.

Heaven Scent (830-232-5600; Hwy. 83, Leakey, TX 78873) offers imports and gifts.

Josh's Landing (830-232-6292; Hwy. 83, Leakey, TX 78873) "Leakey's only bait and tackle headquarters," they say. This is the place for live bait and fishing tackle as well as camping supplies, swimming gear, river tubes, and hunting supplies. Mon.–Sat. 9:30am–5:30pm, Sun. 9:30am–noon.

Camp Wood

Campwood Trading Post (830-597-4220; PO Box 549, Camp Wood, TX 78833, on Hwy. 55) "This is the Camp Wood mall," Billy Joe says as he displays a coffeepot with a steer skull sitting on the top. "Been here for years, wholesale prices." Calling itself an old-fashioned general store, the trading post spreads out along the highway behind a raggedy wooden fence, and inside you go from room to room (three in all), looking at the myriad collection of, well, stuff, that Linda June and Billy Joe Wilkinson have collected over what looks to be several lifetimes.

Cluttered and crowded, this is a fascinating place for browsing. Gifts like handmade hummingbirds hang down from the ceiling, suspended on ribbons; Garrett & Winchester farm and ranch supplies are stacked on counters below. There's a jumble of hardware, automotive supplies, giftware, everywhere.

Dolores's Unique Designs (830-597-4152; PO Box 352, Camp Wood, TX 78833, on Hwy. 55) Angora goats produce mohair, a durable, lightweight, soft, and warm natural fiber that Dolores weaves into wonderful articles of clothing. A full-length coat of twenty panels may be black and white, many colors, or a solid color. Eye-catching is her "Texas Flag" jacket, a bomber jacket created originally for former Texas governor Ann Richards. You'll be in good company if you decide upon one of Dolores's creations while here in one of the Hill Country's mohair capitals: Hillary Clinton is a customer, too.

Hill Country Furniture (830-597-5353; Llano St. at FM 337, Camp Wood, TX 78833) specializes in fine homemade cedar furniture. They offer tours of the plant.

UVALDE COUNTY

Uvalde County, down in the southwest corner of the Hill Country, was formed in 1850 from part of Bexar (pronounced "bear") County. It was named — more or less — for Gov. Juan de Ugalde of Coahuila, Mexico, a renowned Indian fighter. In 1790 Ugalde united the Comanche, Wichita, and Tawakona Indians and led them against a common enemy, the Mescalero Apache. The successful battle took place in a canyon that became known as Cañón del Ugalde; the county was named for the canyon, with the spelling anglicized to match the way Texans pronounced it.

Since the land is partly on the Edwards Plateau, locals describe Uvalde as having one foot in the Badlands and the other in the Hill Country. But because most of it is below the escarpment and consists of rolling hills, the land also lays claim to being "the back door to the Hill Country." Lots of cool, clear rivers run here, more than 1,100 miles of flowing water — the spring-fed Sabinal, Frio, Leona, and Nueces Rivers — so Uvalde County is a popular place for water enthusiasts. The land is covered with cypresses, cedars, and, in one unique spot (for Texas), maple groves. It's a major deer and turkey hunting area, too.

Uvalde is the county seat; Concan and Utopia are small communities on the sparkling clear Frio River, with resorts, camps and campgrounds, outfitters, and a restaurant or two.

If you drive to Uvalde west on Hwy. 90 you'll pass two towns with amusing signs. At Hondo the road sign cautions: "This is God's Country so don't drive through it like Hell." And at little Knippa the sign just says "Blink."

Concan

North of Uvalde, the great outdoors beckons along the lovely length of the crystal blue and white waters of the picturesque Frio River. A host of Concan area camps on the Frio offer hiking and water sports.

Utopia

Yes, there really is a Utopia, and it's on the Sabinal River across the Frio River from Concan. Originally the town had several other names, until along came a postmaster who happened to read Sir Thomas More's idea of Utopia: "Perfect climate, happy, healthy people . . ." This is it, the postmaster decided, and Utopia it became.

Uvalde

Both "Cactus Jack" Garner (former Vice President John Nance Garner) and former Texas governor Dolph Briscoe hailed from these parts. Uvalde has a tale of gunslinging days: Though some lawmen in the Old West left the law to become criminals, outlaw John King Fisher did the opposite. Fisher had begun a career of lawlessness in the wild border country, but after being carried off to jail a time or two, he reformed and ended up as chief deputy sheriff of Uvalde County. Unfortunately his new occupation was short lived. He was ambushed, so the story goes, while he was in San Antonio on "official business." Thirteen bullets felled him — at the age of 26 — and he's buried in Uvalde's Pioneer Cemetery.

UVALDE COUNTY LODGING

Cabins, camps, bed & breakfasts, motels, and combinations of these offer pleasant choices for places to stay in Uvalde, Concan, and Utopia.

For more information, contact the **Uvalde Convention and Visitors Bureau** (830-278-4115, 800-588-2533; www.uvaldecvb.org; 300 E. Main St., Uvalde, TX 78801).

Concan

CAMP RIVERVIEW
Host: Jim Meyer.
830-232-5412.
1636 County Road 350, Concan, TX 78838.
Price: Inexpensive.
Credit Cards: MC, V.
Handicap Access: Yes.

Also close to Garner State Park, this is a fine place for family camping on the Frio River, with campsites, shelters, RV sites, cabins, tubing on the river, and lots of picturesque picnicking places. There's a country store here, too.

J & L RIVER CAMP
Host: John Clark.
830-232-5758.
HCR 70, Box 480, Concan, TX 78838.
Price: Inexpensive to Moderate.
Credit Cards: None.
Handicap Access: No.

On the Rio Frio, close to Garner State Park, J & L offers cabins and shelter, full RV hookups, and tent sites with water and electricity. They offer shuttle service, too, to tubers who want to float lazily down the river without worrying about how they're going to get back to camp.

NEAL'S LODGES & CAFE
Host: Mary Anna Roosa.
830-232-6118.
Hwy. 127, PO Box 165, Concan, TX 78838.
On the Rio Frio.
Price: Inexpensive to Expensive.
Credit Cards: D, MC, V.
Handicap Access: Yes.

This complex includes 60 cabins, a riverside camping area, RV hookups, a dining room, general store, game room, stables, post office, and laundromat. Besides camping, swimming, and tubing, there are hayrides, horseback rides, and bird-watching weekends.

Utopia

UTOPIA ON THE RIVER
Host: Karyn Jones.
830-966-2444.
www.utopiaontheriver.com.
Hwy. 187, PO Box 847,
Utopia, TX 78884.
Price: Moderate.
Credit Cards: AE, D, MC, V.
Handicap Access: Yes.

Utopia on the River may resemble a motel in that the rooms are all in a row along a common walkway, but it's more like a bed & breakfast because you get a full country breakfast every morning, served in the lodge/gift shop. Banana-bran pancakes or scrambled eggs and biscuits will fortify you for the walk down to the river to inspect the old cypress trees that's between 750 and 800 years old. There's a hot tub, sauna, volleyball, and horseshoes; hiking trails, fishing, and tubing on the Sabinal River; and swimming in the pool.

Uvalde

**GRANNY'S BED &
BREAKFAST**
Host: Mary Lou Berry.
830-278-8803.
319 S. Getty St., Uvalde, TX
78801.
Price: Inexpensive.
Credit Cards: AE, D, MC, V.
Handicap Access: No.

Granny's is located in a 1910 Victorian house shaded by leafy pecan trees. The porch all along the front of the house is made just for relaxing. "Take your shoes off and enjoy the fresh country air," says Mary Lou. The front room has two comfortable sofas for lounging, and the three guest rooms, one with a private bath, are invitingly decorated. For breakfast Mary Lou will perhaps feed you an egg casserole, and she likes to serve either breakfast steaks or both ham and bacon with that, along with cinnamon toast. And of course coffee, juice, and fresh fruit.

MOTELS

Uvalde

Amber Sky Motel (830-278-5602; 2005 E. Main, Uvalde, TX 78802) 40 units, all on ground floor.

Best Western Continental Inn (830-278-5671; 701 E. Main, Uvalde, TX 78802) 87 units, pool, playground, picnic area, handicap access.

Holiday Inn (830-278-4511; 920 E. Main, Uvalde, TX 78802) 151 units, pool, restaurant, cocktail lounge, handicap access.

Inn of Uvalde (830-278-9173; 810 E. Main, Uvalde, TX 78802) 70 units, pool, restaurant, handicap access.

UVALDE COUNTY RESTAURANTS AND FOOD PURVEYORS

"This is the country of chicken-fried steak, barbecue, and Mexican, so if you're a vegetarian you'll starve to death," say the friendly folks of the Uvalde Convention & Visitors Bureau.

Concan

NEAL'S CAFE
830-232-6118.
Hwy. 127, PO Box 165, Concan, TX 78838.
On the Rio Frio.
Price: Moderate.
Cuisine: Country.
Serving: B, L Fri.–Sun., D weekends only.
Credit Cards: D, MC, V.
Handicap Access: Yes.

From the outdoor stone terrace of this restaurant on the grounds of Neal's Lodges (see "Lodging"), you get a gorgeous view of Rio Frio. Indoors, you get generous portions of fried catfish, chicken-fried steak, beef tips, fried chicken — or chalupas to remind you of the locale. "If people don't see what they want on the menu, they order it anyway," says waitress Mary. "The fried chicken is Mrs. Neal's grandmother's recipe!"

Utopia

The Lost Maples Cafe in Utopia.

Eleanor S. Morris

LOST MAPLES CAFE
830-966-2221.
Main St., Utopia, TX 78884.
Hwy. 187, 45 miles north of Uvalde.
Price: Inexpensive.
Cuisine: Family-style

A surprise in this quaint country place, named for Lost Maples State Park just up the road in Real County, is the antique English church-pew booths. Rustic is the word otherwise, with wood floors, rough beam ceilings — and antiques for sale upstairs! The stools along the tin counter facing the

American-Mexican.
Serving: B, L, D.
Credit Cards: MC, V.
Handicap Access: Yes.

kitchen walls were fully occupied, as was almost all the other seating in this popular place. Appetizers include cheese sticks and nachos. There are burgers and club sandwiches, with side orders including fries, onion rings, or Texas toast with gravy. Dinner choices are Mexican meals, steaks, even a fish or shrimp platter — all in all, a pretty complete menu. Delectable pies, meringues of lemon, coconut creme, chocolate, come from Iva Rae's Bakeshop down the street.

Uvalde

EVETT'S BARBECUE
830-278-6204.
301 E. Main St., Uvalde, TX 78801.
Price: Inexpensive.
Cuisine: Barbecue.
Serving: L, D Tues.–Sat.
Credit Cards: None.
Handicap Access: No.

The entire 300 block of Main Street is redolent with delicious mouthwatering odors, thanks to the outdoor barbecuing of this longtime Uvalde tradition. Bob Gagliardi is responsible, as he bastes the meat and stokes the fire alongside the small wooden building. Eating is done inside at picnic tables, and the decor is a windowful of paper towels. Evett's specializes in brisket, smoking anywhere from 14 to 20 a day, and ribs, which are gone by 3pm — so if it's ribs you want, don't dawdle.

JOE TOM'S TEXAS GRILL
830-278-4422.
2217 E. Main St., Uvalde, TX 78801.
Price: Moderate.
Cuisine: Mexican-American.
Serving: L, D.
Credit Cards: AE, D, MC, V.
Handicap Access: Yes.

You can dine indoors or out under the shade in the festive atmosphere of the patio. The large menu is a mix of Mexican specialties, pizza, steak, seafood, and the ubiquitous chicken-fried steak.

LUNKER PEABUCKET
830-278-9754.
810 E. Main St., Uvalde, TX 78801.
Price: Inexpensive.
Cuisine: American.
Serving: L, D.
Credit Cards: AE, D, MC, V.
Handicap Access: Yes.

"World's best mesquite-grilled steak" is the claim here, but you also can choose from chicken-fried steak, the Lily Langtry or the Texas Combo (sirloin and shrimp), other seafood choices, chicken dishes, salads, and more. The large room is pleasant, with terra-cotta walls and western prints, the folks are very friendly, and the baked potatoes are the largest grown. "That's because we got complaints that ours were too small," waitress Amanda explains.

MR. C'S RESTAURANT
830-278-6420.
1296 W. Main St., Uvalde, TX 78801.

For real Mexican food, this is the place. As proof, there's *menudo* (Sundays only), not to mention *cabrito* and *tatema*, as well as your more typical tamales, enchiladas, etc. And if you're not in the

Price: Inexpensive.
Cuisine: Mexican.
Serving: L, D daily.
Credit Cards: Yes.
Handicap Access: Yes.

mood for Mexican cuisine, there are steaks, seafood, and sandwiches on the menu.

**TOWN HOUSE
RESTAURANT**
830-278-2428.
2105 E. Main St., Uvalde, TX 78801.
Price: Inexpensive.
Cuisine: Mexican-American.
Serving: B, L, D, SB.
Credit Cards: AE, D, MC, V.
Handicap Access: Yes.

The lunch buffet Sunday to Friday is fresh and tasty, as is the breakfast buffet both Friday and Saturday night as well as Sunday morning. The menu, like many in the Hill Country, ranges from enchiladas and chalupas to steaks and seafood. But it also has a few items that are different if you yearn for a change: liver smothered in onions, and ham steak crowned with grilled pineapple. And the chicken breast offers a choice: grilled or breaded and topped with cream gravy. Steaks and seafood are served with the restaurant's signature French toast, and there is a "Healthy Menu" low in fat and seasonings.

Though the service was slow, nobody seemed to mind; this popular eatery either sets the town pace or goes along with it.

UVALDE COUNTY FOOD PURVEYORS

Rexall Drug and Soda Fountain (830-278-2589; 201 N. Getty, Uvalde, TX 78884) has been in continuous operation since 1883, and Mary Chapoy has been working there for 40 years. (She says 43, but owner/pharmacist Alan Carmichael says she exaggerates; it's only been 40.) Typical of this extremely friendly town, for years he's opened up half an hour early for a sort of open-house coffee time at the fountain counter. "I get to visit with a lot of tourists as well as town folks," he says. "People wander in." Sandwiches, burgers, Mexican food, and fountain favorites like ice cream sodas and hot fudge sundaes, made with that Texas favorite, Blue Bell ice cream.

UVALDE COUNTY CULTURE

HISTORIC BUILDINGS AND MUSEUMS

A self-guided driving tour of the town's Heritage Homes starts at the Grand Opera House, winds past 16 old homes, and takes in Pioneer Cemetery, where John Nance Garner and outlaw-turned-lawman John King Fisher are buried. A free tour map, created by the **Uvalde Convention & Visitors Bureau**, is available at the bureau (830-278-4115, 800-588-2533; 300 E. Main St., Uvalde, TX 78801).

FIRST STATE BANK OF UVALDE
830-278-6231.
200 E. Nopal St., Uvalde, TX 78801.
Open: Mon.–Fri. 9am–3pm.
Admission: Free.

The extensive $2.5 million art collection of former Gov. and Mrs. Dolph Briscoe is housed in this large local bank. It's an amazing collection, from Rembrandt etchings of 1633 to works of Gainsborough and Reynolds, plus such western artists as Warren and Salinas.

JOHN NANCE GARNER MUSEUM
830-278-5018.
333 N. Park, Uvalde, TX 78801.
Open: Mon.–Sat. 9am–5pm, closed noon–1pm.

This museum in the former home of John Nance "Cactus Jack" Garner, congressman under Theodore Roosevelt and vice president under Franklin D. Roosevelt, is now the property of the University of Texas VP Library, and has been renovated with new exhibits. Garner earned the nickname for his Texas plain-speaking: He once said that the office of vice president "isn't worth a bucket of warm spit." When his wife died in 1948, he gave the home to the city as a memorial to her. He died in 1967 a few weeks before his 99th birthday.

The museum is a treasure house of memorabilia, reflecting the personality of this Texas original. When he broke his gavel during his first day as new Speaker of the House, friends sent more than a hundred gavels as replacement, all now on display.

The Uvalde Grand Opera House, with its "drunken dragon" weather vane atop its cupola.

Eleanor S. Morris

UVALDE GRAND OPERA HOUSE
830-278-4184.
100 W. North St., Uvalde, TX 78801.
Open: Mon.–Fri. 9am–noon & 1–5pm, Sat. 10am–2pm.
Admission: Free; donations accepted.

Built in 1891 and fully restored in 1982, this historic opera house offers a variety of dance and theater year-round. When most of Uvalde's buildings were one-story wooden places, this two-story brick edifice was a local marvel. As in many small-town opera houses, the stage is upstairs. The charming peak-roofed bay window looking out over the street was used as an office by John Nance Gardner; although he bought the building in 1916, the show went on. The sculpture draped around the weather vane on the cupola is known as the "drunken dragon" — according to Uvalde folklore, the artist went out drinking with a buddy before getting to work, and this dragon was the result.

Nowadays, about four performances a year showcase area talent in music and drama. A small museum of local history is on the ground floor, as well as a gift shop with dragon prints, armadillos, mugs, plaques, and charms.

NIGHTLIFE

The hot spot in town is the **Lone Star Saloon** (830-591-9191; Hwy. 83 N., Uvalde, TX 78801).

SEASONAL EVENTS

The year begins with the **Uvalde County Junior Livestock Show** in JANUARY.

In FEBRUARY, catch the **Sahawe Indian Dancers Winter Ceremonials** (830-278-3361).

MARCH brings Sabinal's **Wildhog Festival & Crafts fair** (830-988-2010).

In APRIL there are **Nature Quest Tours** and seminars on birds, bays, butter-flies, and wildflowers (800-210-0380).

In MAY, the Garner State Park **Songwriters Festival** brings arts and crafts as well as performances by singers and songwriters (830-232-6131).

In JUNE take in the **Utopia Rodeo and EMS BBQ** at Utopia Park (830-966-2435).

July brings the **Uvalde Patriotic Celebration,** and the **Sahawe Indian Dancers** return as well.

In AUGUST, you can take in both the **National Soaring Competition** (830-278-4481) and the **Tennis Tournament** (830-278-2004).

In SEPTEMBER there's the **Uvalde Taste of the Town** (830-278-3361).

OCTOBER brings the Uvalde **Holiday Crafts Show** at the Civic Center (830-278-3361) and the **S.W. Texas Junior Rodeo** (830-591-7232).

In NOVEMBER, there's the **Chamber Arts & Crafts Show & Sale** and the Uvalde **City of Lights** on the Plaza.

In DECEMBER, catch **Christmas at the Crossroads** at the downtown plaza (830-278-3361).

UVALDE COUNTY RECREATION

Many of Uvalde County's recreational activities are based at the camps, lodges, and other places along the Leona, Frio, and Sabinal Rivers (see "Lodging"). For additional places to camp, fish, golf, get in or on the water, go hiking or bird-watching, and generally relax and enjoy the scenery, visit the county's parks (see below). Another place for a swim is Uvalde's local pool (830-278-7531, Nopal and Wood), open from May to mid-August.

PARKS

Garner State Park (830-232-6132; www.tpwd.state.tx.us/park; HCR #70 Box 599, Concan, TX 78838, 31 miles north of Uvalde on Hwy. 83) The 1,420-acre park was constructed in the 1930s by the WPA and named for John Nance Garner, vice president under FDR. With more than 10 acres of frontage on the Frio River, the beautiful park is pretty popular, so camping reservations are almost a necessity, at least during the summer months. The park has 211 campsites with water, 146 with water and electricity, screened shelters, rest rooms, showers, dump stations, cabins, a grocery store, laundromat, and various shops.

A riverside forest, a gallery of bald cypress, and pecan and live oak dominating the main developed area make the park a haven for birds and heaven for bird-watchers. The Texas Parks and Wildlife Department offers a helpful pamphlet, "Birds of Garner State Park." For a copy, contact them at 800-792-1112; 4200 Smithville Rd., Austin, TX 78744.

Jardin de los Heroes Park (801 W. Main, Uvalde, TX 78801) The "Garden of the Heroes" honors Uvalde Vietnam War veterans. Picnic facilities and playground equipment are provided.

Park Chalk Bluff (830-278-5515; www.chalkbluff.com; HC 33 Box 566, Uvalde, TX 78801, 15 miles north of Uvalde on Hwy. 55) This family vacation center on the beautiful Nueces River offers shady camping sites, primitive or with amenities, RV sites, cabins (some with air-conditioning), shelters with picnic tables and barbecue pits, tubing, swimming, scuba diving, fishing, put-put golf, and bird-watching. There's also a children's playground with swings and slides, and games such as volleyball, tetherball, and horseshoes. Rest rooms with shower pavilion, full RV hookups, horseback riding.

Uvalde Memorial Park and Golf Course (830-278-6155; 329 E. Garden, Uvalde, TX 78801) Set on the shady banks of the Leona River, which flows through town, the park has a long jogging and walking trail along the river, a covered pavilion, and the Sahawe Indian Outdoor Theater. Municipal tennis courts and the golf course are open to the public. Golfers can play Tues.–Sun. 8am–8pm; fees are $10 weekdays, $12 weekends for 18 holes, $15 for cart rentals. (The word is that the course is not so easy that it's not fun — but not so hard you wish it were time to go home.)

TENNIS

Uvalde High School has 12 lit courts, no reservations required. There are two more lit courts at **Uvalde Memorial Park** (830-278-6155; 329 E. Garden, Uvalde, TX 78801).

UVALDE COUNTY SHOPPING

U valde is a large center for wool and mohair — angora goats were brought to Texas in 1849, and since the 1920s Texas has been the largest producer of mohair in the country. You'll find western wear and accessories here, too.

Concan

Neal's General Store (830-232-6118; Hwy. 127, PO Box 165, Concan, TX 78838, at Neal's Lodges on the Rio Frio) T-shirts, caps, and scarves among the convenience store items — and used paperbacks, in case you want to loll alongside the river and read.

Uvalde

Joe Pena's Saddle Shop (830-278-6531; 2521 E. Main, Uvalde, TX 78801) Leather gear has been hand-tooled here for such celebrities as John Wayne, Joe Namath, and Nick Nolte as well as the Texas Rangers.

Market Square Antiques (830-278-1294; 103 N. West St., Uvalde, TX 78801) This multidealer shop in the old Horner's Building on the square in downtown Uvalde displays antiques, classic furniture, jewelry, glassware, accents, collectibles, and gifts. Open Mon.–Sat. 10am–5pm, Sun. "by chance."

South Texas Fine Woods (830-278-1832; 4326 Hwy. 90 E., Uvalde, TX 78801) Shop here for handcarved mesquite furniture and take a tour of the workshop. Open Mon.–Fri. 8am–5pm.

Uvalde Producers Wool & Mohair Co. (830-278-5663; Hwy. 90 E., Uvalde, TX 78801) All sorts of wool and luxury fibers are for sale here, both in the wholesale showrooms and the retail shop, which is open Mon.–Fri. 8am–noon, 1–5pm.

CHAPTER SEVEN
Hill Country Help
INFORMATION

Eleanor S. Morris

A wall of brochures at the Austin Visitors Center.

Here is a brief compendium of miscellaneous information that may prove valuable for visitors — and perhaps residents as well.

AMBULANCE/FIRE/POLICE

Dial **911** to request an ambulance, to report a fire or any situation requiring immediate police response, or to get help for any and all emergencies in the Hill Country.

AREA CODES

There are four area codes for the Hill Country: **210, 512, 915**, and **830**. Here are the codes for each county:

County	Area Code
Bandera	830
Bexar (San Antonio)	210
Blanco	830
Burnet	512, 830
Comal	830
Gillespie	830
Hays	512
Kendall	830
Kerr	830
Kimble	915
Llano	915
Mason	915
Medina	830
Real	830
Travis (Austin)	512
Uvalde	830

BANKS

A ustin and San Antonio have dozens of banks and ATM machines, so perhaps the easiest thing to do is obtain whatever cash you might need in either city before heading out to the Hill Country. Two good sources of bank information are a town's visitors' guide, which you can usually pick up at the chamber of commerce or visitors center, and the local weekly newspaper. Nowadays, though, convenience stores throughout the Hill Country have ATM machines.

BOOKS ABOUT TEXAS AND THE HILL COUNTRY

H ere are just a few of the many books available about the Texas Hill Country and Texas in general.

Chariton, Wallace O. *One Hundred Days in Texas: The Alamo Letters*. Plano, TX: Wordware Publishing, 1990.

Chipman, Donald E. *Spanish Texas 1519-1821*. Austin: University of Texas Press, 1992.

Crow, Melinda. *The Rockhound's Guide to Texas*. Helena, MT: Falcon Press, 1994.

Douglas, Curran. *Austin Overview*. Austin: Eakin Press, 1995.

Frantz, Joe B. *Texas: A Bicentennial History*. New York: W. W. Norton & Company, 1976.

A Guide to San Antonio Architecture. The San Antonio Chapter of the American Institute of Architects, 1986.

Haley, James L. *Texas: An Album of History*. New York: Doubleday & Company, 1985.

——. *Texas: From the Frontier to Spindletop*. New York: St. Martin's Press, 1985.

Haram, Karen, ed. *San Antonio Cuisine*. Kansas City, MO: Two Lane Press, 1994.

Hill Country Oasis: Barton Springs. Barton Creek. Edwards Aquifer. Austin Parks and Recreation Department, 1992.

Lind, Michael. *The Alamo: An Epic*. Boston: Houghton Mifflin, 1997.

Loughmiller, Campbell, and Lynn Loughmiller. *Texas Wildflowers: A Field Guide*. Foreword by Lady Bird Johnson. Austin: University of Texas Press, 1996.

Michener, James A. *Texas*. New York: Random House, 1985.

Morris, Eleanor S. *Country Roads of Texas*. Oaks, PA: Country Roads Press, 1997.

——. *Country Towns of Texas*. Oaks, PA: Country Roads Press, 1999.

——. *Fairs and Festivals of Texas*. Oaks, PA: Country Roads Press, 1996.

——. *Recommended Country Inns of the Southwest: Arizona, New Mexico and Texas*. Old Saybrook, CT: Globe Pequot Press, 1997.

Permenter, Paris, and John Bigley. *Day Trips from San Antonio and Austin*. Kansas City, MO: Two Lane Press, 1995.

——. *Insider's Guide: San Antonio*. Old Saybrook, CT: Globe Pequot Press, 2002.

——. *Texas Barbecue*. Kansas City, MO: Pig Out Publications, 1994.

——. *Texas Getaways for Two*. Kansas City, MO: Two Lane Press, 1996.

Spearing, Darwin. *Roadside Geology of Texas*. Missoula, MT: Mountain Press Publishing, 1991.

Weems, John Edward. *Dream of Empire: A Human History of the Republic of Texas 1836-1846*. New York: Simon and Schuster, 1971.

Zelade, Richard. *Texas Monthly Guide to the Hill Country*. Houston: Gulf Publishing, 1997.

——. *Texas Monthly Guide to Austin*. Houston: Gulf Publishing, 1996.

CLIMATE AND WEATHER

The Hill Country's location on many rivers and streams ensures a mild climate with an average annual temperature of 70 degrees F. The climate in and around Austin is humid subtropical; but although summer daytime temperatures are hot, summer nights are often more pleasant, with average minimums in the lower 70s.

The Hill Country is less humid than either Austin or San Antonio, and it becomes drier as you head west. The average annual rainfall varies from one location to another (Austin's average is 27.86 inches). The heaviest rain occurs in spring, usually a steady, light rain. Summer rains are usually thundershowers, with large amounts falling in a short time. Snow is very rare and completely insignificant as a source of moisture. When it does fall, it melts soon after reaching the ground.

Prevailing winds are southerly throughout most of the year. The occasional northerly winds, accompanying colder air masses in winter, move over the Gulf of Mexico and soon shift to southerly. Damaging hailstorms and destructive winds are infrequent. Although strong winds, along with sharp drops in temperature, sometimes occur during the winter months as the result of cold fronts, these are of short duration, rarely lasting more than a day or two.

About the only drawback to this temperate climate is the occasional dry spring, during which drought dries up the Hill Country rivers, followed by a season of torrential rains that flood the very same rivers. When this occurs, Hill Country roads can be dangerous to drive. Be sure to heed the cautions in the text (and the signs along the roads); people have drowned trying to drive across low-water crossings during rainy seasons.

But such deluges are infrequent. The Hill Country usually enjoys an average of 300 days of sunshine each year, and winters are truly mild, with below-freezing temperatures rarely occurring more than a few days each year.

COUNTY SHERIFFS

Travelers rarely need the services of county sheriffs, but it's reassuring to know that they're there. Here are numbers to call — "nonemergency" numbers if you have business that doesn't require the use of 911:

Bandera	830-796-3771
Bexar	210-270-6000
Blanco	830-868-7104
Boerne	830-249-9721
Burnet	512-756-8080
Castroville	830-931-4020
Comal	830-620-3400
Gillespie	830-997-7578
Hays	512-393-7896
Kerr	830-896-1216
Kendall	830-995-2688
Kimball	915-446-2766
Llano	915-247-5767
Mason	915-347-5252
Medina	830-931-4020
Real	830-232-5201, or
	911 if no answer
Travis	512-473-9770
Uvalde	830-278-4111

HOSPITALS AND HEALTH CARE

Austin

St. David's Hospital (512-476-7111; 919 E. 32 St., Austin, TX 78705)
Seton Medical Center (512-324-1000; 1201 W. 38 St., Austin, TX 78705)
South Hospital (512-447-2211; 901 W. Ben White Blvd., Austin, TX 78704)

San Antonio

Baptist Medical Center (210-297-7000; 111 Dallas St., San Antonio, TX 78229)
Methodist Hospital (210-575-4000; 7700 Floyd Curl Dr., San Antonio, TX 78229)
Metropolitan Methodist Hospital (210-208-2200; 1310 McCullouch Ave., San Antonio, TX 78229)

Hill Country

Hospitals are located in the major Hill Country towns. Some examples:

Burnet/Marble Falls: Seton Highland Lakes (512-756-6000; Hwy. 281 S., Burnet, TX 78611)
Castroville: See San Antonio hospitals.
Fredericksburg/Mason: Hill Country Memorial Hospital (830-997-4353; 1020 Kerrville Hwy., Fredericksburg, TX 78624) serves Gillespie, Mason, Blanco, and other surrounding counties.
Kerrville: Sid Peterson Memorial Hospital (830-896-4200; 710 Water St., Kerrville, TX 78028)
Kimble: Kimble Hospital (915-446-3321; 2101 N. Main, Junction, TX 76849)
Llano: Llano Memorial Hospital (915-247-5040; 200 W. Ollie, Llano, TX 76843)
New Braunfels: McKenna Memorial Hospital (830-606-9111; 143 E. Garza, New Braunfels, TX 78130)
San Marcos/Wimberley: Central Texas Medical Center (512-353-8979; 1301 Wonder World Dr., San Marcos, TX 78666)
Uvalde: Uvalde Memorial Hospital (830-278-6251; 1025 Garner Field Rd., Uvalde, TX 78801)

LATE-NIGHT FOOD AND FUEL

Out in the Hill Country, folks tend to retire early. But there's still help for those out and about late at night.

If you're benighted in *Bandera*, the **Gas Go Market** at 1001 Main St. is open late at night. In *Burnet* there's **Country Corner** on Hwy. 29 W. In Castroville several gas stations stay open until 11pm weekdays, midnight on weekends. In

Comfort the **Mini Mart #6**, Hwy. 87 and Lindner Ave., 830-995-3232, is open 24 hours and has an ATM machine. **Jek's Pit Stop** in *Fredericksburg* is open 24 hours. In *Kerrville* the **Town & Country** and **Circle K** gas and convenience stores are open late or all night. In *Marble Falls* there are **TravelMart Convenience Store** (830-693-8431; 1301 Hwy. 281 N.) and **Pardner Chevron** (830-693-2034; 1710 Hwy. 281 N.), which is open 24 hours.

Diamond Shamrock in *Leakey* is open until 10 pm. In *Mason* the **Short Stop** is open 24 hours. **Pit Stop Food Mart** is on I-35 in *New Braunfels*. In *San Marcos* both the north and the south **Phillips 66** stations are open late. *Stonewall* has two gas/convenience stores on Hwy. 290, which are open late. In Boerne, there's **Five Star Wrecker** (139 N. Wagon Wheel, 830-981-9193). In *Uvalde* the **Kettle**, 629 E. Main St., is open 24 hours. In *Wimberley* the **Texaco** and **Diamond Shamrock** gas stations are open late or all night.

If all else fails, call the local sheriff's office.

NEWSPAPERS AND MAGAZINES

The Hill Country's proximity to its two gateway cities of Austin and San Antonio means that folks in the Hill Country are likely to read the *Austin American-Statesman* or the *San Antonio Express-News* for their daily news fix, while counting on weeklies like Kendall County's *Hill Country Recorder* for local news.

Austin

The Austin American Statesman (512-445-3500; 305 S. Congress Ave., Austin, TX 78704) The only daily newspaper in Austin. The paper publishes a comprehensive entertainment section every Thurs.

The Austin Business Journal (512-494-2500; 111 Congress, Suite 750, Austin, TX 78701) Covers Austin business news; look for it on Fri.

The Austin Chronicle (512-454-5766; 4000 N. IH-35, Austin, TX 78751) Weekly newspaper covering arts, culture, entertainment, politics.

San Antonio

The San Antonio Business Journal (210-341-3202; 70 NE Loop 410, Ste. 350, San Antonio, TX 78216) Weekly business newspaper.

San Antonio Current (210-828-0044; 1500 N. St. Mary's St., San Antonio, TX 78215) A free newsweekly all about the Alamo City.

The San Antonio Express-News (210-250-3000; 400 Third St., San Antonio, TX 78205) The only daily newspaper in San Antonio. The paper publishes a comprehensive entertainment section every Fri.

Hill Country

You'll find an array of Hill Country (mostly) weekly newspapers with news and information geared not only to the locals but also to visitors. Here are some:

Bandera Bulletin, Bandera County.
Blanco County News, Blanco County.
Boerne Star, Kendall County.
Burnet Bulletin, Burnet County.
Castroville News Bulletin, Medina County.
Comfort News, Kendall County.
Cowboy Country Express (published monthly in Rio Frio), Real County.
Fredericksburg Standard-Radio Post, Gillespie County.
Hill Country Recorder, Blanco, Hays, Kendall County.
Junction Eagle, Kimble County.
Kerrville Daily Times, Kerr County.
Llano News, Llano County.
Mason County News, Mason County.
Mountain Sun, Kerr County.
New Braunfels Herald-Zeitung, Comal County.
San Marcos Daily Record, Hays County.
Traveler Magazine, Uvalde County.
Uvalde Leader News, Uvalde County.
Wimberley View, Hays County.

RELIGIOUS SERVICES

Hill Country towns have virtually hundreds of churches. You'll find a complete listing of churches and other places of worship in the Saturday edition of the *Austin American Statesman* and the *San Antonio Express-News* as well as in local weeklies like the *Hill Country Recorder* and the *Fredericksburg Standard* (see "Newspapers and Magazines").

Another good source for church information is a town's visitors guide, which you can usually pick up at the local chamber of commerce or visitors center.

For both a religious and historic experience, visit one of the San Antonio missions, all of which still function as parish churches (see the chapter on San Antonio, "Historic Sites and Districts").

ROADSIDE SERVICE

The following is a selected list, by town, of service stations providing emergency towing service.

Bandera: Hill Country Towing, 830-535-4592.
Boerne: Five Star Wrecker, 830-981-9198.
Burnet: Advantage Towing, 512-756-7995; Gary's Wrecker Service, 512-756-6666.
Castroville: McVay's Wrecker Service, 830-538-2207.
Fredericksburg: Behrends Tire and Auto Center, 830-997-2668.
Kerrville: Krauss Wrecker and Road Service, 830-257-3477.
Leakey: Leakey Auto Supply and Wrecker Service, 830-232-6656.
Mason: Beatty's, 915-347-5759.
New Braunfels: Hernandez Service Center, 830-629-4102.
Stonewall: Eckert & Son Wrecking, 830-644-2388.
Wimberley: Davis Tire Service, 512-847-2260.

TOURIST INFORMATION

There are numerous public or volunteer agencies ready to serve you with visitor and tourist information:

Austin Convention & Visitors Bureau: 512-474-5171, 800-926-2282; www.austintexas.org; 201-B E. 2nd, Austin, TX 78701.
Bandera County Convention & Visitors Bureau: 830-796-3045, 800-364-3833; www.banderacowboycapital.com; 1206 Hackberry, PO Box 171, Bandera, TX 78003.
Blanco Chamber of Commerce: 830-833-5101; www.blancotex.com; PO Box 626, Blanco, TX 78606.
Burnet County Chamber of Commerce: 512-756-4297; www.burnetchamber.org; 703 Buchanan Dr., Burnet, TX 78611.
Castroville Chamber of Commerce: 830-538-3142, 800-778-6775; www.castroville.com; 802 London St., PO Box 572, Castroville, TX 78009.
Comfort Chamber of Commerce: 830-995-3131; www.comfort-texas.com; PO Box 777, Comfort, TX 78013.
Fredericksburg Chamber of Commerce: 830-997-6523; www.fredericksburg-texas.com; 302 E. Austin, Fredericksburg, TX 78624.
Frio Canyon Chamber of Commerce: 830-232-5222; www.friocanyonchamber.com; PO Box 743, Leakey, TX 78873.
Greater Boerne Area Chamber of Commerce: 830-249-8000; www.boerne.org; 126 Rosewood Ave., Boerne, TX 78006.
Greater New Braunfels Chamber of Commerce: 830-625-2385, 800-572-2626; www.nbcham.org; 390 S. Seguin, PO Box 311417, New Braunfels, TX 78131.
Johnson City Chamber of Commerce: 830-868-7684 and 830-868-7805; www.lbjcountry.com; 406 W. Main St., PO Box 485, Johnson City, TX 78636.
Kerrville Convention & Visitors Bureau: 830-792-3535, 800-221-7958; www.ktc.net/kerrcvb.com; 2108 Sidney Baker, Kerrville, TX 78028.

Kimble County Chamber of Commerce & Tourism Board: 915-446-3190, 800-KIMBLE-4; www.junctiontexas.net; 402 Main St., Junction, TX 76849.

Llano Chamber of Commerce: 915-247-5354; www.llanochamber.org; 700 Bessemer, Llano, TX 78643.

Marble Falls/Lake LBJ Chamber of Commerce: 830-693-4449, 800-759-8178; www.marblefalls.org; 801 Hwy. 281, Marble Falls, TX 78654.

Mason County Chamber of Commerce: 915-347-5758; www.masontxcoc.com; 108 Ft. McKavitt, PO Box 156, Mason, TX 76856.

Nueces Canyon Chamber of Commerce: 830-597-6241; www.campwood.com; PO Box 369, Camp Wood, TX 78833.

San Antonio Convention & Visitors Bureau: 210-207-6700, 800-447-3372; www.sanantoniocvb.com; PO Box 2277, San Antonio, TX 78298.

San Marcos Convention & Visitors Bureau: 512-396-2495, 800-782-7653; www.sanmarcostexas.com; PO Box 2310, San Marcos, TX 78667.

Stonewall Chamber of Commerce: 830-644-2735; www.stonewalltexas.com; PO Box 1, Stonewall, TX 78671.

Uvalde Convention & Visitors Bureau: 830-278-4115, 800-588-2533; www.uvaldecvb.org; 300 E. Main St., Uvalde, TX 78801.

Wimberley Chamber of Commerce: 512-847-2201; www.wimberley.org; PO Box 12, Wimberley, TX 78676.

IF TIME IS SHORT

A lthough we've tried to cover everything that makes the Hill Country special, how do you know what to choose if you have time for only one or two destinations or sights? Here are some highlights for those who have only a short time in the hills.

AUSTIN

In Austin, stay at the **Driskill,** even for only one night, to absorb some of the elegance that was so exceptional when everything else was pretty much raw frontier. Then take a look at that Texas pride, the tall **Texas State Capitol** of native pink limestone with fossils imbedded in the stone. If it's the right time of year, around sunset join the crowd waiting to watch the world's largest colony of Mexican freetail bats come out from under the **Congress Avenue Bridge** for the nightly insect feast. Another special Austin sunset is watching that spectacle over **Lake Travis** from the **Oasis Restaurant.**

And don't miss the new **Bob Bullock State History Museum,** which, not surprisingly, is a Texas-size museum. The expansive lobby features a four-story rotunda rising over a 40-foot terrazzo design incorporating themes from Texas's past. Passing through the rotunda, visitors enter the Grand Lobby to stand on a 50-foot granite map of the state. There are three floors of state-of-the-art exhibits and 17 different media and interactive experiences tracing Texas history.

WEST AND SOUTH OF AUSTIN

BURNET COUNTY: In the town of _Burnet,_ **Longhorn Caverns** has sheltered everything from cavemen to Confederate gunpowder makers to a subterranean nightclub as an escape from Hill Country summer heat. Take a light sweater or jacket and wear rubber-soled shoes for the tour. And up the road a piece at Canyon of the Eagles Lodge and Nature Park, the **Vanishing Texas** cruise on Lake Buchanan views waterfalls and, in the fall, nesting bald eagles.

GILLESPIE COUNTY: Not to be missed is _Fredericksburg_. With its German-pioneer history, food, and _Gemütlichkeit_ (friendliness), it's one of the Hill Country's most popular tourist spots. Check out the **National Museum of the Pacific War,** an outstanding record of the Pacific theater of World War II. Admiral Chester Nimitz was a local boy who made good, and the museum is housed in his grandfather's Steamboat Hotel.

And you wouldn't want to pass up a chance to take a look at — and possibly climb — nearby **Enchanted Rock,** one of three such domes in the world. Touring nearby **LBJ Ranch** in Johnson country is perfect for history buffs.

HAYS COUNTY: It would be a pity to miss the flavor, both gustatory and atmospheric, of the **Salt Lick,** that quintessential Texas barbecue pit just west of *Wimberley*.

SAN ANTONIO

Of course the **Alamo** in San Antonio is a must, as is the **River Walk,** even for an hour or so. Take some refreshment in the historic **Menger Hotel**'s bar, where Teddy Roosevelt recruited his Rough Riders. And the **Zoological Gardens and Aquarium** are counted among the best in the nation.

WEST AND NORTH OF SAN ANTONIO

BANDERA COUNTY: For a Hill Country Wild West experience, take in a **rodeo** in *Bandera* and follow it with some boot-scootin' across the sawdust at **Arkey Blue's Silver Dollar** honky-tonk. And if you have time to spend a night or a weekend at the **Mayan** or the **Dixie Dude Ranch,** all the better.

COMAL COUNTY: In *New Braunfels* feast on goodies from **Naegelin's,** the oldest German bakery in these parts, before taking a look at the model of Prince Solms's German castle at the **Sophienburg Museum.** He's the nobleman who founded the town and fled.

KERR COUNTY: Don't miss the **Cowboy Artists of America Museum** in *Kerrville*, and try to spend a night at **Ye Kendall Inn** in *Boerne*. Maybe you'll see the ghosts that are rumored to roam there.

MEDINA COUNTY: At one time, *Castroville*'s **Landmark Inn** was the only place to take a bath between San Antonio and California. Check out the room where Robert E. Lee spent the night.

REAL COUNTY: For the scenic roller-coaster hill ride of your life, drive **FM 337** — slowly — from *Vanderpool* through *Leakey* to *Camp Wood*.

UVALDE COUNTY: In *Uvalde* the extensive art collection of former Governor and Mrs. Dolph Briscoe is exhibited in the elegant **First State Bank of Uvalde,** an amazing group ranging from Rembrandt etchings of 1633 through works of Gainsborough and Reynolds. And be sure to see the historic **Uvalde Opera House,** crowned with its "Drunken Dragon" weather vane.

Index

LODGING BY PRICE CODE

Price Codes:
Inexpensive: Up to $65
Moderate: $65 to $100
Expensive: $100 to $175
Very Expensive: Over $175

**AUSTIN AND TRAVIS
COUNTY**

Inexpensive
Resort Ranch of Lake Travis,
    67

Moderate–Expensive
Carrington's Bluff B&B, 26
The Miller-Crockett House, 26
Trail's End Bed & Breakfast,
    68

Woodburn House, 27

Moderate–Very Expensive
Robin's Nest bed & Breakfast,
    68

Expensive
The Driskill, 25
Governor's Inn, 26

Expensive–Very Expensive
Barton Creek Resort & Spa,
    66
Lakeway Inn, 67

Very Expensive
Four Seasons Hotel, 25

**WEST AND SOUTH OF
AUSTIN**
(Blanco, Burnet, Gillespie,
    Hayes, Kimble, Llano,
    Mason Counties)

Inexpensive
Dabbs Railroad Hotel, 148
Days Inn, Junction, 140
Slumber Inn, 140

Inexpensive–Moderate
Mason Square B&B, 159

Inexpensive–Very Expensive
Thunderbird Resort, 95

Moderate
Badu House, 148

RESTAURANTS BY PRICE CODE

Price Codes:
Austin & San Antonio:
Inexpensive   Up to $20
Moderate $20 to $30
Expensive $30 to $50
Very Expensive
Over $50

In the Counties:
Inexpensive   Up to $10
Moderate $10 to $20
Expensive $20 to $35
Very Expensive
Over $35

AUSTIN & TRAVIS COUNTY

RESTAURANTS BY CUISINE

About the Author

Eleanor S. Morris is a world traveler, author, and photographer based in Austin, Texas. Widely published in national magazines, she has written several books about Texas and the Southwest: *City Smart: Austin; Country Roads of Texas; Country Towns of Texas; Fairs and Festivals of Texas;* and *Recomended Country Inns of the Southwest: Arizona, New Mexico and Texas.*